TOEFL
TEST OF ENGLISH AS A FOREIGN LANGUAGE

EDITH H. BABIN
CAROLE V. CORDES
HARRIET H. NICHOLS

Department of English
Louisiana State University

ARCO PUBLISHING, INC.
NEW YORK

Third Edition, Second Printing, 1984

Published by Arco Publishing, Inc.
215 Park Avenue South, New York, N.Y. 10003

Copyright © 1983, 1978, 1974 by Arco Publishing, Inc.

Library of Congress Cataloging in Publication Data

Babin, Edith H.
  TOEFL (Test of English as a foreign language)

  Rev. ed. of: TOEFL (Test of English as a foreign
language) / Harriet N. Moreno. New 2nd ed. c1978.
  Bibliography: p.
  1. English language—Text-books for foreign speakers.
2. English language—Examinations, questions, etc.
I. Cordes, Carole V. II. Nichols, Harriet H.
III. Moreno, Harriet N. TOEFL (Test of English as
a foreign language) IV. Title: T.O.E.F.L.
(Test of English as a foreign language)
PE1128.B2   1983   428.2′4′076   82-22809
ISBN 0-668-05446-8 (Paper Edition)

Printed in the United States of America

CONTENTS

PART I: THE TEST OF ENGLISH AS A FOREIGN LANGUAGE

PART II: SIX PRACTICE TOEFL TESTS

PART III: APPENDIX

PART I
THE TEST OF ENGLISH AS
A FOREIGN LANGUAGE

Preface

WHY USE THIS BOOK?

If you are planning to take the TOEFL (Test of English as a Foreign Language), this book will be indispensable for a higher score.

You are well aware that the TOEFL is one of the most important examinations that you will ever take. Your entire future may well depend on your performance on the TOEFL. The results of this test will determine, in great measure, whether you will be admitted to the school of your choice. There will be many candidates taking the TOEFL—and not all will score well enough to be accepted by the schools they choose.

This book is designed to guide you in your study so that you will *score high* on the TOEFL. This claim—that this book will help you to achieve a higher rating—has both educational and psychological validity, for these reasons:

1. You will know what to study. A candidate will do better on a test if he or she knows what to study. The questions in this book will show you what is required and therefore help you get the most benefit from your study time.

2. You will spotlight your weaknesses. Using this book, you will discover where your weaknesses lie. This self-diagnosis will provide you with guidelines for spending your time where it will do the most good.

3. You will get the "feel" of the exam. It is important to get the "feel" of the entire examination. Gestalt (meaning *configuration* or *pattern*) psychology stresses that true learning results in a grasp of the entire situation. Gestaltists tell us that we learn by "insight." One of the salient principles of this kind of learning is that we succeed in "seeing through" a problem as a consequence of experiencing previous similar situations. This book contains many "similar situations"—as you will discover when you take the actual examination.

4. You will gain confidence. While preparing for the exam you will build up confidence, and you will retain this confidence when you enter the exam room. This feeling of confidence will be a natural consequence of getting the "feel" of the exam.

5. You will add to your knowledge. In going over the practice questions in this book, you will not—if you use this book properly—be satisfied merely with the answer to a particular question. You will want to do additional research on the other choices for the same question. In this way, you will broaden your background to be prepared adequately for the exam to come, since it is quite possible that a question on the exam which you are going to take may require your knowing the meaning of one of these other choices.

WHAT YOU SHOULD KNOW ABOUT THE TEST OF ENGLISH AS A FOREIGN LANGUAGE

Background and Purpose

The Test of English as a Foreign Language (TOEFL) is given each year to hundreds of thousands of students who plan to enter schools in the United States and Canada and whose native language is not English. Admission committees in the various schools throughout North America use the individual scores from the TOEFL to determine a student's competence in English. Begun in 1963, the TOEFL program was first administered by the Modern Language Association. In 1965, the College Entrance Examination Board and Educational Testing Service became jointly responsible for the program.

A bulletin for candidates explaining the TOEFL may be obtained by writing to:

Test of English as a Foreign Language
Box 899
Princeton, New Jersey, U.S.A. 08541

This "Bulletin of Information and Application Form" is free, although there is a fee for taking the TOEFL that must be paid at the time you send in your application. The bulletin contains fee information and a calendar of TOEFL test dates. It discusses test admissions, procedures, and scoring information. The bulletin also identifies Test Centers and sketches TOEFL services provided by Educational Testing Service. There is a brief description of TOEFL materials available from Educational Testing Service that candidates will find particularly valuable.

Plan to take the TOEFL examination in plenty of time to have your scores reported to the institutions to which you wish to apply before their application deadlines. Allow at least six weeks for your score reports to reach these institutions.

TOEFL Scores and University Admission

Since there are no passing or failing scores on the TOEFL, each institution usually sets its own standards. Generally speaking, a total score of 600 is considered excellent, while any score falling below 400 is regarded as poor. (Note: This book contains a Scoring Chart modeled after that used by ETS with which to assess your progress on the practice tests. See page 17.) You can learn the required score of individual universities by writing and requesting such information.

After you take the TOEFL, your official score can be sent to individual schools where you have applied for admission. These reports must come from Educational Testing Service, Princeton, New Jersey. Institutions do not usually accept your personal copy of the score report as a substitute for the official score. A publication discussing interpretation of your scores will accompany your TOEFL score report. This leaflet, published by Educational Testing Service, provides detailed information regarding the highest, average, and lowest part scores received by over 100,000 individuals who took the TOEFL over a period of about five years.

Because the majority of American colleges and universities use the TOEFL scores in considering foreign students for admission, it is wise to use this book to help you prepare for the test. Most admission committees rely heavily on the TOEFL scores, since even high academic ability in a student's chosen field may be rendered insufficient if his or her command of English is inadequate. It is true that admission committees will be looking at grade point averages. However, remember that they will also be viewing the TOEFL scores as a valid indication of academic success or failure on the American campus.

Introduction:
The Nature of the TOEFL

The goal of the TOEFL is to measure the foreign student's English proficiency objectively. The examination is divided into three parts that test different language skills individually. The test is given in a single session of about 3 hours, which includes the time required for completing admission procedures.

SECTION I: LISTENING COMPREHENSION

(50 Questions—40 Minutes)

This section of the test measures your ability to understand *spoken* English. There are three parts to this section.

Part A

In this part of the test, you will hear twenty brief statements that do not appear in your test booklet. When you have heard a statement, select the answer nearest in meaning to what you have heard. Record your answer on the answer sheet.

Example

You will hear:
"Mary called on Susan."

You will read:
(A) Mary telephoned Susan.
(B) Mary ate with Susan.
(C) Mary visited Susan.
(D) Mary shouted at Susan.

Answer (C), "Mary visited Susan," is the closest in meaning to the statement "Mary called on Susan." You should have chosen (C).

Part B

Fifteen short conversations between two speakers are presented in this part. At the end of each, a third voice asks a question about what was said in the conversation. You will hear the question only once. You will be given about fifteen seconds to answer each item.

Example

You will hear:

(Man) "Martha certainly has strange illnesses. They come and go as quickly as anything else I know of."

(Woman) "Yes. She's sick when there's work to be done, but well when there's a party."

(Third voice) "How does the woman feel about Martha's illnesses?"

You will read:
(A) Martha's illnesses are serious.
(B) Martha's illnesses are pretended.
(C) Martha's illnesses are brief but real.
(D) Martha's illnesses occur only when there is a party.

You should have chosen (B). From the conversation, we can conclude that Martha uses sickness as an excuse whenever she has to work. On the other hand, she is never sick when a party is going on.

Part C

This part consists of several short lectures and conversations that you will hear only once. They do not appear in the test booklet. You will be asked several questions about each lecture or conversation. When a question is asked, choose the best answer from the four answers given. Record your answer on the answer sheet. Part C consists of 15 questions.

Example

You will hear:

Alaska belonged to Russia until the United States purchased the territory just after the Civil War. Influences of the Russian period are to be seen in Southeast, Southwest, and Central Alaska today. You drive to quiet, peaceful communities on the Kenai Peninsula, or fly to Kodiak or Sitka, and step back into a simpler, less hurried time. Strolling through the grounds of a Russian Orthodox church is like stepping back into nineteenth-century Russia, but you're still in the United States. What an incredible buy, you realize. Russia sold us this magnificent land for only two cents an acre.

Anchorage, the commercial hub and home for nearly half of the state's 400,000 residents, is one of the youngest major cities in the United States. Anchorage today is an "air crossroads" to more than 1.5 million passengers who shuttle each year over the Pole between Europe and the Far East or who fly on direct flights to Alaska from West Coast and Midwest cities.

You don't know quite what to expect when your jet lands at Anchorage. The name sounds nautical, but driving into town you realize you've entered a familiar, modern city. Here Alaskans have pushed a hole in the frontier and made an exciting urban oasis. Your surprise makes it all the more exciting.

You will hear:
1. Russian influence is obvious in Alaska in all of the regions below except which one?

You will read:
(A) The Southeast.
(B) The Northwest.
(C) The South.
(D) The central part of the country.

You will hear:
2.. How much did the United States pay for Alaska?

You will read:
(A) A hundred dollars an acre.
(B) Five hundred dollars an acre.
(C) Two cents an acre.
(D) Ten dollars an acre.

You will hear:
3. According to the lecture, approximately how many residents are there in Anchorage?

You will read:
(A) 200,000.
(B) 300,000.
(C) 100,000.
(D) 400,000.

Answers

1. You should have chosen (B).
2. You should have chosen (C).
3. You should have chosen (A).

SECTION II: STRUCTURE AND WRITTEN EXPRESSION

(40 Questions—25 Minutes)

In this section, your ability to recognize standard *written* English is tested. This section consists of two parts, each having special directions.

Part A

Each one of 15 items consists of an incomplete sentence which you are required to complete by selecting one of the four answers given. After you have chosen the one word or phrase that best completes the sentence, mark your answer in the appropriate space on the answer sheet.

Example

I wonder_____.
- (A)   how much costs that book
- (B)   what of that book the price is
- (C)   how much does that book cost
- √(D)   what that book costs

You should have chosen (D). In correct English, the sentence would be, "I wonder what that book costs."

All of the questions in Part A should be answered this way. As soon as you understand the directions completely, begin working on the test.

Part B

In this part, you will find that in each sentence four words or phrases <u>have been underlined</u>. You should select the *one* underlined word or phrase that would not be acceptable in standard, written English. Find the appropriate space on the answer sheet, and record your answer.

Example

If I <u>had known</u> that chemistry <u>was</u> going to be
       A   B
taken
<u>such a difficult subject</u>, I never would have <u>took</u>
       C   D
it up during my first semester.

You should have marked (D). After "never would have," you should use the correct past participial form of the verb. The correct form is *taken*.

SECTION III: READING COMPREHENSION AND VOCABULARY

(60 Questions—45 Minutes)

This section tests your knowledge of English vocabulary and your ability to understand what you read. You cannot sit down the night before a test in vocabulary or reading comprehension and "cram" for it. Some aids for increasing your vocabulary are given in the Appendix of this workbook. Once you have used those aids to build a larger vocabulary, you are ready for the vocabulary section of the practice tests that follow.

Part A

In this part you are required to choose a word or phrase that could be substituted for an underlined word in a given sentence without changing the meaning of the sentence. Note that all four of the possible choices could replace the underlined word and still produce a meaningful sentence. The context, then, does not give you much help in choosing the correct answer. In order to answer the question correctly, you must know the meaning of the underlined word. There are 30 questions in Part A.

Example

That room is spacious enough to be a good place for the party.

(A) attractive
(B) convenient
(C) colorful
√(D) large

First, read the sentence carefully. Notice that if any of the four choices were used to replace the underlined word, the sentence would still make sense. For example, you could describe a place for a party as "attractive," "convenient," "colorful," or "large." The only way that you can decide which of the four words would keep the meaning of the original sentence is by knowing the meaning of the underlined word, *spacious.* If you know that *spacious* means "large," your task is simple. If you do not know the meaning of *spacious,* you still might be able to find the answer if you look for the root of the word. The root of *spacious* is "space," a word that can refer to size, and since only choice (D) refers to size, you would choose (D) as your answer.

Part B

In Part B, although the emphasis is on reading comprehension, you will also frequently be asked the meaning of a particular word in the sentence or paragraph. Even when you are not directly asked what a particular word means, you may be asked questions about the meaning of a sentence or paragraph whose answers depend on your understanding of a particular word. In such cases the underlying meaning of the given sentence can help you. There are 30 questions in Part B.

Example

(1)   Wilson Thompson was such an eloquent speaker that at a camp meeting in an Indiana maple grove, he once held the rapt attention of an audience of between seven and eight thousand for only a few
(5) minutes less than three hours.

1.   The word *rapt* (line 3) means most nearly
     (A)   restless
     (B)   unwilling
     (C)   resentful
     (D)   interested

First, read the sentence carefully. If you know the meaning of the word *rapt,* you will have no problem. If you do not know the meaning of *rapt,* you must look to the context of the sentence to help you find the meaning. You will note that the word *rapt* is being used to describe the attention of the audience. What do you know about that audience? The sentence tells you that the audience is large (seven or eight thousand) and that it has continued listening for a long time (almost three hours). This suggests that the audience must really want to hear what the speaker is saying. Also, Mr. Thompson must be a good speaker, since he is described as being "eloquent." Now, look at the four choices. Choice (A), "restless," suggests that the audience is not paying much attention, and since you know that the listeners have not moved for almost three hours, you can eliminate (A). Choices (B) "unwilling" and (C) "resentful" suggest that the audience does not want to listen and does not like what it hears. Neither of these possible meanings for *rapt* fits the context in which the word is used. Choice (D) "interested," on the other hand, fits the description of the audience's behavior, and would be the kind of attention you would expect an audience to give a speaker who is described as "eloquent." Choice (D) is the answer.

Part B may also include questions in which you are given a sentence and four restatements of that sentence. You are asked to choose the answer that is the closest restatement of the original sentence. Note that more than one of the statements may be factually correct.

Example

Traveling by commercial airplane is cheaper than traveling by a chartered yacht.
(A)   A yacht, which may be privately chartered, is more expensive than a private airplane.
(B)   Traveling on a chartered yacht costs less than traveling on a commercial airplane.

(C) It is cheaper to travel on a commercial airplane than to travel on a chartered yacht.

(D) Because the yacht is chartered, it is more expensive than the airplane.

First, read the given sentence carefully. Next, consider each of the possible choices separately, comparing the information each gives with that given in the original sentence. Choice (A) states that yacht travel costs more than plane travel, which, at first, seems to be the same information given in the original sentence. However, the original sentence was comparing a chartered yacht to a commercial plane, and choice (A) compares a chartered yacht to a private plane. Choice (B) is clearly incorrect, since the information it gives is exactly opposite that given in the original sentence. In choice (C), although the sentence pattern is different from that of the original sentence, the meaning seems to be the same. Choice (C) seems like the answer, but take a quick look at choice (D) to be certain. Choice (D) may well be factually correct: that the yacht is chartered may possibly account for the difference in cost. However, the original sentence does not tell the reader *why* the cost of the yacht is more, so choice (D) can be eliminated. Choice (C) is the answer.

The major portion of Part B consists of short paragraphs or advertisements. To do well on this section of the test, you must build up your reading skill by practicing systematically. There are certain steps you can follow which will help you to arrive at the right answer most of the time. An explanation of those steps and suggestions for improving reading comprehension are given in the Appendix of this workbook. Let us apply those suggestions to an example passage and questions.

Example

(1) When the power of Carthage was at its height, a Punic admiral named Hanno reputedly made a voyage down the West African coast. He appears to have sailed to within 8° of the equator and to (5) have established settlements on the way. An account attributed to Hanno says that he took thirty thousand settlers with him on his expedition. About the time that Hanno was exploring the African coast, a fellow countryman, Himilco, (10) was traveling northward to explore the remoter shores of Europe. He may have been in search of the Tartessan source of tin. The account of his voyage is nebulously preserved in the works of ancient authors. The *Ora Maritima* of Avienus (15) attributed a horrendous description of the Atlantic to him.

1. Hanno and Himilco both
    (A) explored the African coast.
    (B) took thousands of settlers with them on their expeditions.
    (C) came from the same country.
    (D) were in search of the Tartessan source of tin.

2. Himilco's account of his voyage was recorded in the writings of
    (A) Hanno.
    (B) Avienus.
    (C) an unknown Carthaginian sailor.
    (D) a Punic admiral.

Step-by-Step Explanations

Step 1. Read the selection through quickly to get the general sense of it.

Step 2. Read each question, but do not read the possible answers.

Step 3. Reread the passage selectively, noting that the answer to Question 1 is in sentence four, and that the answer to Question 2 is in sentences six and seven.

Step 4. Concentrate on each question. Now that you have located the areas in which each question and answer are discussed, you will reread only those sections.

Question 1 involves both Hanno and Himilco and so you reread sentence 4, which mentions both men. Choice (A) cannot be correct since sentence 4 says that Himilco was exploring not the African but the European coast. Choice (B) could be correct, but although sentence 3 mentions that Hanno took settlers, no mention is made of any settlers traveling with Himilco. Choice (C) looks like the right answer—Hanno and Himilco are said to be "fellow countrymen" but it is best to check further. Choice (D) can be eliminated, since the paragraph nowhere mentions any connection between Hanno and the Tartessan source of tin. So, you return to choice (C) as the best possible answer.

Next, concentrate on Question 2 with its four possible answers, remembering that the answer lies in sentences 6 and 7, which contain the key words "account of his voyage." Choice (A) is obviously wrong; Hanno was an explorer, not a writer. Choice (B) certainly seems to be correct, but you should look quickly at the remaining choices, just to be sure. (C) is not even mentioned and can be easily eliminated; choice (D) is incorrect, since the only Punic admiral mentioned is Hanno, whom you have already eliminated. Choice (B) is the answer.

Step 5. Go back to the selection. Check to see that you have answered each question and marked the answer in the proper space on the answer sheet. If you follow the outlined procedure in answering the reading comprehension question, you will find that you are answering most questions correctly and quickly. Most passages will require at least two readings, one complete, rapid reading for general sense, and a second, selective reading of the sections which contain the key words or ideas of the questions. The important thing is to know where to find the answers and to remain calm when examining the possible choices.

NOTE: ETS administers different forms of the TOEFL, and the particular form you take may vary in length from the practice tests given in this book. If so, the time allowed to complete the individual sections and the number of questions to be answered will be in approximately the same proportion as they are in the practice tests.

How to Take the TOEFL

TEST-TAKING STRATEGY

- Approach the test confidently. Take it calmly.

- Remember to review during the week before the test.

- Arrive on time . . . and ready.

- Choose a good seat. Get comfortable and relax.

- Bring the complete kit of "tools" you'll need.

- Listen carefully to all directions.

- Budget your time intelligently.

- Read all directions carefully—twice if necessary. Pay particular attention to the scoring plan.

- Start right in, if possible. Stay with it. Use every second effectively.

- Do the easy questions first; postpone the more difficult questions until later.

- Read each question carefully. Make sure you understand each one before you answer. Re-read, if necessary.

- Think! Avoid hurried answers. If you must guess, guess intelligently.

- Note your watch and your time budget, but do a little balancing of the time you devote to each question.

- Get all the help you can from "cue" words.

- Rephrase difficult questions for yourself.

- Refresh yourself with a few, well-chosen rest pauses during the test.

- Now that you're a "cool" test-taker, stay calm and confident throughout the test. Don't let anything upset you.

- Keep working until the proctor calls time.

USING YOUR ANSWER SHEET

The present popularity of standardized tests requires the use of electrical test scoring machines. With these machines, scoring that would require the labor of several people for hours can be handled by one person in a fraction of the time. The TOEFL uses a machine-scored answer sheet.

The scoring machine is an amazingly intricate and helpful device, but the machine is not human. It cannot, for example, tell the difference between an intended answer and a stray pencil mark, and will count either indiscriminately. The machine cannot count a pencil mark that is not brought in contact with the electrodes. For these reasons, specially printed answer sheets with response spaces properly located and properly filled in must be employed. Since not all pencil leads contain the necessary ingredients, a number two lead pencil must be used and a solid, heavy, black mark must be made to indicate answers. Each mark must entirely fill the space that corresponds to the number and the letter of your answer choice. All stray pencil marks on the paper, clearly not intended as answers, must be completely erased. Every question may have only one answer indicated. Otherwise, the machine will give you *no* credit for your correct answer.

Here's how to mark your answers on machine-scored answer sheets: 25. Ⓐ Ⓑ ● Ⓓ Ⓔ

We repeat: make only *one* mark for each answer. Additional and stray marks may be counted as mistakes. In making corrections erase errors *completely*.

In order for your answer sheet to be identified as yours, it is important that the blanks at the top be filled in completely and correctly. The proctors will try to check this, but it is your responsibility to be certain that your paper is complete.

Guessing. Many examinations penalize a student for guessing, but on the TOEFL it is better to guess than to omit any item. If you are forced to guess completely at random, you have at least a 25 percent chance of getting the answer. Of course, each time you can use some knowledge to eliminate a wrong choice, you have increased your chances. One choice eliminated will give you a 33⅓ percent chance of guessing right; two choices eliminated will give you a 50 percent chance of getting the right answer.

Time. A time limit is set for each section on the examination. Therefore, follow the time instructions carefully. This book tells you how much time is available for each section of the test. You should calculate in advance about how much time you can afford to spend on each question. Your watch can help you here. Even if you haven't finished a section when the time limit is up, you *must* pass on to the next section. If the examination paper bears the instruction "Do not turn over page until signal is given," or "Do not start until signal is given," follow the instruction. Otherwise, you may be disqualified.

Pay Close Attention. Be sure you understand what you're doing at all times. It is natural to feel stress when taking an examination, and it is easy to skip a word or jump to a false conclusion, which may cost you points off your score. Examiners sometimes deliberately insert plausible-appearing false answers, in order to catch the candidate who is not alert.

Record your answers carefully on the answer sheet one by one as you answer the questions. Double-check to be sure that these answers are recorded next to the appropriate numbers on your answer sheet. It is poor practice to write your answers first on the test booklet and then to transfer all at one time to the answer sheet. This procedure causes many errors, and there is always the possibility that you will run out of time before you have a chance to transfer all the answers.

HOW TO PREPARE FOR THE TOEFL

Before the Test

An important goal of your test preparation is to help you to give the best possible account of yourself by effectively using your knowledge to answer the examination questions.

First, get rid of any negative attitudes toward the test. Your attitude is negative if you view the test as a device to "trip you up" rather than an opportunity to show how effectively you have learned.

Practice Your English. Even the fortunate students who travel to the U.S. to enroll in intensive English courses often make the mistake of spending too much time with people of their own nationality while abroad. These students may spend five or six hours in English classes each day. However, all free time is spent with fellow students who speak their native language. Individuals who refuse to interact with native speakers of English are missing perhaps the greatest opportunity of all in language learning. They may well finish an intensive English course with an understanding of grammatical rules and no ability to communicate their thoughts in English.

If you are presently enrolled in an English course for foreigners in the United States, seize your chance to become fully saturated with the language. You will no doubt eat at least some of your meals in the university cafeteria. Make a point of sitting with Americans. Many of them will be willing to converse with you and some will be glad to offer constructive corrections of your use of English at your request. Take advantage of the many good movies and television programs available to American audiences. Try to view some of these with English-speaking friends. Afterwards, you can discuss the presentation with them in English. In short, attending class is not enough. You must have many contact hours with

English after class is over if you are to obtain a mastery of the language.

Those of you who do not have the opportunity to study English in the United States must be industrious in seeking out English speakers who are living in your city. In all probability, books, magazines, and newspapers in English are available to you. Keep several copies handy. Reading will improve your English vocabulary. American movies and television are no doubt available to you as well. Be certain to investigate all the different ways for you to come in contact with spoken English. You may be surprised at the number of opportunities there are.

In the back of this book you will find a list of books printed in the United States that will provide you with a strong review of the language. Try to obtain one or more of these texts from the publisher, and then set a few hours aside each day for self-instruction.

Approach the Test with Self-Confidence. Working through this book is a difficult job, and after you've done it you will probably be better prepared than 90 percent of the people taking the TOEFL. Self-confidence is one of the biggest strategic assets you can bring to the testing room.

Nobody likes tests, but some people actually permit themselves to get upset or angry when they see what they think is an unfair test. This can only hurt your score. Keep calm and move right ahead. After all, everyone is taking the same test. Anger, resentment, and fear all slow you down and impair your judgment.

Besides, every test you take, including this one, is a valuable experience that improves your skill. Since you will undoubtedly be taking other tests in the years to come, it may help you to regard the TOEFL as training to perfect your skill.

Keep calm; there's no point in panic. If you've done your work, there's no need for it; if you haven't, a cool head is your very first requirement.

At the very least, this book should remove some of the fear and mystery that surrounds examinations. A certain amount of concern is normal and good, but excessive worry saps your strength and keenness. In other words, be prepared *emotionally*.

Pretest Review

If you know any others who are taking this test, you'll probably find it helpful to review the book and your notes with them. The group should be small, certainly not more than four. Team study at this stage should seek to review the material in a different way than you learned it originally; strive for an exchange of ideas. Be selective in sticking to important ideas, and stress the vague and the unfamiliar rather than that which you all know well. End sessions as soon as you get tired.

One of the worst strategies in test-taking is to try to do all your preparation the night before the exam. Cramming is a very good way to guarantee poor test results. Schedule your study properly so as not to suffer from the fatigue and emotional disturbance that come from cramming the night before.

However, you would be wise to review your notes in the 48 hours preceding the exam. You shouldn't have to spend more than two or three hours in this way. Stick to salient points. The others will fall into place quickly.

Don't confuse cramming with a final, calm review that helps you focus on the significant areas of this book and further strengthens your confidence in your ability to handle the test questions. In other words, prepare yourself *factually*.

Keep Fit. Mind and body work together. Poor physical condition will lower your mental efficiency. In preparing for an examination, observe the common sense rules of health. Get sufficient sleep and rest, eat proper foods, plan recreation and exercise. In relation to health and examinations, two cautions are in order. Don't miss your meals prior to an examination in order to get extra time for study. Likewise, don't miss your regular sleep by sitting up late to "cram" for the examination. Cramming is an attempt to learn in a very short period of time what should have been learned through regular and consistent study. Not only are these two habits detrimental to health, but seldom do they pay off in terms of effective learning. It is likely that you will be more confused rather than better prepared on the day of the examination if you have broken into your daily routine by missing your meals or sleep.

On the night before the examination, go to bed at your regular time and try to get a good night's sleep. Don't go to the movies. Don't date. In other words, prepare yourself *physically*.

On the Day of the Test

After a very light, leisurely meal, get to the examination room ahead of time, perhaps ten minutes early. The reason for coming early is to help you get accustomed to the room. It will help you to a better start.

Bring All Necessary Equipment. Three or four sharpened pencils, watch, and eraser are needed. No pencils or erasers will be provided at the test center. You may not take any books, dictionaries, notes, etc., into the examination room. Scores of those individuals taking part in any form of cheating will be canceled.

Get Settled. Find your seat and stay in it. If no special seats have been assigned, take one in the front to facilitate the seating of others who come in after you.

The test will be given by a test supervisor who reads the directions and otherwise tells you what to do. The people who walk about passing out the test papers and assisting with the examination are test proctors. If you're not able to see or hear properly, notify the supervisor or a proctor. If you have any other difficulties during the examination, like a defective test booklet, scoring pencil, or answer sheet, or if it's too hot or cold or dark or drafty, let them know. You're entitled to favorable test conditions, and if you don't have them you won't be able to do your best. Don't be a crank, but don't be shy either. An important function of the proctor is to see to it that you have favorable test conditions.

Relax. Don't bring on unnecessary tenseness by worrying about the difficulty of the examination. If necessary, wait a minute before beginning to write. If you're still tense, take a couple of deep breaths, look over your test equipment, or do something which will take your mind away from the examination for a moment.

If your collar or shoes are tight, loosen them.

You'll give your best test performance if you have:

1. A good test environment,
2. a complete understanding of directions and
3. a desire to do your best.

PART II
SIX PRACTICE TOEFL TESTS

How to Score Your Practice Tests

The TOEFL is scored by converting your raw score, that is, the number of questions you answered correctly, to a scaled score or score range established according to statistical procedures. When you receive your TOEFL score, you will see that each section has been scored individually on a scale of 20 to 80, and that you have also been given a total score in the 200 to 800 range. The section scores are based on a correlation of your raw score with statistical norms, shown on a chart you will find in Educational Testing Service's TOEFL Test Kit "TOEFL Workbook." The score ranges for each section are found in the chart, added, and then converted again to a total score by using a mathematical formula. This procedure makes it possible for Educational Testing Service to compare your score fairly with that of others who have taken different forms of the test or who have taken it at different times or in different places.

The chart below can be used to measure your performance on the practice tests in this book. This is not an actual ETS chart, but you can use it to evaluate your scores on the practice tests and thus get a reasonably accurate idea of your TOEFL proficiency.

First, add up the number of correct answers you scored in each of the three sections of the test. This is your total score for the Practice Test. Locate your total score in the Raw Score column below. Then, look in the Scaled Score column for an equivalent score on a scale of 200 to 800. This scaled score is strictly a proportion (with a raw score of 150, or all questions answered correctly, equated to 800). It is *not* based on the Educational Testing Service formula.

Raw Score (number right)	Scaled Score (on a scale of 800–200)
135–150	720–800
120–135	640–720
105–120	560–640
90–105	480–560
75–90	400–480
60–75	320–400
45–60	240–320
0–45	200–240

SELF-EVALUATION SCALE FOR THE INDIVIDUAL TOEFL SECTIONS

Use the following chart to estimate your strengths and weaknesses and to help you plan your study schedule.

TOEFL Mastery	*Listening Comprehension*	*Structure and Written Expression*	*Reading Comprehension and Vocabulary*
Excellent	45–50	35–40	50–60
Good	35–44	25–34	40–49
Fair	30–34	20–24	30–39
Poor	under 30	under 20	under 30

ANSWER SHEET FOR TEST 1

Tear out this answer sheet and use it to record your answers to all the questions in this examination.

SECTION I

1 Ⓐ Ⓑ Ⓒ Ⓓ	11 Ⓐ Ⓑ Ⓒ Ⓓ	21 Ⓐ Ⓑ Ⓒ Ⓓ	31 Ⓐ Ⓑ Ⓒ Ⓓ	41 Ⓐ Ⓑ Ⓒ Ⓓ
2 Ⓐ Ⓑ Ⓒ Ⓓ	12 Ⓐ Ⓑ Ⓒ Ⓓ	22 Ⓐ Ⓑ Ⓒ Ⓓ	32 Ⓐ Ⓑ Ⓒ Ⓓ	42 Ⓐ Ⓑ Ⓒ Ⓓ
3 Ⓐ Ⓑ Ⓒ Ⓓ	13 Ⓐ Ⓑ Ⓒ Ⓓ	23 Ⓐ Ⓑ Ⓒ Ⓓ	33 Ⓐ Ⓑ Ⓒ Ⓓ	43 Ⓐ Ⓑ Ⓒ Ⓓ
4 Ⓐ Ⓑ Ⓒ Ⓓ	14 Ⓐ Ⓑ Ⓒ Ⓓ	24 Ⓐ Ⓑ Ⓒ Ⓓ	34 Ⓐ Ⓑ Ⓒ Ⓓ	44 Ⓐ Ⓑ Ⓒ Ⓓ
5 Ⓐ Ⓑ Ⓒ Ⓓ	15 Ⓐ Ⓑ Ⓒ Ⓓ	25 Ⓐ Ⓑ Ⓒ Ⓓ	35 Ⓐ Ⓑ Ⓒ Ⓓ	45 Ⓐ Ⓑ Ⓒ Ⓓ
6 Ⓐ Ⓑ Ⓒ Ⓓ	16 Ⓐ Ⓑ Ⓒ Ⓓ	26 Ⓐ Ⓑ Ⓒ Ⓓ	36 Ⓐ Ⓑ Ⓒ Ⓓ	46 Ⓐ Ⓑ Ⓒ Ⓓ
7 Ⓐ Ⓑ Ⓒ Ⓓ	17 Ⓐ Ⓑ Ⓒ Ⓓ	27 Ⓐ Ⓑ Ⓒ Ⓓ	37 Ⓐ Ⓑ Ⓒ Ⓓ	47 Ⓐ Ⓑ Ⓒ Ⓓ
8 Ⓐ Ⓑ Ⓒ Ⓓ	18 Ⓐ Ⓑ Ⓒ Ⓓ	28 Ⓐ Ⓑ Ⓒ Ⓓ	38 Ⓐ Ⓑ Ⓒ Ⓓ	48 Ⓐ Ⓑ Ⓒ Ⓓ
9 Ⓐ Ⓑ Ⓒ Ⓓ	19 Ⓐ Ⓑ Ⓒ Ⓓ	29 Ⓐ Ⓑ Ⓒ Ⓓ	39 Ⓐ Ⓑ Ⓒ Ⓓ	49 Ⓐ Ⓑ Ⓒ Ⓓ
10 Ⓐ Ⓑ Ⓒ Ⓓ	20 Ⓐ Ⓑ Ⓒ Ⓓ	30 Ⓐ Ⓑ Ⓒ Ⓓ	40 Ⓐ Ⓑ Ⓒ Ⓓ	50 Ⓐ Ⓑ Ⓒ Ⓓ

SECTION II

1 Ⓐ Ⓑ Ⓒ Ⓓ	9 Ⓐ Ⓑ Ⓒ Ⓓ	17 Ⓐ Ⓑ Ⓒ Ⓓ	25 Ⓐ Ⓑ Ⓒ Ⓓ	33 Ⓐ Ⓑ Ⓒ Ⓓ
2 Ⓐ Ⓑ Ⓒ Ⓓ	10 Ⓐ Ⓑ Ⓒ Ⓓ	18 Ⓐ Ⓑ Ⓒ Ⓓ	26 Ⓐ Ⓑ Ⓒ Ⓓ	34 Ⓐ Ⓑ Ⓒ Ⓓ
3 Ⓐ Ⓑ Ⓒ Ⓓ	11 Ⓐ Ⓑ Ⓒ Ⓓ	19 Ⓐ Ⓑ Ⓒ Ⓓ	27 Ⓐ Ⓑ Ⓒ Ⓓ	35 Ⓐ Ⓑ Ⓒ Ⓓ
4 Ⓐ Ⓑ Ⓒ Ⓓ	12 Ⓐ Ⓑ Ⓒ Ⓓ	20 Ⓐ Ⓑ Ⓒ Ⓓ	28 Ⓐ Ⓑ Ⓒ Ⓓ	36 Ⓐ Ⓑ Ⓒ Ⓓ
5 Ⓐ Ⓑ Ⓒ Ⓓ	13 Ⓐ Ⓑ Ⓒ Ⓓ	21 Ⓐ Ⓑ Ⓒ Ⓓ	29 Ⓐ Ⓑ Ⓒ Ⓓ	37 Ⓐ Ⓑ Ⓒ Ⓓ
6 Ⓐ Ⓑ Ⓒ Ⓓ	14 Ⓐ Ⓑ Ⓒ Ⓓ	22 Ⓐ Ⓑ Ⓒ Ⓓ	30 Ⓐ Ⓑ Ⓒ Ⓓ	38 Ⓐ Ⓑ Ⓒ Ⓓ
7 Ⓐ Ⓑ Ⓒ Ⓓ	15 Ⓐ Ⓑ Ⓒ Ⓓ	23 Ⓐ Ⓑ Ⓒ Ⓓ	31 Ⓐ Ⓑ Ⓒ Ⓓ	39 Ⓐ Ⓑ Ⓒ Ⓓ
8 Ⓐ Ⓑ Ⓒ Ⓓ	16 Ⓐ Ⓑ Ⓒ Ⓓ	24 Ⓐ Ⓑ Ⓒ Ⓓ	32 Ⓐ Ⓑ Ⓒ Ⓓ	40 Ⓐ Ⓑ Ⓒ Ⓓ

SECTION III

1 Ⓐ Ⓑ Ⓒ Ⓓ	11 Ⓐ Ⓑ Ⓒ Ⓓ	21 Ⓐ Ⓑ Ⓒ Ⓓ	31 Ⓐ Ⓑ Ⓒ Ⓓ	41 Ⓐ Ⓑ Ⓒ Ⓓ	51 Ⓐ Ⓑ Ⓒ Ⓓ
2 Ⓐ Ⓑ Ⓒ Ⓓ	12 Ⓐ Ⓑ Ⓒ Ⓓ	22 Ⓐ Ⓑ Ⓒ Ⓓ	32 Ⓐ Ⓑ Ⓒ Ⓓ	42 Ⓐ Ⓑ Ⓒ Ⓓ	52 Ⓐ Ⓑ Ⓒ Ⓓ
3 Ⓐ Ⓑ Ⓒ Ⓓ	13 Ⓐ Ⓑ Ⓒ Ⓓ	23 Ⓐ Ⓑ Ⓒ Ⓓ	33 Ⓐ Ⓑ Ⓒ Ⓓ	43 Ⓐ Ⓑ Ⓒ Ⓓ	53 Ⓐ Ⓑ Ⓒ Ⓓ
4 Ⓐ Ⓑ Ⓒ Ⓓ	14 Ⓐ Ⓑ Ⓒ Ⓓ	24 Ⓐ Ⓑ Ⓒ Ⓓ	34 Ⓐ Ⓑ Ⓒ Ⓓ	44 Ⓐ Ⓑ Ⓒ Ⓓ	54 Ⓐ Ⓑ Ⓒ Ⓓ
5 Ⓐ Ⓑ Ⓒ Ⓓ	15 Ⓐ Ⓑ Ⓒ Ⓓ	25 Ⓐ Ⓑ Ⓒ Ⓓ	35 Ⓐ Ⓑ Ⓒ Ⓓ	45 Ⓐ Ⓑ Ⓒ Ⓓ	55 Ⓐ Ⓑ Ⓒ Ⓓ
6 Ⓐ Ⓑ Ⓒ Ⓓ	16 Ⓐ Ⓑ Ⓒ Ⓓ	26 Ⓐ Ⓑ Ⓒ Ⓓ	36 Ⓐ Ⓑ Ⓒ Ⓓ	46 Ⓐ Ⓑ Ⓒ Ⓓ	56 Ⓐ Ⓑ Ⓒ Ⓓ
7 Ⓐ Ⓑ Ⓒ Ⓓ	17 Ⓐ Ⓑ Ⓒ Ⓓ	27 Ⓐ Ⓑ Ⓒ Ⓓ	37 Ⓐ Ⓑ Ⓒ Ⓓ	47 Ⓐ Ⓑ Ⓒ Ⓓ	57 Ⓐ Ⓑ Ⓒ Ⓓ
8 Ⓐ Ⓑ Ⓒ Ⓓ	18 Ⓐ Ⓑ Ⓒ Ⓓ	28 Ⓐ Ⓑ Ⓒ Ⓓ	38 Ⓐ Ⓑ Ⓒ Ⓓ	48 Ⓐ Ⓑ Ⓒ Ⓓ	58 Ⓐ Ⓑ Ⓒ Ⓓ
9 Ⓐ Ⓑ Ⓒ Ⓓ	19 Ⓐ Ⓑ Ⓒ Ⓓ	29 Ⓐ Ⓑ Ⓒ Ⓓ	39 Ⓐ Ⓑ Ⓒ Ⓓ	49 Ⓐ Ⓑ Ⓒ Ⓓ	59 Ⓐ Ⓑ Ⓒ Ⓓ
10 Ⓐ Ⓑ Ⓒ Ⓓ	20 Ⓐ Ⓑ Ⓒ Ⓓ	30 Ⓐ Ⓑ Ⓒ Ⓓ	40 Ⓐ Ⓑ Ⓒ Ⓓ	50 Ⓐ Ⓑ Ⓒ Ⓓ	60 Ⓐ Ⓑ Ⓒ Ⓓ

Test 1

I: LISTENING COMPREHENSION

(50 Questions–40 Minutes)

This section of the test requires a demonstration of your ability to understand spoken English. Each of the three parts has special directions. **The spoken parts of this test are on the Arco TOEFL cassette tape.** *(See page 343 for ordering information.) If you cannot use the tape, have a friend read the spoken parts of questions 1 to 50 to you from the script on page 241.*

Part A

Directions. In this part of the test, you will hear a brief statement. Each statement will be spoken only once. The statement does not appear in your test booklet. When you have heard a statement, select the answer nearest in meaning to what you have heard. Record your answer on the answer sheet.

Example

You will hear: The Wagners seem to take their large family in stride.

You will read:
- (A) Mr. Wagner comes from a large family.
- (B) Mrs. Wagner comes from a large family.
- (C) Mr. and Mrs. Wagner are the parents of many children.
- (D) The Wagners dislike small families.

The correct answer to the example is (C).

1.
- (A) Mrs. Jones went out to buy coffee.
- (B) Mrs. Jones doesn't have any coffee.
- (C) Mrs. Jones has a great deal of coffee.
- (D) Mrs. Jones has a little coffee.

2.
- (A) We must ask the question.
- (B) We must remember the question.
- (C) The question is not important.
- (D) We must try to forget the question.

3.
- (A) The woman wanted to hide her accident.
- (B) The woman wanted to explain her accident to her friends.
- (C) The woman wanted to report her accident.
- (D) The woman wanted to talk about her accident quietly.

4.
- (A) I'm going to wear these clothes.
- (B) I'm going to keep these clothes.
- (C) I'm going to wash these clothes.
- (D) I'm going to discard these clothes.

5.
- (A) Bill went to New York in December.
- (B) Bill runs a business in New York.
- (C) Bill will open a business in New York in December.
- (D) Bill shouldn't go to New York.

6.
- (A) The teacher gave the test.
- (B) The teacher postponed the test.
- (C) The teacher canceled the test.
- (D) The teacher gave the test orally.

21

7. (A) Mark became curious.
   (B) Mark became worried.
   (C) Mark became angry.
   (D) Mark became nervous.

8. (A) All of the passengers on the train were killed.
   (B) Mary Peters was the only passenger killed.
   (C) None of the train's passengers were killed.
   (D) Mary Peters was the only passenger not killed in the plane crash.

9. (A) The company offered Bill a job.
   (B) The company rejected Bill's offer.
   (C) The company accepted Bill's offer.
   (D) The company discussed Bill's offer.

10. (A) Mr. Black is a mechanic.
    (B) Mr. Black is a plumber.
    (C) Mr. Black is an electrician.
    (D) Mr. Black is a builder.

11. (A) Mary asked the teacher a question.
    (B) Mary's idea was reasonable.
    (C) Mary's question was off the subject.
    (D) Mary's idea was impossible.

12. (A) After you get your money at the bank, go to the store.
    (B) Banks and stores are often robbed.
    (C) Keep your money hidden in public places.
    (D) Keep your money in a bank, not in a store.

13. (A) William must do a lot of reading during his next English course.
    (B) William read some short stories but no novels.
    (C) English is a refreshing course for William to take.
    (D) William read more short stories than novels.

14. (A) You should buy your ticket at eight.
    (B) The plane departs at eight.

(C) The plane is arriving at seven-thirty.
(D) You should go to the ticket counter as soon as the plane leaves.

15. (A) Many banks offer photographs to drivers.
    (B) Almost all banks photograph their customers.
    (C) Many banks require customer identification.
    (D) Banks must have a valid license in order to cash checks.

16. (A) The boys took a wrong turn during the trip.
    (B) Bill did most of the driving during the trip.
    (C) John drove Bill to New York.
    (D) The boys divided the driving time.

17. (A) The test was not the least bit difficult.
    (B) The test was the least difficult of all.
    (C) The test was very difficult.
    (D) The test was as difficult as previous ones.

18. (A) The van and the truck are the same price.
    (B) The van is more expensive than the truck.
    (C) The truck is as practical as the van.
    (D) The truck is a little more expensive than the van.

19. (A) Our children hardly use the furniture.
    (B) Our children dislike the furniture.
    (C) Our children treat the furniture roughly.
    (D) Our children want us to replace the furniture.

20. (A) Bill surpasses John in math.
    (B) John surpasses Bill in math.
    (C) Bill always does John's math for him.
    (D) John and Bill make the same grades in math.

Part B

Directions. This section of the Listening Comprehension test consists of fifteen short conversations between two people. When each conversation ends, you will be asked a question by a third voice about what was said. You will hear the question only once and you must choose the answer from the four choices given. When you have chosen what you believe to be the best answer to the question, record your answer on the answer sheet.

Example

You will hear:

(Man) "I've never understood how to use the card catalogue, and I need to get this information today."

(Woman) "Why don't you pick up one of the guidebooks at the front desk? It will help you, I'm sure."

(Third voice) "Where did this conversation most likely occur?"

You will read: (A) At a museum.
(B) In a store.
(C) In a classroom.
(D) In a library.

The correct answer to the example is (D).

21. (A) The train is crowded.
(B) The train is late.
(C) The train is empty.
(D) The train is on time.

22. (A) A surprise party.
(B) A picnic.
(C) A meeting.
(D) An appointment.

23. (A) A movie.
(B) A lecture.
(C) A play.
(D) A speech.

24. (A) She misplaced her class card for biology.
(B) She arrived for registration too early.
(C) She missed registration.
(D) The man cannot spell her name.

25. (A) She found it interesting.
(B) She found it boring.
(C) She found it informative.
(D) She found it enjoyable.

26. (A) The woman is afraid of thunderstorms.
(B) The man works for a roofing company.
(C) The roof of the woman's house needs repairing.
(D) The man's roof is leaking.

27. (A) 12.
(B) 48.
(C) 36.
(D) 24.

28. (A) A plumber.
(B) An electrician.
(C) A salesman.
(D) A telephone repairman.

29. (A) By bus.
(B) By plane.
(C) By car.
(D) By train.

30. (A) In a hotel.
(B) At home.
(C) In a hospital.
(D) In a dentist's office.

31. (A) She was at the movies.
(B) She was in bed.
(C) She was in the hospital.
(D) She was watching another channel.

32. (A) Life is less expensive in the city.
(B) Jobs are easier to find in the city.
(C) Her job is in the city.
(D) Living in the suburbs is expensive.

33. (A) A newspaper.
    (B) A suit.
    (C) A coat.
    (D) A blouse.

34. (A) The woman thinks the salesman was realistic.
    (B) The woman thinks the salesman exaggerated his part.
    (C) The woman thinks the salesman was not dramatic enough.
    (D) The woman thinks the salesman played his part well.

35. (A) The model.
    (B) The lens.
    (C) The price.
    (D) The flash attachment.

Part C

Directions. In this part of the test, you will be required to listen to several short lectures and conversations. You will hear the lectures and conversations only once. They do not appear in your test booklet. When a question is asked, choose the best answer from the four given. Record your answer on the answer sheet.

36. (A) Liston was claimed winner by decision after only two rounds.
    (B) Ali knocked Liston out in the seventh round.
    (C) Liston was unable to answer the bell in the ninth round.
    (D) Ali was proclaimed champion after six rounds.

37. (A) He spent five years in prison.
    (B) He was accepted into the Black Muslim religious group.
    (C) He was denied his boxing rights.
    (D) He was immediately exempted from military service.

38. (A) He announced that he had become a Black Muslim after defeating Liston in a championship fight.
    (B) He announced that he had become a Black Muslim while he was still an amateur boxer.
    (C) He announced that he had become a Black Muslim after the Vietnam War.
    (D) He announced that he had become a Black Muslim when he retired from boxing in 1980.

39. (A) The majority of the volcanoes are inactive.
    (B) Most of the volcanoes present a threat to the inhabitants of the island.
    (C) A great many of the volcanoes are still exploding.
    (D) The presence of the volcanoes is making agriculture difficult, if not impossible, on the island.

40. (A) Lanzarote's inhabitants are a brave and flexible people.
    (B) Lanzarote is a dry land without trees.
    (C) Lanzarote's landscape closely parallels that of the moon.
    (D) Lanzarote is located off the southern coast of Africa.

41. (A) The air has a yellowish tinge.
    (B) The sky is very dark.
    (C) The sky is cloudless.
    (D) A red line stretches across the horizon.

42. (A) They fly above the darkened clouds to safety.
    (B) They are unable to navigate.
    (C) Their rate of breathing is increased.
    (D) They die instantly due to low atmospheric pressure.

43. (A) 83.
    (B) 120.
    (C) 300.
    (D) 250.

44. (A) Warm, damp air encounters cooler, arid air.
    (B) Extremely hot, dry air meets with warm, dry air.

(C) Damp air connects with extremely wet air.
(D) Cold, damp air encounters hot, dry air.

45. (A) They are knocked to the ground.
    (B) The wind becomes fast, hot, and humid.
    (C) Air pressure gets progressively lower.
    (D) The black area moves closer.

46. (A) Tennis courts.
    (B) A recreation area.
    (C) A sauna.
    (D) A swimming pool.

47. (A) One hundred dollars.
    (B) Thirty-five dollars.

(C) Fifty dollars.
(D) Two hundred fifty dollars.

48. (A) To secure a two-bedroom apartment.
    (B) To renew a six-month lease.
    (C) To pay for a dishwasher.
    (D) To cover property damage.

49. (A) For a week.
    (B) For two weeks.
    (C) For three weeks.
    (D) For a month.

50. (A) At three-thirty.
    (B) At one-thirty.
    (C) At four o'clock.
    (D) At five o'clock.

II: STRUCTURE AND WRITTEN EXPRESSION

(40 Questions—25 Minutes)

Part A

Directions. In this part each problem consists of an incomplete sentence. Below the sentence are four choices, marked (A), (B), (C), and (D). You should find the one choice which best completes the sentence. Mark your choice on the answer sheet.

Example

Because the United States has little tin, _____ produced in the rest of the world.

(A) tin is used
(B) it uses tin
(C) uses of tin
(D) uses tin

The correct answer to the example is (B).

1. Among the astronomers of ancient Greece, two theories _____ concerning the place of the earth in the universe.

(A) developing
(B) in development
(C) developed
(D) which they developed

2. The geocentric idea was abandoned in the seventeenth century, partly as a result of the writings of Copernicus _____ observations made by other astronomers.

(A) and also were
(B) not only because of
(C) also because were
(D) and also because of

3. The largest meteorite on display is in the American Museum in New York City, _____ over 34 tons.

(A) and it weighs
(B) it weighs
(C) its weight is
(D) which it weighs

4. *Rotation* refers to the turning of the earth _____ to the movement around the sun.

   (A) besides *revolution*
   (B) *revolution* refers
   √(C) and *revolution*
   (D) while *revolution* referring

5. There are several means _____ latitude and longitude.

   (A) can determine
   (B) to determine
   (C) by them can be determined
   (D) we use them to determine

6. Bernard Foucault _____ in 1851 that the earth is rotating.

   (A) who proved
   (B) proved
   (C) he proved
   (D) it was proved

7. The Homestead Act of 1862 _____ to acquire land at a small cost.

   (A) made possible
   (B) made it possible
   (C) made the possibility
   (D) possibly made

8. The earth revolves a little more rapidly _____ it is closer to the sun.

   (A) when
   (B) or
   (C) than
   (D) wherever

9. _____, Sir Isaac Newton described the laws of gravitation.

   (A) Was a seventeenth-century scientist
   (B) Who was a seventeenth-century scientist
   (C) A seventeenth-century scientist
   (D) When was a seventeenth-century scientist

10. The moon is not a planet _____ the planets in many respects.

    (A) resembling
    (B) which resembles
    (C) but resemblance to
    (D) although it resembles

11. Especially important to many people _____.

    (A) there is legislation against pollution
    (B) is legislation against pollution
    (C) it is legislation against pollution
    (D) legislation against pollution is

12. _____, the lion is a member of the cat family.

    (A) Like the tiger
    (B) Alike to the tiger
    (C) Liking the tiger
    (D) It is like the tiger

13. Botanists are not sure where the first plant was grown or even _____.

    (A) what plant was
    (B) it was what plant
    (C) what plant was it
    (D) what plant it was

14. As a Congressman from Ohio, a Republican, and _____ the antiwar movement, the young politician became well known during the 1960's.

    (A) a leader of
    (B) to lead
    (C) leading
    (D) he was leading

15. If a star seems to be moving in a wavy line, _____ of being a double star.

    (A) we suspect
    (B) that we suspect
    (C) we suspect it
    (D) the suspicion

Part B

Directions. In each of the following sentences, four words or phrases have been underlined. You should choose the word or phrase that would *not* be appropriate in standard written English. Mark your choice on the answer sheet.

Example

The average age <u>at which</u> people <u>begin to need</u> eyeglasses <u>vary</u> <u>considerably</u>.
             A   B   C   D

(C)   is incorrect in standard written English.

16.   <u>Not long after</u> Galileo's time, Sir Isaac Newton invented <u>another kind of</u> telescope <u>which he used</u>
       A   B   C
     mirrors <u>instead of</u> lenses.
               D

17.   Despite the <u>disappearance</u> of the Mayan empire, <u>there are still</u> Mayans in the region <u>in which</u> <u>they</u>
                  A   B   C
     once <u>inhabited</u>.
           D

18.   *Treasure Island,* the book <u>that made</u> Robert Louis Stevenson <u>famous</u>, <u>has became</u> a best seller for
                            A   B   C
     readers <u>young and old</u>.
              D

19.   <u>To be good for</u> agricultural purposes, soil <u>must have</u> <u>in it</u> the minerals <u>plants required</u>.
            A   B   C   D

20.   In spite of <u>its small size</u>, Europe <u>has</u> a greater <u>impact on</u> world history than <u>any other</u> continent.
                A   B   C   D

21.   Because the farms of Europe <u>produce</u> <u>less food</u> than <u>the people</u> need, some products must be to
                                  A   B   C
     <u>bring</u> from other lands.
       D

22.   <u>Among</u> the most remarkable eyes are <u>those of the dragonfly</u>, <u>for this insect</u> has compound eyes
      A   B   C
     <u>make up</u> of tiny eyes.
        D

23.   The <u>police investigation</u> <u>revealed that</u> the thieves <u>have planned</u> the robbery <u>carefully</u> before they
              A   B   C   D
     stole the jewelry.

24.   <u>By watching</u> sunspots, great storms <u>which rage</u> on the surface of the sun, scientists discovered
          A   B
     <u>whether</u> the sun <u>spins on</u> its axis.
        C   D

25.   These early people did not learn <u>how to make</u> bronze until 1500 B.C., but <u>they have done</u> <u>excellent</u>
         A   B   C   D
     <u>work</u> with other metals.

26. It is not known <u>exactly when</u> the first immigrants <u>arrived in</u> the New World, but where <u>did that</u>
                       A   B   C
   event occur is certain.
             D

27. <u>Unlike</u> many other people, the <u>America Indians</u> had to <u>discover</u> agriculture <u>for themselves</u>.
     A   B   C   D

28. Although the Indians <u>lacking animals</u>, they <u>had the ability</u> to <u>cultivate</u> plants <u>suitable for</u> daily use.
                                 A   B   C   D

29. <u>The element</u> uranium, which is <u>a hard, silvery</u> metal and <u>it was discovered</u> in 1789, <u>was named for</u>
       A   B   C   D
   the planet Uranus.

30. In the New World <u>as in</u> Europe, each region developed <u>its own</u> distinct pattern of culture <u>adapted</u>
                    A   B   C
   to local conditions <u>and influential</u>.
                           D

31. The government troops <u>were very fortunate</u> than the rebels <u>in having</u> large numbers of <u>foot</u>
                                 A   B   C
   soldiers <u>ready for</u> combat.
            D

32. This region of the Andes, <u>where</u> tin <u>was mixed</u> with copper to make bronze, was <u>the greater</u>
                              A   B   C
   <u>center of</u> metallurgy.
      D

33. The Mayan priests, <u>who were not only</u> excellent mathematicians <u>but also outstanding</u> scientists,
                        A   B
   <u>calculated the correct revolution</u> of several planets and <u>even predict</u> eclipses.
                       C   D

34. The natives, who were <u>used to get</u> most of <u>their living</u> from the sea, <u>seldom if ever</u> ventured inland
                         A   B   C
   <u>to search for</u> food.
          D

35. One of <u>the most famous men</u> of ancient times <u>Socrates was</u>, <u>whose teachings</u> <u>are reflected</u> in
                A   B   C   D
   Plato's writings.

36. Our civilization is <u>so commonplace</u> to us <u>that</u> rarely <u>we stop</u> to think about <u>its complexity</u>.
                         A   B   C   D

37. When archeologists <u>begin digging</u>, <u>they generally have</u> a good idea <u>of what</u> they are looking for
                    A   B   C
   and where <u>they are like</u> to find it.
                D

38. Through the study of <u>trees rings</u>, <u>which originated</u> in Arizona, the houses <u>in which</u> the Anasazi
                        A   B   C
   lived can <u>accurately</u> be dated.
              D

39. In Mesopotamia kings <u>were regarded as</u> the servants <u>of the gods</u>, but in Egypt, <u>on the other hand</u>,
                       A   B   C

   the pharaoh was thought <u>he was</u> divine.
                          D

40. The composer Verdi <u>has written</u> the opera *Aïda* <u>to celebrate</u> <u>the opening of</u> the Suez Canal, but
                            A   B   C

   the opera <u>was not performed</u> until 1871.
                        D

III: READING COMPREHENSION AND VOCABULARY

(60 Questions—45 Minutes)

Part A

Directions. Each problem in this part consists of a sentence in which one word or phrase has been underlined. From the four choices given, you should choose the one word or phrase which could be substituted for the underlined word or phrase without changing the meaning of the sentence. Mark your choice on the answer sheet.

Example

The <u>frown</u> on the man's face showed that he was displeased.

(A) look of fear
(B) look of anger
(C) look of delight
(D) look of surprise

The best answer is (B).

1. It is impossible for parents to <u>shield</u> their children from every danger.

   (A) protect
   (B) conserve
   (C) relieve
   (D) free

2. That student is <u>discourteous</u>; he <u>grumbles</u> no matter how one tries to please him.

   (A) giggles
   (B) scolds
   (C) complains
   (D) sneers

3. Do not leave the iron on that delicate fabric or the heat will <u>scorch</u> it.

   (A) melt
   (B) press
   (C) discolor
   (D) wrinkle

4. The new contact lenses made the woman <u>blink</u> her eyes much more than usual.

   (A) strain and stretch
   (B) open and close
   (C) rub
   (D) shade

5. The man walked <u>briskly</u> to keep warm on the very cold night.

   (A) quickly
   (B) excitedly
   (C) aimlessly
   (D) steadily

6. Michael was such a <u>shrewd</u> businessperson that he never lost money in any transaction.

   (A) fortunate
   (B) clever
   (C) wealthy
   (D) well-liked

7. There was no trace of poison in the coffee the chemist analyzed.

    √ (A) indication
    (B) taste
    (C) color
    (D) smell

8. The intricate directions were difficult to understand.

    (A) vague
    (B) unusual
    (C) routine
    (D) complicated

9. The little boy had had a long day; he was feeling drowsy.

    (A) lazy
    (B) sleepy
    (C) exhausted
    (D) sad

10. Since I have been ill, my appetite has diminished.

    (A) desire for exercise
    (B) desire for visitors
    (C) desire for sleep
    (D) desire for food

11. He stayed late to tell his hostess how much he had enjoyed the party.

    (A) neglected
    (B) attempted
    (C) lingered
    (D) struggled

12. The night was so foggy that the murderer was easily able to escape his pursuers.

    (A) misty
    (B) moist
    (C) mild
    (D) messy

13. The horse finally came to a halt on the very rim of the cliff.

    (A) top
    (B) edge
    (C) slope
    (D) base

14. Her husband is very competent; he will repair the roof himself.

    (A) capable
    (B) industrious
    (C) thrifty
    (D) careful

15. Mr. Henderson was determined to remain neutral.

    (A) untroubled
    (B) unhurried
    (C) unmarried
    (D) uncommitted

16. The stray dog was picked up by the dog-catcher because he had no collar.

    (A) dirty
    (B) sick
    (C) unfriendly
    (D) homeless

17. The time for discussing the problem is over; now we must act.

    (A) talking about
    (B) thinking about
    (C) arguing about
    (D) putting off

18. His apparel showed him to be a successful man.

    (A) clothing
    (B) confidence
    (C) answer
    (D) manner

19. He agreed to the plan of his own accord.

    (A) enthusiastically
    (B) voluntarily

(C)   unwillingly
(D)   unhesitatingly

20. <u>Ignoring</u> something will not make it go away.

(A)   Taking an interest in
(B)   Looking closely at
√(C)   Paying no attention to
(D)   Studying the causes of

21. During the war, the shipping lanes proved <u>vulnerable</u> to attack.

(A)   susceptible
(B)   dangerous
(C) . futile
(D)   feasible

22. The charges brought against the government official finally hurt nothing but his <u>vanity</u>.

(A)   family
(B)   prospects
(C)   pride
(D)   image

23. According to investigators, the recent report of a sea monster was a <u>hoax</u>.

(A)   breakthrough
(B)   mistake
(C)   trick
(D)   crime

24. In his statements to the press, the administrator was consistently <u>equivocal</u>.

(A)   ambiguous
(B)   reasonable
(C)   friendly
(D)   frank

25. The holiday crowds <u>littered</u> the park.

(A)   dirtied
(B)   filled
(C)   cleaned
(D)   left

26. The President's greatest <u>asset</u> was his reputation for honesty.

(A)   deception
(B)   advantage
(C)   liability
(D)   pride

27. The scientist <u>examined</u> the fossils closely to determine their age.

(A)   processed
(B)   cleaned
(C)   compared
√(D)   inspected

28. <u>Affluent</u> nations have an obligation to help their neighbors.

(A)   large
(B)   industrialized
(C)   advanced
(D)   wealthy

29. The governor's <u>impromptu</u> remarks caused his political party much embarrassment.

(A)   unrehearsed
(B)   forceful
(C)   unrestrained
(D)   absurd

30. Few people like someone who <u>meddles</u> in the affairs of others.

(A)   participates
(B)   delights
(C)   interferes
(D)   dabbles

Part B

Directions. You will be given a series of different types of reading material (sentences, short paragraphs, advertisements, etc.). Each selection is followed by questions about the meaning of the material. You are to choose the one best answer to each question from the four choices given.

Read the following sample passage.

(1)   Marianne Moore was born in St. Louis in 1887 and graduated from Bryn Mawr College in 1909. She taught stenography for a few years and then worked as a librarian in New York. She was a
(5)   member of the editorial staff of the famous literary magazine *The Dial* from 1925 to 1929. Although a book of her poems, titled *Observations,* was published in America in 1924, Miss Moore has only recently received the full acclaim
(10) she deserves.

Example 1

When did Miss Moore graduate from college?

(A)   1887
(B)   1909
(C)   1925
(D)   1924

The passage says that Miss Moore graduated from Bryn Mawr in 1909. Therefore, you should choose answer (B).

Example 2

The one profession *not* mentioned as being pursued by Miss Moore is that of

(A)   poet.
(B)   teacher.
(C)   scientist.
(D)   librarian.

The passage mentioned that Miss Moore taught stenography, worked as a librarian, and wrote poetry. Therefore, you should choose (C) as the best completion of the sentence.
     As soon as you understand the directions, begin work on the problems.

Questions 31–33

(1)   The minute investigations of the historians, the political scientists, and even the sociologists have not succeeded in destroying or even seriously modifying the mental pictures created by the
(5)   romantic Southerners for themselves.

31.   Romantic Southerners have

(A)   done much research in the history of their area.
(B)   not radically changed their views.
(C)   modified their views as a result of investigations.
(D)   become more realistic.

32.   Historians, political scientists, and sociologists have

(A)   investigated only a little.
(B)   succeeded in changing romantic Southerners.
(C)   investigated carefully and thoroughly.
(D)   created mental pictures.

33.   Romantic Southerners' views are

(A)   not affected by exposure to facts.
(B)   clearly based on real fact.
(C)   not very firmly held.
(D)   the same as those of the historians.

Questions 34–37

(1)   Upper-class English life in the last quarter of the seventeenth century had been characterized by artificiality in dress, manners, and conversation—an elaborate surface of formality and grace
(5)   covering a certain amount of vice and a great deal of plain silliness.

34.   The period being discussed was

(A)   from 1700 to 1725.
(B)   from 1675 to 1700.
(C)   from 1775 to 1800.
(D)   from 1800 to 1825.

35.   The period referred to in the paragraph was criticized for

(A)   a lack of naturalness.
(B)   not enough formality.
(C)   a lack of grace.
(D)   poor manners.

36. Generally, upper-class English people of this period probably lived

    (A) very simple lives.
    (B) very wicked lives.
    (C) very virtuous lives.
    (D) very conventional lives.

37. The author does *not* suggest that some upper-class English people of this period were

    (A) hypocritical.
    (B) silly.
    (C) formal.
    (D) witty.

Questions 38–39 refer to the following news item.

The stock market fell to a 16-month low in active trading Thursday, amid concern about the president's ability to trim the budget and a noted analyst's reiteration that prices will slump further.

38. At the time of this news release, trading in the stock market

    (A) was lower than ever before.
    (B) had been much higher 16 months ago.
    (C) had reached its lowest point in 16 months.
    (D) had been low for 16 months.

39. According to the release, the market has been affected by doubts about the president's ability to

    (A) prevent prices from slumping further.
    (B) cut the budget.
    (C) stay within the budget.
    (D) keep trading active.

Questions 40–44 refer to the following newspaper advertisement.

(1)   **EDGEMONT**

Absolutely one of the finest buys on the market. Spacious home with large living room, separate 15-foot dining room with crystal chandelier and built-in buffet,
(5) paneled family room with fireplace, huge kitchen with lots of cabinets, big cheery breakfast room, 2½ baths, 4 huge bedrooms (one is separate and could be a

playroom or offers complete privacy with separate entrance for guests). There is a covered patio and
(10) landscaped yard. Better than new with draperies and new air compressor. $160,000. Call Lane Hitcher (home) 926–6043.

40. What room in the above advertisement is described as having several possible uses?

    (A) the dining room
    (B) the family room
    (C) one bedroom
    (D) the playroom

41. Which room is described in the most detail?

    (A) the living room
    (B) the dining room
    (C) the family room
    (D) the kitchen

42. What detail is emphasized in the description of most rooms?

    (A) cheerfulness
    (B) built-ins
    (C) type of chandeliers
    (D) size

43. One feature of the house that is *not* mentioned is

    (A) the draperies.
    (B) the walk-in closet in the bedroom.
    (C) the landscaped yard.
    (D) the paneling in the family room.

44. The "buffet" mentioned in the description (line 4) is

    (A) a light fixture
    (B) a large meal.
    (C) a bookcase.
    (D) a serving table for food.

Questions 45–50

(1)   Today every major anthology of nineteenth-century poetry includes examples of the work which Christina Rossetti produced during her long literary career. Born in 1830, she began compos-

(5) ing verse at the age of eleven and continued to write for the remaining fifty-three years of her life. Her brother Dante Gabriel Rossetti, himself a poet and painter, soon recognized her genius and urged her to publish her poems. By the time (10) of her death in 1894, Christina had written more than eleven hundred poems and had published over nine hundred of them. Although this work has earned her recognition as the greatest woman poet of the Victorian Age, there is still no (15) authoritative edition of her poetry.

45. The word "anthology" (line 1) probably means

(A) writer.
(B) collection.
(C) poem.
(D) poet.

46. Christina Rossetti began writing poetry

(A) only after her brother urged her to do so.
(B) when she was fifty-three years old.
(C) when she was very young.
(D) when her genius was recognized.

47. Christina's brother was probably a good judge of her work because

(A) he loved his sister very much.
(B) he himself published poems.
(C) he was a poet.
(D) he was a famous painter.

48. The word "urged" (line 9) means closest to

(A) forbade.
(B) dared.
(C) encouraged.
(D) forced.

49. By 1894, Christina

(A) had published only a few of the many poems she had written.
(B) had published all the poems she had written.
(C) had published more than eleven hundred poems.
(D) had published over nine hundred poems.

50. At the time this passage was written, Christina Rossetti's poetry

(A) was almost unknown.
(B) was rarely published.
(C) had made her known as the greatest woman poet of the eighteenth century.
(D) had not been collected in an authoritative edition.

Questions 51–56

(1) Early French visitors to the wilderness of the Lower Mississippi Valley were impressed by the hostility of the Natchez Indians. The LaSalle voyagers, who in 1682 stopped beneath the steep (5) bluff on which the tribe resided, were sure that the Indians were plotting "some evil design" and were "resolved to betray and kill us." Jesuits journeyed to the Natchez villages soon after the birth of the Louisiana colony at Biloxi in 1699, but (10) so fruitless was their work that the mission was abandoned eight years later. The priests were shocked by the "barbarous" and "vicious" natives. Whether the Natchez were more unreceptive to Gallic ways than were neighboring Indians (15) is moot, but certainly the French encountered in them a strong and unusual tribe.

51. The Jesuits began their work at the Natchez villages

(A) in 1699.
(B) in 1682.
(C) around 1707.
(D) around 1680.

52. How did the Natchez respond to the French?

(A) They abandoned their mission.
(B) They founded the Louisiana colony at Biloxi.
(C) They were very hostile to the French.
(D) They were receptive to French ways.

53. The one thing about the Natchez that most impressed early French settlers was

(A) their unfriendliness.
(B) their numbers.

(C) their highly developed civilization.
(D) their method of government.

54. The word "fruitless" (line 10) probably means

(A) successful.
(B) unpredictable.
(C) that the fruit trees the Jesuits planted were barren.
(D) unproductive.

55. What quality was *not* attributed to the Natchez?

(A) barbarity
(B) viciousness
(C) insanity
(D) strength

56. The word "resided" (line 5) means

(A) hunted.
(B) lived.
(C) hid.
(D) waited.

Questions 57–60

Directions. For each of the following questions, choose the answer whose *meaning is closest* to that of the given sentence. Although more than one of the choices may be factually correct, you should choose the one that *most closely restates the original sentence.*

57. The artist's job in the beginning is not unlike the job of a writer.

(A) The artist's job in the beginning is very different from the job of a writer.
(B) The jobs of artists and writers are identical.
(C) In the beginning, the jobs of artists and writers are similar.
(D) In the beginning, the job of an artist is not like the job of a writer.

58. Cancer cells multiply faster and spread more rapidly than normal cells do.

(A) Normal cells, which multiply more rapidly than cancer cells, spread more slowly.
(B) Cancer cells, which multiply faster than normal cells, also spread faster.
(C) Cancer cells spread more slowly, although they multiply more rapidly, than normal cells.
(D) Because normal cells spread more slowly, they also multiply more slowly than cancer cells.

59. Zoysia grass, which is good in Southern areas, may be very poor in cooler areas where it turns green too late in spring and goes brown too early in the fall.

(A) Zoysia grass gets brown early in the fall and turns green early in spring in cooler areas.
(B) Zoysia grass turns green earlier in Southern areas than it does in cooler areas.
(C) Zoysia grass is good in Southern areas, because it turns green late in spring and does not turn brown in fall.
(D) Zoysia grass is not good for cooler areas, where it becomes green only late in spring and stays green only until early fall, but it works well in Southern areas.

60. More is known of conditions on Mars than of conditions on Pluto.

(A) Conditions on Pluto are better known than conditions on Mars.
(B) Neither conditions on Mars nor the conditions on Pluto are well known.
(C) We know less about conditions on Mars than about conditions on Pluto.
(D) Conditions on Pluto are less well known than conditions on Mars.

Test 1—Answer Key

I: LISTENING COMPREHENSION

Part A

1.	B	6.	C	11.	D	16.	D
2.	B	7.	C	12.	C	17.	C
3.	A	8.	D	13.	D	18.	D
4.	D	9.	B	14.	B	19.	C
5.	D	10.	B	15.	C	20.	A

Part B

21.	B	26.	C			31.	D
22.	A	27.	D			32.	C
23.	C	28.	B			33.	D
24.	B	29.	B			34.	B
25.	B	30.	C			35.	C

Part C

36.	D	41.	C			46.	D
37.	C	42.	B			47.	A
38.	A	43.	B			48.	D
39.	A	44.	A			49.	C
40.	D	45.	C			50.	D

II: STRUCTURE AND WRITTEN EXPRESSION

Part A

1.	C	6.	B	11.	B
2.	D	7.	B	12.	A
3.	A	8.	A	13.	D
4.	C	9.	C	14.	A
5.	B	10.	D	15.	C

36

Part B

16. C		25. C		34. A
17. C		26. C		35. B
18. C		27. B		36. C
19. D		28. A		37. D
20. B		29. C		38. A
21. D		30. D		39. D
22. D		31. A		40. A
23. C		32. C		
24. C		33. D		

III: READING COMPREHENSION AND VOCABULARY

Part A

1. A	9. B	17. A	25. A
2. C	10. D	18. A	26. B
3. C	11. C	19. B	27. D
4. B	12. A	20. C	28. D
5. A	13. B	21. A	29. A
6. B	14. A	22. C	30. C
7. A	15. D	23. C	
8. D	16. D	24. A	

Part B

31. B	39. B	47. C	55. C
32. C	40. C	48. C	56. B
33. A	41. B	49. D	57. C
34. B	42. D	50. D	58. B
35. A	43. B	51. A	59. D
36. D	44. D	52. C	60. D
37. D	45. B	53. A	
38. C	46. C	54. D	

Test 1—Explanatory Answers

II: Structure and Written Expression

1. Among the astronomers of ancient Greece, two theories _____ concerning the place of the earth in the universe.
   (This sentence is made complete by a finite verb.)

(A)	*developing*	*Developing* is not a verb.
(B)	*in development*	This choice is incorrect because it contains no finite verb.
(C)	*developed*	CORRECT ANSWER
(D)	*which they developed*	This choice is incorrect because it is a dependent adjective clause.

2. The geocentric idea was abandoned in the seventeenth century, partly as a result of the writings of Copernicus _____ observations made by other astronomers.
   (This sentence contains two modifying phrases connected by a coordinating conjunction.)

(A)	*and also were*	This choice is wrong because it contains a verb.
(B)	*not only because of*	The conjunction *not only* is grammatically incorrect in this choice.
(C)	*also because were*	This choice does not contain a coordinating conjunction.
(D)	*and also because of*	CORRECT ANSWER

3. The largest meteorite on display is in the American Museum in New York City, _____ over 34 tons.
   (This sentence contains two independent clauses connected by a coordinating conjunction.)

(A)	*and it weighs*	CORRECT ANSWER
(B)	*it weighs*	This choice does not contain a conjunction and results in a comma splice (two independent clauses connected by a comma).
(C)	*its weight is*	This choice results in a comma splice. See (B).
(D)	*which it weighs*	The word *it* makes this choice a faulty adjective clause. Also, the relative pronoun *which* is misplaced. The following sentence would be an acceptable choice: "The largest meteorite on display, which weighs over 34 tons, is in the American Museum in New York City."

4. *Rotation* refers to the turning of the earth _____ to the movement around the sun.

    (in this sentence, the verb *refers* is implied, although not written, in the second part of the sentence.)

    (A) *besides* revolution — This choice is wrong because the word *besides* is not a conjunction. It is used here as a preposition.

    (B) revolution *refers* — Since there is no conjunction, this choice results in a comma splice. See 3(B).

    (C) *and* revolution — CORRECT ANSWER

    (D) *while* revolution *referring* — The word *referring* makes this choice incorrect. *While revolution refers* would be an acceptable choice.

5. There are several means _____ latitude and longitude.

    (This answer choice illustrates the use of an infinitive as a modifier.)

    (A) *can determine* — This is a verb and not a modifier.

    (B) *to determine* — CORRECT ANSWER

    (C) *by them can be determined* — The word *them* makes this choice incorrect. *By which we can determine* would be an acceptable choice.

    (D) *we use them to determine* — The omission of the word *them* would make this answer choice acceptable. Likewise, the words *which we use to determine* would be correct.

6. Bernard Foucault _____ in 1851 that the earth is rotating.

    (A finite verb makes this sentence complete.)

    (A) *who proved* — This choice results in an incomplete sentence.

    (B) *proved* — CORRECT ANSWER

    (C) *he proved* — The word *he* is incorrect because it repeats the subject of the sentence (Bernard Foucault).

    (D) *it was proved* — The use of the passive voice is incorrect in this choice. The following sentence would be an acceptable choice: "It was proved by Bernard Foucault in 1851 that the earth is rotating."

7. The Homestead Act of 1862 _____ to acquire land at a small cost.

    (This sentence is made complete by a verb, an object, and a complement.)

    (A) *made possible* — This choice lacks an object.

    (B) *made it possible* — CORRECT ANSWER

    (C) *made the possibility* — The use of *the possibility* makes this choice incorrect.

    (D) *possibly made* — The words *possibly made* do not make sense in this sentence.

8. The earth revolves a little more rapidly _____ it is closer to the sun. (In this sentence, a connecting word referring to time is needed.)

(A)	*when*	CORRECT ANSWER
(B)	*or*	The conjunction *or* does not refer to time. It makes no sense in this sentence.
(C)	*than*	The conjunction *than* is used in clauses of comparison. There is no comparison in this sentence.
(D)	*wherever*	The conjunction *wherever* refers to place and not to time. The word *whenever* would be an acceptable choice.

9. _____, Sir Isaac Newton described the laws of gravitation. (This sentence is complete as written. However, a dependent clause or modifying phrase can be added at the beginning of the sentence.)

(A)	*Was a seventeenth-century scientist*	The addition of the verb *was* makes this choice wrong.
(B)	*Who was a seventeenth-century scientist*	This choice, an adjective clause, is grammatically correct, but it is misplaced. *Who was a seventeenth-century scientist* must be placed after *Sir Isaac Newton*.
(C)	*A seventeenth-century scientist*	CORRECT ANSWER
(D)	*When was a seventeenth-century scientist*	The omission of the subject *he* before the verb *was* makes this choice wrong.

10. The moon is not a planet _____ the planets in many respects. (This sentence includes an independent clause followed by a dependent clause of contrast.)

(A)	*resembling*	This choice does not make any sense.
(B)	*which resembles*	Although this choice is grammatically correct, it does not show contrast.
(C)	*but resemblance to*	The noun *resemblance* makes this choice incorrect. *But it resembles* would be an acceptable choice.
(D)	*although it resembles*	CORRECT ANSWER

11. Especially important to many people _____. (This sentence is an example of inverted word order, where the subject comes at the end of the sentence.)

(A)	*there is legislation against pollution*	The addition of the word *there* makes this choice incorrect.
(B)	*is legislation against pollution*	CORRECT ANSWER
(C)	*it is legislation against pollution*	The word *it* makes this choice incorrect. Notice that the sentence, "It is legislation against pollution that is especially important to many people," would be correct.

(D) *legislation against pollution is*   The word order in this choice is incorrect. See (B).

12. _____, the lion is a member of the cat family.
(This sentence is complete as written, but an introductory prepositional phrase can be added at the beginning of the sentence.)

(A) *Like the tiger*   CORRECT ANSWER
(B) *Alike to the tiger*   *Alike* is not a preposition.
(C) *Liking the tiger*   This choice does not make sense because the sentence is not trying to indicate that the lion likes the tiger. Rather, the sentence shows in which way the lion may be compared to the tiger.
(D) *It is like the tiger*   This choice is an independent clause and results in a comma splice. See 3(B).

13. Botanists are not sure where the first plant was grown or even _____.
(This sentence is made complete by a noun clause.)

(A) *what plant was*   The omission of the word *it* before the verb *was* makes this choice incorrect.
(B) *it was what plant*   The word order is incorrect in this choice.
(C) *what plant was it*   This choice is not a noun clause but rather a simple question. A noun clause does not follow question word order.
(D) *what plant it was*   CORRECT ANSWER

14. As a Congressman from Ohio, a Republican, and _____ the antiwar movement, the young politician became well known during the 1960's.
(In this sentence, the preposition *as* has three nouns as its objects. The principle of parallelism—or making grammatical elements equal—is illustrated.)

(A) *a leader of*   CORRECT ANSWER
(B) *to lead*   This choice does not make sense.
(C) *leading*   This choice results in a sentence which is not parallel.
(D) *he was leading*   *He was leading* contains a subject and a verb. This construction is not parallel with the nouns *Congressman* and *Republican*.

15. If a star seems to be moving in a wavy line, _____ of being a double star.
(Since the first clause is a dependent clause of condition, an independent clause is needed to complete the sentence.)

(A) *we suspect*   This choice lacks an object.
(B) *that we suspect*   This choice is not an independent clause.
(C) *we suspect it*   CORRECT ANSWER
(D) *the suspicion*   This answer choice is wrong since it does not include a subject and a verb.

16. (C) Include the preposition *in*. You should say *in which he used*.

17. (C) Omit the preposition *in*. Notice that the preposition *in* already occurs before *the region*. The last part of the sentence should read ". . . in the region *which* they once inhabited."

18. (C) You should say *has become* since *become* is the correct form of the verb to use with the auxiliary *has* in forming the present perfect tense.

19. (D) This phrase contains a mistake in tense. You should say *plants require* since the present tense instead of the past tense is indicated.

20. (B) Change the present tense verb *has* to the present perfect tense verb *has had*. The present perfect tense is often used to describe an action which began in the past and includes the present. In other words, the impact of Europe on world history began a long time ago and that impact continues into the present.

21. (D) The infinitive *to bring* is used incorrectly in this phrase. You should say *brought* in order to form the passive voice. The last part of the sentence should read ". . . some products must be *brought* from other lands."

22. (D) You should say *made up*. The past participle *made* is used here as an adjective to describe compound eyes.

23. (C) The tense in this phrase is wrong. You should use the past perfect tense *had planned*. The past perfect tense is used to describe an action that took place before another action in the past. In this sentence, the thieves planned before they stole the jewelry.

24. (C) You should use the connecting word *that* instead of *whether* to introduce the noun clause in this sentence. The connecting word *whether* is used to introduce a noun clause only when the principal verb is negative or when the principal verb has a negative implication. For example: "Scientists have *not* discovered *whether*. . ." would be grammatically correct.

25. (C) You should use the past tense verb *did* instead of the present perfect *have done* because the action was completed long ago. If the people were still doing excellent work, the present perfect tense would be correct.

26. (C) You should say *that event occurred* since a noun clause instead of a question form is indicated.

27. (B) You should use the adjective *American* to describe the noun *Indians*.

28. (A) You should use the phrase *lacked animals* since the word *lacking* is not a verb. Notice that the first part of the sentence forms a subordinate clause introduced by the subordinating conjunction *although*. Then the sentence will read "Although the Indians *lacked animals*. . ."

29. (C) The construction in this phrase is not parallel with *which is a hard, silvery metal* (a dependent clause). You should say *which was discovered*.

30. (D) The noun *influences* should be used. *Local conditions* and *influences* are the objects of the preposition *to*.

31. (A) This phrase contains an incorrect word. You should use the adverb *more* to form a comparison with the conjunction *than*. Then the sentence will say that the government troops were "*more* fortunate *than* the rebels. . ."

32. (C) You should say *the greatest* since the superlative degree of comparison is indi-

cated. The sentence should be "This region of the Andes . . . was *the greatest* center of metallurgy."

33. **(D)** This choice contains a shift in tense. You should use the past tense *predicted,* and now the verb is in the same time sequence as the verb *calculated.*

34. **(A)** You should say *used to getting,* since *used* in this phrase is an adjective meaning "accustomed." Notice that the corrected phrase consists of the adjective *used* followed by the preposition *to* followed by the gerund *getting.* The verb phrase *used to get* has a different meaning from *used (accustomed) to getting.*

35. **(B)** This choice contains a mistake in word order. You should say *was Socrates.*

36. **(C)** You should use the question word order *do we stop* because the clause is preceded by the negative word *rarely.* Notice that either *rarely do we stop* or *we rarely stop* would be equally correct.

37. **(D)** Use the adverb *likely,* which means "probably."

38. **(A)** You should use the singular noun *tree* since in this sentence *tree* is used as an adjective which modifies the noun *rings.* In English we say *tree rings.*

39. **(D)** You should use the infinitive *to be.* Then the last part of the sentence is ". . . the pharaoh was thought *to be* divine."

40. **(A)** This phrase contains a mistake in verb tense. You should use the past tense verb *wrote* since the action occurred at a specific time in the past (sometime before 1871).

III: READING COMPREHENSION AND VOCABULARY

Part A

Following are explanations of questions 1–30. In this section, the correct answers are placed first, so that they can be used to help explain the other choices.

1. (A) CORRECT: *Protect* means "to guard or to keep from harm," as does shield in the sentence.
   (B) *Conserve* means "to keep from being damaged, lost, or wasted." It cannot be used with the preposition *from.*
   (C) *Relieve* means "to free from pain, discomfort, or anxiety."
   (D) *Free* as a verb means "to let go of, to release from restraints."

2. (C) CORRECT: *Complains* and grumbles both mean "to express discontent."
   (A) *Giggles* means "high-pitched, rapid laughter," and would be expressive of pleasure, not discontent.
   (B) *Scolds* means "to rebuke," not "to grumble."
   (D) *Sneers* means "to show scorn or contempt."

3. (C) CORRECT: *Discolor* means "to cause a change in color by superficial burning." It can be substituted for scorch in the original sentence.

(A)	*Melt* means "to change from a solid to a liquid state."
(B)	In the sentence, *press* would mean "to iron," but not "to scorch."
(D)	*Wrinkle* means "to pucker" or "crease." Usually, an iron removes wrinkles.

4. **(B) CORRECT:** To <u>blink</u> one's eyes is *to open and close them.*

(A)	Although eyes can be *strained,* "injured by overexertion," and *stretched,* "opened to their greatest extent," neither word means the same as <u>blink</u>.
(C)	*Rub* means "to move one's hand, a cloth, etc., over a surface."
(D)	*Shade* means "to protect or screen from light." Exposure to light is not the only reason one blinks.

5. **(A) CORRECT:** *Quickly* means the same thing as the underlined word, <u>briskly</u>.

(B)	*Excitedly* means "emotionally aroused; agitated." It is possible that the man was excited, but the underlined word does not say so.
(C)	*Aimlessly* means "without purpose." A brisk walk may or may not be purposeful.
(D)	*Steadily* means to walk "without stopping." One might walk slowly but steadily.

6. **(B) CORRECT:** *Clever* and <u>shrewd</u> both mean "quick-witted in action and speech."

(A)	*Fortunate* means "lucky." A businessperson's success may be due to good luck, but *fortunate* does not mean <u>shrewd</u>.
(C)	*Wealthy* means "rich," and being rich will not make a person quick-witted nor prevent a person from losing money in a transaction.
(D)	No matter how *well-liked* a businessperson Michael is, being popular will not make him clever nor bring financial success.

7. **(A) CORRECT:** *Indication* means a "sign" or "evidence of something" and is synonymous with <u>trace</u>.

(B)	*Taste* is too specific to replace the underlined word. It is a particular kind of evidence.
(C)	*Color* is also a particular type of evidence.
(D)	*Smell* is too specific as well.

8. **(D) CORRECT:** *Complicated* means "complex" and can replace <u>intricate</u> without changing the meaning of the sentence.

(A)	*Vague* means "ambiguous; not clearly expressed." Vague directions may be "difficult to understand," but they are not necessarily <u>intricate</u>.
(B)	*Unusual* means "not common or ordinary."
(C)	*Routine* directions should not be "difficult to understand" since they are "in accordance with established procedure."

9. **(B) CORRECT:** *Sleepy* and drowsy are synonyms.
   (A)   *Lazy* means "unwilling to work."
   (C)   *Exhausted* means "tired."
   (D)   *Sad* means "unhappy." A long day will not ordinarily make one unhappy.

10. **(D) CORRECT:** A *desire for food* could replace appetite without loss of meaning.
    (A)   A *desire for exercise* means a "wish for activity or physical exertion."
    (B)   One might have a *desire for visitors* without wanting to eat.
    (C)   A *desire for sleep* probably would not diminish, "grow less," with illness, and it does not have anything to do with hunger.

11. **(C) CORRECT:** In this sentence, *lingered* means stayed late.
    (A)   *Neglected* means "failed to do."
    (B)   *Attempted* means "tried."
    (D)   *Struggled* means "exerted muscular energy; strove."

12. **(A) CORRECT:** In this sentence, *misty* and foggy both refer to a "mass of fine droplets of water in the atmosphere," droplets that decrease visibility.
    (B)   *Moist* means "slightly wet" and is not usually used to describe a night.
    (C)   *Mild* means "temperate; neither too hot nor too cold," and a mild night would not help or hinder a murderer's escape.
    (D)   *Messy* means "cluttered; untidy."

13. **(B) CORRECT:** *Edge* or rim means "brink or crest, as of a cliff or ridge of hills."
    (A)   *Top* means "the highest point of something," but not necessarily the edge.
    (C)   A *slope* here means "a stretch of ground forming a natural or artificial incline."
    (D)   *Base* here would mean the bottom of the cliff.

14. **(A) CORRECT:** *Capable* and competent both mean "efficient and able."
    (B)   *Industrious* means "hardworking," but not necessarily "efficient" or "able."
    (C)   *Thrifty* means "economical" or "frugal."
    (D)   In the context of this sentence, *careful* would mean "thorough; conscientious."

15. **(D) CORRECT:** *Uncommitted* is synonymous with neutral and means "taking no side; impartial."
    (A)   *Untroubled* means "free from worry."
    (B)   *Unhurried* means "not rushed."
    (C)   *Unmarried* means "single; not having a husband or wife."

16. **(D) CORRECT:** In this context, *homeless* means <u>stray</u>.
    (A) *Dirty* means "unclean, filthy." A <u>stray</u> dog may be dirty, but not all dirty dogs are strays.
    (B) *Sick* means "unwell; ill." Sick dogs are not necessarily <u>stray</u> dogs.
    (C) *Unfriendly* means "not disposed to friendship; hostile." Not all unfriendly dogs are strays, and not all strays are unfriendly.

17. **(A) CORRECT:** *Talking about* a problem is the same as <u>discussing</u> it.
    (B) *Thinking about* a problem does not involve speaking and would not be a synonym for <u>discussing</u>.
    (C) *Arguing about* suggests that those doing the talking are disagreeing, something not implied by <u>discussing</u>.
    (D) *Putting off* means "delaying."

18. **(A) CORRECT:** *Clothing* and <u>apparel</u> are synonyms.
    (B) *Confidence* means "trust or faith in oneself or in another." Whether or not a man is confident has little to do with his clothing.
    (C) An *answer* is a "response," usually to a question.
    (D) In this sentence, *manner* would mean "one's way of acting; a person's bearing or behavior."

19. **(B) CORRECT:** Both to do something of one's <u>own accord</u> and to do it *voluntarily* mean to do it "willingly."
    (A) *Enthusiastically* means "eagerly; ardently." Many who agree to do something of their <u>own accord</u> do not act enthusiastically.
    (C) Doing something *unwillingly* is the opposite of doing it of one's <u>own accord</u>.
    (D) In this sentence, *unhesitatingly* would mean "promptly, without pausing or faltering," and one can act of one's <u>own accord</u> and still hesitate.

20. **(C) CORRECT:** *Paying no attention to* something means <u>ignoring</u> it.
    (A) *Taking an interest in* something means the opposite of <u>ignoring</u> it.
    (B) *Looking closely at* something means examining it carefully, not <u>ignoring</u> it.
    (D) *Studying the causes of* something would involve paying a great deal of attention to it.

21. **(A) CORRECT:** In this sentence, <u>vulnerable</u> and *susceptible* mean that the shipping lanes were "unprotected from danger, open to physical attack, insufficiently defended."
    (B) In this context, *dangerous* to attack would mean that the attacker would be in peril, not the shipping lanes.
    (C) *Futile* means "useless."
    (D) *Feasible* means "possible."

22. **(C) CORRECT:** *Pride* and vanity are synonyms here. Both mean one's "high opinion of oneself."
    (A) One's *family* are those people related to one by blood or marriage.
    (B) In this sentence, *prospects* would mean "chances for success."
    (D) Here *image* would mean "the concept of someone that is held by the public."

23. **(C) CORRECT:** A *trick* and a hoax describe "acts intended to deceive, either as a joke or a serious fraud."
    (A) A *breakthrough* here would mean "a major achievement or success."
    (B) A *mistake* is an "error."
    (D) A *crime* is an "act that breaks the law," and although some hoaxes may be illegal, not all hoaxes are crimes.

24. **(A) CORRECT:** In this sentence, *ambiguous* and equivocal mean "capable of two interpretations; evasive."
    (B) Here *reasonable* would mean "in accordance with sound thinking."
    (C) *Friendly* means "not antagonistic; amicable."
    (D) To be *frank* would mean "to be open and honest," almost the opposite of equivocal.

25. **(A) CORRECT:** Littered means "to make *dirty* by discarding rubbish carelessly."
    (B) In this sentence, *filled* the park suggests that the crowd "occupied" the park.
    (C) *Cleaned* the park would mean the opposite of littered the park.
    (D) *Left* the park would mean that the crowd had gone out of the park.

26. **(B) CORRECT:** In this context, an asset, a "useful or valuable quality," means an *advantage*.
    (A) *Deception* means "fraud," or "trickery."
    (C) *Liability* is "something that works to one's disadvantage."
    (D) Here, *pride* means "a high opinion of oneself," or "self-satisfaction."

27. **(D) CORRECT:** *Inspected* means examined or "looked at carefully."
    (A) *Processed* means "prepared or treated."
    (B) *Cleaned* means "washed."
    (C) Here, *compared* means to note the similarities among different fossils.

28. **(D) CORRECT:** Affluent and *wealthy* nations are both "rich."
    (A) *Large* means "big" in size, not wealth.
    (B) *Industrialized* means "having highly developed industries."
    (C) *Advanced* nations are "ahead of their contemporaries," usually in technology and thought.

29. (A) CORRECT: An *unrehearsed* remark is "impromptu, made without preparation; spontaneous."

    (B) *Forceful* means "effective or persuasive." A spontaneous remark is not necessarily forceful.

    (C) *Unrestrained* here would mean "unchecked." A remark may be unrestrained without being impromptu.

    (D) *Absurd* means "foolish or ridiculous." An impromptu remark might be absurd or sensible.

30. (C) CORRECT: *Interferes* and meddles both mean "to intrude in other people's affairs or business."

    (A) *Participates* means "to take part in," or "to join and share with." There is no suggestion that "participation" is unwelcome or intrusive.

    (B) *To delight in* is "to take pleasure in" or "to enjoy."

    (D) In this sentence, *dabbles* would mean "to undertake something superficially or without serious intent."

Part B

31. This question tests the main idea.

    (A) The statement asserts that others have done research, not romantic Southerners.

    (B) CORRECT: No investigations have persuaded romantic Southerners *to change their views.*

    (C) The investigations have not modified their views.

    (D) "Romantic mental pictures" imply that their views, in contrast to the results of the "minute investigations," are not realistic.

32. This question tests a subordinate idea asserted in the statement.

    (A) "Minute" here suggests exhaustive and detailed investigation.

    (B) See 31(C) above.

    (C) CORRECT: See 32(A) above.

    (D) The passage asserts that romantic Southerners have created mental pictures, not those who have conducted the investigations.

33. The question tests the implied sense of the statement.

    (A) CORRECT: The facts result from the "minute investigations," and they have no appreciable effect on the views of the romantic Southerner.

    (B) See 31 (D) above.

    (C) The statement implies that the views are so strongly held that no facts can shake them.

    (D) The historians' views are based on the "minute investigations" which, the statement implies, contradict the "mental pictures" of the romantic Southerner.

34. This question tests a subordinate idea asserted in the statement.

    (A)   See 34(B) below.

    (B) CORRECT: "Quarter" here refers to a one-fourth part. A quarter of a century (100 years) is twenty-five years. The passage refers to the "last quarter," and a century is named one number higher than the first two digits in the numbered years of the century; accordingly, the "*last quarter* of the *seventeenth century*" is 1675–1700. When terms like "quarter" and "half" refer to part of a century, the reference almost always is to be only *approximate.*

    (C)   See 34(B) above.

    (D)   See 34(B) above.

35. This question tests the main idea of the statement.

    (A) CORRECT: "Artificiality" and "formality" are usually contrary to *naturalness.*

    (B)   The period is criticized for being too formal.

    (C)   The passage states that *grace* was a characteristic of the time.

    (D)   The passage suggests that the class of people criticized exhibited good manners (*manners* here refers to the forms and rituals of social behavior). Their behavior was formal and graceful. The good manners of this class, however, were superficial.

36. This question tests an idea implied in the statement.

    (A)   "Artificiality" and "elaborate" in this context suggest just the opposite of *simple.*

    (B)   The statement asserts that the lives of these people were more silly (foolish) than *wicked* (evil).

    (C)   *Virtuous* suggests a morally good life; "vice" and "silliness" are inconsistent with goodness.

    (D) CORRECT: *Conventional* suggests being governed or bound by conventions. The passage implies this is the most noticeable characteristic of the lives of these people.

37. This question tests a distinction between what the statement asserts and what it does not.

    (A)   They were *hypocritical:* they behaved in public as though they were courteous and serious, but they showed themselves otherwise to be vicious and silly.

    (B)   See 35(A) above.

    (C)   See 35(B) above.

    (D) CORRECT: The author does not indicate directly whether he considers the people of this class *witty* or not. One may infer from the passage that he does not consider them to be especially witty. Usually one does not consider something "simultaneously" silly and witty; but persons may be sometimes silly, sometimes witty.

38. This statement tests an idiomatic expression (implied idea) in the main clause.

    (A)   It was as low 16 months earlier.

    (B)   See 38(C) below.

    (C) CORRECT: "16-month low" is an idiomatic expression which means that the last time the market was so low was 16 months earlier.

    (D)   See 38(C) above.

39. This question tests a supporting idea in the statement.

    (A)   A "noted analyst" has said again that prices will *slump* (go down) *further*.

    (B) CORRECT: "Trim" means "to cut off of," in this context "to make smaller."

    (C)   *Stay within* means not to exceed the budget. It does not mean to make it smaller.

    (D)   "In active trading" in the statement describes the kind of "low" the market has suffered.

40. This question tests for a detail in the description.

    (A)   The room's use is implied in name but not otherwise mentioned.

    (B)   Same as 40(A) above.

    (C) CORRECT: "One" in line 7 refers back to "bedrooms." The statement in parentheses suggests possible uses for the room.

    (D)   One bedroom could be made into a playroom.

41. This question tests for a comparison of details in the description.

    (A)   Described as "large," line 3.

    (B) CORRECT: Described as (1) "separate," (2) "15-foot," (3) "with crystal chandelier," and (4) "built-in buffet," lines 2–3.

    (C)   Described as (1) "paneled," (2) "with fireplace," line 5.

    (D)   Described as (1) "huge," (2) "with lots of cabinets," lines 5–6.

42. This question tests for a comparison of details.

    (A)   Only the breakfast room is described as "cheery," line 6.

    (B)   Only the buffet in the dining room is described as "built-in," line 4.

    (C)   Only the chandelier in the dining room is mentioned, line 4.

    (D) CORRECT: The living room is "large" (line 3), the dining room is "15-foot" (line 3), the kitchen is "huge" (line 5), the breakfast room is "big" (line 6), the bedrooms are "huge" (line 7).

43. This question tests for attention to details.

    (A)   Mentioned in line 10.

    (B) CORRECT: Not mentioned.

    (C)   Mentioned in line 10.

    (D)   Mentioned in line 5.

44. This question tests for word recognition.

    (A)   See 44(D) below.
    (B)   "Buffet" can mean a meal, but not in this context.
    (C)   See D below.
    (D) CORRECT: This "buffet" is an article of furniture used for serving food; "built-in" means that it is attached to the wall and cannot be removed.

45. This question tests for word recognition.

    (A)   *Writer* means "a person who writes."
    (B) CORRECT: An "anthology" is a *collection* of writings, usually, as in this case, by various writers.
    (C)   The anthologies referred to are collections of poems by various 19th-century poets.
    (D)   A *poet* is "a person who writes poems."

46. This question tests for attention to detail.

    (A)   Her brother "urged her to publish her poems" (line 9) after she had written many of them.
    (B)   She wrote poems for fifty-three years (lines 5–6).
    (C) CORRECT: She began writing poems at the age of eleven.
    (D)   Her genius could only be recognized *after* she had written poems.

47. This question tests for the ability to draw inferences.

    (A)   No mention is made of his affection for his sister, nor would affection necessarily make him a good judge of her poems.
    (B)   He did publish poems, but this information is not given in the passage.
    (C) CORRECT: See lines 7–8.
    (D)   He was a painter. The passage does not indicate whether or not he was famous as a painter; nor would being a *famous painter* qualify him as a judge of poetry.

48. This question tests for word recognition.

    (A)   *Forbade*, past tense form of *forbid*, would mean in this context "to have commanded not to" publish—almost the opposite sense of "urged" here.
    (B)   *Dared* would mean here "to have challenged" her to publish. See 48(C) below.
    (C) CORRECT: "Urged" in this context has the sense "strongly encouraged."
    (D)   *Forced* would mean in this context "that he compelled her to publish by applying some power he had over her."

49. This question tests for attention to detail.

    (A)   See 49(D) below.
    (B)   See 49(C, D) below.

(C)   She had written "more than eleven hundred poems" (line 11).

(D) CORRECT: "And had published over nine hundred" (lines 11–12).

50. This question tests for comprehension.

(A)   The passage was written after her death, by which time more than nine hundred of her poems had been published.

(B)   See 50(A) above.

(C)   She lived in the nineteenth century (lines 1–2, 4, 10).

(D) CORRECT: "There is still . . ." (line 14) means that, as of the time the passage was written, "no authoritative edition of her poetry" had been published.

51. This question tests for attention to detail.

(A) CORRECT: The Jesuits began their work in the Natchez villages at about this time (lines 7–9).

(B)   This is the year the LaSalle party stopped where the Natchez tribe lived.

(C)   This is when the Jesuits left the Natchez mission (about eight years after they began it in 1699) (line 11).

(D)   This date is not mentioned in the passage.

52. This question tests for comprehension.

(A)   The Natchez did not have a mission.

(B)   The French founded the colony.

(C) CORRECT: Their hostility is suggested throughout the passage.

(D)   That they were hostile implies that they were not receptive to French ways.

53. This question tests for the main idea of the paragraph.

(A) CORRECT: This idea is stated in the topic sentence of the paragraph (lines 1–3); "hostility" (line 3) suggests *unfriendliness*.

(B)   The size of the tribe is not mentioned in the paragraph.

(C)   The quality of their civilization is not mentioned.

(D)   The paragraph does not mention *their method of government*.

54. This question tests for word recognition.

(A)   "Fruitless" here suggests just the opposite.

(B)   *Unpredictable* means "not able to be foretold." See 54(D) below.

(C)   No mention is made of the Jesuits planting trees.

(D) CORRECT: "Fruitless" here means *unproductive*.

55. This question tests for attention to detail.

(A)   Mentioned in line 12.

(B)   Mentioned in line 12, implied in the whole paragraph.

(C) CORRECT: Not mentioned in the paragraph.

(D)   The tribe is specifically described as "strong" (line 16).

56. This question tests for word recognition.

    (A)   *Hunted* in this context would mean "went out to kill game for food."

    (B) CORRECT: *Lived* and "resided" are synonyms.

    (C)   *Hid* in this context would mean "concealed," probably in order to attack.

    (D)   *Waited* would mean, in this context, "to stay in readiness."

57. (A)   *Is very different from* means almost the opposite of "is not unlike."

    (B)   *Identical* means "alike in every way"; see 57(C) below.

    (C) CORRECT: "Not unlike" means "like" or "similar to"—alike in many ways.

    (D)   *Not like* means almost the opposite of "not unlike"—its sense is comparable to 57(A) above.

58. (A)   The original sentence states that cancer cells multiply more rapidly than normal cells.

    (B) CORRECT: Same sense as original, but different emphasis.

    (C)   The original sentence states that cancer cells spread more rapidly than normal cells.

    (D)   This sentence asserts a causal relation between the speed of spreading and the speed of multiplying in cells. The original does not.

59. (A)   In cooler areas, zoysia grass turns green "late" in spring.

    (B)   This statement is consistent with the original, but not the closest restatement available. See 59(D) below.

    (C)   The original implies that zoysia grass turns green *earlier* in spring in Southern areas, and nowhere suggests that it does *not* turn brown in fall.

    (D) CORRECT: Same sense as original, but with different emphasis.

60. (A)   States just the opposite of the original.

    (B)   May be true, but the original *compares* degrees of knowledge about the two heavenly bodies.

    (C)   Means the same as 60(A) above.

    (D) CORRECT: Same sense as original, but different emphasis.

ANSWER SHEET FOR TEST 2

Tear out this answer sheet and use it to record your answers to all the questions in this examination.

SECTION I

1 Ⓐ Ⓑ Ⓒ Ⓓ	11 Ⓐ Ⓑ Ⓒ Ⓓ	21 Ⓐ Ⓑ Ⓒ Ⓓ	31 Ⓐ Ⓑ Ⓒ Ⓓ	41 Ⓐ Ⓑ Ⓒ Ⓓ
2 Ⓐ Ⓑ Ⓒ Ⓓ	12 Ⓐ Ⓑ Ⓒ Ⓓ	22 Ⓐ Ⓑ Ⓒ Ⓓ	32 Ⓐ Ⓑ Ⓒ Ⓓ	42 Ⓐ Ⓑ Ⓒ Ⓓ
3 Ⓐ Ⓑ Ⓒ Ⓓ	13 Ⓐ Ⓑ Ⓒ Ⓓ	23 Ⓐ Ⓑ Ⓒ Ⓓ	33 Ⓐ Ⓑ Ⓒ Ⓓ	43 Ⓐ Ⓑ Ⓒ Ⓓ
4 Ⓐ Ⓑ Ⓒ Ⓓ	14 Ⓐ Ⓑ Ⓒ Ⓓ	24 Ⓐ Ⓑ Ⓒ Ⓓ	34 Ⓐ Ⓑ Ⓒ Ⓓ	44 Ⓐ Ⓑ Ⓒ Ⓓ
5 Ⓐ Ⓑ Ⓒ Ⓓ	15 Ⓐ Ⓑ Ⓒ Ⓓ	25 Ⓐ Ⓑ Ⓒ Ⓓ	35 Ⓐ Ⓑ Ⓒ Ⓓ	45 Ⓐ Ⓑ Ⓒ Ⓓ
6 Ⓐ Ⓑ Ⓒ Ⓓ	16 Ⓐ Ⓑ Ⓒ Ⓓ	26 Ⓐ Ⓑ Ⓒ Ⓓ	36 Ⓐ Ⓑ Ⓒ Ⓓ	46 Ⓐ Ⓑ Ⓒ Ⓓ
7 Ⓐ Ⓑ Ⓒ Ⓓ	17 Ⓐ Ⓑ Ⓒ Ⓓ	27 Ⓐ Ⓑ Ⓒ Ⓓ	37 Ⓐ Ⓑ Ⓒ Ⓓ	47 Ⓐ Ⓑ Ⓒ Ⓓ
8 Ⓐ Ⓑ Ⓒ Ⓓ	18 Ⓐ Ⓑ Ⓒ Ⓓ	28 Ⓐ Ⓑ Ⓒ Ⓓ	38 Ⓐ Ⓑ Ⓒ Ⓓ	48 Ⓐ Ⓑ Ⓒ Ⓓ
9 Ⓐ Ⓑ Ⓒ Ⓓ	19 Ⓐ Ⓑ Ⓒ Ⓓ	29 Ⓐ Ⓑ Ⓒ Ⓓ	39 Ⓐ Ⓑ Ⓒ Ⓓ	49 Ⓐ Ⓑ Ⓒ Ⓓ
10 Ⓐ Ⓑ Ⓒ Ⓓ	20 Ⓐ Ⓑ Ⓒ Ⓓ	30 Ⓐ Ⓑ Ⓒ Ⓓ	40 Ⓐ Ⓑ Ⓒ Ⓓ	50 Ⓐ Ⓑ Ⓒ Ⓓ

SECTION II

1 Ⓐ Ⓑ Ⓒ Ⓓ	9 Ⓐ Ⓑ Ⓒ Ⓓ	17 Ⓐ Ⓑ Ⓒ Ⓓ	25 Ⓐ Ⓑ Ⓒ Ⓓ	33 Ⓐ Ⓑ Ⓒ Ⓓ
2 Ⓐ Ⓑ Ⓒ Ⓓ	10 Ⓐ Ⓑ Ⓒ Ⓓ	18 Ⓐ Ⓑ Ⓒ Ⓓ	26 Ⓐ Ⓑ Ⓒ Ⓓ	34 Ⓐ Ⓑ Ⓒ Ⓓ
3 Ⓐ Ⓑ Ⓒ Ⓓ	11 Ⓐ Ⓑ Ⓒ Ⓓ	19 Ⓐ Ⓑ Ⓒ Ⓓ	27 Ⓐ Ⓑ Ⓒ Ⓓ	35 Ⓐ Ⓑ Ⓒ Ⓓ
4 Ⓐ Ⓑ Ⓒ Ⓓ	12 Ⓐ Ⓑ Ⓒ Ⓓ	20 Ⓐ Ⓑ Ⓒ Ⓓ	28 Ⓐ Ⓑ Ⓒ Ⓓ	36 Ⓐ Ⓑ Ⓒ Ⓓ
5 Ⓐ Ⓑ Ⓒ Ⓓ	13 Ⓐ Ⓑ Ⓒ Ⓓ	21 Ⓐ Ⓑ Ⓒ Ⓓ	29 Ⓐ Ⓑ Ⓒ Ⓓ	37 Ⓐ Ⓑ Ⓒ Ⓓ
6 Ⓐ Ⓑ Ⓒ Ⓓ	14 Ⓐ Ⓑ Ⓒ Ⓓ	22 Ⓐ Ⓑ Ⓒ Ⓓ	30 Ⓐ Ⓑ Ⓒ Ⓓ	38 Ⓐ Ⓑ Ⓒ Ⓓ
7 Ⓐ Ⓑ Ⓒ Ⓓ	15 Ⓐ Ⓑ Ⓒ Ⓓ	23 Ⓐ Ⓑ Ⓒ Ⓓ	31 Ⓐ Ⓑ Ⓒ Ⓓ	39 Ⓐ Ⓑ Ⓒ Ⓓ
8 Ⓐ Ⓑ Ⓒ Ⓓ	16 Ⓐ Ⓑ Ⓒ Ⓓ	24 Ⓐ Ⓑ Ⓒ Ⓓ	32 Ⓐ Ⓑ Ⓒ Ⓓ	40 Ⓐ Ⓑ Ⓒ Ⓓ

SECTION III

1 Ⓐ Ⓑ Ⓒ Ⓓ	11 Ⓐ Ⓑ Ⓒ Ⓓ	21 Ⓐ Ⓑ Ⓒ Ⓓ	31 Ⓐ Ⓑ Ⓒ Ⓓ	41 Ⓐ Ⓑ Ⓒ Ⓓ	51 Ⓐ Ⓑ Ⓒ Ⓓ
2 Ⓐ Ⓑ Ⓒ Ⓓ	12 Ⓐ Ⓑ Ⓒ Ⓓ	22 Ⓐ Ⓑ Ⓒ Ⓓ	32 Ⓐ Ⓑ Ⓒ Ⓓ	42 Ⓐ Ⓑ Ⓒ Ⓓ	52 Ⓐ Ⓑ Ⓒ Ⓓ
3 Ⓐ Ⓑ Ⓒ Ⓓ	13 Ⓐ Ⓑ Ⓒ Ⓓ	23 Ⓐ Ⓑ Ⓒ Ⓓ	33 Ⓐ Ⓑ Ⓒ Ⓓ	43 Ⓐ Ⓑ Ⓒ Ⓓ	53 Ⓐ Ⓑ Ⓒ Ⓓ
4 Ⓐ Ⓑ Ⓒ Ⓓ	14 Ⓐ Ⓑ Ⓒ Ⓓ	24 Ⓐ Ⓑ Ⓒ Ⓓ	34 Ⓐ Ⓑ Ⓒ Ⓓ	44 Ⓐ Ⓑ Ⓒ Ⓓ	54 Ⓐ Ⓑ Ⓒ Ⓓ
5 Ⓐ Ⓑ Ⓒ Ⓓ	15 Ⓐ Ⓑ Ⓒ Ⓓ	25 Ⓐ Ⓑ Ⓒ Ⓓ	35 Ⓐ Ⓑ Ⓒ Ⓓ	45 Ⓐ Ⓑ Ⓒ Ⓓ	55 Ⓐ Ⓑ Ⓒ Ⓓ
6 Ⓐ Ⓑ Ⓒ Ⓓ	16 Ⓐ Ⓑ Ⓒ Ⓓ	26 Ⓐ Ⓑ Ⓒ Ⓓ	36 Ⓐ Ⓑ Ⓒ Ⓓ	46 Ⓐ Ⓑ Ⓒ Ⓓ	56 Ⓐ Ⓑ Ⓒ Ⓓ
7 Ⓐ Ⓑ Ⓒ Ⓓ	17 Ⓐ Ⓑ Ⓒ Ⓓ	27 Ⓐ Ⓑ Ⓒ Ⓓ	37 Ⓐ Ⓑ Ⓒ Ⓓ	47 Ⓐ Ⓑ Ⓒ Ⓓ	57 Ⓐ Ⓑ Ⓒ Ⓓ
8 Ⓐ Ⓑ Ⓒ Ⓓ	18 Ⓐ Ⓑ Ⓒ Ⓓ	28 Ⓐ Ⓑ Ⓒ Ⓓ	38 Ⓐ Ⓑ Ⓒ Ⓓ	48 Ⓐ Ⓑ Ⓒ Ⓓ	58 Ⓐ Ⓑ Ⓒ Ⓓ
9 Ⓐ Ⓑ Ⓒ Ⓓ	19 Ⓐ Ⓑ Ⓒ Ⓓ	29 Ⓐ Ⓑ Ⓒ Ⓓ	39 Ⓐ Ⓑ Ⓒ Ⓓ	49 Ⓐ Ⓑ Ⓒ Ⓓ	59 Ⓐ Ⓑ Ⓒ Ⓓ
10 Ⓐ Ⓑ Ⓒ Ⓓ	20 Ⓐ Ⓑ Ⓒ Ⓓ	30 Ⓐ Ⓑ Ⓒ Ⓓ	40 Ⓐ Ⓑ Ⓒ Ⓓ	50 Ⓐ Ⓑ Ⓒ Ⓓ	60 Ⓐ Ⓑ Ⓒ Ⓓ

-15

Test 2

I: LISTENING COMPREHENSION

(50 Questions—40 Minutes)

This section of the test requires a demonstration of your ability to understand spoken English. Each of the three parts has special directions. **The spoken parts of this test are on the Arco TOEFL cassette tape.** (See page 343 for ordering information.) If you cannot use the tape, have a friend read the spoken parts of questions 1 to 50 to you from the script on page 249.

Part A

Directions. In this part of the test you will hear a brief statement. Each statement will be spoken only once. The statement does not appear in your test booklet. When you have heard a statement, select the answer nearest in meaning to what you have heard. Record your answer on the answer sheet.

Example

You will hear: The Wagners seem to take their large family in stride.

You will read: (A) Mr. Wagner comes from a large family.
(B) Mrs. Wagner comes from a large family.
(C) Mr. and Mrs. Wagner are the parents of many children.
(D) The Wagners dislike small families.

The correct answer to the example is (C).

1. (A) I pay my rent before the middle of each month.
(B) I do not pay my rent until after the fifteenth of the month.
(C) I have fifteen bills a month, including my rent.
(D) I rarely pay my rent when it is due.

2. (A) Both bedspreads cost the same amount.
(B) The green bedspread is the same size as the blue one.
(C) The blue bedspread isn't as pretty as the other one.
(D) One of the bedspreads has blue checks.

3. (A) Mary will graduate in June, and then she's going away.
(B) Mary intends to do graduate work in chemistry after June.
(C) Mary won't graduate in June because of chemistry.
(D) Mary must take another chemistry course before she can graduate in June.

4. (A) The machine does not spin if you close the top.
(B) The top of the machine spins during operation.
(C) Do not open the machine when it is spinning.
(D) The operation of the machine requires you to spin.

5. (A) John likes to take chances.
(B) John dislikes eating sweets.

(C) John never turns down sweets when they are offered to him.

(D) John will not take a chance on eating sweets.

6. (A) We knew almost every person at the party.

(B) We knew none of the people at the party.

(C) We guess we had a better time at the party than the other people.

(D) We had a good time with the guests at the party.

7. (A) Tigers occasionally consume human beings when they are hungry.

(B) People rarely scare tigers.

(C) Tigers are scarce today, just like food.

(D) Food is available for human beings but not for tigers.

8. (A) I like Bill Jones, but he doesn't like me.

(B) Bill Jones and I don't know each other very well.

(C) Most fellows are acquainted with Bill Jones.

(D) Bill Jones is a well-known, likeable fellow.

9. (A) The shoe shop is not located in the shopping center.

(B) The cafeteria is on the east side of the shopping center.

(C) The shoe shop closes at the same time as the cafeteria.

(D) The shoe shop near the cafeteria is closed.

10. (A) Peter wants his father to be an architect.

(B) Peter and his father wish to become architects.

(C) Peter would like to be an architect.

(D) Peter wants the architect to like his father.

11. (A) Mary got into bed without setting the alarm.

(B) Mary was alarmed when she couldn't get to sleep.

(C) Mary's sleep was interrupted by the alarm.

(D) Mary almost slept through the alarm.

12. (A) Carolyn is a better math student than her tutor.

(B) Tutors cannot be found this semester.

(C) Carolyn needs to do better in math.

(D) Carolyn has improved in math this semester.

13. (A) He was surprised when I came.

(B) I was not surprised by his actions.

(C) He told me that he was not surprised.

(D) His behavior surprised me.

14. (A) More men than women have insurance.

(B) Male insurance agents outnumber female agents.

(C) Women are twice as likely as men to have insurance.

(D) Insurance is twice as difficult to sell to women as to men.

15. (A) Mr. Moore's secretary delivered the lawyer's message.

(B) Mr. Moore and his lawyer had lunch together in the office.

(C) Mr. Moore advised his secretary to deliver lunch to his lawyer.

(D) The lawyer asked the secretary to have lunch with him.

16. (A) The plane landed at 5:30.

(B) The plane was on time.

(C) The landing was delayed for half an hour.

(D) The plane didn't land until 6:30.

17. (A) Frank wants Harriet to stay.

(B) Harriet will stay, but Frank wants her to leave.

(C) Harriet wants to leave unless Frank stays.

(D) Whatever Harriet does is all right with Frank.

18. (A) When I saw him, he tried to escape.
    (B) His face seemed unfamiliar to me when I saw him.
    (C) When I saw him, I couldn't recall his name.
    (D) As soon as I saw him, I remembered his name.

19. (A) Walter is sorry about his engagement to Susan.
    (B) Susan has decided not to marry Walter.
    (C) Susan is upset that Walter broke their engagement.
    (D) Susan and Walter regret their marriage.

20. (A) Mr. Conner wore old clothes to the bank.
    (B) Mr. Conner's bank was old and large.
    (C) Mr. Conner wore old clothes in a large size.
    (D) Mr. Conner did not spend money on clothes.

Part B

Directions. This section of the Listening Comprehension test consists of fifteen short conversations between two people. When each conversation ends, you will be asked a question by a third voice about what was said. You will hear the question only once and you must choose the answer from the four choices given. When you have chosen what you believe to be the best answer to the question, record your answer on the answer sheet.

Example

You will hear:

(Man) "I've never understood how to use the card catalogue, and I need to get this information today."

(Woman) "Why don't you pick up one of the guidebooks at the front desk? It will help you, I'm sure."

(Third voice) "Where did this conversation most likely occur?"

You will read: (A) At a museum.
(B) In a store.
(C) In a classroom.
(D) In a library.

The correct answer to the example is (D).

21. (A) The test consisted of one page.
    (B) The exam was difficult for the woman.
    (C) The woman found the exam easy.
    (D) The woman completed the exam in one hour.

22. (A) Parents.
    (B) A teacher and a student.
    (C) Two friends.
    (D) A parent and a child.

23. (A) Play the piano.
    (B) Learn to sing.
    (C) Keep her company.
    (D) Teach her to sing.

24. (A) Leave work early.
    (B) Call the telephone company at noon.
    (C) Go to work during the afternoon.
    (D) Go to the telephone company between one and three.

25. (A) On a college campus.
    (B) In a bank.
    (C) In a doctor's clinic.
    (D) In a hardware store.

26. (A) He was speeding.
    (B) He ran a red light.
    (C) He went through a stop sign.
    (D) He turned a corner too fast.

27. (A) To save her money for a long time.
    (B) To buy a new car.
    (C) To purchase a used car.
    (D) To get a second car.

28. (A) Her guests don't like punch.
    (B) The man left two gallons of punch on the shelf.
    (C) She has too many gallons of punch.
    (D) She will run out of punch.

29. (A) His advisor.
    (B) His teacher.
    (C) His partner.
    (D) His boss.

30. (A) Frank's car was accidentally lost.
    (B) Frank was killed in a car accident.
    (C) Frank fell out of a car.
    (D) Frank survived a car accident.

31. (A) They are faded.
    (B) They are dirty.
    (C) They are dyed.
    (D) They are blue.

32. (A) They have two children already.
    (B) Mrs. Taylor wishes to have children, but her husband doesn't.
    (C) They will start a family as soon as they get married.
    (D) They don't want children for the time being.

33. (A) Four contestants failed to win prizes.
    (B) The man ate during the show.
    (C) The woman missed the show.
    (D) Five contestants won cars.

34. (A) Change apartments.
    (B) Look for a less expensive place to live.
    (C) Move to the mountains.
    (D) Find an older apartment away from the lakes.

35. (A) Cough medicine.
    (B) Honey and whiskey.
    (C) Antibiotics.
    (D) Over-the-counter remedies.

Part C

Directions. In this part of the test, you will be required to listen to several short lectures and conversations. You will hear the lectures and conversations only once. They do not appear in your test booklet. When a question is asked, choose the best answer from the four given. Record your answer on the answer sheet.

36. (A) They thought there was gold in western Kansas.
    (B) They found slave labor too expensive.
    (C) They considered the land unproductive.
    (D) They liked the rich soil.

37. (A) By giving away gold.
    (B) By offering cheap land.
    (C) By constructing flour mills.
    (D) By opposing slave labor.

38. (A) The population is small, but the state is large.
    (B) It is a large state with a large population.
    (C) The state is small and it has few people.
    (D) Its sparse population inhabits 50,000 acres.

39. (A) Farming.
    (B) Running railroads.
    (C) Weaving baskets.
    (D) Mining.

40. (A) A survey done by Friends of Animals, Inc.
    (B) A report prepared by the city of Chicago.
    (C) A survey sponsored by the federal government.
    (D) A study done by the city of New York.

41. (A) A tax-funded organization.
    (B) A society that roams the streets.
    (C) A control center for destroying strays.
    (D) An agency interested in animals.

42. (A) Chicago.
    (B) New York City.
    (C) Friends of Animals, Inc.
    (D) The American Society for the Prevention of Cruelty to Animals.

43. (A) All of the lakes are located within the United States.
    (B) The lakes have salty water.
    (C) Many ships sail the lakes.
    (D) Lake Superior is the fifteenth largest lake in the world.

44. (A) Erie.
    (B) Michigan.
    (C) Huron.
    (D) Canada.

45. (A) To improve the lakes as a waterway.
    (B) To form a boundary between the United States and Canada.
    (C) To make all the lakes among the fifteen largest lakes in the world.
    (D) To keep fresh water in the lakes running.

46. (A) Huron.
    (B) Ontario.

    (C) Superior.
    (D) Erie.

47. (A) In the library on campus.
    (B) In a classroom.
    (C) In the professor's office.
    (D) In the corridor between classes.

48. (A) Eight weeks.
    (B) Six weeks.
    (C) Four weeks.
    (D) Two weeks.

49. (A) The professor believes that the student's work was not completely his own.
    (B) The professor believes that the student's work is inferior to that of the other students in the class.
    (C) The professor believes that the student's project is incomplete.
    (D) The professor believes that the student should discuss his project at the faculty meeting.

50. (A) Write a report.
    (B) Revise his project.
    (C) Give a talk to the class.
    (D) Take an examination.

II: STRUCTURE AND WRITTEN EXPRESSION

(40 questions—25 minutes)

Part A

Directions. In Part A each problem consists of an incomplete sentence. Below the sentence are four choices, marked (A), (B), (C), and (D). You should find the one choice which best completes the sentence. Mark your choice on the answer sheet.

Example

Because the United States has little tin, _____ produced in the rest of the world.

(A) tin is used
(B) it uses tin
(C) uses of tin
(D) uses tin

The correct answer to the example is (B).

1. The principle of a rocket motor is simple, _____ rockets are very complicated machines.

(A) large but which powerful
(B) but large, powerful

(C) large although powerful
(D) so large, powerful

2. The universe _____ we know it might have begun with a great explosion.

(A) as
(B) that
(C) and which
(D) and

3. _____ to find stars in pairs.

(A) It is very common
(B) Being very common
(C) Very common is
(D) That is very common

4. Some areas of the moon are so full of craters _____ an extremely rough surface.

(A) that they present
(B) presenting
(C) which present
(D) to present

5. James Cook, _____, also discovered the Hawaiian Islands.

(A) by exploring the South Sea he reached Australia
(B) explored the South Sea and reaching Australia
(C) who explored the South Sea and reached Australia
(D) explored the South Sea then reached Australia

6. _____, but it also filters out harmful sun rays.

(A) The atmosphere gives us air to breathe
(B) Not only the atmosphere gives us air to breathe
(C) The atmosphere which gives us air to breathe
(D) Not only does the atmosphere give us air to breathe

7. One of the most obvious characteristics of the moon is the way in which it continuously changes _____.

(A) in appearing
(B) its appearance
(C) are appearing
(D) for appearance

8. The total influence of literature upon the course of human history _____.

(A) an evaluation is difficult
(B) is difficult to evaluate
(C) difficult to evaluate it
(D) it is difficult to evaluate

9. _____, John Glenn was a pioneer in the U.S. space program.

(A) Despite the first American who orbited the earth
(B) That the first American orbited the earth
(C) The first American to orbit the earth
(D) He was the first American to orbit the earth

10. _____ with the size of the whole earth, the highest mountains do not seem high at all.

(A) When compared
(B) Compare them
(C) If you compare
(D) A comparison

11. Determining the mineral content of soil samples is an exacting process; _____, experts must perform detailed tests to analyze soil specimens.

(A) so that
(B) however
(C) afterwards
(D) therefore

12. The amount of gravitational attraction between two objects depends on the mass of
the objects and _____ between them.

   (A) what is the distance
   (B) the distance is
   (C) the distance
   (D) the distance what is

13. For the first time _____, large portions of
the universe can be observed simultaneously.

   (A) since history
   (B) in history
   (C) history began
   (D) of the beginning of history

14. _____ that it might be easier to prepare a
better map of the moon than of the earth.

   (A) To say
   (B) They say
   (C) The saying
   (D) It is said

15. Early settlers needed trees, so they sent
back to Europe for seedlings _____
around their houses.

   (A) to plant
   (B) and planted
   (C) and plants
   (D) which planted

Part B

Directions. In each of the following sentences, four words or phrases have been underlined. You should choose the one word or phrase that would *not* be appropriate in standard written English. Mark your choice on the answer sheet.

Example

The average age at which people begin to need eyeglasses vary considerably.
               A   B   C   D

(C) is incorrect in standard written English.

16. Ever since the world began, nations have difficulty in keeping peace with their neighbors.
        A   B   C   D

17. Sugar provides man with quick energy, but it has neither vitamins, minerals, and other body-build-
          A   B
ing material necessary for an adequate diet.
             C   D

18. From archeological evidence, we know that the Egyptians were highly organized, civilized, and
   A   B
they were skillful in using crafts.
      C   D

19. Although tea drinking is a considerably old custom in the Far East, this custom first reached
               A   B
Europe for the first time during the seventeenth century.
            C   D

20. A virus, which is too small to be seen except with a powerful microscope, is causing measles.
               A   B   C   D

21. The Mediterranean, a large sea surrounded by land, is a mile deep on the average and more than
                         A   B   C
2,000 miles length.
     D

22. The findings of Gregor Mendel were published in 1866, but scientists paid little attention to it for
                            A   B   C D
    about fifty years.

23. During the Middle Ages people were willing to pay a great deal for spices because disguised the
                            A   B   C
    bad taste of spoiled food.
            D

24. When a spider catches an insect, it releases some poison into an insect with its fangs, but the
            A   B
    poison of most spiders is harmless to man.
                C   D

25. Many people enjoy stamp collecting, and they will pay often large sums for stamps on which a
                     A   B   C
    mistake was made.
         D

26. Statesmen are people who have attained fame because of which they have achieved in the field of
                            A   B   C   D
    government.

27. Whether have individuals served good or evil governments, these individuals are remembered if
               A   B
    their actions have altered historical events.
        C   D

28. William Pitt urged that the English colonists were given the same constitutional rights to which
                  A   B   C
    other English subjects were entitled.
                   D

29. John Calhoun objected to creating a federal strong government because he believed that each
                           A   B
    state should decide most issues for itself.
            C   D

30. Sir Winston Churchill, as the British Prime Minister, leads his country to victory during the
                      A   B   C   D
    Second World War.

31. Although violent, tornadoes are small storms which paths are not usually more than a quarter of a
          A   B   C
    mile in width.
        D

32. Since 1975, the economy has been growing steadily, and today the country ranks as a one of the
                        A   B   C
    world's most rapidly developing nations.
             D

33. In 1954, the United States Navy decided to add the *Nautilus,* the first submarine to be driven for
                               A   B   C
    atomic power, to its fleet.
             D

34. Ships which <u>use to have</u> to <u>sail</u> around Africa <u>to get to</u> India from Europe can <u>now pass through</u>
             A   B   C   D
the Suez Canal.

35. <u>It is generally known</u> that the natural habitat of <u>these types</u> of monkeys <u>are</u> the central and eastern
      A   B   C   D
forests of Africa.

36. Sir James Dewar invented the thermos in 1892 <u>to keep</u> heat <u>away from</u> the liquefied gas <u>with</u>
                                       A   B   C
<u>which he was experiment.</u>
          D

37. Not only <u>did the Egyptians preserve</u> the dead bodies of important people, but they also buried
                   A
<u>with the dead person</u> <u>every which object</u> he <u>might possibly</u> use in an afterlife.
        B   C   D

38. The vibrations that <u>make</u> musical sounds are <u>more pleasanter</u> than <u>those</u> <u>causing</u> noise.
                    A   B   C   D

39. We see lightning <u>before we hear</u> the thunder <u>it causes</u> because sound travels <u>more slowly</u> than <u>light</u>
                      A   B   C   D
<u>is.</u>

40. Bats <u>are able</u> to <u>guide them</u> by producing sound waves <u>too high</u> for us <u>to hear.</u>
        A   B   C   D

III: READING COMPREHENSION AND VOCABULARY

(60 Questions—45 Minutes)

Part A

Directions. Each problem in Part A consists of a sentence in which one word or phrase has been underlined. From the four choices given, you should choose the one word or phrase which could be substituted for the underlined word or phrase without changing the meaning of the sentence. Mark your choice on the answer sheet.

Example

The <u>frown</u> on the man's face showed that he was displeased.

(A) look of fear
(B) look of anger
(C) look of delight
(D) look of surprise

The best answer is (B).

1. The two companies are going to <u>merge</u> by the first of the year.

(A) become one
(B) divide into two
(C) dissolve
(D) change owners

2. The old woman is too <u>feeble</u> to cross the street without her nephew's help.

(A) tired
(B) weak

(C) timid
(D) blind

3. There is no alternative; the president must approve the bill if Congress passes it.

(A) chance of agreement
(B) doubt
(C) other choice
(D) mistake

4. It is futile to argue with him once he has made up his mind.

(A) unpleasant
(B) encouraging
(C) helpful
(D) useless

5. He hurled the statue to the floor with such force that it shattered.

(A) dropped
(B) pulled
(C) pushed
(D) threw

6. He is the most intrepid explorer in the present century.

(A) successful
(B) fearless
(C) reliable
(D) fearsome

7. It is not easy to remain tranquil when events suddenly change your life.

(A) superior
(B) serious
(C) severe
(D) serene

8. One symptom of the disease is a high fever.

(A) symbol
(B) sign
(C) cause
(D) pain

9. He was greatly vexed by the new and unexpected development.

(A) astonished
(B) annoyed
(C) enlightened
(D) contented

10. The clerk had been insolent to his superior once too often; now he was without a job.

(A) affectionate
(B) rude
(C) dishonest
(D) sly

11. The picture is tilted; please straighten it.

(A) high
(B) level
(C) crooked
(D) adjustable

12. His employer appeared to be in such an affable mood that Tom decided to ask for a raise.

(A) despondent
(B) irresponsible
(C) agreeable
(D) uncertain

13. The boy felt disgraced because he knew that he had been wrong to steal.

(A) ashamed
(B) worried
(C) tempted
(D) phony

14. Since he had never been in such a situation before, his apprehension was understandable.

(A) eagerness
(B) fear
(C) hesitation
(D) excitement

15. A sealed bottle thrown into the ocean often floats aimlessly before it reaches land.

    (A) sinks
    (B) leaks
    (C) disintegrates
    (D) drifts

16. His face was flushed because he had run all the way from the dormitory.

    (A) red
    (B) shaking
    (C) pale
    (D) wet

17. The initial step is often the most difficult.

    (A) quickest
    (B) longest
    (C) last
    (D) first

18. The noise was so faint that it was impossible to be sure what it was or even where it came from.

    (A) frightening
    (B) general
    (C) loud
    (D) indistinct

19. The clerk had to break off the conversation in order to wait on a customer.

    (A) interrupt
    (B) hurry
    (C) continue
    (D) begin

20. The mother soothed the disappointed child and then promised to take him on a picnic as soon as it stopped raining.

    (A) hugged
    (B) comforted
    (C) whipped
    (D) praised

21. The new tax law is explicit; that type of certificate is tax-exempt.

    (A) definite
    (B) deficient
    (C) harsh
    (D) imprecise

22. Zinnia seeds will begin to germinate in seven to ten days.

    (A) grow
    (B) rot
    (C) sink
    (D) bloom

23. The union's grievance committee met with the school board to protest the teacher's firing.

    (A) personnel
    (B) scholarship
    (C) investment
    (D) complaint

24. Argon, an inert gas, constitutes nearly one percent of the atmosphere.

    (A) inflammable
    (B) colorless
    (C) inactive
    (D) odorless

25. Most high school students look up to the star player on the football team.

    (A) envy
    (B) respect
    (C) trust
    (D) pursue

26. Quito's 9,350-foot elevation makes it the third loftiest capital in the world.

    (A) mildest
    (B) highest
    (C) largest
    (D) flattest

27. The <u>concurrence</u> of the heads of state was totally unexpected.

    (A) rejection
    (B) proposal
    (C) agreement
    (D) objection

28. The police <u>confiscated</u> the stolen goods.

    (A) reported
    (B) located
    (C) released
    (D) seized

29. A <u>conscientious</u> teacher spends hours preparing for classes and correcting students' papers.

    (A) creative
    (B) leading
    (C) skillful
    (D) careful

30. The French detective novelist Georges Simenon is one of the most <u>prolific</u> writers of the twentieth century.

    (A) instructive
    (B) productive
    (C) famous
    (D) pessimistic

Part B

Directions. You will be given a series of different types of reading material (sentences, short paragraphs, advertisements, etc.). Each selection is followed by questions about the meaning of the material. You are to choose the one best answer to each question from the four choices given.

Read the following sample passage.

(1)   Marianne Moore was born in St. Louis in 1887 and graduated from Bryn Mawr College in 1909. She taught stenography for a few years and then worked as a librarian in New York. She was a
(5) member of the editorial staff of the famous literary magazine *The Dial* from 1925 to 1929. Although a book of her poems, titled *Observa-* *tions*, was published in America in 1924, Miss Moore has only recently received the full acclaim
(10) she deserves.

Example 1

When did Miss Moore graduate from college?

    (A) 1887
    (B) 1909
    (C) 1925
    (D) 1924

The passage says that Miss Moore graduated from Bryn Mawr in 1909. Therefore, you should choose answer (B).

Example 2

The one profession *not* mentioned as being pursued by Miss Moore is that of

    (A) poet.
    (B) teacher.
    (C) scientist.
    (D) librarian.

The passage mentions that Miss Moore taught stenography, worked as a librarian, and wrote poetry. Therefore, you should choose (C) as the best completion of the sentence.

As soon as you understand the directions, begin work on the problems.

Questions 31–34

    The white-throated wood rat builds nests of sticks and grasses in crevices in rocks when such cover is available, and on the open desert he constructs bulky "houses" of sticks and cacti.

31. When he nests near rocks, the wood rat likes to build

    (A) on the tops of the rocks.
    (B) beneath the rocks.
    (C) in the cracks of the rocks.
    (D) in the shade of the rocks.

32. Probably the open desert mentioned above

    (A) has many rocks.
    (B) has many cacti.

(C) is covered with grass.
(D) has much cover for the wood rat.

33. In the desert, the wood rat's home is

(A) underground.
(B) made of sticks and grasses.
(C) relatively large.
(D) relatively small.

34. This variety of wood rat probably got its name from

(A) its nesting habits.
(B) the fact that it always uses sticks to build its houses.
(C) its coloring.
(D) the kind of noises it makes.

Questions 35–37 refer to the following newspaper index.

The Index

Classified Ads	Page 1-D
Comics	Page 5-B
Deaths	Page 15-A
Editorials	Page 6-B
Entertainment	Page 6-C
Finance	Page 1-C
Religion	Page 1-E

35. Which page of the newspaper would most likely give you the names and telephone numbers of people who have used cars for sale?

(A) Page 6-C
(B) Page 1-C
(C) Page 1-D
(D) Page 6-B

36. On which page would you find information on the stock exchange?

(A) Page 6-B
(B) Page 1-C
(C) Page 1-D
(D) Page 1-E

37. On which of the following pages would you most likely find the time and station of your favorite television show?

(A) Page 6-C
(B) Page 1-D
(C) Page 5-B
(D) Page 6-B

Questions 38–42 refer to the following directions.

How to Transplant a Tree

(1) In most cases, you can transplant a tree successfully, at any time, if you follow the instructions for planting a tree. The most important thing is to dig out enough roots, but this process is difficult with a large tree.

(5) When you dig out the tree, leave a ball of earth around its roots. This ball of earth should measure about a foot wide for every inch of the tree trunk's diameter. Dig deep enough to avoid cutting off too many taproots.

(10) It is wise to call in a professional tree expert to transplant a tree more than a few inches in trunk diameter.

38. Transplanting a tree is

(A) very different from planting a tree.
(B) so difficult that an expert should always be called in.
(C) much like planting a tree.
(D) done successfully in the right seasons.

39. The larger the trunk of the tree you are transplanting

(A) the less it matters whether you call in a tree expert.
(B) the more you should avoid cutting off the taproots.
(C) the larger the ball of earth you must leave around the roots.
(D) the easier it is to dig out sufficient roots.

40. The taproots are

(A) the heaviest roots.
(B) the principal, deepest roots.
(C) the ball of earth.
(D) the same width as the trunk's diameter.

41. The best time for transplanting a tree is

(A) spring.
(B) fall.

(C) winter.
(D) any season.

42. To decide whether you can successfully transplant a tree yourself, you should

(A) select your location carefully.
(B) measure the ball of earth around the tree roots.
(C) measure the diameter of the tree trunk.
(D) cut off as many taproots as you can reach.

Questions 43–47

(1) The early expansion of the sugar industry was based on cane transported from two different parts of the Orient, first from India and second from the islands of the Southwest Pacific. From
(5) India, sugar cane was carried through the western regions of Asia into Arabia and later into the countries bordering on the Mediterranean. It was established in Sicily in about A.D. 703 and was carried to Spain about A.D. 755. As early as A.D.
(10) 1150, Spain had at least 75,000 acres of cane. During this early period sugar cane was grown largely to supply local wants. The Crusades were partly responsible for the further expansion and improvement of the sugar industry and for inter-
(15) esting Europeans in the use of sugar.

43. From this selection, it appears that sugar cane was first grown in

(A) Europe.
(B) the Orient.
(C) Arabia.
(D) Sicily.

44. Sugar cane was first introduced into Spain in

(A) A.D. 703.
(B) A.D. 755.
(C) A.D. 1150.
(D) A.D. 1419.

45. In the twelfth century, most cane was grown

(A) for exportation.
(B) for industrial uses.

(C) for sale in the large market cities.
(D) for local use.

46. One thing that caused the sugar industry to shift westward was

(A) the favorable climate in the Orient.
(B) better means of transportation.
(C) the Crusades.
(D) that cane came from different parts of the Orient.

47. Cane was transported

(A) from the islands of the Southwest Pacific, to India, to Asia, to Arabia, and then to Spain.
(B) from the islands of the Southwest Pacific, to the western regions of Asia, and then to the countries near the Mediterranean.
(C) from India to the islands of the Southwest Pacific, to Asia, into Arabia, and then to the countries bordering the Mediterranean.
(D) from India to Asia into Arabia, and then to the countries on the border of the Mediterranean.

Questions 48–52

(1) By the end of the first quarter of the nineteenth century a number of our Eastern institutions— Harvard, Yale, Columbia, and Pennsylvania— had some of the necessary ingredients of a
(5) university, but hardly yet the point of view. They were little clusters of schools and institutes. Indeed, just after the Revolution, the schools of Pennsylvania and Harvard had assumed the somewhat pretentious title of university, and,
(10) shortly after, the University of Virginia was founded under the guidance of Thomas Jefferson. In the South, Georgia and later North Carolina began to rise. The substance in all these was mainly lacking, though the title was honored.
(15) There were rather feeble law, medical, and divinity schools, somewhat loosely attached to these colleges. It has been commonly recognized, however, that the first decade after the close of the Civil War, that is, from about 1866 to 1876,
(20) was the great early flowering of the university idea in America.

48. In the opinion of the author of this passage, in 1825

    (A) only Harvard, Yale, Columbia, and Pennsylvania could truly be called universities.
    (B) all American educational institutions could justifiably claim to be universities.
    (C) those institutions which called themselves universities were not justified in doing so.
    (D) no American institution of higher education had any of the necessary ingredients of a university.

49. Thomas Jefferson founded

    (A) the University of Pennsylvania.
    (B) Harvard.
    (C) the University of Virginia.
    (D) the University of Georgia.

50. The Civil War ended

    (A) about 1866.
    (B) about 1876.
    (C) about 1856.
    (D) during the decade from 1866 to 1876.

51. The words "little clusters" (line 6) most nearly means

    (A) small groups.
    (B) small colleges.
    (C) small buildings.
    (D) small organizations.

52. The university idea really began to develop

    (A) in the first quarter of the nineteenth century.
    (B) just after the Revolution.
    (C) during the last quarter of the nineteenth century.
    (D) just after the Civil War.

Questions 53–56

(1)　In a very broad sense, legislation plays the same role in civil law countries as judicial decisions play in common law countries. Legislative rules pro-(5) vide the starting point from which lawyers and judges work toward their goal, the most just solution for the problem at hand. Usually the statute provides a clear answer to the problem. In those cases, the statute is strictly applied, more because it is just than because it is a statute. (10) Because of this it often appears that legislation is the law and that the judge's role is simply to apply automatically the ready-made solutions provided by the legislature. Nevertheless, there are a great many cases where the judge's role is far more (15) creative.

53. When civil law lawyers and judges strictly apply a statute, it is usually because

    (A) it provides a just solution to a problem.
    (B) statutes are laws, and must be obeyed.
    (C) the judge's role is always simply to apply automatically the ready-made solutions provided by the legislature.
    (D) the role of the civil law judiciary is never really creative.

54. Judicial decisions in common law countries play the same role as

    (A) legislation in common law countries.
    (B) legislation in civil law countries.
    (C) U.S. Supreme Court interpretations.
    (D) common law decisions in civil law countries.

55. A "statute" is

    (A) a judicial decision.
    (B) a just solution to a problem.
    (C) a law.
    (D) the goal of lawyers and judges.

56. When the author says that "the judge's role is far more creative" (lines 14–15) he means that

    (A) the judge, not the legislature, makes the law.
    (B) the judge applies the solution provided by the legislature.
    (C) the judge creates some cases he tries.
    (D) the judge often does more than just apply the law.

Questions 57–60

Directions. For each of the following questions, choose the answer whose *meaning is closest* to that of the given sentence. Although more than one of the choices may be factually correct, you should choose the one that *most closely restates the original sentence.*

57. The adventures of Donald Duck reached a wider audience than did the adventures of Don Juan.

    (A) Donald Duck's adventures are less well-known than Don Juan's adventures.
    (B) The audience for Donald Duck's adventures was smaller than the audience for Don Juan's adventures.
    (C) Fewer people know about the adventures of Donald Duck than about the adventures of Don Juan.
    (D) More people know about the adventures of Donald Duck than about the adventures of Don Juan.

58. College students would be better prepared for independent thinking if there were less emphasis on conformity in high school.

    (A) Because of emphasis on conformity in high school, students are frequently poorly prepared to think independently in college.
    (B) Although there is great emphasis on conformity in high school, college students are generally able to think independently.
    (C) If one emphasized independent thinking in college, there would be less conformity in high school.
    (D) Because of great emphasis on independent thinking in high school, students are able to think independently in college.

59. Britain aroused the American colonists' anger in 1763 by prohibiting the pioneers from settling and trading in lands west of the Appalachians.

    (A) Britains were aroused by the American colonists, who prohibited the pioneers from settling and trading in lands west of the Appalachians in 1763.
    (B) In 1763, the American colonists were angered by the British decision to forbid the pioneers to settle and trade in lands west of the Appalachians.
    (C) In 1763, the American colonists angered the British, who prohibited the pioneers from settling and trading in lands west of the Appalachians.
    (D) The lands west of the Appalachians were forbidden to the British by the angry American colonists in 1763.

60. A computer can become obsolete within only a few years because computer technology is constantly improving and changing.

    (A) Although computer technology is constantly improving and changing, a computer can become obsolete in only a few years.
    (B) Computer technology is constantly improving and changing; therefore, a computer can become obsolete within only a few years.
    (C) Since a computer can become obsolete within only a few years, computer technology is constantly improving and changing.
    (D) Computers improve and change constantly, so their technology can become obsolete in only a few years.

Test 2—Answer Key

I: LISTENING COMPREHENSION

Part A

1.	A	6.	B	11.	A	16.	A
2.	C	7.	A	12.	C	17.	D
3.	D	8.	B	13.	B	18.	C
4.	C	9.	B	14.	B	19.	B
5.	C	10.	C	15.	A	20.	D

Part B

21.	B	26.	B	31.	A
22.	A	27.	B	32.	D
23.	A	28.	D	33.	C
24.	A	29.	D	34.	A
25.	C	30.	D	35.	B

Part C

36.	C	41.	D	46.	C
37.	B	42.	B	47.	C
38.	A	43.	C	48.	C
39.	A	44.	D	49.	A
40.	A	45.	A	50.	C

II: STRUCTURE AND WRITTEN EXPRESSION

Part A

1.	B	6.	D	11.	D
2.	A	7.	B	12.	C
3.	A	8.	B	13.	B
4.	A	9.	C	14.	D
5.	C	10.	A	15.	A

Part B

16. C	23. C	30. B	37. C
17. B	24. B	31. B	38. B
18. C	25. B	32. C	39. D
19. C	26. C	33. C	40. B
20. D	27. A	34. A	
21. D	28. B	35. D	
22. C	29. B	36. D	

III: READING COMPREHENSION AND VOCABULARY

Part A

1. A	9. B	17. D	25. B
2. B	10. B	18. D	26. B
3. C	11. C	19. A	27. C
4. D	12. C	20. B	28. D
5. D	13. A	21. A	29. D
6. B	14. B	22. A	30. B
7. D	15. D	23. D	
8. B	16. A	24. C	

Part B

31. C	39. C	47. D	55. C
32. B	40. B	48. C	56. D
33. C	41. D	49. C	57. D
34. C	42. C	50. A	58. A
35. C	43. B	51. A	59. B
36. B	44. B	52. D	60. B
37. A	45. D	53. A	
38. C	46. C	54. B	

TEST 2—Explanatory Answers

II: STRUCTURE AND WRITTEN EXPRESSION

1. The principle of a rocket motor is simple, _____ rockets are very complicated machines.
   (This sentence consists of two independent clauses connected by a coordinating conjunction. The word *simple* in the first clause and the word *complicated* in the second clause indicate that a contrast is being made.)

(A)	*large but which powerful*	The word *which* is used incorrectly because it has no antecedent.
(B)	*but large, powerful*	CORRECT ANSWER
(C)	*large although powerful*	The word order in this choice is wrong. *Although large, powerful* would be an acceptable choice.
(D)	*so large, powerful*	The conjunction *so* shows that a result follows. Therefore, this choice is incorrect.

2. The universe _____ we know it might have begun with a great explosion.
   (A connecting word of manner is used to make this sentence correct.)

(A)	*as*	CORRECT ANSWER
(B)	*that*	The use of the relative pronoun *that* together with the object pronoun *it* (after the verb *know*) is incorrect.
(C)	*and which*	The conjunction *and* (showing equal ideas) is incorrect. Also, the relative pronoun *which* cannot be used in this sentence. See (B).
(D)	*and*	This answer choice results in a sentence that is not parallel.

3. _____ to find stars in pairs.
   (The "false" subject *it* and a finite verb are used to complete this sentence. Notice that the real subject *to find stars in pairs* comes at the end of the sentence.)

(A)	*It is very common*	CORRECT ANSWER
(B)	*Being very common*	The word *being* is not a finite verb.
(C)	*Very common is*	This choice lacks a subject.
(D)	*That is very common*	It is incorrect to use *that* instead of *it* in expressions like *it is common, it is clear, it is tragic, it is surprising,* etc.

75

4. Some areas of the moon are so full of craters _____ an extremely rough surface.
   (In this sentence, the correct choice is a clause of result.)

   (A) *that they present*   **CORRECT ANSWER**
   (B) *presenting*   The word *presenting* results in an incomplete sentence.

   (C) *which present*   This choice is not a clause of result, and the sentence is incomplete. However, the sentence, "Some areas of the moon are full of craters which present an extremely rough surface," would be correct.

   (D) *to present*   *To present*, used here as an infinitive of purpose, makes no sense.

5. James Cook, _____, also discovered the Hawaiian Islands.
   (This sentence is correct as written. However, a modifying phrase or a dependent clause can be added after the subject *James Cook*.)

   (A) *by exploring the South Sea he reached Australia*   The words *he reached* make this choice incorrect. However, *who reached Australia by exploring the South Sea* would be an acceptable choice.

   (B) *explored the South Sea and reaching Australia*   This choice is incorrect because the verb *explored* is not a modifier. Notice that *exploring the South Sea and reaching Australia* would be an acceptable choice.

   (C) *who explored the South Sea and reached Australia*   **CORRECT ANSWER**

   (D) *explored the South Sea then reached Australia*   This choice is incorrect because the verb *explored* lacks a subject. Also, the word *then* is not a conjunction.

6. _____, but it also filters out harmful sun rays.
   (The correct choice in this sentence must include information which is additional to *it also filters out harmful sun rays*.)

   (A) *The atmosphere gives us air to breathe*   This choice is incorrect because it cannot be used with the conjunction *but also*. The sentence, "The atmosphere gives us air to breathe, and it also filters out harmful sun rays," would be correct.

   (B) *Not only the atmosphere gives us air to breathe*   This choice is wrong because the conjunction *not only* must be followed here by question word order. Refer to (D).

   (C) *The atmosphere which gives us air to breathe*   This choice is incorrect because it is not an independent clause. Also, it lacks the conjunction *not only*, which is used in connection with *but also*. "The atmosphere, which gives us air to breathe, also filters out harmful sun rays," would be a correct sentence.

   (D) *Not only does the atmosphere give us air to breathe*   **CORRECT ANSWER**

7. One of the most obvious characteristics of the moon is the way in which it continuously changes _____.
   (This sentence is correctly completed by adding an object.)

   (A) *in appearing*   The word *appearing* makes this choice wrong. Change *appearing* to *appearance*.

   (B) *its appearance*   CORRECT ANSWER

   (C) *are appearing*   *Are appearing* is a verb and cannot be the object of the verb *changes*.

   (D) *for appearance*   The preposition *for* is incorrect. *In appearance* would be an acceptable choice.

8. The total influence of literature upon the course of human history _____.
   (A finite verb is needed to make this sentence complete.)

   (A) *an evaluation is difficult*   The subject of the verb *is* is not *an evaluation,* but rather *the total influence.* Therefore, this choice is wrong.

   (B) *is difficult to evaluate*   CORRECT ANSWER

   (C) *difficult to evaluate it*   This choice is incorrect since it does not contain a finite verb.

   (D) *it is difficult to evaluate*   The word *it* in this choice repeats the subject of the sentence.

9. _____, John Glenn was a pioneer in the U.S. space program.
   (This sentence is grammatically complete, but a dependent clause or modifying phrase can be added at the beginning of the sentence.)

   (A) *Despite the first American who orbited the earth*   The word *despite* makes no sense in this sentence.

   (B) *That the first American orbited the earth*   This answer choice, a noun clause, cannot be used to modify *John Glenn.* Also, when a noun clause is the subject of a sentence, it must be followed by a finite verb.

   (C) *The first American to orbit the earth*   CORRECT ANSWER

   (D) *He was the first American to orbit the earth*   *He was* makes this choice incorrect and results in a comma splice (two independent clauses connected by a comma).

10. _____ with the size of the whole earth, the highest mountains do not seem high at all.
    (An introductory modifying phrase is used to make this sentence grammatically correct.)

    (A) *When compared*   CORRECT ANSWER

    (B) *Compare them*   This choice results in a comma splice. See 9(D).

    (C) *If you compare*   In this choice, the object *them* has been omitted after the verb *compare*.

    (D) *A comparison*   *A comparison* is a noun and cannot be used to modify *the highest mountains.*

11. Determining the mineral content of soil samples is an exacting process; _____, experts must perform detailed tests to analyze soil specimens.
(In this sentence a connecting word showing result is needed to show the relationship between the two clauses.)

(A)	*so that*	*So that* indicates purpose and not result.
(B)	*however*	The word *however* shows a contrast between two ideas and cannot be used here.
(C)	*afterwards*	*Afterwards* refers to time and does not make sense in this sentence.
(D)	*therefore*	CORRECT ANSWER

12. The amount of gravitational attraction between two objects depends on the mass of the objects and _____ between them.
(The correct choice in this sentence is a direct object.)

(A)	*what is the distance*	This choice is incorrect because it is a simple question.
(B)	*the distance is*	This choice is incorrect because it makes no sense.
(C)	*the distance*	CORRECT ANSWER
(D)	*the distance what is*	The word *what* makes this choice incorrect. If it were changed to *the distance which is,* this choice would be acceptable.

13. For the first time _____, large portions of the universe can be observed simultaneously.
(A modifying phrase or dependent clause can be added to make this sentence complete.)

(A)	*since history*	*Since history* is a faulty clause because it lacks a verb. *Since history began* would be an acceptable choice. As a modifying phrase (that is, without a verb following), *since history* is not idiomatic English.
(B)	*in history*	CORRECT ANSWER
(C)	*history began*	This choice is incorrect because *history began* is an independent clause.
(D)	*of the beginning of history*	The first *of* makes this choice incorrect. The prepositional phrase *since the beginning of history* would be an acceptable choice.

14. _____ that it might be easier to prepare a better map of the moon than of the earth.
(A subject and a finite verb are needed in this answer choice.)

(A)	*To say*	*To say* is not a finite verb.
(B)	*They say*	The subject *they* is a poor choice because it is unclear who "they" refers to.
(C)	*The saying*	This choice is incorrect since it lacks a verb.
(D)	*It is said*	CORRECT ANSWER

15. Early settlers needed trees, so they sent back to Europe for seedlings
    _____ around their houses.
    (In this sentence, the correct answer choice is an infinitive of purpose which
    tells why the early settlers sent home for seedlings.)

(A)	*to plant*	**CORRECT ANSWER**
(B)	*and planted*	This answer choice is incomplete. Notice that *and planted them* would be an acceptable choice.
(C)	*and plants*	This choice makes no sense because the words *around their house* indicate that something is being done to the seedlings.
(D)	*which planted*	*Which planted* is a faulty adjective clause because it lacks a subject. *Which they planted* would be an acceptable choice.

16. (C) The correct verb form is *have had* instead of *have*. The present perfect tense is often used to show an action that began in the past and continues into the present.

17. (B) The correct conjunction to use here is *nor* in combination with the conjunction *neither*. The sentence should read ". . . but it has *neither* vitamins, minerals, *nor* other body-building material . . ."

18. (C) For the sake of parallelism, omit *they were*. You should say ". . . the Egyptians were highly organized, civilized, *and skillful* . . ."

19. (C) Omit this entire phrase since the adverb *first* was used before the verb *reached*. The second part of the sentence should be ". . . this custom first reached Europe during the seventeenth century."

20. (D) The present perfect continuous cannot be used here. Say *causes* or *is the cause of*.

21. (D) Use the adjective *long* and say *2,000 miles long*.

22. (C) Change the pronoun *it* to the pronoun *them*, since the antecedent is *the findings*. You should say *to them*.

23. (C) Include the subject *they* and say *because they disguised*. The pronoun *they* in this sentence refers to *spices*.

24. (B) You should say *into the insect*. Always use the definite article *the* to refer to a specific noun. In this case, the specific noun is *the insect* which a spider catches.

25. (B) The adverb *often* is misplaced. Change the phrase to *will often pay*.

26. (C) Instead of *which*, say *what they have achieved*.

27. (A) You should say *whether individuals have*.

28. (B) You should say *be given* since it is correct to use the subjunctive form of the verb after the expression *urged that*.

29. (B) In this phrase, the word order is incorrect. The words *federal government* form a noun phrase and are used as a single noun would be. Therefore, the adjective *strong* modifies *federal government* and should be placed before *federal*.

30. (B) *Leads* is the present tense of the verb. Change it to the past tense, *led*.

31. (B) Instead of the relative pronoun *which*, use the possessive pronoun *whose*. The sentence should read, ". . . tornadoes are small storms *whose paths* . . .". The sentence is talking about the paths of small storms.

32. (C) Omit the article *a* and say, ". . . the country ranks *as one* of the world's most rapidly developing nations."

33. (C) The preposition *for* is incorrect. You should say *driven by*.

34. (A) The verb tense is incorrect. Change *use* to *used*. The sentence means that some ships *used to* have to sail around Africa (but they don't anymore).

35. (D) Since the subject *habitat* is singular, change the verb *are* to the verb *is*. Verbs must agree with their subjects. Now the sentence reads ". . . the natural *habitat* of these types of monkeys *is* . . ."

36. (D) *Was experiment* is not an acceptable construction. You should use the past continuous tense *was experimenting*.

37. (C) The word order is incorrect. Change the phrase to *every object which*. *Which* here is a relative pronoun, and relative pronouns follow the nouns to which they refer. Notice that the pronoun *which* refers to the noun *object*.

38. (B) This phrase contains an incorrect comparative form. The comparative of *pleasant* is *more pleasant*.

39. (D) Change *is* to *does*. Notice that the present tense auxiliary *does* is a substitute for the verb *travels*. The second part of the sentence should read ". . . sound travels more slowly than *light does*."

40. (B) It is correct to use the reflexive pronoun *themselves* in this phrase. Therefore, you should say "Bats are able *to guide themselves* . . ."

READING COMPREHENSION AND VOCABULARY

Part A

Following are explanations of questions 1–30. In this section, the correct answers are placed first, so that they can be used to help explain why the other choices are incorrect.

1. (A) CORRECT: <u>Merge</u> means *to become one.*
   (B) *To divide into two* would be "to separate," the opposite of to <u>merge</u>.
   (C) *To dissolve* in this context would mean "to break up; to end."
   (D) *To change owners* has nothing to do with merging.

2. (B) CORRECT: *Weak* and <u>feeble</u> are synonyms; both mean "lacking strength."
   (A) *Tired* means "worn out; exhausted." A tired person might feel weaker than usual, but not all feeble people are tired.

(C)	*Timid* means "shy" or "fearful." It refers to an emotional rather than a physical state.
(D)	*Blind* means "without the sense of sight." A blind person may be very strong.

3. (C) CORRECT: *Other choice* is a synonym for <u>alternative</u>. Both mean "another possibility."
   (A)   *Chance of agreement* means a "possibility" of agreement.
   (B)   *Doubt* here would mean that the point of law being discussed in the sentence is certain.
   (D)   *Mistake* would have the same sense as "doubt" in 3(B).

4. (D) CORRECT: *Useless* and <u>futile</u> are synonyms.
   (A)   *Unpleasant* does not suggest that arguing would be useless, only disagreeable.
   (B)   *Encouraging* suggests the opposite of "useless," that it might be possible to change his mind.
   (C)   Like encouraging, *helpful* suggests that arguing might have some effect.

5. (D) CORRECT: To <u>hurl</u> and *to throw* mean the same thing.
   (A)   *Dropped* does not suggest the intention or the force of <u>hurl</u>.
   (B)   *Pulled* means "to cause motion toward the source of the force," while with <u>hurl</u> the motion is away from the source of the force.
   (C)   *Pushed* suggests "thrusting" or "shoving," not "throwing."

6. (B) CORRECT: *Fearless* and <u>intrepid</u> both mean "brave" or "courageous."
   (A)   *Successful* refers to the results of his explorations, not to his character.
   (C)   *Reliable* means "trustworthy; dependable." Bravery and reliability do not always go together.
   (D)   *Fearsome* here would mean "to be feared" not "without fear."

7. (D) CORRECT: *Serene* and <u>tranquil</u> mean "calm."
   (A)   *Superior* means "above those about one; indifferent." Indifference may allow one to remain tranquil, but tranquility is not always due to indifference.
   (B)   *Serious* might mean "earnest" or "solemn" here.
   (C)   *Severe* means "harsh," "stern," or "strict." One can be severe without being calm.

8. (B) CORRECT: A *sign* and a <u>symptom</u> are both indications of something.
   (A)   A *symbol* is not used to describe the signs of an illness. It is often used in literature, music, and mathematics to mean "something that represents something else."

(C)	Symptoms are the manifestations, not the *causes*, of an illness.
(D)	A *pain* is "a feeling of suffering or distress." A particular type of pain may be a symptom of a disease, but not all symptoms are pains.

9. (B) CORRECT: *Annoyed* and vexed mean "to irritate" or "bother."
    (A) *Astonished* means "surprised."
    (C) *Enlightened* means "informed or instructed."
    (D) *Contented* means "satisfied with things as they are," almost the opposite of vexed.

10. (B) CORRECT: To be *rude* or insolent is to be "insulting in manner or speech."
    (A) *Affectionate* means "loving."
    (C) *Dishonest* means "disposed to lie, cheat, defraud, or deceive." Many dishonest people are careful not to be insolent.
    (D) *Sly* means "secret; underhanded; deceitful."

11. (C) CORRECT: *Crooked* and tilted both mean "sloping," or "not level."
    (A) A *high* picture may be tilted or straight.
    (B) *Level* means the opposite of tilted in this sentence.
    (D) To be *adjustable* is "to be able to change so as to match or fit."

12. (C) CORRECT: *Agreeable* and affable mean "easy to speak to; approachable" in this context.
    (A) *Despondent* means "disheartened; dejected." A despondent person is unhappy, the opposite of affable.
    (B) *Irresponsible* means "undependable; unreliable; untrustworthy."
    (D) In this context, *uncertain* might mean "not known or established" or "subject to change."

13. (A) CORRECT: In this context, both *ashamed* and disgraced suggest that the boy felt that he had lost "honor, respect, or reputation" by his actions.
    (B) *Worried* here would mean "uneasy about some threatening matter; troubled." One can feel worried without feeling disgraced.
    (C) *Tempted* here means "enticed to commit an unwise or immoral act." One would be tempted before, not after, stealing.
    (D) *Phony* means "fake; not genuine or real."

14. (B) CORRECT: *Fear* can be substituted for apprehension without changing the meaning of the sentence.
    (A) *Eagerness* here would mean "impatiently expectant." To be eager is to look forward to something; to be apprehensive is to dread it.

(C)   *Hesitation* would mean "to hold back in uncertainty; waver." Such behavior might be the *result* of <u>apprehension</u>, but it is not fear itself.

(D)   *Excitement* would be very close to *eagerness* in this context.

15. (D) CORRECT: *Drifts* means to <u>float aimlessly</u>, or to move without any particular destination in view.

(A)   *Sinks* here would mean "to go beneath the surface," not to float ("stay on the surface") at all.

(B)   *Leaks* means "to permit the escape of something through an opening." In this case, water would be entering the bottle through some opening and the bottle would soon sink.

(C)   *Disintegrates* means "to separate into components; fragment."

16. (A) CORRECT: In this context <u>flushed</u> means "turned *red* in the face from exertion."

(B)   *Shaking* means "trembling." *Shaking* might also be caused by exertion, but does not mean <u>flushed</u>."

(C)   Here *pale* means "a loss of color," almost the opposite of <u>flushed</u>.

(D)   *Wet* means "covered or saturated with a liquid, especially water."

17. (D) CORRECT: *First* and <u>initial</u> are synonyms here.
(A)   *Quickest* means the "fastest," not the "first."
(B)   *Longest* means "having the greatest length."
(C)   *Last* is the opposite of <u>initial</u>.

18. (D) CORRECT: In this sentence, <u>faint</u> means *indistinct* or "barely perceptible; dim."
(A)   *Frightening* means "causing fear."
(B)   *General* here means "widespread; prevalent."
(C)   *Loud* would be the opposite of <u>faint</u> in this sentence.

19. (A) CORRECT: To *interrupt* the conversation is to <u>break it off</u>, or "to stop suddenly, as in speaking."
(B)   *Hurry* would mean "to speed up" or "go faster."
(C)   *Continue* would mean "to keep on speaking" in this sentence. It would thus be the opposite of "interrupt."
(D)   *Begin* means to "start," the opposite of <u>break off</u> in this sentence.

20. (B) CORRECT: *Comforted* and <u>soothed</u> both mean "to calm; mollify; placate."

(A)   *Hugged* means "to embrace; to hold in one's arms." In this sentence, to hug might be a specific means of soothing.

(C)   *Whipped* means "to punish by striking with repeated strokes."

(D)   *Praised* means "an expression of warm approval or admiration."

21. (A) CORRECT: *Definite* and <u>explicit</u> both mean "expressed with precision; specific."

   (B)   *Deficient* means "lacking a necessary quality" or "incomplete."

   (C)   *Harsh* means "severe" or "stern." An <u>explicit</u> tax law is not necessarily harsh.

   (D)   *Imprecise* means the opposite of <u>explicit</u>.

22. (A) CORRECT: In this context, *grow* and <u>germinate</u> are synonyms.
   (B)   *Rot* means "to decay."
   (C)   Here *sink* would mean "to go deeper into the ground."
   (D)   *Bloom* means "to blossom" or "to produce a flower." Zinnia seeds do not bloom in only seven to ten days.

23. (D) CORRECT: A <u>grievance</u> or *complaint* would mean a "protest."
   (A)   Here *personnel* would refer to the "people who work in this educational system."
   (B)   *Scholarship* would refer to an "award" or "grant-in-aid" for further study.
   (C)   *Investment* means "money, time, or effort spent to gain future security or profit."

24. (C) CORRECT: *Inactive* and <u>inert</u> here mean "not reacting chemically."
   (A)   *Inflammable* means "capable of burning easily."
   (B)   *Colorless* means "without color."
   (D)   *Odorless* means "without an odor or smell."

25. (B) CORRECT: To *respect* someone is to <u>look up to</u> or "to admire" that person.
   (A)   To *envy* is "to be jealous of" someone; "to want what someone else has."
   (C)   To *trust* is "to have faith or confidence."
   (D)   To *pursue* means "to chase" or "to try to catch."

26. (B) CORRECT: Here *highest* and <u>loftiest</u> are synonyms.
   (A)   *Mildest* here would mean "the most temperate; not too hot or too cold."
   (C)   *Largest* has nothing to do with Quito's high elevation.
   (D)   *Flattest* means "the most level; smoothest."

27. (C) CORRECT: <u>Concurrence</u> means *agreement*.
   (A)   *Rejection* means "refusal to agree."
   (B)   *Proposal* means "plan" or "suggestion."
   (D)   *Objection* suggests disagreement or "opposition," almost the opposite of <u>concurrence</u>.

28. **(D) CORRECT:** *Seized* and <u>confiscated</u> are synonyms here. Both mean "to take private property, usually as a penalty."
    (A)   *Reported* means "notified."
    (B)   In this sentence, *located* means "found."
    (C)   *Released* means "to let go"; here, it would be the opposite of <u>confiscated</u>.

29. **(D) CORRECT:** *Careful* and <u>conscientious</u> are synonyms here.
    (A)   *Creative* would mean "innovative," someone who thinks of new ways to do things. A person can be creative without being <u>conscientious</u>.
    (B)   *Leading* here would mean "most important; foremost."
    (C)   *Skillful* means "competent; having ability." Skill does not guarantee care or thoroughness.

30. **(B) CORRECT:** *Productive* and <u>prolific</u> both mean "producing a great deal," in this context, many detective novels.
    (A)   *Instructive* here would mean "giving knowledge or information." A prolific writer may or may not be instructive.
    (C)   *Famous* means "well-known." Most very prolific writers are well-known, but not all famous writers are prolific.
    (D)   *Pessimistic* means "expecting the worst."

Part B

31. This question tests for word recognition.

    (A)   See 31(C) below.
    (B)   See 31(C) below.
    (C) **CORRECT:** In this context, "crevices" are splits or *cracks* in rocks.
    (D)   See 31(C) above.

32. This question tests for the ability to draw inferences.

    (A)   In the passage, the "open desert" is "contrasted" to rocky areas; the open desert does not have *many rocks*.
    (B) **CORRECT:** On the "open desert," the wood rat builds "houses" of sticks and cacti, so sufficient cacti are available for its use.
    (C)   The statement does not indicate whether or not grass is plentiful on the desert, but implies that it is not plentiful.
    (D)   That the wood rat must build "houses" for cover suggests that natural cover is not available to it in the desert.

33. This question tests for comprehension and word recognition.

    (A)   The statement suggests that the house is built above ground.
    (B)   The rat's nest in rocky areas is *made of sticks and grasses*.
    (C) **CORRECT:** "Bulky" (line 4) implies that the structure is *relatively large*.
    (D)   See 33(C) above.

34. This question tests for the ability to draw inferences and for word recognition.

    (A)   See 34(C) below.
    (B)   See 34(C) below.
    (C) CORRECT: This variety of wood rat is the "white-throated wood rat," which suggests that the fur in the area of its throat is white.
    (D)   See 34(C) above.

Questions 35–37 test for word recognition and the ability to draw inferences.

35. (A)   *Page 6-C* is the entertainment section and would give information about television, movies, restaurants, etc.
    (B)   *Page 1-C* is the finance section and would contain the business news; for example, information on the stock exchange.
    (C) CORRECT: *Page 1-D* is the classified section. Since it would carry "For Sale by Owner" ads, it would be a likely place to find *someone selling a used car.*
    (D)   *Page 6-B* is the editorial section and would contain columns by local and national journalists.

36. (A)   See 35(D) above.
    (B) CORRECT: See 35(B) above.
    (C)   See 35(C) above.
    (D)   *Page 1-E* is the religion section and would contain information about the services and activities of the local churches and articles pertaining to religion.

37. (A) CORRECT: See 35(A) above.
    (B)   See 35(C) above.
    (C)   *Page 5-B* is the comics. It would feature cartoons.
    (D)   See 35(D) above.

38. This question tests for attention to details.

    (A)   Lines 1–3 state just the opposite.
    (B)   Lines 1–3 state that the reader can transplant most trees.
    (C) CORRECT: Clearly implied in lines 1–3.
    (D)   "At any time" (line 2) means that a tree can be "successfully transplanted in any season."

39. This question tests for a main idea in the passage.

    (A)   The passage (lines 10–12) suggests the opposite.
    (B)   You must always *avoid cutting off the taproots.*
    (C) CORRECT: Lines 6–8 explain how to *determine the size of the ball of earth,* which increases in correlation to the diameter of the tree trunk.
    (D)   Lines 3–4 suggest the opposite.

40. This question tests for word recognition.

    (A)   Taproots are often *the heaviest roots,* but this is not their defining characteristic.

    (B) CORRECT: This definition is implied in lines 8–9.

    (C)   A root is not a *ball of earth.*

    (D)   This is possible, but rarely the case in larger trees, and not taproots' defining characteristic.

41. This question tests for attention to details.

    (A)   No one season is mentioned as best for transplanting trees.

    (B)   See 41(A) above, 41(D) below.

    (C)   See 41(A) above, 41(D) below.

    (D) CORRECT: Usually, trees can be successfully transplanted "at any time" (line 2).

42. This question tests for the ability to draw inferences.

    (A)   This consideration is not mentioned.

    (B)   This instruction implies that it is carried out after the tree is dug up, which is too late.

    (C) CORRECT: This test is clearly implied in lines 10–12, which explain how to decide whether or not to call in a tree expert.

    (D)   One must always be careful *not* to do this (lines 8–9).

43. This question tests for attention to detail.

    (A)   The passage describes how the growing of cane was gradually established in *Europe.*

    (B) CORRECT: Lines 2–4 explain that cane was brought from two areas of *the Orient.*

    (C)   Cane originating in India was brought into *Arabia* (lines 4–6).

    (D)   Cane was brought into *Sicily* only after it was brought from India through Asia and Arabia and finally into the Mediterranean (lines 5–8).

44. This passage tests for attention to detail.

    (A)   It was established on this date in Sicily (line 8).

    (B) CORRECT: See line 9.

    (C)   By this date, cane was well established in Spain (lines 9–10).

    (D)   This date is not mentioned in the passage.

45. This question tests for attention to detail.

    (A)   The passage states just the opposite (lines 11–12).

    (B)   Industrial use of sugar is not mentioned.

    (C)   *Large market cities* are not mentioned and the sense of this statement is contrary to the passage.

    (D) CORRECT: By the middle of the twelfth century (1150), cane was well established in Spain, and was grown mainly for local consumption (lines 9–12).

46. This question tests for attention to detail and inferences.

   (A)   The Orient is East; a favorable climate there does not guarantee that cane can be cultivated in the West.

   (B)   This may be true, but the passage does not say that improved transportation caused the sugar industry to shift *westward*.

   (C) CORRECT: *Westward* here means toward Europe, and lines 12–15 note the influence of *the Crusades* on the expansion of the sugar industry into Europe.

   (D)   This statement does not explain why the industry shifted *westward*.

47. This question tests for attention to detail.

   (A)   The passage does not indicate where sugar from the Southwest Pacific islands was brought to. See lines 2–7.

   (B)   See 47(A) above, lines 2–7.

   (C)   Sugar was brought from both India and the Pacific islands, not from India *to* the Pacific islands.

   (D) CORRECT: See lines 4–7.

48. This question tests for a main idea in the paragraph.

   (A)   Lines 1–6 suggest that these institutions could not yet properly be called universities.

   (B)   The passage suggests just the opposite.

   (C) CORRECT: See lines 7–9, 13–14. In the opinion of this writer, many of these institutions had the title of the university, but not yet the "substance" (line 13) or "point of view" (line 5) to warrant it.

   (D)   Lines 1–5 contradict this statement.

49. This question tests for attention to detail.

   (A)   See lines 10–11.

   (B)   See lines 10–11.

   (C) CORRECT: See lines 10–11.

   (D)   See lines 10–11.

50. This question tests for attention to detail.

   (A) CORRECT: The decade immediately following the Civil War began *about 1866* (lines 17–19).

   (B)   See above.

   (C)   This date is neither mentioned nor implied in the passage.

   (D)   This was the decade "after" the war (lines 17–19).

51. This question tests for word recognition.

   (A) CORRECT: A *cluster* is a group of objects or persons in close proximity to one another and set off from other objects or groups of the same kind. "Little clusters" (line 6) means *small groups*.

(B)   One can have a *cluster* of colleges. See 51(A) above.

(C)   There can exist a *cluster* of buildings.

(D)   See 51(A) above.

52. This question tests for a main idea of the paragraph.

(A)   Lines 1–5 describe the situation at this time.

(B)   Lines 7–11 describe what happened *just after the Revolution.*

(C)   The idea began to develop just before this period. See 52(D) below.

(D) CORRECT: This point is made in the last sentence of the paragraph (lines 17–21).

53. This question tests for a supporting idea in the paragraph.

(A) CORRECT: This idea is stated in lines 3–6.

(B)   This is what the situation often "appears" to be, not what it is (lines 8–13).

(C)   See 53(B) above.

(D)   Lines 13–15 assert just the opposite.

54. This question tests for a main idea in the paragraph.

(A)   The passage does not state the role of legislation in common law countries.

(B) CORRECT: This is stated clearly, but with a different emphasis, in lines 1–3.

(C)   These are not mentioned in the paragraph.

(D)   The passage implies that there are no *common law decisions* in civil law countries.

55. This question tests for word recognition and the ability to draw inferences.

(A)   The paragraph makes clear that statutes and judicial decisions are different from one another (lines 1–3, 6–13).

(B)   A statute may be, and often is, *a just solution to a problem,* but it is not so by definition.

(C) CORRECT: "Legislation," "legislative rules," "law," and "statute" are close synonyms in this paragraph.

(D)   A statute may be someone's goal, but "statute" does not mean "goal."

56. This question tests for word recognition and the ability to draw inferences.

(A)   Laws are created through *legislation,* by a *legislature.* See 56(D) below.

(B)   The author is distinguishing another function of a judge from his function of automatically applying a statute.

(C)   The judge must sometimes create solutions to cases; his function as a judge is not to create the cases.

(D) CORRECT: The implication (lines 13–15) is that the judge must often provide solutions for situations that existing legislation does not cover.

The following four questions test for the sense of the sentences.

57. (A)   This is the opposite sense of the original.
    (B)   Same as 57(A) above.
    (C)   Same as 57(A) above.
    (D) CORRECT: A "wider audience" contains "more people."

58. (A) CORRECT: This is the same idea stated with a slightly different emphasis.

    (B)   The original implies that college students are not sufficiently able to think independently.

    (C)   This sentence reverses the causal relation asserted in the original.

    (D)   This sentence states the exact opposite of the original.

59. (A)   This sentence reverses the relation between Britain and the colonists stated in the original.
    (B) CORRECT: This is the same idea restated.
    (C)   The colonists were angered, not the British.
    (D)   The lands were forbidden to the colonists by Britain.

60. (A)   This statement suggests that computers *can become obsolete despite* the constant improvement of computer technology. See 60(B) below.

    (B) CORRECT: This statement suggests that a computer can become obsolete within a few years *because* computer technology is constantly improving. This is the sense of the original sentence.

    (C)   This statement reverses the causal relation in the original sentence. See 60(B) above.

    (D)   In this statement, the predicates in the clauses are reversed, changing the sense of each clause. See 60(B) above.

ANSWER SHEET FOR TEST 3

Tear out this answer sheet and use it to record your answers to all the questions in this examination.

SECTION I

1 Ⓐ Ⓑ Ⓒ Ⓓ	11 Ⓐ Ⓑ Ⓒ Ⓓ	21 Ⓐ Ⓑ Ⓒ Ⓓ	31 Ⓐ Ⓑ Ⓒ Ⓓ	41 Ⓐ Ⓑ Ⓒ Ⓓ
2 Ⓐ Ⓑ Ⓒ Ⓓ	12 Ⓐ Ⓑ Ⓒ Ⓓ	22 Ⓐ Ⓑ Ⓒ Ⓓ	32 Ⓐ Ⓑ Ⓒ Ⓓ	42 Ⓐ Ⓑ Ⓒ Ⓓ
3 Ⓐ Ⓑ Ⓒ Ⓓ	13 Ⓐ Ⓑ Ⓒ Ⓓ	23 Ⓐ Ⓑ Ⓒ Ⓓ	33 Ⓐ Ⓑ Ⓒ Ⓓ	43 Ⓐ Ⓑ Ⓒ Ⓓ
4 Ⓐ Ⓑ Ⓒ Ⓓ	14 Ⓐ Ⓑ Ⓒ Ⓓ	24 Ⓐ Ⓑ Ⓒ Ⓓ	34 Ⓐ Ⓑ Ⓒ Ⓓ	44 Ⓐ Ⓑ Ⓒ Ⓓ
5 Ⓐ Ⓑ Ⓒ Ⓓ	15 Ⓐ Ⓑ Ⓒ Ⓓ	25 Ⓐ Ⓑ Ⓒ Ⓓ	35 Ⓐ Ⓑ Ⓒ Ⓓ	45 Ⓐ Ⓑ Ⓒ Ⓓ
6 Ⓐ Ⓑ Ⓒ Ⓓ	16 Ⓐ Ⓑ Ⓒ Ⓓ	26 Ⓐ Ⓑ Ⓒ Ⓓ	36 Ⓐ Ⓑ Ⓒ Ⓓ	46 Ⓐ Ⓑ Ⓒ Ⓓ
7 Ⓐ Ⓑ Ⓒ Ⓓ	17 Ⓐ Ⓑ Ⓒ Ⓓ	27 Ⓐ Ⓑ Ⓒ Ⓓ	37 Ⓐ Ⓑ Ⓒ Ⓓ	47 Ⓐ Ⓑ Ⓒ Ⓓ
8 Ⓐ Ⓑ Ⓒ Ⓓ	18 Ⓐ Ⓑ Ⓒ Ⓓ	28 Ⓐ Ⓑ Ⓒ Ⓓ	38 Ⓐ Ⓑ Ⓒ Ⓓ	48 Ⓐ Ⓑ Ⓒ Ⓓ
9 Ⓐ Ⓑ Ⓒ Ⓓ	19 Ⓐ Ⓑ Ⓒ Ⓓ	29 Ⓐ Ⓑ Ⓒ Ⓓ	39 Ⓐ Ⓑ Ⓒ Ⓓ	49 Ⓐ Ⓑ Ⓒ Ⓓ
10 Ⓐ Ⓑ Ⓒ Ⓓ	20 Ⓐ Ⓑ Ⓒ Ⓓ	30 Ⓐ Ⓑ Ⓒ Ⓓ	40 Ⓐ Ⓑ Ⓒ Ⓓ	50 Ⓐ Ⓑ Ⓒ Ⓓ

SECTION II

1 Ⓐ Ⓑ Ⓒ Ⓓ	9 Ⓐ Ⓑ Ⓒ Ⓓ	17 Ⓐ Ⓑ Ⓒ Ⓓ	25 Ⓐ Ⓑ Ⓒ Ⓓ	33 Ⓐ Ⓑ Ⓒ Ⓓ
2 Ⓐ Ⓑ Ⓒ Ⓓ	10 Ⓐ Ⓑ Ⓒ Ⓓ	18 Ⓐ Ⓑ Ⓒ Ⓓ	26 Ⓐ Ⓑ Ⓒ Ⓓ	34 Ⓐ Ⓑ Ⓒ Ⓓ
3 Ⓐ Ⓑ Ⓒ Ⓓ	11 Ⓐ Ⓑ Ⓒ Ⓓ	19 Ⓐ Ⓑ Ⓒ Ⓓ	27 Ⓐ Ⓑ Ⓒ Ⓓ	35 Ⓐ Ⓑ Ⓒ Ⓓ
4 Ⓐ Ⓑ Ⓒ Ⓓ	12 Ⓐ Ⓑ Ⓒ Ⓓ	20 Ⓐ Ⓑ Ⓒ Ⓓ	28 Ⓐ Ⓑ Ⓒ Ⓓ	36 Ⓐ Ⓑ Ⓒ Ⓓ
5 Ⓐ Ⓑ Ⓒ Ⓓ	13 Ⓐ Ⓑ Ⓒ Ⓓ	21 Ⓐ Ⓑ Ⓒ Ⓓ	29 Ⓐ Ⓑ Ⓒ Ⓓ	37 Ⓐ Ⓑ Ⓒ Ⓓ
6 Ⓐ Ⓑ Ⓒ Ⓓ	14 Ⓐ Ⓑ Ⓒ Ⓓ	22 Ⓐ Ⓑ Ⓒ Ⓓ	30 Ⓐ Ⓑ Ⓒ Ⓓ	38 Ⓐ Ⓑ Ⓒ Ⓓ
7 Ⓐ Ⓑ Ⓒ Ⓓ	15 Ⓐ Ⓑ Ⓒ Ⓓ	23 Ⓐ Ⓑ Ⓒ Ⓓ	31 Ⓐ Ⓑ Ⓒ Ⓓ	39 Ⓐ Ⓑ Ⓒ Ⓓ
8 Ⓐ Ⓑ Ⓒ Ⓓ	16 Ⓐ Ⓑ Ⓒ Ⓓ	24 Ⓐ Ⓑ Ⓒ Ⓓ	32 Ⓐ Ⓑ Ⓒ Ⓓ	40 Ⓐ Ⓑ Ⓒ Ⓓ

SECTION III

1 Ⓐ Ⓑ © Ⓓ   11 Ⓐ Ⓑ © Ⓓ   21 Ⓐ Ⓑ © Ⓓ   31 Ⓐ Ⓑ © Ⓓ   41 Ⓐ Ⓑ © Ⓓ   51 Ⓐ Ⓑ © Ⓓ

2 Ⓐ Ⓑ © Ⓓ   12 Ⓐ Ⓑ © Ⓓ   22 Ⓐ Ⓑ © Ⓓ   32 Ⓐ Ⓑ © Ⓓ   42 Ⓐ Ⓑ © Ⓓ   52 Ⓐ Ⓑ © Ⓓ

3 Ⓐ Ⓑ © Ⓓ   13 Ⓐ Ⓑ © Ⓓ   23 Ⓐ Ⓑ © Ⓓ   33 Ⓐ Ⓑ © Ⓓ   43 Ⓐ Ⓑ © Ⓓ   53 Ⓐ Ⓑ © Ⓓ

4 Ⓐ Ⓑ © Ⓓ   14 Ⓐ Ⓑ © Ⓓ   24 Ⓐ Ⓑ © Ⓓ   34 Ⓐ Ⓑ © Ⓓ   44 Ⓐ Ⓑ © Ⓓ   54 Ⓐ Ⓑ © Ⓓ

5 Ⓐ Ⓑ © Ⓓ   15 Ⓐ Ⓑ © Ⓓ   25 Ⓐ Ⓑ © Ⓓ   35 Ⓐ Ⓑ © Ⓓ   45 Ⓐ Ⓑ © Ⓓ   55 Ⓐ Ⓑ © Ⓓ

6 Ⓐ Ⓑ © Ⓓ   16 Ⓐ Ⓑ © Ⓓ   26 Ⓐ Ⓑ © Ⓓ   36 Ⓐ Ⓑ © Ⓓ   46 Ⓐ Ⓑ © Ⓓ   56 Ⓐ Ⓑ © Ⓓ

7 Ⓐ Ⓑ © Ⓓ   17 Ⓐ Ⓑ © Ⓓ   27 Ⓐ Ⓑ © Ⓓ   37 Ⓐ Ⓑ © Ⓓ   47 Ⓐ Ⓑ © Ⓓ   57 Ⓐ Ⓑ © Ⓓ

8 Ⓐ Ⓑ © Ⓓ   18 Ⓐ Ⓑ © Ⓓ   28 Ⓐ Ⓑ © Ⓓ   38 Ⓐ Ⓑ © Ⓓ   48 Ⓐ Ⓑ © Ⓓ   58 Ⓐ Ⓑ © Ⓓ

9 Ⓐ Ⓑ © Ⓓ   19 Ⓐ Ⓑ © Ⓓ   29 Ⓐ Ⓑ © Ⓓ   39 Ⓐ Ⓑ © Ⓓ   49 Ⓐ Ⓑ © Ⓓ   59 Ⓐ Ⓑ © Ⓓ

10 Ⓐ Ⓑ © Ⓓ   20 Ⓐ Ⓑ © Ⓓ   30 Ⓐ Ⓑ © Ⓓ   40 Ⓐ Ⓑ © Ⓓ   50 Ⓐ Ⓑ © Ⓓ   60 Ⓐ Ⓑ © Ⓓ

Test 3

I: LISTENING COMPREHENSION

(50 questions—40 minutes)

This section of the test requires a demonstration of your ability to understand spoken English. Each of the three parts has special directions. **The spoken parts of this test are on the Arco TOEFL cassette tape.** *(See page 343 for ordering information.) If you cannot use the tape have a friend read the spoken parts of questions 1 to 50 to you from the script on page 257.*

Part A

Directions. In this part of the test, you will hear a brief statement. Each statement will be spoken only once. The statement does not appear in your test booklet. When you have heard a statement, select the answer nearest in meaning to what you have heard. Record your answer on the answer sheet.

Example

You will hear: The Wagners seem to take their large family in stride.

You will read:
  (A) Mr. Wagner comes from a large family.
  (B) Mrs. Wagner comes from a large family.
  (C) Mr. and Mrs. Wagner are the parents of many children.
  (D) The Wagners dislike small families.

The correct answer to the example is (C).

1. (A) You can pick up your film in two days.
  (B) You can get your film tomorrow.
  (C) Your film is ready now.
  (D) You can pick up your film either today or tomorrow.

2. (A) We need to get some gas soon.
  (B) We have about twenty gallons of gas left.
  (C) We have traveled about twenty miles so far.
  (D) There are about twenty gas stations on this road.

3. (A) You can buy the television set on credit.
  (B) You can arrange to use the television set for twelve months.
  (C) You must pay cash for the television set.
  (D) You can return the television set to the credit manager after twelve months.

4. (A) The woman will go to the doctor's office first.
  (B) The woman will go to the post office first.
  (C) The woman will go to the grocery store first.
  (D) The woman will go to the cleaners first.

5. (A) The performance lasts two hours.
  (B) The man got a seat in the second row.
  (C) The man got a seat in the front row.
  (D) The man failed to get a ticket to the performance.

6. (A) Jack must memorize his notes.
   (B) Jack must review his notes.
   (C) Jack must type his notes.
   (D) Jack must summarize his notes.

7. (A) Yale won the game.
   (B) The score of the game was 30–30.
   (C) A player from Yale scored the winning touchdown.
   (D) Harvard won the game.

8. (A) The total price of the lawn mower is $225.
   (B) There is no charge to assemble the lawn mower.
   (C) A lawn mower comes assembled for $100.
   (D) The price is cheaper if you assemble the lawn mower yourself.

9. (A) Dave lost his job.
   (B) Dave had an accident on the job.
   (C) Dave's salary was lowered.
   (D) Dave was given a salary increase.

10. (A) Bill was given a speeding ticket by the patrolman.
    (B) Bill was speeding when he saw the patrolman.
    (C) Bill was about to speed when he saw the patrolman.
    (D) Bill told the patrolman that he (Bill) had not been speeding.

11. (A) Bob wants to begin work immediately.
    (B) Bob wants to begin working tomorrow.
    (C) Bob wants to forget about the work.
    (D) Bob wants to begin working on Wednesday.

12. (A) I answered only the first question.
    (B) The last question was the most difficult for me.
    (C) I failed to get to the last question.
    (D) I found the final question easier than the other questions.

13. (A) On Tuesdays, the store closes at 8.
    (B) On Tuesdays, the store closes at 6.
    (C) On Tuesdays, the store closes at 4.
    (D) On Tuesdays, the store closes at 12.

14. (A) The student continued talking.
    (B) The student asked for permission to talk.
    (C) The student stopped talking.
    (D) The student prevented the teacher from talking.

15. (A) Mrs. Jones asked Linda to bathe the baby.
    (B) Mrs. Jones asked Linda to walk the baby.
    (C) Mrs. Jones asked Linda to feed the baby.
    (D) Mrs. Jones asked Linda to take care of the baby.

16. (A) The father broke the window.
    (B) The father mistakenly accused his child of breaking the window.
    (C) The child was responsible for breaking the window.
    (D) The father never learned who had broken the window.

17. (A) The hostess was reluctant to offer her guests food and drinks.
    (B) The hostess tried hard to please her guests.
    (C) The guests refused the food and drinks prepared by the hostess.
    (D) Neither the guests nor the hostess had food or drinks.

18. (A) John attended college in New York City.
    (B) John attended college in Chicago.
    (C) John received a poor education in school.
    (D) John studied education in college.

19. (A) Bill is studying more this year.
    (B) Bill is in his second year of college.
    (C) Bill made a statement about the university.
    (D) Bill is in his fourth year of college.

20. (A) Mark hasn't gone to the library.
    (B) Mark hasn't begun the semester.
    (C) Mark hasn't studied at all this semester.
    (D) Mark hasn't bought any books.

Part B

Directions. This section of the Listening Comprehension test consists of fifteen short conversations between two people. When each conversation ends, you will be asked a question by a third voice about what was said. You will hear the question only once and you must choose the answer from the four choices given. When you have chosen what you believe to be the best answer to the question, record your answer on the answer sheet.

21. (A) He must see the dentist.
    (B) He must give a speech.
    (C) He has a meeting to attend.
    (D) He must travel to a business conference.

22. (A) A new restaurant.
    (B) A new hotel.
    (C) A new hospital.
    (D) A new airport.

23. (A) John should not talk to Bill anymore.
    (B) John should tell Bill not to think negatively.
    (C) John should take Bill's remarks seriously.
    (D) John should pay little attention to what Bill says.

24. (A) The woman buys all her clothes in Chicago.
    (B) The woman purchased no dresses in Chicago.
    (C) The woman can sew.
    (D) The woman bought one dress in Chicago.

25. (A) He arrived at the subway station late.
    (B) The subway is not on time.

(C) The subway left an hour ago.
(D) The woman kept him from boarding the subway.

26. (A) It will probably rain.
    (B) It will probably be foggy.
    (C) It will probably not rain.
    (D) It will probably be cold.

27. (A) Take four pills.
    (B) Hesitate to take any pills.
    (C) Take the doctor's advice.
    (D) Take eight pills.

28. (A) In Rome.
    (B) In Paris.
    (C) In London.
    (D) In Madrid.

29. (A) By plane.
    (B) By car.
    (C) By bus.
    (D) By train.

30. (A) In a park.
    (B) In a museum.
    (C) In a zoo.
    (D) In a pet store.

31. (A) Get directions to the bus station.
    (B) Get to the grocery store.
    (C) Give the man directions to the bus station.
    (D) Find out where the stoplight is.

32. (A) She's a maid.
    (B) She sells stoves and refrigerators.
    (C) She's an apartment manager.
    (D) She's a real estate agent.

33. (A) Four hundred dollars.
    (B) A little less than four hundred dollars.
    (C) No money at all.
    (D) A great deal less than four hundred dollars.

34. (A) A bus station.
    (B) An airport.
    (C) A super highway.
    (D) A train station.

35. (A) He got angry with his boss.
    (B) He always got to work late.
    (C) He was frequently sick and absent from work.
    (D) He prepared a financial report incorrectly.

Part C

Directions. In this part of the test, you will be required to listen to several short lectures and conversations. You will hear the lectures and conversations only once. They do not appear in your test booklet. When a question is asked, choose the best answer from the four given. Record your answer on the answer sheet.

36. (A) Six years old.
    (B) Two years old.
    (C) Three months old.
    (D) Seven years old.

37. (A) Helen's hearing was restored.
    (B) Helen learned to speak.
    (C) Helen's sight was restored.
    (D) Helen was able to teach other blind children.

38. (A) In 1887.
    (B) In 1830.
    (C) In 1867.
    (D) In 1840.

39. (A) Her son.
    (B) Her brother.
    (C) Her father.
    (D) Her nephew.

40. (A) Fifty dollars.
    (B) Ten dollars.
    (C) Thirty dollars.
    (D) Twenty dollars.

41. (A) A chess set.
    (B) A pen and pencil set.
    (C) A book on athletics.
    (D) A handball set.

42. (A) The rattlesnake is a dangerous snake.
    (B) The rattlesnake's rattles are rings of hardened skin.
    (C) The rattlesnake is the only species of snake that has rattles.
    (D) The rattlesnake is one of many poisonous snakes that give warning before they strike.

43. (A) The snake sheds its skin.
    (B) The snake becomes transparent.
    (C) The skin hardens and releases a poisonous liquid.
    (D) The snake forms an additional protective skin over the original.

44. (A) They believe that the snake is able to control the rattle.
    (B) They believe that the snake is unaware of its rattle.
    (C) They believe that the rattle is a nervous action.
    (D) They believe that the rattle is a deliberate warning.

45. (A) The water snake.
    (B) The bull snake.
    (C) The cobra.
    (D) The cat snake.

46. (A) One-half.
    (B) One-fourth.
    (C) One-third.
    (D) Two-thirds.

47. (A) They always have the same blood type.
    (B) They occur at random in the population.
    (C) They can be of different sexes.
    (D) They have the same genes.

48. (A) Single-egg twins.
    (B) Mirror twins.
    (C) Fraternal twins.
    (D) Separate-egg twins.

49. (A) A secret language.
    (B) The same genes.

(C) The same careers.
(D) A different bone structure.

50. (A) How twins are born.
    (B) Fraternal twins and their parents.
    (C) Characteristics of identical twins.
    (D) The marriages of twins.

II: STRUCTURE AND WRITTEN EXPRESSION

(40 questions—25 minutes)

Part A

Directions. In this part of the test each problem consists of an incomplete sentence. Below the sentence are four choices, marked (A), (B), (C), and (D). You should find the one choice which best completes the sentence. Mark your choice on the answer sheet.

Example

Because the United States has little tin, _____ produced in the rest of the world.

(A) tin is used
(B) it uses tin
(C) uses of tin
(D) uses tin

The correct answer to the example is (B).

1. Michael Faraday made a great discovery _____ that electricity can be made to flow in a coil of wire.

   (A) when he found
   (B) to find
   (C) was found
   (D) he found

2. Solid-fuel engines are simpler than liquid-fuel engines, _____ have important uses.

   (A) both of them
   (B) so both
   (C) both however
   (D) but both

3. In 1939 the Ohio and Mississippi rivers overflowed _____ the worst flood ever known in the United States.

   (A) the cause of
   (B) which caused
   (C) and caused
   (D) they caused

4. The city's transport system, which is extremely old, _____ prove difficult to modernize.

   (A) it might
   (B) and might
   (C) might
   (D) that might

5. Many craters on the earth's surface were probably formed by very large meteorites _____.

   (A) smashing into the ground and exploding
   (B) which smashed into the ground and an explosion
   (C) when smashed into the ground was an explosion
   (D) they smashed into the ground and exploded

6. Galileo's experiments with falling bodies, Pasteur's work with disease germs, _____ on heredity are significant events in the story of science.

   (A) also Mendel's research
   (B) and Mendel's research

(C)   and Mendel did research
(D)   despite Mendel's research

7. Throughout history, the moon has inspired . not only song and dance _____.

(A)   and also poetry and prose
(B)   but poetry also prose
(C)   together with poetry and prose
(D)   but poetry and prose as well

8. The accomplishments of modern medicine would be impossible _____ highly specialized instruments.

(A)   without
(B)   but without
(C)   but there are
(D)   among

9. The earth might look like a perfect sphere, but careful measurements _____.

(A)   show is not
(B)   show that it is not
(C)   that show it is not
(D)   show it that is not

10. Nebraska is a state whose name comes from an Indian word _____ "river in the flatness."

(A)   means
(B)   the meaning of
(C)   meaning
(D)   is meant

11. Claudius Ptolemy, _____ of the first century A.D., left a good description of the geocentric theory.

(A)   he was an astronomer and a philosopher
(B)   being an astronomer and a philosopher
(C)   who was an astronomer and a philosopher
(D)   an astronomer and who was a philosopher

12. Near the White House is another famous landmark _____ the Washington Monument.

(A)   is which
(B)   which call
(C)   called
(D)   it is called

13. _____ coming of the Space Age, a new dimension has been added to the study of the planets.

(A)   While
(B)   It is the
(C)   When the
(D)   With the

14. It is useful to science _____ the earth as an object in space.

(A)   to consider
(B)   which considers
(C)   considers
(D)   the consideration of

15. For many children, nothing seems so exciting _____ their first airplane ride.

(A)   so does
(B)   as
(C)   on
(D)   is

Part B

Directions.   In each of the following sentences, four words or phrases have been underlined. You should choose the one word or phrase that would *not* be appropriate in standard written English. Mark your choice on the answer sheet.

Example

The average age <u>at which</u> people <u>begin to need</u> eyeglasses <u>vary</u> <u>considerably</u>.
              A   B   C   D

(C)   is incorrect in standard written English.

16. The capital city <u>is noted for</u> its many modern improvements, but in other parts of the country, <u>lack</u>
    A B
    <u>of enough good</u> roads <u>have delayed</u> progress.
       C   D

17. With the <u>marriage of</u> Isabella and Ferdinand, the rise <u>of Spain</u> began <u>and secured</u> <u>a rich and</u>
              A   B   C   D
    <u>extensive</u> empire.

18. Before an <u>explorer Norwegian</u> reached the South Pole in 1911, many other explorers <u>had tried to</u>
                A   B
    <u>reach it</u> and <u>failed</u>.
       C   D

19. West of the <u>Missouri River</u> there <u>are vast</u>, open <u>grazing</u> lands, an area that receives <u>little rain</u> than
                A   B   C   D
    the farming region.

20. Plantation life in South Carolina <u>lasted until</u> the Civil War, <u>after which</u> most of the state <u>suffering</u>
                                       A   B   C
    <u>badly</u>.
       D

21. A book of many pages <u>would be needed</u> to <u>just list</u> <u>all the</u> animals <u>native to</u> South America.
                         A   B   C   D

22. From the chart <u>shown</u> <u>on</u> page 115, <u>one can easily see</u> how large each country is and how many
                    A   B   C
    inhabitants <u>does it have</u>.
                D

23. Some of the land in that region is <u>so wet</u> and hot and <u>covered with</u> jungle that <u>a few people</u> live
                                        A   B   C
    <u>there</u>.
       D

24. <u>Between</u> the two rivers, where Charleston <u>now stands</u>, <u>the first English</u> settlement <u>there was</u>
       A   B   C   D
    established in 1680.

25. <u>Wealthy</u> people have always desired <u>and wear</u> precious stones because <u>their beauty</u> <u>is lasting</u>.
       A   B   C   D

26. The Taj Mahal, <u>that</u> took twenty-two years <u>to construct</u>, <u>is possibly</u> the most beautiful building <u>in</u>
                    A   B   C
    the world.
       D

27. <u>While visiting</u> a cotton plantation, Eli Whitney got the idea for the cotton gin, <u>which</u> soon helped
       A   B
    to increase <u>the production cotton</u> throughout the South.
                C   D

28. Every one of us <u>has read</u> that when <u>any substance</u> burns, <u>that it</u> <u>unites with</u> oxygen.
                    A   B   C   D

29. Michelangelo's father <u>sent him</u> to school, <u>hoping that</u> he <u>would be</u> a scholar, but the boy was fond
                        A   B   C

    <u>only in</u> sculpture.
      D

30. Cortés, <u>who conquered</u> Mexico City and <u>destroyed it lately</u>, considered Mexico <u>to be</u> the most
                 A   B   C

    beautiful city <u>he had ever seen</u>.
                D

31. From <u>its</u> name, <u>one might guess</u> <u>that</u> meteorology is the study of meteors, <u>but instead of</u>, it is the
       A   B   C   D

    study of weather.

32. <u>Unless</u> we polish metals <u>frequently</u>, they <u>rust or tarnish</u> when <u>exposure</u> to air.
      A   B   C   D

33. Some mercury <u>exists free</u> in nature; most of it, <u>however</u>, is found <u>in combination</u> <u>to</u> sulfur.
                      A   B   C   D

34. <u>Someone who</u> has ever tried <u>to pick up</u> spilled mercury will <u>agree that</u> this element is hard <u>to</u>
         A   B   C

    handle.
      D

35. <u>By 1910</u>, other scientists <u>had carried out</u> experiments which were much <u>like Mendel</u>, and their
        A   B   C

    results were <u>the same as his</u>.
               D

36. <u>The medical science</u> began with the <u>Greek Hippocrates</u>, who earned <u>for himself</u> <u>the title</u> of Father
               A   B   C   D

    of Medicine.

37. <u>After exploring</u> the coast <u>for a month</u>, the Pilgrims <u>founded</u> a new colony <u>and named</u> Plymouth.
            A   B   C   D

38. A person <u>on a diet</u> should keep <u>in mind</u> that <u>the worst time</u> <u>to eat heavy</u> is just before bedtime.
              A   B   C   D

39. <u>Approximately</u> one in <u>every</u> three marriages <u>in America</u> today <u>end in</u> divorce.
          A   B   C   D

40. Sulfuric acid is used <u>so extensively</u> <u>in manufacturing</u> that thousands of factories would go <u>out of</u>
                           A   B

    business if this acid <u>is unattainable</u>.
      C   D

III: READING COMPREHENSION AND VOCABULARY

(60 Questions—45 Minutes)

Part A

Directions. Each problem in this part of the test consists of a sentence in which one word or phrase has been underlined. From the four choices given, you should choose the one word or phrase which could be substituted for the underlined word or phrase without changing the meaning of the sentence. Mark your choice on the answer sheet.

Example

The frown on the man's face showed that he was displeased.

(A) look of fear
(B) look of anger
(C) look of delight
(D) look of surprise

The best answer is (B).

1. His winning the award was the highest attainment of his career.

   (A) desire
   (B) spectacle
   (C) achievement
   (D) joy

2. Your mood seems very meditative this evening.

   (A) gleeful
   (B) thoughtful
   (C) desperate
   (D) stern

3. He was too obstinate to admit he had been wrong.

   (A) stubborn
   (B) frightened
   (C) selfish
   (D) cautious

4. I knew my father would discipline me for my actions.

   (A) reward
   (B) reprove
   (C) congratulate
   (D) punish

5. Samuel Morse's painting ability has been obscured by his other accomplishments.

   (A) revealed
   (B) hidden
   (C) exposed
   (D) popularized

6. The earth is usually represented by a sphere.

   (A) cube
   (B) globe
   (C) block
   (D) cylinder

7. He was able to mend the cup and saucer.

   (A) wash
   (B) repair
   (C) decorate
   (D) mold

8. The girl took a long hike on her first morning at camp.

   (A) horseback ride
   (B) walk
   (C) bicycle ride
   (D) swim

9. Before taking such a test, one had better brush up on his or her vocabulary.

   (A) outline
   (B) translate
   (C) revise
   (D) review

10. It is ridiculous to become angry about such an insignificant matter.

    (A) sinful
    (B) tragic
    (C) absurd
    (D) unpardonable

11. The official hinted at startling new developments that would soon be made public.

    (A) openly announced
    (B) carefully concealed
    (C) indirectly suggested
    (D) reluctantly revealed

12. The orchid is an exotic plant to see blooming in most North American gardens.

    (A) a common
    (B) a colorful
    (C) a beautiful
    (D) an unusual

13. The crowd swelled until the noise made could be heard for miles.

    (A) shouted
    (B) cheered
    (C) grew
    (D) scattered

14. The flowers will wither in a few hours.

    (A) blossom
    (B) dry up
    (C) open
    (D) revive

15. The indecisive man was readily persuaded to change his mind again.

    (A) easily
    (B) hardly
    (C) subtly
    (D) abruptly

16. He was too old to keep up the pace for more than a few miles.

    (A) pretense
    (B) speed
    (C) appearance
    (D) practice

17. The candidate's victory at the polls was overwhelming.

    (A) treachery
    (B) defeat
    (C) triumph
    (D) popularity

18. By taking larger seams, it is a simple matter to alter the pattern to fit you.

    (A) enlarge
    (B) change
    (C) shorten
    (D) design

19. It is useless to attempt to flee from every danger; some risks must be taken.

    (A) hide oneself
    (B) run away
    (C) protect oneself
    (D) hesitate

20. The political leader was revered by the people of his country.

    (A) loved
    (B) detested
    (C) distrusted
    (D) assassinated

21. The history professor gave a synopsis of the events leading to World War I.

    (A) discussion
    (B) summary
    (C) report
    (D) preview

22. The noisy throng of teenagers jammed the hall to hear the rock concert.

    (A) parents
    (B) quartet
    (C) crowd
    (D) class

23. That matter is so <u>confidential</u> that it must not be discussed outside this office.

    (A) important
    (B) secret
    (C) interesting
    (D) alarming

24. The Department of Resources notified the town council that the water supply was <u>contaminated</u>.

    (A) polluted
    (B) tinted
    (C) diluted
    (D) diverted

25. The automobile's exhaust system <u>gave off</u> foul-smelling fumes.

    (A) attracted
    (B) neutralized
    (C) emitted
    (D) condensed

26. The espionage agent agreed not to <u>divulge</u> the top-secret plans.

    (A) reveal
    (B) destroy
    (C) duplicate
    (D) market

27. The surgeon examined the <u>gash</u> in the victim's head.

    (A) large bruise
    (B) deep cut
    (C) big bump
    (D) long scratch

28. In last year's Grand Prix, two cars <u>overturned</u>, severely injuring both drivers.

    (A) collided
    (B) boiled over
    (C) flipped over
    (D) overheated

29. The last weeks before Christmas are usually <u>hectic</u>, as people rush to get last-minute gifts.

    (A) happy
    (B) very expensive
    (C) exciting
    (D) very busy

30. At the stockholder's meeting, the company spokesperson gave the shareholders the <u>gist</u> of the annual report.

    (A) copy
    (B) main idea
    (C) full details
    (D) good news

Part B

Directions. You will be given a series of different types of reading material (sentences, short paragraphs, advertisements, etc.). Each selection is followed by questions about the meaning of the material. You are to choose the one best answer to each question from the four choices given.

Read the following sample passage.

(1) Marianne Moore was born in St. Louis in 1887 and graduated from Bryn Mawr College in 1909. She taught stenography for a few years and then worked as a librarian in New York. She was a
(5) member of the editorial staff of the famous literary magazine *The Dial* from 1925 to 1929. Although a book of her poems, titled *Observations,* was published in America in 1924, Miss Moore has only recently received the full acclaim
(10) she deserves.

Example 1

When did Miss Moore graduate from college?

    (A) 1887
    (B) 1909
    (C) 1925
    (D) 1924

The passage says that Miss Moore graduated from Bryn Mawr in 1909. Therefore, you should choose answer (B).

Example 2

The one profession *not* mentioned as being pursued by Miss Moore is that of

(A) poet.
(B) teacher.
(C) scientist.
(D) librarian.

The passage mentions that Miss Moore taught stenography, worked as a librarian, and wrote poetry. Therefore, you should choose (C) as the best completion of the sentence.

As soon as you understand the directions, begin work on the problems.

Questions 31–33

(1)   Before the founding of Rome, before the golden age of Athens, and about the same time as the pyramids were built, a seed germinated in what is now California, and the tree that grew from that
(5) seed is still alive—the world's oldest living thing, a 4,600-year-old bristlecone pine.

31.   You can see the world's oldest living thing if you go to

   (A)   Rome.
   (B)   Athens.
   (C)   Egypt.
   (D)   California.

32.   The founding of Rome, the golden age of Athens, and the building of the pyramids are mentioned to show

   (A)   that man was alive when the tree began to grow.
   (B)   that man has created lasting monuments.
   (C)   how very old the tree is.
   (D)   that the tree is one of man's monuments.

33.   According to this passage, about 4,600 years ago

   (A)   the world's oldest tree was already grown.

(B)   Rome had been founded.
(C)   Athens was experiencing its "golden age."
(D)   the pyramids were being built.

Questions 34–35

In the seventeenth century, although three hundred crimes in English law were punishable by death, the Massachusetts Body of Liberties listed only ten, and in some of the other colonies there were fewer.

34.   Massachusetts law

   (A)   punished more crimes by death than did English law.
   (B)   punished fewer crimes by death than did any other colony.
   (C)   punished fewer than a dozen crimes by death.
   (D)   punished three hundred crimes by death.

35.   In the seventeenth century,

   (A)   the colonies had fewer crimes than England did.
   (B)   England had fewer crimes than the colonies did.
   (C)   English law was more severe than the law of the colonies.
   (D)   colonial law was more severe than English law.

Questions 36–39 refer to the following newspaper advertisement.

(1)   U.S. CENSUS BUREAU NEEDS
         TEMPORARY PART-TIME
         FIELD INTERVIEWERS

         $6.56 Per Hour
(5)   15½¢ Per Mile Car Allowance

   Six temporary part-time field interviewers needed to conduct personal household interviews to collect social and economic data. Eight-hour day required during work periods. Approxi-
(10) mately 40–100 hours per month (May through June). Paid training. Requirements: U.S. citizen, high school or equivalent, pass 30-minute written test, have automobile, must be available for day, evening, and Saturday work. Attend a 3-day

(15) training session. Transportation paid, expenses reimbursed. Qualified applicants will be tested and interviewed by a Census representative. Persons meeting the above requirements apply in person, 1991 Wooddale Boulevard, on or before
(20) Wednesday, April 6, 1983.

U.S. DEPARTMENT OF COMMERCE
BUREAU OF THE CENSUS
EQUAL OPPORTUNITY EMPLOYER
(Employer Paid Ad)

36. One qualification *not* required by an applicant for the position described above is

   (A) a high school diploma or its equivalent.
   (B) United States citizenship.
   (C) an automobile.
   (D) at least thirty hours of university credit.

37. A person who accepts this position can be assured of

   (A) six months' employment.
   (B) approximately 40–100 months' employment.
   (C) approximately two months' employment.
   (D) eight hours per day for an unspecified time.

38. Benefits of this position do *not* include

   (A) paid training.
   (B) paid vacation.
   (C) $6.56 per hour.
   (D) 15½¢ per mile car allowance.

39. Applicants accepting this position will

   (A) be expected to work only three days per month.
   (B) be expected to work only on weekdays.
   (C) be expected to work some evenings.
   (D) be expected to work every weekend.

Questions 40–43

(1) Two key figures in American command arrangements in World War II were President Franklin D. Roosevelt and General George C.

Marshall, Chief of Staff of the army, who enjoyed
(5) Roosevelt's almost complete confidence. Even now historians are not agreed on the extent of Roosevelt's role as commander-in-chief, nor on the nature of his relations with Marshall and the other staff heads comprising the Joint Chiefs of
(10) Staff. According to one view, Roosevelt was a somewhat passive war director, concerned only with winning the war quickly and largely reliant on the advice of his top military assistants. Professor Samuel P. Huntington, in *The Soldier*
(15) *and the State* (1957), states flatly that "the military ran the war." Nevertheless, says Professor William Emerson in *Military Affairs* (Winter, 1958–1959), the picture of the passive Roosevelt is deceiving. When the President wanted to, he
(20) could intervene in military affairs powerfully and decisively.

40. Professors Huntington and Emerson

   (A) agree that Roosevelt was a somewhat passive war director.
   (B) agree that the military ran the war.
   (C) disagree as to the extent of Roosevelt's role as Commander-in-Chief.
   (D) both believe that the President could, and often did, intervene in military affairs powerfully and decisively.

41. It seems to be generally agreed that President Franklin D. Roosevelt

   (A) allowed General George C. Marshall to make all major military decisions.
   (B) made all major military decisions himself.
   (C) intervened in military affairs powerfully and decisively.
   (D) trusted General George C. Marshall and, whether or not he always followed his policy, listened carefully to his advice.

42. According to Professor Emerson, Roosevelt

   (A) sometimes took an active role in making military decisions.
   (B) had a passive role in military affairs.
   (C) was closely supervised by the Joint Chiefs of Staff.
   (D) had little control of the war machine.

43. The phrase "two key figures" (line 1) means that

   (A) these men trusted each other.
   (B) these men were important military leaders.
   (C) these men held the keys to American defense headquarters.
   (D) these men equally shared the responsibility of command.

Questions 44-47

(1) The alligator (*Alligator mississippiensis*), whose great size is legendary, is one of two members of the order *Crocodilia* found in the U.S. The anatomy of the alligator has been studied from (5) the middle of the last century up to the present, and hundreds of papers have been written on the subject. A fairly comprehensive treatise published by Reese in 1915 has been a guide for much of the more recent work, and is still helpful to (10) those using the alligator for research. Neither the physiology nor the biochemistry of the alligator had been studied in much detail prior to the work described here. In the early years of the century when metabolism was being investigated in many (15) different types of animals, several experiments were conducted on reptiles. Benedict, Krehl, and Soetbeer, and others used the alligator, and comparisons were made of the caloric requirements of cold- and warm-blooded animals.

44. Krehl and Soetbeer studied

   (A) the size of the alligator.
   (B) the metabolism of the alligator.
   (C) the natural history of the alligator.
   (D) the anatomy of the alligator.

45. *Crocodilia*

   (A) has only one member, *Alligator mississippiensis*.
   (B) has two members.
   (C) has two members which are found in the U.S.
   (D) has one member which is found in the U.S.

46. The aspect of the alligator that has been studied the longest is

   (A) its great size.
   (B) its metabolism.
   (C) its anatomy.
   (D) its caloric requirements.

47. The word "legendary" (line 2) means

   (A) famous.
   (B) enormous.
   (C) incredible.
   (D) interesting.

Questions 48-52

(1) According to the census of 1800, the United States of America contained 5,308,483 persons. In the same year the British Islands contained upwards of fifteen million; the French Republic, (5) more than twenty-seven million. Nearly one-fifth of the American people were black slaves; the true political population consisted of four and a half million free whites, or less than one million able-bodied males, on whose shoulders fell the (10) burden of a continent. Even after two centuries of struggle the land was still untamed; forest covered every portion, except here and there a strip of cultivated soil; the minerals lay undisturbed in their rocky beds, and more than two-thirds of the (15) people clung to the seaboard within fifty miles of tidewater, where alone the wants of civilized life could be supplied.

48. In the United States of America in 1800

   (A) one out of every twenty-five Americans was a black slave.
   (B) one out of every four Americans was a black slave.
   (C) two out of every three Americans were black slaves.
   (D) one out of every five Americans was a black slave.

49. Free white men in America numbered

   (A) about four-fifths of the population.
   (B) about four and one-half million.
   (C) 5,308,483.
   (D) less than one million.

50. Two-thirds of the American people

    (A) lived where the wants of civilized life could not be supplied.
    (B) lived in Washington.
    (C) lived on the seaboard.
    (D) lived within fifteen miles of tidewater.

51. The struggle to tame the American continent had been going on

    (A) about two hundred years.
    (B) about fifty years.
    (C) a little more than a century.
    (D) since 1750.

52. This description of the United States in 1800 suggests that

    (A) most of the new nation was undeveloped.
    (B) the people of the new nation had succeeded in taming the continent.
    (C) strips of cultivated land were everywhere.
    (D) settlers were beginning to mine the valuable minerals of the new continent.

Questions 53–56

(1) Since the original sections of New Orleans had been built upon a natural levee or embankment, which had been further heightened as the years passed, the natural drainage of all streets was
(5) away from the river in the direction of the swamp leading ultimately to Lake Pontchartrain. Whatever may have been the disadvantages of this drainage system, it was possible to flush the gutters by means of hydrants located at the heads
(10) of those streets running diagonally from the river. In its aim to keep the streets as clean as possible, the Board of Health ordered that public hydrants on the main streets be opened for one hour each morning and evening. The sixty-inch annual
(15) rainfall in New Orleans originally had been sufficient to clean out the gutters, but as the population grew and the dirt and refuse accumulated, the rainwater soon proved inadequate. Whatever impact flushing the gutters may have
(20) had on health—and this is a debatable point—the aesthetic results must have justified the practice.

53. The city of New Orleans seems

    (A) to have been located in a valley.
    (B) to have been located between a river and a lake.
    (C) to have had no natural levee to help in its drainage.
    (D) to have been built on land so high that it needed no further heightening.

54. The streets of New Orleans drained

    (A) into the river.
    (B) away from the lake.
    (C) into Lake Pontchartrain.
    (D) away from the swamp.

55. New Orleans usually had

    (A) little rainfall.
    (B) sixty inches of rainfall a month.
    (C) sixty inches of rainfall a year.
    (D) enough rainfall to eliminate completely the need for extra drainage systems.

56. The flushing of the gutters

    (A) definitely improved the health of the New Orleanians.
    (B) had no real effect on the health of the New Orleanians.
    (C) may have made an improvement in the health of the New Orleanians.
    (D) had some effect on the health of the citizens of New Orleans, but no other noticeable effect.

Questions 57–58

Directions. For each of the following questions, choose the answer whose *meaning is closest* to that of the given sentence. Although more than one of the choices may be factually correct, you should choose the one that *most closely restates the original sentence.*

57. Though considered good by local standards, my salary was not enough to feed and clothe my family.

(A) My salary was worse than that of my neighbors, and was not enough to feed and clothe my family.

(B) Because my salary was not enough to feed and clothe my family, it was not considered good by local standards.

(C) I earned as much money as most people in my locality; however, I did not earn enough to provide for my family.

(D) My salary was sufficient to provide for my family, although it was considered poor by local standards.

58. The Secretary of State usually attracts more criticism than any other member of the President's cabinet.

(A) The Secretary of State is more attractive than any other member of the President's cabinet.

(B) Other members of the President's cabinet attract more criticism than the Secretary of State does.

(C) Less criticism is usually directed at the Secretary of State than at other members of the President's cabinet.

(D) Other members of the President's cabinet usually attract less criticism than the Secretary of State does.

59. Most of the Roman Empire surrounding the Mediterranean Sea enjoyed a climate somewhat like that of southern California, mild in winter and hot in summer.

(A) Southern California's climate, which is mild in winter and hot in summer, is identical to the climate enjoyed by most of the Roman Empire surrounding the Mediterranean Sea.

(B) The Roman Empire, most of which surrounded the Mediterranean Sea, had the same climate (mild in winter and hot in summer) as that of southern California.

(C) Most of the Roman Empire surrounding the Mediterranean Sea had a climate rather similar to southern California's, which is mild in winter and hot in summer.

(D) Southern California has a climate (mild in winter and hot in summer) that resembles that of the Roman Empire, most of which surrounded the Mediterranean Sea.

60. Roses grow in so many different kinds of soils and climates, and thrive so well under cultivation, that thousands of different varieties have been developed.

(A) Because roses grow in many different soils and climates and can be very successfully cultivated, thousands of different varieties have been developed.

(B) Even though roses grow in many different kinds of soil and climate, and thrive so well under cultivation, thousands of different varieties have been developed.

(C) Thousands of different varieties have been developed so that roses will grow in many different kinds of soil and climate and will thrive under cultivation.

(D) Since thousands of different varieties have been developed, roses grow in many different soils and climates and can be successfully cultivated.

Test 3—Answer Key

I: LISTENING COMPREHENSION

Part A

1.	A	6.	B	11.	A	16.	B
2.	A	7.	D	12.	B	17.	B
3.	A	8.	D	13.	B	18.	B
4.	A	9.	C	14.	A	19.	B
5.	C	10.	C	15.	D	20.	C

Part B

21.	B	26.	C	31.	A
22.	C	27.	C	32.	C
23.	D	28.	C	33.	D
24.	C	29.	A	34.	B
25.	B	30.	D	35.	D

Part C

36.	A	41.	B	46.	C
37.	B	42.	D	47.	C
38.	A	43.	A	48.	A
39.	D	44.	C	49.	A
40.	D	45.	B	50.	C

II: STRUCTURE AND WRITTEN EXPRESSION

Part A

1.	A	6.	B	11.	C
2.	D	7.	D	12.	C
3.	C	8.	A	13.	D
4.	C	9.	B	14.	A
5.	A	10.	C	15.	B

Part B

16.	D	25.	B	34.	A
17.	C	26.	A	35.	C
18.	A	27.	D	36.	A
19.	D	28.	C	37.	D
20.	C	29.	D	38.	D
21.	B	30.	B	39.	D
22.	D	31.	D	40.	D
23.	C	32.	D		
24.	D	33.	D		

III: READING COMPREHENSION AND VOCABULARY

Part A

1.	C	11.	C	21.	B
2.	B	12.	D	22.	C
3.	A	13.	C	23.	B
4.	D	14.	B	24.	A
5.	B	15.	A	25.	C
6.	B	16.	B	26.	A
7.	B	17.	C	27.	B
8.	B	18.	B	28.	C
9.	D	19.	B	29.	D
10.	C	20.	A	30.	B

Part B

31.	D	41.	D	51.	A
32.	C	42.	A	52.	A
33.	D	43.	B	53.	B
34.	C	44.	B	54.	C
35.	C	45.	C	55.	C
36.	D	46.	C	56.	C
37.	C	47.	A	57.	C
38.	B	48.	D	58.	D
39.	C	49.	D	59.	C
40.	C	50.	C	60.	A

Test 3—Explanatory Answers

II: Structure and Written Expression

1. Michael Faraday made a great discovery _____ that electricity can be made to flow in a coil of wire.
   (A subordinating conjunction of time followed by a subject and a finite verb are used to make this sentence complete.)

   (A) *when he found*   CORRECT ANSWER

   (B) *to find*   *To find* is an infinitive of purpose. This choice does not contain a conjunction or a subject.

   (C) *was found*   This answer is incorrect because there is no subject for the passive verb *was found*.

   (D) *he found*   Without a conjunction, this choice results in a run-together sentence (two independent clauses joined without a conjunction).

2. Solid-fuel engines are simpler than liquid-fuel engines, _____ have important uses.
   (The correct choice in this sentence will show the contrast between the first and the second clauses.)

   (A) *both of them*   This choice is wrong because the resulting sentence is a comma splice (two independent clauses connected by a comma).

   (B) *so both*   The conjunction *so,* which means result, makes no sense in this sentence.

   (C) *both however*   The punctuation makes this choice incorrect. The following change in punctuation would make this answer acceptable: "Solid-fuel engines are simpler than liquid-fuel engines; both, however, have important uses."

   (D) *but both*   CORRECT ANSWER

3. In 1939 the Ohio and Mississippi rivers overflowed _____ the worst flood ever known in the United States.
   (This sentence is illustrative of a simple sentence with a compound subject and a compound verb. The correct answer choice completes the compound verb.)

   (A) *the cause of*   *The cause of* is not a verb. It does not make any sense following the verb *overflowed*.

(B)	*which caused*	The word *which* is a relative pronoun, but it cannot be used in this sentence since it does not refer to a specific noun.
(C)	*and caused*	CORRECT ANSWER
(D)	*they caused*	This choice results in a run-together sentence. See 1(D).

4. The city's transport system, which is extremely old, _____ prove difficult to modernize.
(An auxiliary verb is needed to make this sentence complete.)

(A)	*it·might*	The word *it* is incorrect because it repeats the subject of the sentence (*the city's transport system*).
(B)	*and might*	The word *and* makes this choice wrong because the result is a sentence fragment (an incomplete sentence).
(C)	*might*	CORRECT ANSWER
(D)	*that might*	The word *that* makes this choice incorrect since it repeats the subject of the sentence.

5. Many craters on the earth's surface were probably formed by very large meteorites _____.
(This sentence can be completed correctly by the use of a modifying phrase or a dependent clause.)

(A)	*smashing into the ground and exploding*	CORRECT ANSWER
(B)	*which smashed into the ground and an explosion*	The noun *an explosion* makes this choice incorrect. Instead, the verb *exploded* would make this choice acceptable.
(C)	*when smashed into the ground was an explosion*	The omission of several key words makes this choice wrong. Notice that *when they smashed into the ground and there was an explosion* would be an acceptable choice.
(D)	*they smashed into the ground and exploded*	The use of the word *they* instead of the relative pronoun *which* makes this answer incorrect.

6. Galileo's experiments with falling bodies, Pasteur's work with disease germs, _____ on heredity are significant events in the story of science.
(This answer choice shows how to make parts of a sentence parallel.)

(A)	*also Mendel's research*	The word *also* cannot join the three subjects of the sentence. The addition of the word *and* before *also* would be an acceptable choice.
(B)	*and Mendel's research*	CORRECT ANSWER
(C)	*and Mendel did research*	This answer choice results in a sentence that is not parallel.
(D)	*despite Mendel's research*	The word *despite* makes no sense in this sentence.

7. Throughout history, the moon has inspired not only song and dance
   _____.

   (This sentence is completed correctly with a conjunction and an object.)

   (A) *and also poetry and prose*   The word *and* makes this choice incorrect. The use of *but also poetry and prose* would be acceptable.

   (B) *but poetry also prose*   The word *also* is not a conjunction and cannot be used to connect the noun *poetry* to the noun *prose*.

   (C) *together with poetry and prose*   Since the conjunction *not only* occurs previously in the sentence, *together with* does not make sense in this choice.

   (D) *but poetry and prose as well*   CORRECT ANSWER

8. The accomplishments of modern medicine would be impossible _____ highly specialized instruments.
   (The correct answer choice in this sentence is a preposition.)

   (A) *without*   CORRECT ANSWER
   (B) *but without*   The conjunction *but* makes this choice wrong.

   (C) *but there are*   This answer choice does not logically complete the idea of how the accomplishments of modern medicine would be impossible.

   (D) *among*   The preposition *among* makes no sense in this sentence.

9. The earth might look like a perfect sphere, but careful measurements
   _____.

   (This sentence is completed correctly by adding a finite verb and a noun clause as the object.)

   (A) *show is not*   *Is not* cannot be the object of the verb *show*.

   (B) *show that it is not*   CORRECT ANSWER
   (C) *that show it is not*   The word *that* is misplaced. It must follow the verb *show* to introduce the noun clause.

   (D) *show it that is not*   The words *it* and *that* must be interchanged to make this choice correct.

10. Nebraska is a state whose name comes from an Indian word _____ "river in the flatness."
    (The last part of this sentence consists of a modifying phrase.)

    (A) *means*   The verb *means* is not a modifier. However, *which means* would be an acceptable answer.

    (B) *the meaning of*   This answer choice results in an incomplete idea. Notice that *the meaning of which is* would be an acceptable choice.

(C)	*meaning*	CORRECT ANSWER
(D)	*is meant*	The passive voice verb *is meant* is grammatically incorrect in this sentence.

11. Claudius Ptolemy, _____ of the first century A.D., left a good description of the geocentric theory.
(This answer choice illustrates the use of an adjective clause to describe the subject of the sentence.)

(A)	*he was an astronomer and a philosopher*	The pronoun *he* is incorrect because it repeats the subject of the sentence.
(B)	*being an astronomer and a philosopher*	The word *being* must be omitted in order for this answer to be correct.
(C)	*who was an astronomer and a philosopher*	CORRECT ANSWER
(D)	*an astronomer and who was a philosopher*	The word order in this choice is wrong.

12. Near the White House is another famous landmark _____ the Washington Monument.
(A dependent clause or phrase can be added to make this sentence complete.)

(A)	*is which*	Instead of *is which*, you must say *which is*.
(B)	*which call*	This modifier is incomplete because it lacks a subject. The adjective clause *which we call the Washington Monument* would be an acceptable choice.
(C)	*called*	CORRECT ANSWER
(D)	*it is called*	The pronoun *it* cannot be used as the subject of a dependent clause. The substitution of *which* for *it* would make this choice acceptable.

13. _____ coming of the Space Age, a new dimension has been added to the study of the planets.
(This answer choice involves choosing the correct words for an introductory phrase.)

(A)	*While*	The word *while* makes no sense in this sentence.
(B)	*It is the*	This choice, an independent clause, results in a comma splice. See 2(A).
(C)	*When the*	This choice results in an incomplete idea. Another sentence, such as "When the Space Age began, a new dimension was added to the study of the planets," would be an acceptable answer.
(D)	With the	CORRECT ANSWER

14. It is useful to science _____ the earth as an object in space.
(In order to complete this sentence correctly, an infinitive that shows the meaning of *it* is used.)

   (A) *to consider* — CORRECT ANSWER

   (B) *which considers* — *Which considers* introduces an adjective clause, but the "false" subject *it* must be followed by a finite verb and a noun structure.

   (C) *considers* — The verb *considers* cannot substitute for an infinitive.

   (D) *the consideration of* — This noun phrase is grammatically incorrect in this sentence. Notice that "The consideration of the earth as an object in space is useful to science" would be an acceptable sentence.

15. For many children, nothing seems so exciting _____ their first airplane ride.
(This answer choice involves choosing the correct conjunction to complete a dependent clause of comparison.)

   (A) *so does* — The word *so* does not complete this comparison.

   (B) *as* — CORRECT ANSWER

   (C) *on* — The word *on* is not a conjunction. The resulting sentence is an incomplete comparison.

   (D) *is* — A verb cannot substitute for a conjunction.

16. (D) This phrase contains an error in agreement. Change it to *has delayed* since the subject *lack* is singular. The sentence should read ". . . lack of enough good roads *has delayed* progress."

17. (C) This phrase contains an omission that makes the sentence sound illogical. You should say *and Spain secured*. Now the sentence will read ". . . the rise of Spain began *and Spain secured* . . ." Notice that the subject of the verb *secured* is not *the rise* but rather *Spain*.

18. (A) The word order is incorrect. In English, most adjectives come before the noun or pronoun they describe. You should say *a Norwegian explorer*.

19. (D) In order to form a comparison with the conjunction *than*, you should say *less rain*.

20. (C) Change *suffering* to *suffered* so that the last part of the sentence forms a dependent clause.

21. (B) You should say *just to list*. Notice that an infinitive should usually not be separated by other words.

22. (D) The word order is incorrect since this phrase is part of a noun clause. You should say *it has*. Now the sentence will read ". . . one can easily see how large each country is and how many inhabitants *it has*."

23. (C) You should say *few* people because the sentence has a negative implication. Notice

that *few* means "not many." *A few* means "some." The sentence means that *not many* people live in that region because it is wet, hot, and covered with jungle.

24. (D) Omit the expletive *there* since the settlement's location has already been mentioned. Now the sentence will read, ". . . the first English settlement *was established* in 1680."

25. (B) This phrase is in conjunction with *have always desired.* Therefore, you should say, ". . . have always desired *and worn* . . ."

26. (A) You should use the relative pronoun *which* instead of *that.* The pronoun *that* is never used in an adjective clause which modifies an identified noun. In this case, the identified noun is *The Taj Mahal.* The corrected sentence is "The Taj Mahal, *which* took twenty-two years to construct, is possibly . . ."

27. (D) There is a word omitted in this phrase. You should say *the production of cotton* or *cotton production.*

28. (C) Omit the conjunction *that* in this phrase because it is repetitive. Notice that the conjunction *that* already appears after the verb *has read.*

29. (D) The preposition *in* cannot be used here. The preposition *of* is correctly used with the adjective *fond.* You should say, ". . . the boy was *fond* only *of* sculpture."

30. (B) The adverb *lately* is wrong in this phrase. You should say *destroyed it later.* *Later* means "afterwards," and *lately* means "recently."

31. (D) Omit the preposition *of* in this phrase because it is not followed by an object. Say *but instead,* which means "but rather."

32. (D) A modifying phrase or clause is needed here. You should say *when exposed* or *when they are exposed.*

33. (D) The preposition *to* is wrong. You should say *in combination with* or *combined with.*

34. (A) Change the pronoun *someone* to the pronoun *anyone.* *Anyone* means "any person."

35. (C) This phrase contains a faulty comparison. Notice that you are not comparing the experiments of other scientists to Mendel. The experiments of other scientists are being compared to the experiments of Mendel. Therefore, you should say *like Mendel's* or *like those of Mendel.* The corrected sentence is ". . . other scientists had carried out experiments which were much *like Mendel's* . . ."

36. (A) Omit the article *the.* In English we do not usually use the article *the* when the noun phrase refers to something in a very general way. However, if the noun phrase is followed by an identifying phrase, *the* is often used. For example, you would say *the science of medicine* (*of medicine* is an identifying phrase).

37. (D) A word is omitted in this phrase. You should say *and named it.* Here, the pronoun *it* refers to *a new colony.*

38. (D) You should use the adverb *heavily* and say *to eat heavily.*

39. (D) This phrase contains a mistake in agreement. You should use the singular form of the verb, since the subject of the verb is *one,* which is singular.

40. (D) Since the last part of the sentence contains a contrary-to-fact conditional clause, you should say *were unattainable.*

III: READING COMPREHENSION AND VOCABULARY

Part A

Following are explanations of questions 1–30. In this section, the correct answers are placed first, so that they can be used to help explain the other choices.

1. **(C) CORRECT:** *Achievement* and attainment are synonyms. They mean an "accomplishment," some goal that has been reached.
   (A) *Desire* means a "longing," something one wants very much. Not every desire becomes an attainment.
   (B) A *spectacle* is a "public show; display."
   (D) A *joy* is a "delight; pleasure." Many attainments are joys, but not all joys are things one has achieved.

2. **(B) CORRECT:** *Thoughtful* means meditative.
   (A) *Gleeful* means "full of joy," or "full of mirth."
   (C) *Desperate* means "hopeless; despairing; despondent."
   (D) *Stern* means "severe; austere; strict." A *stern, gleeful* 2(A), or *desperate* 2(C) person may also be meditative, perhaps thinking about the causes of his severity, despair, or joy.

3. **(A) CORRECT:** *Stubborn* and obstinate both mean "unwilling to change."
   (B) *Frightened* means "afraid" or "fearful."
   (C) *Selfish* suggests "caring only for oneself."
   (D) *Furious* means "violently angry."

4. **(D) CORRECT:** In this sentence, *punish* and discipline are synonyms, both meaning "to correct or teach by penalizing."
   (A) *Reward*, "something given in return for good" is almost the opposite of discipline in this sentence.
   (B) To *reprove* is "to blame; rebuke; reprimand." It is related to discipline, but suggests words, not the punishment of discipline.
   (C) *Congratulate* is "to compliment with words of sympathetic pleasure or satisfaction." It is related to *reward* much as *reprove* is related to discipline.

5. **(B) CORRECT:** *Hidden* can be substituted for obscured here without loss of meaning.
   (A) In this context, *revealed,* meaning "disclosed; made known; divulged," is almost the opposite of obscured.
   (C) In the sense of "to lay open" or "to present to view," *exposed* is also almost opposite to obscured.
   (D) To *popularize* something is "to make ordinary people accept and like it."

6. **(B) CORRECT:** A *globe* and a sphere are both "hollow balls."
   (A) A *cube* is "a solid having six equal sides."

| (C) | Here, a *block* is "a solid mass of wood, stone, etc." |
| (D) | A *cylinder* is "any solid having two parallel planes and a curved surface." |

7. (B) CORRECT: *Repair* and <u>mend</u> both mean "to fix" or "to make whole."

(A)	To *wash* is "to apply a liquid, usually water, in order to clean."
(C)	To *decorate* is "to add ornamentation."
(D)	To *mold* is "to shape or form."

8. (B) CORRECT: Here <u>hike</u> means "a long *walk.*"

(A)	A *horseback ride* is a ride on a horse.
(C)	A *bicycle ride* is a ride on a bicycle.
(D)	To *swim* is "to move through the water by using one's arms and legs."

9. (D) CORRECT: To <u>brush up on</u> something is to *review* it, to "refresh one's memory."

(A)	*Outline* means "to summarize" or to write the main points of something.
(B)	*Translate* means "to put into different words or into a different language."
(C)	*Revise* means "to correct, improve, or update."

10. (C) CORRECT: *Absurd* means <u>ridiculous</u>, or "foolish; silly."

(A)	*Sinful* means "morally wrong."
(B)	*Tragic* means "mournful; melancholy; dreadful; fatal."
(D)	*Unpardonable* means "unforgivable, not excusable."

11. (C) CORRECT: <u>Hinted at</u> and *indirectly suggested* both mean "to give a slight indication," but not to say directly.

(A)	*Openly announced* would mean "to say publicly."
(B)	*Carefully concealed* means "to keep secret."
(D)	*Reluctantly revealed* would mean "to make known," but to do so unwillingly.

12. (D) CORRECT: Here <u>exotic</u> and *unusual* both mean "strange" or "uncommon."

(A)	*Common* here would be the opposite of <u>exotic</u>.
(B)	*Colorful* here would mean "vivid; having much color."
(C)	*Beautiful* means "delighting the eye." Both *beautiful* and *colorful* 12(B) plants may be <u>exotic</u> or *common.*

13. (C) CORRECT: Here *grew* and <u>swelled</u> both mean "increased in number."

(A)	*Shouted* means "to call or cry out loudly and vigorously."
(B)	*Cheered* suggests that the shouts 13(A) are "of encouragement or approval."
(D)	*Scattered* here would mean that the crowd "separated and went off; dispersed."

14. (B) CORRECT: *Dry up* and <u>wither</u> here both mean "to shrivel from loss of moisture; to lose freshness; fade."
    (A) To *blossom* is "to bloom," the "state of having buds open into flowers."
    (C) To *open* here also means "to bloom."
    (D) *Revive* would mean "to restore to life." In this sense *revive* is almost the opposite of <u>wither</u>.

15. (A) CORRECT: *Easily* and <u>readily</u> are synonyms here.
    (B) *Hardly* here means "barely; with trouble or difficulty." It is almost the opposite of *easily*.
    (C) *Subtly* in this context means "with craft or cunning; not obviously or openly."
    (D) *Abruptly* means "suddenly."

16. (B) CORRECT: <u>Pace</u> means "*speed*, often a speed set by others."
    (A) *Pretense* means "make believe; a false show of something."
    (C) *Appearance* here means "outward aspect or look" and is almost a synonym for *pretense*.
    (D) *Practice* means a "custom" or a "performance."

17. (C) CORRECT: A *triumph* and a <u>victory</u> are both "wins."
    (A) *Treachery* means "betrayal of faith or trust; disloyalty."
    (B) A *defeat* is "a loss." *Defeat* is the opposite of <u>victory</u>.
    (D) *Popularity* means that someone or something is "regarded with favor or approval by others." In the sentence, *popularity* might be the *cause* of the candidate's victory.

18. (B) CORRECT: Here to *change* and to <u>alter</u> are synonyms.
    (A) To *enlarge* is too specific here; it is a special way of <u>altering</u>, "to make bigger."
    (C) To *shorten*, "to reduce the length" is also a specific way of <u>altering</u>.
    (D) To *design* here is "to plan and fashion skillfully."

19. (B) CORRECT: To *run away* and to <u>flee</u> are synonyms.
    (A) To *hide oneself* is "to prevent oneself from being seen; to cover up; to conceal."
    (C) To *protect oneself* means "to cover or shield from injury; to defend from harm."
    (D) To *hesitate* is to "hold back" or "delay temporarily."

20. (A) CORRECT: *Loved* and <u>revered</u> both mean "to feel admiration and affection for."
    (B) *Detested* means "hated," the opposite of <u>revered</u>.
    (C) *Distrusted* means "lacked faith or confidence" in the leader.
    (D) *Assassinated* means "killed, usually for political reasons."

21. (B) CORRECT: A *summary* here means a <u>synopsis</u>, a "brief outline" of the subject.

   (A)   A *discussion* suggests the consideration of a subject by a group. It also suggests that the subject would be covered in more detail than would be given in a <u>synopsis</u>.

   (C)   A *report* is an "account." It does not suggest the brevity of a <u>synopsis</u>.

   (D)   A *preview* suggests an "advance" showing.

22. (C) CORRECT: Here *crowd* and <u>throng</u> are synonyms; both mean many people.

   (A)   *Parents* refers to the mothers and fathers of the teenagers.

   (B)   A *quartet* means "four," here, four teenagers. Four is not a <u>throng</u>.

   (D)   A *class* suggests a group having attributes in common. Such a group may be very few in number.

23. (B) CORRECT: <u>Confidential</u> and *secret* both suggest that the matter being discussed in private must not be revealed.

   (A)   *Important* means having significance or "value."

   (C)   *Interesting* means "exciting curiousity or attention."

   (D)   *Alarming* suggests that the matter being discussed is "frightening."

24. (A) CORRECT: *Polluted* and <u>contaminated</u> both mean that the water supply contained dangerous impurities.

   (B)   *Tinted* means "lightly colored."

   (C)   *Diluted* suggests that a substance has been mixed with something else and is not at full strength.

   (D)   *Diverted* means "turned from its course; deflected."

25. (C) CORRECT: *Emitted* means <u>gave off</u>, "sent out" or "discharged."

   (A)   *Attracted* means "pulled or drawn toward."

   (B)   *Neutralized* would mean "made less powerful; made ineffective."

   (D)   *Condensed* means "made more compact; reduced in size."

26. (A) CORRECT: *Reveal* and <u>divulge</u> both mean "to make known."

   (B)   *Destroy* means "to ruin completely."

   (C)   *Duplicate* means "to copy."

   (D)   *Market* in this context means "to sell."

27. (B) CORRECT: A *deep cut* or "wound" is a <u>gash</u>.

   (A)   A *large bruise* is an area of discoloration of the skin usually caused by a blow. It does not break the skin as a <u>gash</u> does.

   (C)   A *big bump* here means a raised or swollen area caused by a blow. As with a bruise, the skin is not broken.

   (D)   A *long scratch* is a "thin or shallow cut," not as deep as a <u>gash</u>.

28. (C) CORRECT: *Flipped over* here means <u>overturned</u>, so that, in the final position, what was on top is now on the bottom.
    (A) *Collided* here means "ran into each other; hit together."
    (B) *Boiled over* is used to refer to a liquid that gets so hot that it overflows its container.
    (D) *Overheated* means to become "too hot."

29. (D) CORRECT: *Very busy* and <u>hectic</u> are synonyms here.
    (A) *Happy* here means "having or demonstrating pleasure or satisfaction."
    (B) *Very expensive* means "costly."
    (C) *Exciting* means "emotionally arousing; stirring."

30. (B) CORRECT: The *main* or most important *idea* is the <u>gist</u> of something.
    (A) A *copy* is a "duplicate."
    (C) *Full details* would mean a report more complete than <u>gist</u> suggests.
    (D) *Good news* tells what the report says, not how many or few details are given.

PART B

31. This question tests for the main idea of the statement.

    (A) See 31(D) below.
    (B) See 31(D) below.
    (C) See 31(D) below.
    (D) CORRECT: The seed from which the oldest living thing grew "germinated in what is now California" (lines 3–4).

32. This question tests for the ability to draw inferences.

    (A) This is true, but not the emphasis of the passage. See 32(C) below.
    (B) This might be true, but is not the sense of the passage. See 32(C) below.
    (C) CORRECT: The references to Rome, Athens, and the pyramids show how old the tree is in terms of human history.
    (D) The statement makes no such assertion. See 32(C) above.

33. This question tests for a supporting idea in the statement.

    (A) The seed only "germinated" (began to grow) at this time.
    (B) 4,600 years ago Rome was not yet founded (line 1).
    (C) 4,600 years ago was Athens' golden age (lines 1–2).
    (D) CORRECT: 4,600 years ago, when the bristlecone pine seed germinated, the pyramids were being built (lines 2–3).

34. This question tests for the main idea.

    (A) The sentence states the opposite.
    (B) The sentence states that other colonies punished fewer crimes by death than did Massachusetts.

(C) CORRECT: Massachusetts punished ten crimes by death.
(D)   England punished 300 crimes by death.

35. This question tests for the ability to draw inferences.

(A)   The statement concerns the laws in England and the colonies, not the number of crimes in these places.
(B)   See 35(A) above.
(C) CORRECT: In England, 300 crimes were punishable by death; in the colonies, 10 or fewer were so punishable. English law, then, was more severe, or more harsh.
(D)   See 35(C) above.

36. This question tests for attention to detail.

(A)   Mentioned in line 12.
(B)   Mentioned in line 11.
(C)   Mentioned in line 13.
(D) CORRECT: Not mentioned as a requirement for the job.

37. This question tests for attention to detail.

(A)   See 37(C) below.
(B)   The person can be assured of 40–100 *hours* of work during each month that he works.
(C) CORRECT: "May through June" (lines 10–11) equals two months.
(D)   The time is specified as two months.

38. This question tests for attention to detail.

(A)   Stated in line 11.
(B) CORRECT: Not stated.
(C)   Stated in line 4.
(D)   Stated in line 5.

39. This question tests for attention to detail.

(A)   Applicants will work 8-hour days for a minimum of 40 hours a month. Three 8-hour days equal only 24 hours.
(B)   See C below.
(C) CORRECT: See lines 13–14. Applicants must be willing and able to work evenings and Saturdays, but they will not necessarily be required to work always at these times.
(D)   See 39(C) above.

40. This question tests for a main idea of the paragraph.

(A)   They disagree on this point (lines 10–19).
(B)   Only Huntington believes this (lines 14–16).
(C) CORRECT: Stated in lines 14–21.
(D)   Only Emerson believes this (lines 16–21).

41. This question tests for a main idea of the paragraph.

(A)   This point is not agreed on. See lines 3–21.
(B)   Apparently no one holds that view.

(C)   Some persons believe this, but not all (lines 16–21).

(D) CORRECT: The author states without qualification (lines 3–5) Roosevelt's confidence in Marshall. The rest of the paragraph describes the disagreement over whether or not Roosevelt always followed the advice of the military, including that of General Marshall.

42. This question tests for a supporting idea in the paragraph.

(A) CORRECT: Emerson's view is stated in lines 16–21.

(B)   This is Huntington's view (lines 10–16).

(C)   See 42(A) above.

(D)   Emerson argues the opposite (lines 16–21).

43. This question tests for word recognition.

(A)   See 43(B) below. Key does not refer to trust.

(B) CORRECT: "Key" in this context means being of major importance.

(C)   *Key* in this answer means a metal instrument which is inserted into a lock to open it.

(D)   This answer may be true, but *key* does not imply equal responsibility.

44. This question tests for a supporting idea.

(A)   Its *size* is easily determined.

(B) CORRECT: This assertion is made in lines 14–17.

(C)   The various studies described would all be parts of *natural history*.

(D)   Reese has a treatise on the alligator's *anatomy*. See lines 7–10.

45. This question tests for attention to detail.

(A)   See 45(C) below.

(B)   See 45(C) below.

(C) CORRECT: See lines 1–3.

(D)   See 45(C) above.

46. This question tests for a main idea of the paragraph.

(A)   Its size can be determined by simple observation.

(B)   This began to be investigated only in the early twentieth century (lines 13–19).

(C) CORRECT: This was studied from the middle of the nineteenth century.

(D)   See 46(B) above.

47. This question tests for word recognition.

(A) CORRECT: In this context, "legendary" means well known and widely known for a long time.

(B)   "Great size" (line 2) means "large or enormous."

(C)   *Incredible* means "hard to believe" (literally it means "not believable").

(D)   Something "legendary," however, is often—or usually—of interest.

48. This question tests for attention to detail.

(A)   See 48(D) below.
(B)   See 48(D) below.
(C)   See 48(D) below.
(D) CORRECT: If "nearly one-fifth of Americans were black slaves" (lines 5–6), then approximately one out of five was a slave.

49. This question tests for attention to detail.

(A)   See 49(D) below.
(B)   See 49(D) below.
(C)   This was the total population of the United States.
(D) CORRECT: This is stated in lines 7–9.

50. This question tests for attention to detail.

(A)   They lived in the only area where these wants could be supplied.
(B)   Washington is not mentioned in the paragraph.
(C) CORRECT: "clung to" (line 15) suggests that they would not move away from this area.
(D)   They lived within "fifty" miles of tidewater (lines 15–16).

51. This question tests for attention to detail.

(A) CORRECT: "After two centuries" (line 10) means "about two hundred years."
(B)   See 51(A) above.
(C)   See 51(A) above.
(D)   See 51(A) above.

52. This question tests for the main idea of the paragraph.

(A) CORRECT: The nation did not have a large population, and most of its territory was unsettled.
(B)   The land was still untamed (lines 10–11).
(C)   Most portions of the land were covered by forests, with only occasional strips of cultivated land (lines 11–13).
(D)   The minerals were not yet being mined—they "lay undisturbed" (lines 13–14).

53. This question tests for the ability to draw inferences.

(A)   No valley is mentioned or implied.
(B) CORRECT: The city's drainage was away from the river and toward the lake (lines 1–6).
(C)   It had a natural embankment on the river (lines 1–2).
(D)   The passage does not say how high the land was, but the levee suggests that it was not high above the river.

54. This question tests for attention to detail.

 (A) They drained "away from" the river (line 5).
 (B) They drained toward the lake (line 6).
 (C) CORRECT: They drained "into" the swamp that led to the lake (lines 4–6).
 (D) See 54(C) above.

55. This question tests for attention to detail.

 (A) See 55(C) below.
 (B) See 55(C) below.
 (C) CORRECT: "The sixty-inch annual rainfall" means *sixty inches of rainfall a year* (lines 14–15).
 (D) As the population grew, the rainfall became inadequate to flush the gutters (lines 16–18). "Flush" in this context means "clean out" (line 19).

56. This question tests for a supporting idea in the paragraph.

 (A) See 56(C) below.
 (B) See 56(C) below.
 (C) CORRECT: It is not clear ("debatable") whether or not flushing the gutters made the city healthier to live in (lines 19–21).
 (D) The most noticeable effect was "aesthetic" (line 21), in this case cleaner and better-smelling.

The following questions test for the sense of the sentences.

57. (A) If it was worse than my neighbors', it would be considered poor—not good—by local standards.
 (B) It *was* considered good by local standards.
 (C) CORRECT: This is the same sense as the original, but with change in details.
 (D) This states just the opposite of the original.

58. (A) *Attractive* here means "handsome, good-looking."
 (B) This statement contradicts the original.
 (C) See 58(B) above.
 (D) CORRECT: This reverses the order of the original, but retains the sense.

59. (A) "Somewhat like" is not the same as *identical,* which means "exactly the same."
 (B) This statement asserts that most of the Roman Empire surrounded the Mediterranean; the original does not.
 (C) CORRECT: "Somewhat like" means *rather similar to.*
 (D) See 59(B) above.

60. (A) CORRECT: Both statements have the same sense, and assert the same causal relation.
 (B) *Even though* here means "despite the fact that."
 (C) This statement reverses the causal relation of the original.
 (D) See 60(C) above.

ANSWER SHEET FOR TEST 4

Tear out this answer sheet and use it to record your answers to all the questions in this examination.

SECTION I

1 Ⓐ Ⓑ Ⓒ Ⓓ	11 Ⓐ Ⓑ Ⓒ Ⓓ	21 Ⓐ Ⓑ Ⓒ Ⓓ	31 Ⓐ Ⓑ Ⓒ Ⓓ	41 Ⓐ Ⓑ Ⓒ Ⓓ
2 Ⓐ Ⓑ Ⓒ Ⓓ	12 Ⓐ Ⓑ Ⓒ Ⓓ	22 Ⓐ Ⓑ Ⓒ Ⓓ	32 Ⓐ Ⓑ Ⓒ Ⓓ	42 Ⓐ Ⓑ Ⓒ Ⓓ
3 Ⓐ Ⓑ Ⓒ Ⓓ	13 Ⓐ Ⓑ Ⓒ Ⓓ	23 Ⓐ Ⓑ Ⓒ Ⓓ	33 Ⓐ Ⓑ Ⓒ Ⓓ	43 Ⓐ Ⓑ Ⓒ Ⓓ
4 Ⓐ Ⓑ Ⓒ Ⓓ	14 Ⓐ Ⓑ Ⓒ Ⓓ	24 Ⓐ Ⓑ Ⓒ Ⓓ	34 Ⓐ Ⓑ Ⓒ Ⓓ	44 Ⓐ Ⓑ Ⓒ Ⓓ
5 Ⓐ Ⓑ Ⓒ Ⓓ	15 Ⓐ Ⓑ Ⓒ Ⓓ	25 Ⓐ Ⓑ Ⓒ Ⓓ	35 Ⓐ Ⓑ Ⓒ Ⓓ	45 Ⓐ Ⓑ Ⓒ Ⓓ
6 Ⓐ Ⓑ Ⓒ Ⓓ	16 Ⓐ Ⓑ Ⓒ Ⓓ	26 Ⓐ Ⓑ Ⓒ Ⓓ	36 Ⓐ Ⓑ Ⓒ Ⓓ	46 Ⓐ Ⓑ Ⓒ Ⓓ
7 Ⓐ Ⓑ Ⓒ Ⓓ	17 Ⓐ Ⓑ Ⓒ Ⓓ	27 Ⓐ Ⓑ Ⓒ Ⓓ	37 Ⓐ Ⓑ Ⓒ Ⓓ	47 Ⓐ Ⓑ Ⓒ Ⓓ
8 Ⓐ Ⓑ Ⓒ Ⓓ	18 Ⓐ Ⓑ Ⓒ Ⓓ	28 Ⓐ Ⓑ Ⓒ Ⓓ	38 Ⓐ Ⓑ Ⓒ Ⓓ	48 Ⓐ Ⓑ Ⓒ Ⓓ
9 Ⓐ Ⓑ Ⓒ Ⓓ	19 Ⓐ Ⓑ Ⓒ Ⓓ	29 Ⓐ Ⓑ Ⓒ Ⓓ	39 Ⓐ Ⓑ Ⓒ Ⓓ	49 Ⓐ Ⓑ Ⓒ Ⓓ
10 Ⓐ Ⓑ Ⓒ Ⓓ	20 Ⓐ Ⓑ Ⓒ Ⓓ	30 Ⓐ Ⓑ Ⓒ Ⓓ	40 Ⓐ Ⓑ Ⓒ Ⓓ	50 Ⓐ Ⓑ Ⓒ Ⓓ

SECTION II

1 Ⓐ Ⓑ Ⓒ Ⓓ	9 Ⓐ Ⓑ Ⓒ Ⓓ	17 Ⓐ Ⓑ Ⓒ Ⓓ	25 Ⓐ Ⓑ Ⓒ Ⓓ	33 Ⓐ Ⓑ Ⓒ Ⓓ
2 Ⓐ Ⓑ Ⓒ Ⓓ	10 Ⓐ Ⓑ Ⓒ Ⓓ	18 Ⓐ Ⓑ Ⓒ Ⓓ	26 Ⓐ Ⓑ Ⓒ Ⓓ	34 Ⓐ Ⓑ Ⓒ Ⓓ
3 Ⓐ Ⓑ Ⓒ Ⓓ	11 Ⓐ Ⓑ Ⓒ Ⓓ	19 Ⓐ Ⓑ Ⓒ Ⓓ	27 Ⓐ Ⓑ Ⓒ Ⓓ	35 Ⓐ Ⓑ Ⓒ Ⓓ
4 Ⓐ Ⓑ Ⓒ Ⓓ	12 Ⓐ Ⓑ Ⓒ Ⓓ	20 Ⓐ Ⓑ Ⓒ Ⓓ	28 Ⓐ Ⓑ Ⓒ Ⓓ	36 Ⓐ Ⓑ Ⓒ Ⓓ
5 Ⓐ Ⓑ Ⓒ Ⓓ	13 Ⓐ Ⓑ Ⓒ Ⓓ	21 Ⓐ Ⓑ Ⓒ Ⓓ	29 Ⓐ Ⓑ Ⓒ Ⓓ	37 Ⓐ Ⓑ Ⓒ Ⓓ
6 Ⓐ Ⓑ Ⓒ Ⓓ	14 Ⓐ Ⓑ Ⓒ Ⓓ	22 Ⓐ Ⓑ Ⓒ Ⓓ	30 Ⓐ Ⓑ Ⓒ Ⓓ	38 Ⓐ Ⓑ Ⓒ Ⓓ
7 Ⓐ Ⓑ Ⓒ Ⓓ	15 Ⓐ Ⓑ Ⓒ Ⓓ	23 Ⓐ Ⓑ Ⓒ Ⓓ	31 Ⓐ Ⓑ Ⓒ Ⓓ	39 Ⓐ Ⓑ Ⓒ Ⓓ
8 Ⓐ Ⓑ Ⓒ Ⓓ	16 Ⓐ Ⓑ Ⓒ Ⓓ	24 Ⓐ Ⓑ Ⓒ Ⓓ	32 Ⓐ Ⓑ Ⓒ Ⓓ	40 Ⓐ Ⓑ Ⓒ Ⓓ

128 / *TOEFL*

SECTION III

1 Ⓐ Ⓑ Ⓒ Ⓓ   11 Ⓐ Ⓑ Ⓒ Ⓓ   21 Ⓐ Ⓑ Ⓒ Ⓓ   31 Ⓐ Ⓑ Ⓒ Ⓓ   41 Ⓐ Ⓑ Ⓒ Ⓓ   51 Ⓐ Ⓑ Ⓒ Ⓓ

2 Ⓐ Ⓑ Ⓒ Ⓓ   12 Ⓐ Ⓑ Ⓒ Ⓓ   22 Ⓐ Ⓑ Ⓒ Ⓓ   32 Ⓐ Ⓑ Ⓒ Ⓓ   42 Ⓐ Ⓑ Ⓒ Ⓓ   52 Ⓐ Ⓑ Ⓒ Ⓓ

3 Ⓐ Ⓑ Ⓒ Ⓓ   13 Ⓐ Ⓑ Ⓒ Ⓓ   23 Ⓐ Ⓑ Ⓒ Ⓓ   33 Ⓐ Ⓑ Ⓒ Ⓓ   43 Ⓐ Ⓑ Ⓒ Ⓓ   53 Ⓐ Ⓑ Ⓒ Ⓓ

4 Ⓐ Ⓑ Ⓒ Ⓓ   14 Ⓐ Ⓑ Ⓒ Ⓓ   24 Ⓐ Ⓑ Ⓒ Ⓓ   34 Ⓐ Ⓑ Ⓒ Ⓓ   44 Ⓐ Ⓑ Ⓒ Ⓓ   54 Ⓐ Ⓑ Ⓒ Ⓓ

5 Ⓐ Ⓑ Ⓒ Ⓓ   15 Ⓐ Ⓑ Ⓒ Ⓓ   25 Ⓐ Ⓑ Ⓒ Ⓓ   35 Ⓐ Ⓑ Ⓒ Ⓓ   45 Ⓐ Ⓑ Ⓒ Ⓓ   55 Ⓐ Ⓑ Ⓒ Ⓓ

6 Ⓐ Ⓑ Ⓒ Ⓓ   16 Ⓐ Ⓑ Ⓒ Ⓓ   26 Ⓐ Ⓑ Ⓒ Ⓓ   36 Ⓐ Ⓑ Ⓒ Ⓓ   46 Ⓐ Ⓑ Ⓒ Ⓓ   56 Ⓐ Ⓑ Ⓒ Ⓓ

7 Ⓐ Ⓑ Ⓒ Ⓓ   17 Ⓐ Ⓑ Ⓒ Ⓓ   27 Ⓐ Ⓑ Ⓒ Ⓓ   37 Ⓐ Ⓑ Ⓒ Ⓓ   47 Ⓐ Ⓑ Ⓒ Ⓓ   57 Ⓐ Ⓑ Ⓒ Ⓓ

8 Ⓐ Ⓑ Ⓒ Ⓓ   18 Ⓐ Ⓑ Ⓒ Ⓓ   28 Ⓐ Ⓑ Ⓒ Ⓓ   38 Ⓐ Ⓑ Ⓒ Ⓓ   48 Ⓐ Ⓑ Ⓒ Ⓓ   58 Ⓐ Ⓑ Ⓒ Ⓓ

9 Ⓐ Ⓑ Ⓒ Ⓓ   19 Ⓐ Ⓑ Ⓒ Ⓓ   29 Ⓐ Ⓑ Ⓒ Ⓓ   39 Ⓐ Ⓑ Ⓒ Ⓓ   49 Ⓐ Ⓑ Ⓒ Ⓓ   59 Ⓐ Ⓑ Ⓒ Ⓓ

10 Ⓐ Ⓑ Ⓒ Ⓓ   20 Ⓐ Ⓑ Ⓒ Ⓓ   30 Ⓐ Ⓑ Ⓒ Ⓓ   40 Ⓐ Ⓑ Ⓒ Ⓓ   50 Ⓐ Ⓑ Ⓒ Ⓓ   60 Ⓐ Ⓑ Ⓒ Ⓓ

Test 4

I: LISTENING COMPREHENSION

(50 Questions—40 minutes)

This section of the test requires a demonstration of your ability to understand spoken English. Each of the three parts has special directions. Have a friend read the spoken parts of questions 1 to 50 to you from the script on page 265.

Part A

Directions. In this part of the test, you will hear a brief statement. Each statement will be spoken only once. The statement does not appear in your test booklet. When you have heard a statement, select the answer nearest in meaning to what you have heard. Record your answer on the answer sheet.

Example

You will hear: The Wagners seem to take their large family in stride.

You will read: (A) Mr. Wagner comes from a large family.
                 (B) Mrs. Wagner comes from a large family.
                 (C) Mr. and Mrs. Wagner are the parents of many children.
                 (D) The Wagners dislike small families.

The correct answer to the example is (C).

1. (A) John forgot that he needed to correct a mistake.
    (B) John corrected the mistake which he had made.
    (C) Going back was the mistake John made.
    (D) John corrected one mistake but neglected the others.

2. (A) Alice subscribes to more news magazines than her husband.
    (B) Alice told her husband that he should like news magazines.
    (C) Alice's husband considers it worthwhile to subscribe to several news magazines.
    (D) Neither Alice nor her husband reads news magazines.

3. (A) He was too sleepy to take the medicine.
    (B) He took the medicine while he was driving.
    (C) He couldn't drive while he took the medicine.
    (D) He felt drowsy, so he didn't have to take the medicine.

4. (A) The flight attendant piloted the plane.
    (B) The airplane went out of control.
    (C) The pilot assisted the flight attendant.
    (D) The flight attendant suffered a heart attack.

5. (A) Fathers are usually good husbands.
    (B) He is more successful as a husband than as a father.
    (C) His father is better than her husband.
    (D) He tries to be a good husband and father.

6. (A) The problem was solved after several months' discussion.
   (B) The discussion of the problem ceased several months ago.
   (C) Several new problems have arisen and must be discussed.
   (D) The discussion of the problem is not over yet.

7. (A) I like all world religions.
   (B) I'm a very religious person.
   (C) World religions do not concern me.
   (D) I'm interested in learning more about world religions.

8. (A) Richard's wife forgot her own birthday.
   (B) Richard had a birthday which his wife forgot.
   (C) Yesterday, Richard remembered when his wife's birthday was.
   (D) Richard failed to remember the date of his wife's birthday.

9. (A) Mr. Grant is against buying another television set.
   (B) The family is sorry that Mr. Grant bought a television set.
   (C) The family enjoys watching television more than Mr. Grant does.
   (D) Mr. Grant advised his family to find a television set.

10. (A) I used to live in the United States.
    (B) I came to the United States when I was a small child.
    (C) My family lived in the United States for a short time.
    (D) I lived in Canada much longer than in the United States.

11. (A) Working hard ensures success.
    (B) One must work hard to keep secrets.
    (C) One cannot succeed if he has secrets.
    (D) If you keep your work secret, you will succeed.

12. (A) The doctor gave Carol two pairs of glasses.
    (B) Carol's vision is no better now than it was before she went to the doctor.
    (C) Carol has visited two eye doctors.
    (D) Carol's eyesight improved when she went to the doctor.

13. (A) The twins are exactly the same.
    (B) Both twins are overweight.
    (C) One twin is taller than the other.
    (D) The twins have different opinions concerning weight.

14. (A) The car got dirty last week.
    (B) The man's dirty car did not last.
    (C) The man got dirty when he washed the car.
    (D) Someone finally washed the man's car.

15. (A) I'd rather catch fish than clean them.
    (B) I don't know how to clean the fish I catch.
    (C) I enjoy cleaning fish.
    (D) It's no fun to catch fish.

16. (A) The auditorium will not be open for the lecture.
    (B) The public auditorium charged a fee for the lecture.
    (C) The lecture is an open discussion of public matters.
    (D) Admittance to the lecture is free.

17. (A) Mr. Butler rarely takes the subway to work.
    (B) Mr. Butler usually goes to work by bus.
    (C) Mr. Butler missed the bus this morning, so he took the subway.
    (D) Mr. Butler almost always takes the subway to work.

18. (A) Mrs. Capps lives in a strange neighborhood.
    (B) Everyone in the neighborhood wears caps.

(C) Mrs. Capps is a popular person in the neighborhood.

(D) The neighbors act oddly toward Mrs. Capps.

19. (A) The temperature will probably rise.
    (B) The temperature will probably remain cold.
    (C) The temperature will probably fall.
    (D) The temperature will probably stay warm.

20. (A) Don spends more money than his wife.
    (B) Don's wife keeps spending more money.
    (C) Don and his wife both make money.
    (D) Don spends the money his wife makes.

Part B

Directions. This section of the Listening Comprehension test consists of fifteen short conversations between two people. When each conversation ends, you will be asked a question by a third voice about what was said. You will hear the question only once and you must choose the answer from the four choices given. When you have chosen what you believe to be the best answer to the question, record your answer on the answer sheet.

Example

You will hear:

    (Man)   "I've never understood how to use the card catalogue, and I need to get this information today."

    (Woman)   "Why don't you pick up one of the guidebooks at the front desk? It will help you, I'm sure."

    (Third voice)   "Where did this conversation most likely occur?"

You will read: (A) At a museum.
                 (B) In a store.

(C) In a classroom.
(D) In a library.

The correct answer to the example is (D).

21. (A) He publishes books.
    (B) He is an author.
    (C) He collects automobiles.
    (D) He works in industry.

22. (A) He has a promising career.
    (B) He can't sell books.
    (C) He and his boss get along well.
    (D) He prefers to be a fireman.

23. (A) She would've received an A.
    (B) She would've received a C.
    (C) She would've received a D.
    (D) She would've received a B.

24. (A) He prefers his old set of clubs.
    (B) He has little chance to play golf.
    (C) He's playing better golf recently.
    (D) He's too old to play much golf.

25. (A) He suggests that she visit Belgium.
    (B) He suggests that she spend more time studying her textbook.
    (C) He suggests that she spend time in the language laboratory.
    (D) He suggests that she get a tutor.

26. (A) Mow the lawn.
    (B) Weed the flowers.
    (C) Pay $50 a month for a gardener.
    (D) Work in the flowerbeds.

27. (A) The man and woman shopped all over town.
    (B) The woman went to many different stores.
    (C) The woman bought some bookcases on sale.
    (D) The man sold the woman some expensive bookcases.

28. (A) On a farm.
    (B) In a slaughterhouse.

(C) In a market.
(D) In a feed store.

29. (A) He read the newspaper.
(B) One of his students told him.
(C) He listened to a radio report.
(D) He attended a cabinet meeting.

30. (A) Vegetables.
(B) Cereal and vegetables.
(C) Cereal and banana.
(D) Rice and mashed fruit.

31. (A) Setting the table.
(B) Polishing silver.
(C) Sewing napkins.
(D) Stocking a pantry.

32. (A) He went directly to the boss with his problem.
(B) He decided to keep the problem to himself.
(C) He let his mother speak to the boss about the problem.
(D) He told his boss's mother about the problem.

33. (A) To mail a letter.
(B) To buy stamps.
(C) To get a package.
(D) To deliver a check to the postman.

34. (A) She lost a hundred dollars on the way to the health club.
(B) She received a refund of one hundred dollars from the health club.
(C) She refused to sign a contract with the health club.
(D) She failed to keep her contract with the health club.

35. (A) She plans to teach.
(B) She plans to write a book.
(C) She plans to do a great deal of reading.
(D) She plans to stay at home and rest.

Part C

Directions. In this part of the test you will be required to listen to several short lectures and conversations. You will hear the lectures and conversations only once. They do not appear in your test booklet. When a question is asked, choose the best answer from the four given. Record your answer on the answer sheet.

36. (A) Gaily colored.
(B) Very plain.
(C) Like the common crow's.
(D) Symmetrically shaped.

37. (A) They had no scientific name.
(B) Their skins were used in trading.
(C) They were related to the crow.
(D) They kept flying until they died.

38. (A) New Guinea.
(B) Australia.
(C) The East Indies.
(D) Linnaeus.

39. (A) Bright colors.
(B) Flying creatures.
(C) Without feet.
(D) Dancing skins.

40. (A) A majority of Americans voted for it.
(B) Large trucks were causing many accidents.
(C) There was a sudden increase in highway deaths.
(D) A fuel shortage was developing.

41. (A) Easterners.
(B) Westerners.
(C) Older persons.
(D) Automobile industry workers.

42. (A) 75 percent.
(B) 23 percent.
(C) 55 percent.
(D) 66 percent.

43. (A) Trucks do not use crucial fuel.
    (B) Few trucks are involved in accidents.
    (C) Most trucks do not transport consumer goods.
    (D) Trucks run better at higher speeds.

44. (A) He's a scientist.
    (B) He's an electrical engineer.
    (C) He's an inventor.
    (D) He's a chemist.

45. (A) Still air.
    (B) Electricity.
    (C) The power of the wind.
    (D) Solar energy.

46. (A) It is cheaper to construct than a windmill.
    (B) It will produce 80 megawatts of electricity.
    (C) It could produce much more power than the windmill.
    (D) It is currently providing all of the electrical power needed by the United States.

47. (A) He believes that the windmill is more practical than his machine.
    (B) He believes that a network of his machines would be incapable of transferring electricity from one place to another.
    (C) He believes that his machine will probably never be the only device used to produce power in the United States.
    (D) He believes that his machine will never be popular outside the United States.

48. (A) It consists of a couple and four children.
    (B) It includes a man and his wife.
    (C) It has four members.
    (D) It has three members.

49. (A) He read about it in the newspaper.
    (B) He saw it on South Florida Street.
    (C) His wife told him about it.
    (D) He saw it while riding down Churchill Avenue.

50. (A) The size of the house.
    (B) The location of the house.
    (C) The appearance of the house.
    (D) The down payment on the house.

II: STRUCTURE AND WRITTEN EXPRESSION

(40 Questions—25 minutes)

Part A

Directions. In this part of the test each problem consists of an incomplete sentence. Below the sentence are four choices, marked (A), (B), (C), and (D). You should find the one choice which best completes the sentence. Mark your choice on the answer sheet.

Example

Because the United States has little tin, _____ produced in the rest of the world.

(A) tin is used
(B) it uses tin
(C) uses of tin
(D) uses tin

The correct answer to the example is (B).

1. _____ a common belief, fright or excitement causes the flesh of young game fowl to turn a different color.

(A) It is according to
(B) That it is according to
(C) While according to
(D) According to

2. _____, Nathan Hale was a young school-teacher living in Connecticut.

   (A) When the American Revolution began
   (B) The American Revolution began
   (C) It was when the American Revolution began
   (D) The beginning of the American Revolution

3. Some bees make the characteristic monotonous noise known as buzzing _____.

   (A) but their wings are vibrated rapidly
   (B) the vibration of their wings is rapid
   (C) by vibrating their wings rapidly
   (D) and their wings rapidly vibrating

4. _____, James Fenimore Cooper wrote about Indians and pioneers in the forest and sailors on the high seas.

   (A) The first American novelist to achieve world-wide fame who is
   (B) The first American novelist to achieve world-wide fame
   (C) Although he was the first American novelist to achieve world-wide fame
   (D) He was the first American novelist to achieve world-wide fame

5. _____ pioneer days, a group of farmers would bring together the livestock they wanted to sell so that one person could drive the animals to market.

   (A) When
   (B) It was during
   (C) While
   (D) In

6. Nicolaus Copernicus, _____, was born in Zorun, Poland.

   (A) is often considered the founder of modern astronomy
   (B) whose founder of modern astronomy is often considered
   (C) often considered the founder of modern astronomy
   (d) who he is often considered the founder of modern astronomy

7. _____ that modern corn may be a hybrid of teosinte and other wild species that no longer exist.

   (A) Now is thought
   (B) Thinking
   (C) The thought
   (D) It is thought

8. A planetarium is a special kind of educational facility _____ the teaching of astronomy.

   (A) devoted to
   (B) which devotes
   (C) to devote
   (D) to devote to

9. Only when humans employ nonchemical approaches to pest control _____.

   (A) will creatures such as roaches and rodents be successfully eliminated
   (B) creatures such as roaches and rodents will be successfully eliminated
   (C) if creatures such as roaches and rodents will be successfully eliminated
   (D) that creatures such as roaches and rodents will be successfully eliminated

10. Penguins usually do not get wet _____ their feathers are kept oily by tiny oil glands.

   (A) so
   (B) despite
   (C) because
   (D) yet

11. In explaining the theory of relativity, the scientist states that mechanical laws that are true in one place _____ equally valid in any other place.

   (A) being
   (B) they should be
   (C) are
   (D) to be

12. Marine reptiles are among the few creatures that are known to have a possible life span greater than _____.

    (A) man
    (B) the man's
    (C) the one of man's
    (D) that of man

13. Public transportation in most of the nation is expanding. _____, the use of subways and buses is declining in some metropolitan areas.

    (A) Nevertheless
    (B) Consequently
    (C) Despite the fact
    (D) Although

14. _____ the financial means to remain independent, Thomas Edison was compelled to seek employment as a night telegraph operator.

    (A) He was deprived of
    (B) Deprived of
    (C) That he was deprived of
    (D) Although he was deprived of

15. The Egyptians and the Sumerians _____ copper as early as 5,000 years before Christ.

    (A) they were using
    (B) having used
    (C) may have used
    (D) using

Part B

Directions. In each of the following sentences, four words or phrases have been underlined. You should choose the one word or phrase that would *not* be appropriate in standard written English. Mark your choice on the answer sheet.

Example

The average age at which people begin to need eyeglasses vary considerably.
　　　　　　　　A　　　　　　　　B　　　　　　　　C　　D
(C) is incorrect in standard written English.

16. The dense Belgian fogs, like the most inland fogs, are caused by the cooling of humid surface air
　　　　　　　　　　　　　A　　　　　　　　　　　B　　　　　　　　　C
to a relatively low temperature.
　　　D

17. Most bothersome flies belong to the family Sarcophagidae and are popular known as flesh flies
　　　　　　　　　　　A　　　　　　　　　　　　　　　B
because the larvae feed on flesh.
　C　　　　　D

18. That touching toads causes warts are still one of the most widely believed superstitions in America; however, no reputable authority supports this theory.
　　　　　　　　　A　　　　　　　　　　　B　　　　　　　　　C
　　D

19. The cheetah, the fastest of all land animals, can cover a mile in less than a minute, but the cheetah
　　　　　　A　　　　　　　　　B
seems slow compared some birds.
　　C　　　　D

20. Generally, Europe and Asia are regarded as being distinct continents, but they are simply vast
　A　　　　　　　　B　　　　　　　　　　　　　　　C
geography divisions of the larger land mass known as Eurasia.
　D

21. To say that Ferdinand Magellan, the first European to discover the Philippines, did not actually
      A   B
    circumnavigate the earth because he was killed before his famous voyage was completed.
                                                 C   D

22. Because of the large amount of salt, the specific gravity of the water in Great Salt Lake, Utah, is
      A   B   C
    so great that one cannot sink or completely submerging oneself in it.
                                             D

23. Both solar energy or nuclear energy will supply most of America's electrical power in the twenty-
                    A   B
    first century; however, giant windmills will also dot the coastal regions of New England and the
                    C   D
    Middle Atlantic states.

24. Bothered by the heavy traffic along interstates highways, some travelers prefer the more tranquil
       A   B   C
    routes of older, two-lane roads.
                      D

25. Close to 73 percentage of the United States' population is concentrated in metropolitan areas, and
      A   B   C
    more than half the population lives in the South and West.
        D

26. The eggs of eagles are covered with a natural mucilaginous coating what delays the entrance of
                  A   B
    harmful germs into the egg's interior.
      C   D

27. All Middle East peoples believed in life after death, but the Egyptians of ages past carried this
                    A   B
    idea further than any ancient civilization.
        C   D

28. Mountains have helped to protect the Swiss from invaders, and, indeed, Switzerland has remained
                  A   B   C
    at peace while other European nations engaging in war.
      D

29. A collection of Indian artifacts, which was taken from graves in the area and it was lent to
          A   B   C
    Harvard University, will be returned to the museum next week.
               D

30. The backbone of the single-humped camel is not curved upward in the middle, like many people
       A   B   C   D
    suppose.

31. Caviar is generally spread on toast, flavored with a few drops of lemon juice, and eating as an
               A   B   C
    appetizer with various beverages.
            D

32. During <u>election campaigns</u>, politicians <u>frequently often</u> <u>hold debates</u> with other candidates <u>about</u>
    A · B C D
    major issues.

33. The common notion <u>that</u> fish is an excellent food <u>for improving</u> the brain is not <u>supported by</u> any
    A B C
    available <u>scientist</u> information.
    D

34. Popping in corn occurs whenever there <u>is an explosion caused by</u> the <u>expansion under pressure</u> of
    A B
    moisture in the starch grains <u>during the kernel</u> is dry heated.
    C D

35. If allowed to turn <u>yellow</u> while still on the plant, bananas lose <u>their characteristically good</u> flavor,
    A B
    <u>the skin break open</u>, insects <u>enter the inside</u>, and the fruit rots.
    C D

36. Proper lighting is a <u>necessary for good eyesight</u>; <u>however</u>, human night vision <u>can be temporarily</u>
    A B C
    impaired <u>by extreme flashes of light</u>.
    D

37. <u>During</u> a rainstorm, mud rivulets form <u>on the side of</u> a hill and thus <u>move</u> soil from one place to
    A B C
    <u>other</u>.
    D

38. Hand grenades, round shells <u>filled with powder</u> and ignited <u>by means of a fuse</u>, <u>were</u> first used <u>in</u>
    A B C
    warfare during <u>fifteenth century</u>.
    D

39. Naturalists say <u>that there is</u> evidence <u>to support</u> the assertion that anthropoids, whether <u>in captive</u>
    A B C
    or in the native state, sometimes <u>beat their breasts</u>.
    D

40. Fish <u>are</u> unable to sleep, but sometimes a fish in <u>an aquarium</u> will lie on <u>their side</u> and appear to
    A B C
    be <u>completely unaware of</u> everything around it.
    D

III: READING COMPREHENSION AND VOCABULARY

(60 Questions—45 minutes)

Part A

Directions. Each problem in this part of the test consists of a sentence in which one word or phrase has been underlined. From the four choices given, you should choose the one word or phrase which could be substituted for the underlined word or phrase without changing the meaning of the sentence. Mark your choice on the answer sheet.

Example

The <u>frown</u> on the man's face showed that he was displeased.

(A) look of fear
(B) look of anger
(C) look of delight
(D) look of surprise

The best answer is (B).

1. He <u>tramped</u> across the cream-colored carpet, leaving a trail of mud behind him.

(A) walked heavily
(B) skipped
(C) walked unsteadily
(D) limped

2. The <u>tunnel</u> was so dark and clammy that we became frightened.

(A) long corridor
(B) underground passageway
(C) center aisle
(D) open ditch

3. My supply of confidence slowly <u>dwindles</u> as the deadline approaches.

(A) shifts
(B) grows
(C) emerges
(D) diminishes

4. Can this be a <u>duplicate</u> of the document?

(A) a summary
(B) a revision
(C) an outline
(D) a copy

5. The gunfire was <u>sporadic</u>.

(A) intermittent
(B) frequent
(C) continuous
(D) distant

6. The chairman did not <u>rule out</u> the possibility of an agreement.

(A) promise
(B) reject
(C) accept
(D) forestall

7. <u>Punctuality</u> is imperative in your new job.

(A) Being efficient
(B) Being courteous
(C) Being on time
(D) Being cheerful

8. He <u>got nowhere</u> with his plan to balance the budget.

(A) succeeded completely
(B) accomplished nothing
(C) fooled no one
(D) became obsessed

9. He ate a <u>prodigious</u> amount of the home-made bread.

(A) slight
(B) tiny
(C) huge
(D) moderate

10. He is <u>infamous</u> for his dishonesty in business matters.

(A) notorious
(B) dreaded
(C) loathed
(D) investigated

11. We were forced to <u>postpone</u> the picnic.

(A) call off
(B) do without
(C) put off
(D) see about

12. The hunter carefully <u>stalked</u> the deer.

(A) shot
(B) tracked
(C) aimed at
(D) skinned

13. There is a large area of swamp that will have to be cleared before construction can begin.

    (A)   forest
    (B)   soft, wet land
    (C)   dry, sandy soil
    (D)   prairie

14. For once, everything in her life seemed to be in equilibrium.

    (A)   turmoil
    (B)   disarray
    (C)   balance
    (D)   danger

15. The world leaders had a chat before beginning formal negotiations.

    (A)   friendly, unimportant talk
    (B)   disagreement
    (C)   serious discussion
    (D)   high-level conference

16. Where did she acquire all her wealth?

    (A)   gain
    (B)   lose
    (C)   hide
    (D)   steal

17. He resolved to act more wisely in the future.

    (A)   promised
    (B)   hoped
    (C)   consented
    (D)   decided

18. The jeweler reported that the diamonds were genuine.

    (A)   perfect
    (B)   imitations
    (C)   real
    (D)   valuable

19. I decided to go to the party on the spur of the moment.

    (A)   after careful thought
    (B)   for only a short time
    (C)   without previous thought
    (D)   at the earliest possible moment

20. The winners will be selected at random.

    (A)   by interviewing
    (B)   by testing
    (C)   by chance
    (D)   by competition

21. Pilfering by company employees costs many businesses thousands of dollars each year.

    (A)   absenteeism
    (B)   stealing
    (C)   tardiness
    (D)   ignorance

22. The relativity theory is basically made up of two parts: the restricted and the general relativity theory.

    (A)   fundamentally
    (B)   usually
    (C)   frequently
    (D)   approximately

23. The sales representatives were asked to go over the figures in their reports before the conference.

    (A)   relate
    (B)   revise
    (C)   review
    (D)   calculate

24. Doctors prescribe massive doses of penicillin for patients with pneumonia.

    (A)   daily
    (B)   heavy
    (D)   double
    (D)   adequate

25. Tornadoes are violent whirlwinds which vary in their width from a few yards to 1,300 feet.

    (A)   fierce
    (B)   immense
    (C)   rapid
    (D)   chilly

26. The movie critic said that *Airplane*, the parody of disaster movies, was <u>hilarious</u>.

    (A) suspenseful
    (B) very funny
    (C) realistic
    (D) very tragic

27. In spite of medical advances, that disease is usually <u>fatal</u>.

    (A) curable
    (B) painful
    (C) deadly
    (D) disabling

28. The sculptor, Lorenzo Ghiberti, <u>blended</u> medieval grace with Renaissance realism.

    (A) produced
    (B) combined
    (C) invented
    (D) discovered

29. Identical twins are frequently <u>inseparable</u>; they even seem to think alike.

    (A) not able to be distinguished
    (B) not able to be understood
    (C) not able to be parted
    (D) not able to be believed

30. His extreme nervousness <u>impeded</u> his ability to speak in front of large groups of people.

    (A) hindered
    (B) halted
    (C) accelerated
    (D) fostered

Part B

Directions. You will be given a series of different types of reading material (sentences, short paragraphs, advertisements, etc.). Each selection is followed by questions about the meaning of the material. You are to choose the one best answer to each question from the four choices given.

Read the following sample passage.

(1)   Marianne Moore was born in St. Louis in 1887 and graduated from Bryn Mawr College in 1909. She taught stenography for a few years and then worked as a librarian in New York. She was a
(5) member of the editorial staff of the famous literary magazine *The Dial* from 1925 to 1929. Although a book of her poems, titled *Observations*, was published in America in 1924, Miss Moore has only recently received the full acclaim
(10) she deserves.

Example 1

When did Miss Moore graduate from college?

    (A) 1887
    (B) 1909
    (C) 1925
    (D) 1924

The passage says that Miss Moore graduated from Bryn Mawr in 1909. Therefore, you should choose answer (B).

Example 2

The one profession not mentioned as being pursued by Miss Moore is that of

    (A) poet
    (B) teacher.
    (C) scientist.
    (D) librarian.

The passage mentions that Miss Moore taught stenography, worked as a librarian, and wrote poetry. Therefore, you should choose (C) as the best completion of the sentence.

As soon as you understand the directions, begin work on the problems.

Questions 31–33

The Mediterranean climate is little suited to stock-breeding; only sheep and goats can make use of the extensive feeding grounds with their meager rainfall.

31. The Mediterranean climate is described as

    (A) humid.
    (B) dry.
    (C) extremely cold.
    (D) generally moderate, but with heavy rainfall.

32. The Mediterranean area is

    (A) good for raising all varieties of animals.
    (B) poor for raising animals.
    (C) suitable for some animals, but not for sheep and goats.
    (D) well suited to breeding animals.

33. According to this sentence animal feeding grounds in the Mediterranean are

    (A) severely limited in size.
    (B) very steep and rocky.
    (C) large, but not very good for grazing.
    (D) large, but very swampy.

Questions 34–36

An observer sitting on a beach can make at least an intelligent guess whether the surf spilling out onto the sand before him has been produced by a gale close offshore or by a distant storm.

34. An observer sitting on the beach

    (A) can tell nothing about what produced the surf he sees.
    (B) can be certain what produced the surf he sees.
    (C) has no basis on which to choose between two possible sources of the surf he sees.
    (D) has some basis for an opinion about the source of the surf he sees.

35. Surf must be

    (A) a distant storm.
    (B) wave action near the shore.
    (C) wave action far out in the ocean.
    (D) small rocks and seashells.

36. A "gale" is probably

    (A) an island.
    (B) a very strong wind.
    (C) a breeze.
    (D) a tidal wave.

Questions 37–41 refer to the following instructions.

(1)

(5)

(10)

Indications: For the temporary relief of cough and nasal congestion as may occur with the common cold or with inhaled irritants.

Directions for use: Adults: 2 teaspoonfuls every four hours, not to exceed 12 teaspoonfuls in a 24-hour period; children 6 to under 12 years: 1 teaspoonful every four hours, not to exceed 6 teaspoonfuls in a 24-hour period; children 2 to under 6 years: ½ teaspoonful every four hours, not to exceed 3 teaspoonfuls in a 24-hour period; children under 2 years: use as directed by a physician.

37. This medicine in obviously a

    (A) tablet.
    (B) liquid.
    (C) lozenge.
    (D) ointment.

38. According to these directions, the maximum dose for adults is

    (A) 2 teaspoonfuls every four hours.
    (B) 12 teaspoonfuls in a 24-hour period.
    (C) 6 teaspoonfuls in a 24-hour period.
    (D) 3 teaspoonfuls in a 24-hour period.

39. This label suggests that

    (A) coughs and nasal congestion may have a variety of causes.
    (B) all coughs and nasal congestion are temporary.
    (C) this medicine causes drowsiness.
    (D) physicians often prescribe this medicine.

40. The tone of this label suggests that

    (A) it might be dangerous to take a large amount of this medicine at one time.
    (B) this medicine is extremely dangerous and must be used with great caution.
    (C) this medicine is used primarily by adults.
    (D) this medicine is used primarily by children.

41. These directions indicate that a one-year-old child

    (A) should not take this medicine.
    (B) should take less than ½ teaspoonful every fours hours.
    (C) should take the dose prescribed by his or her doctor.
    (D) should be very careful when taking this and all medicines.

Questions 42–44

(1) The normal daytime retreats of bats are the rooms of caves, but individuals commonly live in dry, dark rooms of buildings. Males are usually solitary, but females, especially when they are
(5) young, gather in colonies. The bats do not hide in crevices but, when not hibernating, hang from the open roof of caves or buildings where they can see, and escape from, any intruder. In the dormant condition, which the bats assume when the air
(10) temperature is low, the body temperature drops; and they cling with thumbs and toes to some vertical walls, with their ears closely coiled to conserve body heat.

42. Young female bats

    (A) hide in crevices.
    (B) like to live in groups.
    (C) prefer the dry, dark rooms of buildings.
    (D) hibernate until maturity.

43. When the weather turns cold

    (A) the bats move to the rooms of buildings.
    (B) the bats gather in colonies.
    (C) the bats coil their ears.
    (D) the bats hide in crevices.

44. Bats often hang from the open roof of caves and buildings

    (A) to keep warm.
    (B) to see and escape from intruders.
    (C) to hibernate.
    (D) to lower their body temperature.

Questions 45–48

(1) Embodying the bad as well as the good of America, Theodore Roosevelt was admired by his countrymen almost as much for his failings as for his "finer qualities." If he gave voice to the nobler
(5) aspirations of the nation, his defects were those of a majority of the people. Harry Thurston Peck noted that "the self-consciousness, the touch of the swagger, the love of applause and of publicity, the occasional lapse of official dignity, even the
(10) reckless speech, the unnecessary frankness, and the disregard of form" which characterized Roosevelt were in reality "traits that . . . were national." One of Roosevelt's bitterest critics wrote, "Roosevelt is popular—as popular as any Presi-
(15) dent in our history. America has a hysterical element. Official hysterics appeal to them. With some of our people physical size means greatness. In them Roosevelt touches a responsive chord. Many of our people are boastful and self-asser-
(20) tive. Roosevelt is their ideal. Fulmination, bluster, clamorousness appeal to some of us. Roosevelt satisfies us."

45. Roosevelt's defects

    (A) were peculiarly his own.
    (B) were similar to those of other Americans.
    (C) far outweighed his good qualities.
    (D) were well-hidden.

46. Roosevelt's personality was clearly

    (A) shy and retiring.
    (B) cautious and prudent.
    (C) bold and informal.
    (D) dignified and tactful.

47. Physically, Roosevelt was probably

    (A) short and fat.
    (B) thin and sickly.

(C)   a big man.
(D)   a small man.

48. The unidentified critic quoted in this passage

   (A)   admired Roosevelt as a man, but he questioned his ability as a president.
   (B)   thought that Roosevelt was popular mainly because he was different from the average American.
   (C)   believed that Roosevelt was seen clearly and judged accurately by the American people.
   (D)   disliked and disapproved of Roosevelt.

Questions 49–52

(1)   At the battle of Gettysburg, General George G. Meade, who succeeded General Hooker as commander of the Army of the Potomac, threw back Lee's attacks and hurt the Confederate army
(5) badly. Meade had fought a skillful defensive battle, but he was satisfied with his victory as it was. He was content to see Lee leave his front, and his principal concern was to "herd" Lee back over the Potomac. Like other Federal generals,
(10) he lacked the killer instinct, which all the great battle captains have had, to finish off the enemy. After the engagement he issued a congratulatory order to his troops in which he praised them for having driven the enemy from "our soil." After
(15) all, this was a civil war! When Lincoln read the order, he exclaimed in anguish, "My God! Is that all?"

49. The Battle of Gettysburg

   (A)   was won by the Confederate army.
   (B)   was won by Hooker.
   (C)   was won by Lee.
   (D)   was won by the Federal army.

50. George G. Meade did *not*

   (A)   hurt the Confederate army.
   (B)   fight a good defensive battle.
   (C)   force Lee to retreat.
   (D)   completely destroy the enemy.

51. When Lincoln heard of Meade's order, he

   (A)   was delighted.
   (B)   congratulated the troops.
   (C)   was dismayed.
   (D)   prayed.

52. The implication of the paragraph is that

   (A)   Meade was totally incompetent.
   (B)   Meade was ruthless.
   (C)   Meade should have "finished off" the enemy.
   (D)   Meade was well-loved by his men.

Questions 53–57

(1)   Up to about 1915, movies were short and programs were made up of several works. Then, D. W. Griffith and others began to make longer films which provided the same powerful emo-
(5) tional appeal as did melodrama and presented spectacles far beyond what the theater could offer. Consequently, after World War I increasing numbers of spectators deserted the theater for the movies. This trend was accelerated in the late
(10) 1920's as a result of two new elements. In 1927 sound was added to the previously silent film, and thus one of the theater's principal claims to superiority vanished. In 1929 a serious economic depression began. Since audiences could go to the
(15) movies for a fraction of what it cost to see a play, theatergoing became a luxury which few could afford, especially as the depression deepened.
   By the end of World War II, the American theater had been reduced to about thirty theaters
(20) in New York City and a small number of touring companies originating there.

53. One thing that movies could do better than the theater was

   (A)   provide longer programs.
   (B)   provide emotional appeal.
   (C)   provide more melodrama.
   (D)   provide greater spectacle.

54. Up to the 1920's one objection to films was that

   (A)   they were too short.
   (B)   they were silent.

(C) they were too expensive.
(D) they did not tell a complete story.

55. One thing that made people choose the movies over the theater was

(A) World War I.
(B) the fact that films were less expensive.
(C) the fact that films were silent.
(D) the fact that films were shorter.

56. By the end of World War II,

(A) theater had become entertainment for the masses.
(B) the theater was no longer considered a luxury.
(C) professional theatrical performances were confined mainly to New York City.
(D) there were no theatrical performances outside of New York City.

57. When the author of this paragraph says "this trend was accelerated in the late 1920's" (lines 9 and 10), he means that

(A) many more people went to the theater than to the movies.
(B) the shift away from the movies to the theater was slowed down.
(C) the popularity of the theater was gradually increasing.
(D) the shift away from the theater to the movies was speeded up.

Questions 58–60

Directions. For these questions, choose the answer whose *meaning is closest* to that of the given sentence. Although more than one of the choices may be factually correct, you should choose the one that *most closely restates the original sentence.*

58. In much of Europe, American films are more popular than those of any other country.

(A) All over Europe, American films are the most popular.

(B) Most countries' films are more popular in Europe than those of America.
(C) The films that are most popular in much of Europe are American.
(D) Most American films are more popular in Europe than in other countries.

59. A radio listener in California can hear the sounds of an orchestra sooner than an audience in a New York City concert hall where the broadcast originates.

(A) If a radio broadcasts the sounds of an orchestra concert in a New York City hall, a radio listener in California can hear the music sooner than the audience in the hall in New York.
(B) A radio listener in New York City will hear the sounds of an orchestra in a New York City concert hall sooner than a radio listener in California.
(C) A radio listener in New York City will hear the sounds of an orchestra in a New York City concert hall later than a radio listener in California.
(D) If a radio broadcasts the sounds of an orchestra concert in a New York City hall, a radio listener in California will hear the music later than a listener in New York City.

60. The painter Thomas Gainsborough rivaled Sir Joshua Reynolds in the quality of his work, but not in social success or financial reward.

(A) The painters Thomas Gainsborough and Sir Joshua Reynolds were rivals in art, society, and finance.
(B) Sir Joshua Reynolds was more successful socially, financially, and artistically than the painter Thomas Gainsborough.
(C) The painter Thomas Gainsborough was more successful socially and financially than his rival Sir Joshua Reynolds.
(D) Although the painting of Thomas Gainsborough and Sir Joshua Reynolds was comparable in quality, the latter was more successful socially and financially.

Test 4—Answer Key

I: LISTENING COMPREHENSION

Part A

1. B	6. D	11. A	16. D
2. C	7. D	12. B	17. D
3. C	8. D	13. C	18. C
4. A	9. A	14. D	19. A
5. B	10. B	15. A	20. B

Part B

21. B	26. D	31. A
22. B	27. B	32. D
23. D	28. A	33. A
24. C	29. A	34. D
25. D	30. C	35. B

Part C

36. B	41. B	46. D
37. D	42. A	47. C
38. A	43. D	48. A
39. C	44. C	49. A
40. D	45. C	50. D

II: STRUCTURE AND WRITTEN EXPRESSION

Part A

1. D	6. C	11. C
2. A	7. D	12. D
3. C	8. A	13. A
4. B	9. A	14. B
5. D	10. C	15. C

Part B

16.	A	25.	B	34.	D
17.	B	26.	B	35.	C
18.	A	27.	D	36.	A
19.	D	28.	D	37.	D
20.	C	29.	C	38.	D
21.	A	30.	D	39.	C
22.	D	31.	C	40.	C
23.	A	32.	B		
24.	B	33.	D		

III: READING COMPREHENSION

Part A

1.	A	11.	C	21.	B
2.	B	12.	B	22.	A
3.	D	13.	B	23.	C
4.	D	14.	C	24.	B
5.	A	15.	A	25.	A
6.	B	16.	A	26.	B
7.	C	17.	D	27.	C
8.	B	18.	C	28.	B
9.	C	19.	C	29.	C
10.	A	20.	C	30.	A

Part B

31.	B	41.	C	51.	C
32.	B	42.	B	52.	C
33.	C	43.	C	53.	D
34.	D	44.	B	54.	B
35.	B	45.	B	55.	B
36.	B	46.	C	56.	C
37.	B	47.	C	57.	D
38.	B	48.	D	58.	C
39.	A	49.	D	59.	A
40.	A	50.	D	60.	D

Test 4—Explanatory Answers

II: STRUCTURE AND WRITTEN EXPRESSION

1. _____ a common belief, fright or excitement causes the flesh of young game fowl to turn a different color.
(This sentence needs a choice which correctly completes the introductory phrase.)

(A)	*It is according to*	This choice contains a subject (*it*) and a verb (*was*). Two independent clauses may not be separated by a comma in correct written English.
(B)	*That it is according to*	A noun clause used as a subject must be followed immediately by a finite verb.
(C)	*While according to*	*While* is a word indicating time and is often used to introduce a dependent clause containing a subject and a finite verb.
(D)	*According to*	CORRECT ANSWER

2. _____, Nathan Hale was a young schoolteacher living in Connecticut.
(An introductory dependent clause of time will complete this sentence correctly.)

(A)	*When the American Revolution began*	CORRECT ANSWER
(B)	*The American Revolution began*	This group of words is an independent clause. Two independent clauses should not be separated by a comma.
(C)	*It was when the American Revolution began*	This choice would be acceptable if the words *it was* were omitted. See 2(B) above.
(D)	*The beginning of the American Revolution*	This group of words forms a phrase, rather than a dependent clause. By placing the word *at* in front of the phrase, we form an acceptable choice.

3. Some bees make the characteristic monotonous noise known as buzzing _____.
(A phrase showing manner correctly completes this sentence.)

(A)	*but their wings are vibrated rapidly*	*But* shows contrast and therefore confuses the intended meaning of the sentence.
(B)	*the vibration of their wings is rapid*	This choice is an independent clause which must be separated from the first independent clause by a semicolon or by a period.

(C) *by vibrating their wings rapidly*   CORRECT ANSWER

(D) *and their wings rapidly vi-brating*   The use of the word *and* requires an independent clause to parallel the initial independent clause. A finite verb is needed for the subject *wings*.

4. _____, James Fenimore Cooper wrote about Indians and pioneers in the forest and sailors on the high seas.
(This is a complete sentence as it stands. Only a dependent group of words can be placed at the beginning of the sentence.)

(A) *The first American novelist to achieve world-wide fame who is*   This choice would be correct if *who is* were omitted. If *who is* is left in the sentence, additional information must be given before the comma.

(B) *The first American novelist to achieve world-wide fame*   CORRECT ANSWER

(C) *Although he was the first American novelist to achieve world-wide fame*   This group of words is a dependent clause, but *although* indicates contrast, which makes no sense in this sentence.

(D) *He was the first American novelist to achieve world-wide fame*   This choice is an independent clause. Two independent clauses may not be separated by a comma in formal English.

5. _____ pioneer days, a group of farmers would bring together the live-stock they wanted to sell so that one person could drive the animals to market.
(An introductory time phrase is needed to complete this sentence.)

(A) *When*   *When* indicates time, but this word is normally followed by a clause rather than by a noun phrase.

(B) *It was during*   By placing *it was during* at the beginning of the sentence, an independent clause is formed before the comma. Two independent clauses may not be separated by only a comma in written English. *During pioneer days* would be an acceptable choice.

(C) *While*   *While* is a word indicating time that is normally followed by a subject and a finite verb.

(D) *In*   CORRECT ANSWER

6. Nicolaus Copernicus, _____, was born in Zorum, Poland.
(A dependent clause or phrase used to give additional information about the subject, *Nicolaus Copernicus,* is needed to complete this sentence.)

(A) *is often considered the founder of modern astron-omy.*   This group of words is a faulty adjective clause. The addition of the word *who* before the verb *is* would make the sentence correct.

(B) *whose founder of modern astronomy is often considered*	This is a dependent clause, but the use of the word *whose* makes no sense in the sentence. A correct choice might read *"who is often considered the founder of modern astronomy."*
(C) *often considered the founder of modern astronomy*	CORRECT ANSWER
(D) *who he is often considered the founder of modern astronomy.*	This dependent clause contains two subjects. Omit the word *he* to achieve an acceptable answer.

7. _____ that modern corn may be a hybrid of teosinte and other wild species that no longer exist.

(In this sentence, the "false" subject *it* is followed by a passive verb. In turn, the passive verb is followed by a *that* clause, which is the real subject of the sentence.)

(A) *Now is thought*	This choice is wrong since it does not contain a subject.
(B) *Thinking*	*Thinking* is not a finite verb.
(C) *The thought*	*The thought* is a noun phrase. This choice is wrong because it does not contain a finite verb.
(D) *It is thought*	CORRECT ANSWER

8. A planetarium is a special type of educational facility _____ the teaching of astronomy.

(This sentence needs a modifying phrase after the word *facility*.)

(A) *devoted to*	CORRECT ANSWER
(B) *which devotes*	Because the verb in the modifying phrase is in the present active form, the sentence makes no sense.
(C) *to devote*	*Facility* is a noun that should be followed by a modifying word or phrase. Here, a passive voice is necessary to give full meaning to the sentence; *to devote* is not passive.
(D) *to devote to*	See 8(C) above.

9. Only when humans employ nonchemical approaches to pest control _____.

(A clause containing question order rather than statement order is used to complete this sentence.)

(A) *will creatures such as roaches and rodents be successfully eliminated*	CORRECT ANSWER
(B) *creatures such as roaches and rodents will be successfully eliminated*	Whenever a negative word such as *only, never, rarely*, etc., heads a clause, the sentence requires question order. An auxiliary verb will occur *immediately* after the negative word.

| (C) | *if creatures such as roaches and rodents will be successfully eliminated* | *If* is usually used in conditional sentences and therefore does not make sense in this sentence. A correct choice would be "If humans employ nonchemical approaches to pest control, creatures such as roaches and rodents will be successfully eliminated." |
| (D) | *that creatures such as roaches and rodents will be successfully eliminated* | This choice is incorrect because of the word *that*. Also, the word order is incorrect. See 9(B). |

10. Penguins usually do not get wet _____ their feathers are kept oily by tiny oil glands.
(A subordinating word indicating reason is needed to complete the meaning.)

(A)	*so*	*So* indicates result rather than reason.
(B)	*despite*	*Despite* indicates contrast rather than reason.
(C)	*because*	CORRECT ANSWER
(D)	*yet*	*Yet* indicates contrast rather than reason.

11. In explaining the theory of relativity, the scientist states that mechanical laws which are true in one place _____ equally valid in any other place.
(A finite verb in the simple present tense is needed to give this sentence meaning.)

(A)	*being*	*Being* is not a finite verb.
(B)	*they should be*	This choice consists of a subject and a verb. Only a finite verb is needed. This choice would be acceptable if the word *they* were omitted.
(C)	*are*	CORRECT ANSWER
(D)	*to be*	*To be* is not a finite verb.

12. Marine reptiles are among the few creatures that are known to have a possible life span greater than _____.
(Because this sentence is stating a comparison, *than* must be followed by a word or phrase that makes the comparison both logical and complete.)

(A)	*man*	This comparison is not logical. We are not comparing the life span of the tortoise to man himself, but rather to the life span of man.
(B)	*the man's*	Our comparison involves man in general. The use of the article *the* makes *man* specific.
(C)	*the one of man's*	*Of* shows possession after a noun. It is unnecessary to make man possessive by using an apostrophe.
(D)	*that of man*	CORRECT ANSWER

13. Public transportation in most of the nation is expanding. _____, the use of subways and buses is declining in some metropolitan areas.
    (A connecting word of contrast is needed to define the relationships between these two sentences.)

    (A) *Nevertheless*   CORRECT ANSWER
    (B) *Consequently*   *Consequently* means "as a result," a sentence connector that makes no sense in this sentence.
    (C) *Despite the fact*   *Despite the fact* must be followed immediately by a dependent clause beginning with the word *that*.
    (D) *Although*   *Although* is used to show contrast in a sentence that contains both a dependent and an independent clause.

14. _____ the financial means to remain independent, Thomas Edison was compelled to seek employment as a night telegraph operator.
    (A past participle serves as the introductory word for this phrase used to modify the subject of the main clause, which is *Thomas Edison.*)

    (A) *He was deprived of*   This choice would result in a comma splice, which is two independent clauses separated by only a comma.
    (B) *Deprived of*   CORRECT ANSWER
    (C) *That he was deprived of*   If this group of words is placed at the beginning of the sentence, a noun clause results. A noun clause must be followed immediately by a finite verb.
    (D) *Although he was deprived of*   This choice is grammatically correct, but the word *although*, which indicates contrast, makes no sense in this sentence.

15. The Egyptians and the Sumerians _____ copper as early as 5,000 years before Christ.
    (A finite verb in the past tense is needed to complete this sentence.)

    (A) *they were using*   The word *they* gives the sentence two subjects. The omission of *they* would create an acceptable choice.
    (B) *having used*   *Having used* is not a finite verb.
    (C) *may have used*   CORRECT ANSWER
    (D) *using*   *Using* is not a finite verb.

16. (A) Because in this context *most* means "the majority of," the article *the* is grammatically incorrect in this sentence. The answer should be *like most*.

17. (B) *Known* is a past participle; therefore, *popular,* an adjective, should be changed to the adverb *popularly*.

18. (A) The subject of the sentence is a noun clause. The verb, therefore, should be singular. Change *are* to *is*.

19. (D) A necessary word has been omitted. Add *with* after the word *compared*.

20. (C) *Divisions* is a noun; therefore, change the noun *geography* to the adjective *geographic*. The adjective is the correct modifier.

21. (A) As the statement stands, it is a fragment. To create a complete sentence, change *to say* to *it is said*.

22. (D) *Or* is a conjunction that connects parallel sentence parts. Change *submerging* to *submerge* to form a parallel form for *sink*.

23. (A) *Both* is a conjunction that must be paired with the word *and*. Change *or nuclear energy* to *and nuclear energy*.

24. (B) Noun modifiers, functioning as adjectives, are normally not plural. Change the word *interstates* to *interstate*.

25. (B) The word *percentage* is used when no specific amount or number is mentioned. Because a specific number, *73*, is given, use *percent* instead of *percentage*.

26. (B) The word *what* may not be used as a relative pronoun. Change *what* to *which* or *that*.

27. (D) A superlative comparison is present in this sentence. Therefore, the word *other* must be added after the word *any* because the Egyptians belonged to the group of ancient civilizations.

28. (D) Change *engaging* to *engage* or *have engaged*. Now the sentence is parallel.

29. (C) The coordinating conjunction *and* is used in this sentence to connect parallel parts. Change *it was lent* to simply *lent*, a parallel past participle for *taken*.

30. (D) *Like* is a preposition which must be followed by a noun or a noun phrase, but never by a clause (subject + verb). Change *like* to *as*.

31. (C) *And* must join parallel sentence parts. Change *eating* to *eaten* to create a parallel form for the past participle *flavored*.

32. (B) *Frequently* and *often* have the same meaning. Therefore, this phrase is repetitive. Omit one of these words to correct the sentence.

33. (D) Change *scientist*, a noun, to *scientific*, an adjective, to modify the noun *information* correctly.

34. (D) Change *during* to *when* to direct the reader's attention to a specific moment. *During* involves a greater span of time, whereas *when* indicates an exact point in time.

35. (C) *Skin* is a singular noun requiring a singular verb. Change *break* to *breaks*.

36. (A) A noun is needed after the article *a*. Change *necessary* to *necessity*.

37. (D) The word *place*, a singular noun, is understood at the end of the sentence. *Other* may be followed only by plural nouns or non-countable nouns. Therefore, change *other* to *another*.

38. (D) Because the number word *fifteenth* is an ordinal number in English, it must be preceded by the definite article, *the*. The answer should read *in warfare during the fifteenth century*.

39. (C) *Or* is used to join equal sentence parts. Change *captive* to *captivity*, a noun parallel to the noun *state*.

40. (C) A pronoun referring to *a fish*, a singular noun, must also be singular. Change *their side* to *its side*.

III: READING COMPREHENSION and VOCABULARY

Part A

Following are explanations of questions 1–30. In this section, the correct answers are placed first, so that they can be used to help explain the other choices.

1. (A) CORRECT: *Walked heavily* and <u>tramped</u> are synonyms here.
    (B)   *Skipped* means "moved with a jump or a spring."
    (C)   *Walked unsteadily* means "walked in an uneven or irregular way."
    (D)   *Limped* suggests that one's foot or leg has been injured. It means "walked with a labored, jerky movement; having a lame gait."

2. (B) CORRECT: An *underground passageway* is a <u>tunnel</u>.
    (A)   A long *corridor* is "a long passageway connecting parts of a building."
    (C)   A *center aisle* is "a center passageway connecting parts of a building."
    (D)   An *open ditch* is "an open hollow made in the earth by digging."

3. (D) CORRECT: Both *diminishes* and <u>dwindles</u> means "to grow less."
    (A)   *Shifts* means "changes."
    (B)   *Grows* means "increases," the opposite of "diminishes."
    (C)   *Emerges* in this sentence would mean "to come forth; to come into view."

4. (D) CORRECT: *Copy* and <u>duplicate</u> both mean an "identical" document.
    (A)   A *summary* is "a short version of a longer work," or "a brief statement of main points."
    (B)   A *revision* is "an amended or altered version" of a work.
    (C)   An *outline*, like a *summary*, is "a general sketch indicating only the main features."

5. (A) CORRECT: *Intermittent* and <u>sporadic</u> both describe an activity that is "interrupted by pauses; not continuous."
    (B)   *Frequent* means "constant; habitual; regular."
    (C)   *Continuous* means "without break or interruption," the opposite of sporadic.
    (D)   *Distant* here means "far away." Intermittent gunfire might be nearby or distant.

6. (B) CORRECT: In this sentence, *reject* means to <u>rule out</u> or "eliminate."
    (A)   *Promise* means "to give assurance that one will do something."
    (C)   *Accept* means "to receive with approval or favor; accede; assent to."
    (D)   *Forestall* means "to prevent; hinder; thwart."

7. (C) CORRECT: *Being on time* means "being punctual."
   (A) *Being efficient* would mean "being capable; competent."
   (B) *Being courteous* means "being polite; using good manners."
   (D) *Being cheerful* means "being joyful; happy."

8. (B) CORRECT: <u>Got nowhere</u> and *accomplished nothing* both mean that the attempt failed.
   (A) *Succeeded completely* means the opposite of <u>got nowhere</u>.
   (C) *Fooled no one* means that "no one was tricked or deceived."
   (D) *Became obsessed* means "became abnormally preoccupied."

9. (C) CORRECT: *Huge* and <u>prodigious</u> both mean "very large."
   (A) *Slight* here would mean "small."
   (B) *Tiny* would mean "very small, minute." Both "tiny" and "slight" 9(A) suggest the opposite of <u>prodigious</u>.
   (D) *Moderate* means "not extreme; not very large or very small."

10. (A) CORRECT: *Notorious* and <u>infamous</u> mean "known widely and regarded unfavorably."
    (B) *Dreaded* means "feared greatly" or "regarded with much apprehension."
    (C) *Loathed* means "regarded with hatred or disgust."
    (D) *Investigated* suggests "examined in detail."

11. (C) CORRECT: To *put off* and <u>postpone</u> both mean "to delay until a later time."
    (A) *Call off* means "to cancel."
    (B) To *do without* means "to manage without."
    (D) To *see about* means "to attend to" or "to investigate."

12. (B) CORRECT: *Tracked* and <u>stalked</u> mean "to pursue by following the marks left by the passage of a person, animal, or thing."
    (A) *Shot* means "hit with some projectile"; probably a bullet, but possibly an arrow.
    (C) To *aim at* means "to direct something [a weapon, in this context] at someone or something else."
    (D) *Skinned* means "stripped or deprived of skin."

13. (B) CORRECT: *Soft, wet land* means <u>swamp</u>.
    (A) A *forest* is "a large area of land covered with trees."
    (C) *Dry, sandy soil* would be almost the opposite of a <u>swamp</u>.
    (D) A *prairie* is "a wide area of flat or rolling grassland."

14. (C) CORRECT: <u>Equilibrium</u> and *balance* both indicate "stability."
    (A) *Turmoil* means "confusion."
    (B) *Disarray* means "disorder."
    (D) *Danger* means "peril; liability to pain."

15. (A) CORRECT: A *friendly, unimportant talk* is a <u>chat</u>.
    (B) A *disagreement* is a "conflict or difference of opinion."
    (C) A *serious discussion* is not an "unimportant" talk.
    (D) A *high-level conference* is also too official and serious to be called a chat.

16. (A) CORRECT: To *gain* and <u>acquire</u> are synonyms meaning "get or obtain."
    (B) *Lose* would mean the opposite of <u>acquire</u>.
    (C) *Hide* means "to conceal from sight."
    (D) *Steal* means to "acquire wrongfully or dishonestly; to take what belongs to someone else."

17. (D) CORRECT: *Decided* and <u>resolved</u> both mean "to have made up one's mind."
    (A) *Promised* means "to have given one's word (usually to someone else) to do or not to do something."
    (B) *Hoped* here would mean "expected something desired."
    (C) *Consented* means "agreed."

18. (C) CORRECT: Here *real* and <u>genuine</u> mean the same thing.
    (A) *Perfect* here would mean without "defects" or "flaws." A diamond can be real and still be flawed.
    (B) *Imitations* would be "false" or "fake," the opposite of <u>genuine</u>.
    (D) *Valuable* means "worth money" in this context.

19. (C) CORRECT: *Without previous thought* means <u>on the spur of the moment</u>.
    (A) *After careful thought* would be the opposite of <u>on the spur of the moment</u>.
    (B) *For only a short time* tells how long the stay at the party will be.
    (D) *At the earliest possible moment* tells when the writer of the sentence will go to the party.

20. (C) CORRECT: *By chance* can be substituted for <u>at random</u> without changing the meaning. Both mean "without definite method or purpose; unsystematically."
    (A) *By interview* would mean "by a face-to-face meeting and discussion."
    (B) *By testing* would mean "by means of a trial for evaluating performance."
    (D) *By competition* would mean "by a contest between two (or more)."

21. (B) CORRECT: *Stealing* can be substituted for <u>pilfering</u> without changing the meaning of the sentence.
    (A) *Absenteeism* means "habitual failure to appear for work."
    (C) *Tardiness* means "being late; not being punctual."
    (D) *Ignorance* means "lack of knowledge."

22. (A) CORRECT: *Fundamentally* and *basically* both mean "essentially."
    (B) *Usually* means "normally; customarily; habitually."
    (C) *Frequently* means "often."
    (D) *Approximately* means "about; near; close."

23. (C) CORRECT: To *review* is to *go over* or "to study or examine again."
    (A) To *relate* here would mean "to tell."
    (B) To *revise* means "to change or modify."
    (D) To *calculate* would mean "to perform a mathematical operation."

24. (B) CORRECT: *Heavy* and *massive* both mean "very large" in this context.
    (A) *Daily* means "every day."
    (C) *Double* means "twice as much as usual." Here, it is more specific than *massive*.
    (D) *Adequate* means "enough; sufficient." An adequate dose might be large or small.

25. (A) CORRECT: *Fierce* and *violent* both mean "strong" and "intense."
    (B) *Immense* means "big."
    (C) *Rapid* means "fast."
    (D) *Chilly* means "slightly cold."

26. (B) CORRECT: *Very funny* can be substituted for *hilarious* in the sentence without loss of meaning.
    (A) *Suspenseful* means "full of anxious uncertainty."
    (C) *Realistic* here means "depicting things which are real; true to life."
    (D) *Very tragic* would mean "sad," almost the opposite of *hilarious*.

27. (C) CORRECT: *Fatal* and *deadly* both mean "ending in or causing death."
    (A) *Curable* means "able to be cured or healed."
    (B) *Painful* means "causing suffering; hurting."
    (D) *Disabling* means "crippling; incapacitating."

28. (B) CORRECT: *Combined* and *blended* both mean "completely or thoroughly mixed."
    (A) Here, *produced* would mean "created," or "made."
    (C) *Invented* would mean "produced for the first time; originated."
    (D) *Discovered* means "found for the first time."

29. (C) CORRECT: *Not able to be parted* can be substituted for *inseparable*.
    (A) *Not able to be distinguished* would mean that the twins could not be told apart or identified.
    (B) *Not able to be understood* would mean that the twins' speech was difficult to understand.
    (D) *Not able to be believed* suggests that the twins are "incredible" in some way.

30. (A) CORRECT: *Hindered* and <u>impeded</u> mean "prevented" or "blocked."
    (B)   *Halted* means "completely stopped."
    (C)   *Accelerated* means "speeded up."
    (D)   *Fostered* here would mean "promoted the development of," almost the opposite of <u>impeded</u>.

Part B

31. This question tests for word recognition.

    (A)   It is described as the opposite of *humid*.
    (B) CORRECT: "Meager" (line 4) means "a small, insufficient amount." "Meager rainfall" suggests that the climate is *dry*.
    (C)   The statement does not mention temperature.
    (D)   *Heavy* here suggests the opposite of "meager."

32. This question tests for the main idea.

    (A)   The statement asserts the opposite.
    (B) CORRECT: "Little suited to stock-breeding" in this context (lines 1–2) means "poor for raising animals."
    (C)   "Only" sheep and goats can be raised there.
    (D)   See 32(A) above.

33. This question tests for word recognition.

    (A)   The statement asserts the opposite.
    (B)   The statement does not describe the *kind* of terrain in this area.
    (C) CORRECT: "Extensive" (line 3) in this context means "large" or "covering a large area." The rest of the sentence suggests that the area is not good for grazing. See 32(B) above.
    (D)   That the area receives little rainfall (line 4) suggests that it is not swampy.

34. This question tests for the main idea of the statement.

    (A)   He has some signs or evidence on which to base a reasonable opinion.
    (B)   He can only make "an intelligent guess" (line 2).
    (C)   See 34(A) above.
    (D) CORRECT: If he has *some basis for an opinion*, then he can make "an intelligent guess" (line 2).

35. This question tests for word recognition and the ability to draw inferences.

    (A)   Surf may be produced by *a distant storm* (lines 3–4), so it cannot *be* the storm.
    (B) CORRECT: The observer can see the surf "spilling out onto the sand" (lines 2–3).
    (C)   An observer on the beach could not, then, see the surf on the sand before him.
    (D)   Small rocks and seashells cannot be "produced" by a storm.

36. This question tests for word recognition and for the ability to draw inferences.

    (A)   *An island*—a body of land surrounded by water—cannot itself produce surf.

    (B) CORRECT: A "gale" must share characteristics with a storm, if they have like effects on the sea. Storms always have strong winds.

    (C)   *A breeze*—a gentle wind—is not likely to have the same effect on the sea as a storm.

    (D)   *A tidal wave* is an unusually high wave that may be caused by a gale, a storm, or an earthquake.

37. This question tests for a main assumption in the "Directions."

    (A)   See 37(B) below.

    (B) CORRECT: Of the forms of medication named, only a *liquid* would be measured by teaspoon.

    (C)   See 37(B) above.

    (D)   See 37(B) above.

38. This question tests for word recognition.

    (A)   This is how much an adult should take at one time, and how often to take it.

    (B) CORRECT: The instruction "not to exceed" this amount (lines 5–6) means that this is the maximum dose an adult should take within the time period.

    (C)   This is the maximum dose for children 6–12 years old (lines 6–8).

    (D)   This is the maximum dose for children 2–6 years old (lines 8–10).

39. This question tests for the ability to draw inferences.

    (A) CORRECT: Lines 1–3 identify by their causes the kinds of cough and nasal congestion the medicine will relieve.

    (B)   The relief the medicine may provide is temporary (lines 1–2).

    (C)   The instructions do not mention drowsiness.

    (D)   A physician should be consulted before administering the medicine to children under two years of age.

40. This question tests for a main idea implicit in the passage.

    (A) CORRECT: The detailed instructions on dosages (lines 4–12) indicate that an excessive amount of the medicine may be dangerous.

    (B)   If the medicine is extremely dangerous, the label does not sufficiently indicate its danger. It can be given to children two years and older without consulting a physician.

    (C)   Dosages are indicated for both adults and children.

    (D)   See 40(C) above.

41. This question tests for a main idea in the "Directions."

    (A)   See 41(C) below.
    (B)   See 41(C) below.
    (C) CORRECT: Children less than two years old should be given the medicine only at the direction of a physician (lines 11–12).
    (D)   See 41(C) above.

42. This question tests for a supporting idea in the paragraph.

    (A)   Bats do not *hide in crevices* (lines 5–6).
    (B) CORRECT: They like to "gather in colonies" (line 5).
    (C)   See 42(B) above.
    (D)   See 42(B) above.

43. This problem tests for word recognition and for a supporting idea in the paragraph.

    (A)   Individual bats often live in dry, dark buildings (lines 2–3).
    (B)   Females, especially when young, gather in colonies (lines 4–5).
    (C) CORRECT: "When the air temperature is low" (lines 9–10), that is, when the weather is cold, the bats hang "with their ears closely coiled" (lines 12–13) to keep warm.
    (D)   Bats do not hide in crevices (lines 5–6).

44. This question tests for a supporting idea in the paragraph.

    (A)   See 44(B) below.
    (B) CORRECT: This is clearly stated in lines 6–8.
    (C)   They hang in such places when not hibernating (lines 6–7). See 44(B) above.
    (D)   Their body temperature drops when they are in the dormant condition (lines 8–10), that is, when they are hibernating. See 44(C, B) above.

45. This question tests for the main idea of the paragraph.

    (A)   The sense of the paragraph is that they were *not* peculiarly his own. See 45(B) below.
    (B) CORRECT: The sense of the paragraph is that even in his defects or bad traits he was representative of the national character.
    (C)   The author does not comment on this point in the paragraph. Some persons whom he quotes possibly believed this.
    (D)   The sense of the paragraph is that they were quite obvious.

46. This question tests for word recognition and the ability to draw inferences.

    (A)   See 46(C) below.
    (B)   See 46(C) below.
    (C) CORRECT: Most commentators agree that Roosevelt was not shy but

open and boisterous, not cautious but bold and assertive, not always tactful but reckless and assertive, not always dignified but informal, even swaggering (line 8), blustering (line 21), and clamorous (line 21).

(D)   See 46(C) above.

47. This question tests for ability to draw inferences.

(A)   His physical appearance is not specifically described. See 47(C) below.

(B)   See 47(A) above, 47(C) below.

(C) CORRECT: The statement "physical size means greatness" (see lines 16–17) implies, in the context, that *physical size* means "large."

(D)   He was probably the opposite. See 47(C) above.

48. This question tests for the ability to draw inferences.

(A)   Most likely he did not admire him as a man.

(B)   Roosevelt was popular, he agreed, because he was in many ways like the average American.

(C)   The quote makes clear that he believed neither of these things.

(D) CORRECT: He suggests that Roosevelt was popular because he embodied and appealed to some of the worst characteristics of the American people (lines 14–21).

49. This question tests for the ability to draw inferences.

(A)   Lee commanded the Confederate army, and was beaten by Meade (lines 1–5).

(B)   Hooker was replaced by Meade as commander before the battle.

(C)   See 49(D) below.

(D) CORRECT: Meade won over Lee (lines 1–5), and Meade was a Federal general (lines 5–10).

50. This question tests for the main idea of the paragraph.

(A)   He did *hurt the Confederate army* (lines 3–5).

(B)   He fought "a skillful defensive battle" (lines 5–6).

(C)   He did *force Lee to retreat* (lines 7–9).

(D) CORRECT: He did not "finish off the enemy" (lines 9–11).

51. This question tests for a supporting idea.

(A)   He was "in anguish" (line 16) which means here that he was very displeased and upset.

(B)   He may have, but in the paragraph Meade is described as congratulating the troops (lines 12–14).

(C) CORRECT: He was unhappy that Meade had not pursued and destroyed Lee's army, which would have shortened the war (lines 15–17).

(D)   "My God!" in this context is an expression of dismay.

52. This question tests for the ability to perceive implications.

(A)   He was competent enough to win the battle.
(B)   The author suggests that he was not ruthless enough.
(C) CORRECT: This is the main implication of the paragraph.
(D)   The author does not mention the soldiers' feelings toward Meade.

53. This question tests for a supporting idea.

(A)   At first movies were short (lines 1–2).
(B)   Longer films could provide the *same* emotional appeal as melodramas in theaters (lines 3–7).
(C)   See 53(B) above.
(D) CORRECT: In this respect, films had a clear advantage over theaters (lines 4–7).

54. This question tests for the ability to draw inferences.

(A)   Longer films began to be made by about 1915 (lines 1–4).
(B) CORRECT: When sound was introduced in 1927, more people than ever began to go to movies rather than to the theater (lines 10–13).
(C)   They were less expensive than the theater (lines 14–15).
(D)   Beginnning in about 1915, they did tell complete, longer stories (lines 1–4).

55. This question tests for a main idea in the paragraph.

(A)   More people began going to movies after World War I, but not because of the war.
(B) CORRECT: Movies were much cheaper than the theater, so more people could afford to go (lines 14–17).
(C)   Before sound was introduced, this was a disadvantage to movies in the competition with the theater (lines 10–13).
(D)   After about 1915, films were not shorter (lines 1–4).

56. This question tests for the main idea of the second paragraph.

(A)   The theater was available to relatively few.
(B)   It was a luxury available, because of location at least, to few people in the United States.
(C) CORRECT: In the United States, only about thirty producing theaters in New York remained.
(D)   Some touring companies originating in New York would tour the country.

57. This question tests for word recognition.

(A)   This is possibly true, but it is not the sense of the statement. See 57(D) below.
(B)   This is not the "trend" to which the author refers. See lines 7–10.

(C)   This is the opposite of his meaning.

(D) CORRECT: The trend is that more people were going to movies, and fewer to the theater. "Accelerated" means "speeded up" (lines 7–10).

The following questions test for the sense of the sentence.

58. (A)   "Much of" is less inclusive than *all over*. The second sentence means that American films are the most popular *everywhere* in Europe. The original does not.

     (B)   This almost exactly reverses the sense of the original.

     (C) CORRECT: This sentence changes the emphasis but retains the sense of the original.

     (D)   The original sentence does not say how popular American films are in countries other than those of Europe.

59. (A) CORRECT: This has the same sense as the original but with a different emphasis.

     (B)   This may be true, but the original sentence doesn't mention radio listeners in New York.

     (C)   See 59(B) above.

     (D)   The original says the California listener will hear the music "sooner"; also, *listener in New York City* is not qualified, so the reader cannot determine whether the author means all listeners or only those in the concert hall.

60. (A)   This may be true, but the original sentence does not mention whether or not they were rivals.

     (B)   Artistically, the two men's achievements are comparable.

     (C)   The original states just the reverse.

     (D) CORRECT: The sense is the same but the emphasis is different: the original is a compound sentence (with elements understood), and the revision is a complex sentence.

ANSWER SHEET FOR TEST 5

Tear out this answer sheet and use it to record your answers to all the questions in this examination.

SECTION I

1 Ⓐ Ⓑ Ⓒ Ⓓ	11 Ⓐ Ⓑ Ⓒ Ⓓ	21 Ⓐ Ⓑ Ⓒ Ⓓ	31 Ⓐ Ⓑ Ⓒ Ⓓ	41 Ⓐ Ⓑ Ⓒ Ⓓ
2 Ⓐ Ⓑ Ⓒ Ⓓ	12 Ⓐ Ⓑ Ⓒ Ⓓ	22 Ⓐ Ⓑ Ⓒ Ⓓ	32 Ⓐ Ⓑ Ⓒ Ⓓ	42 Ⓐ Ⓑ Ⓒ Ⓓ
3 Ⓐ Ⓑ Ⓒ Ⓓ	13 Ⓐ Ⓑ Ⓒ Ⓓ	23 Ⓐ Ⓑ Ⓒ Ⓓ	33 Ⓐ Ⓑ Ⓒ Ⓓ	43 Ⓐ Ⓑ Ⓒ Ⓓ
4 Ⓐ Ⓑ Ⓒ Ⓓ	14 Ⓐ Ⓑ Ⓒ Ⓓ	24 Ⓐ Ⓑ Ⓒ Ⓓ	34 Ⓐ Ⓑ Ⓒ Ⓓ	44 Ⓐ Ⓑ Ⓒ Ⓓ
5 Ⓐ Ⓑ Ⓒ Ⓓ	15 Ⓐ Ⓑ Ⓒ Ⓓ	25 Ⓐ Ⓑ Ⓒ Ⓓ	35 Ⓐ Ⓑ Ⓒ Ⓓ	45 Ⓐ Ⓑ Ⓒ Ⓓ
6 Ⓐ Ⓑ Ⓒ Ⓓ	16 Ⓐ Ⓑ Ⓒ Ⓓ	26 Ⓐ Ⓑ Ⓒ Ⓓ	36 Ⓐ Ⓑ Ⓒ Ⓓ	46 Ⓐ Ⓑ Ⓒ Ⓓ
7 Ⓐ Ⓑ Ⓒ Ⓓ	17 Ⓐ Ⓑ Ⓒ Ⓓ	27 Ⓐ Ⓑ Ⓒ Ⓓ	37 Ⓐ Ⓑ Ⓒ Ⓓ	47 Ⓐ Ⓑ Ⓒ Ⓓ
8 Ⓐ Ⓑ Ⓒ Ⓓ	18 Ⓐ Ⓑ Ⓒ Ⓓ	28 Ⓐ Ⓑ Ⓒ Ⓓ	38 Ⓐ Ⓑ Ⓒ Ⓓ	48 Ⓐ Ⓑ Ⓒ Ⓓ
9 Ⓐ Ⓑ Ⓒ Ⓓ	19 Ⓐ Ⓑ Ⓒ Ⓓ	29 Ⓐ Ⓑ Ⓒ Ⓓ	39 Ⓐ Ⓑ Ⓒ Ⓓ	49 Ⓐ Ⓑ Ⓒ Ⓓ
10 Ⓐ Ⓑ Ⓒ Ⓓ	20 Ⓐ Ⓑ Ⓒ Ⓓ	30 Ⓐ Ⓑ Ⓒ Ⓓ	40 Ⓐ Ⓑ Ⓒ Ⓓ	50 Ⓐ Ⓑ Ⓒ Ⓓ

SECTION II

1 Ⓐ Ⓑ Ⓒ Ⓓ	9 Ⓐ Ⓑ Ⓒ Ⓓ	17 Ⓐ Ⓑ Ⓒ Ⓓ	25 Ⓐ Ⓑ Ⓒ Ⓓ	33 Ⓐ Ⓑ Ⓒ Ⓓ
2 Ⓐ Ⓑ Ⓒ Ⓓ	10 Ⓐ Ⓑ Ⓒ Ⓓ	18 Ⓐ Ⓑ Ⓒ Ⓓ	26 Ⓐ Ⓑ Ⓒ Ⓓ	34 Ⓐ Ⓑ Ⓒ Ⓓ
3 Ⓐ Ⓑ Ⓒ Ⓓ	11 Ⓐ Ⓑ Ⓒ Ⓓ	19 Ⓐ Ⓑ Ⓒ Ⓓ	27 Ⓐ Ⓑ Ⓒ Ⓓ	35 Ⓐ Ⓑ Ⓒ Ⓓ
4 Ⓐ Ⓑ Ⓒ Ⓓ	12 Ⓐ Ⓑ Ⓒ Ⓓ	20 Ⓐ Ⓑ Ⓒ Ⓓ	28 Ⓐ Ⓑ Ⓒ Ⓓ	36 Ⓐ Ⓑ Ⓒ Ⓓ
5 Ⓐ Ⓑ Ⓒ Ⓓ	13 Ⓐ Ⓑ Ⓒ Ⓓ	21 Ⓐ Ⓑ Ⓒ Ⓓ	29 Ⓐ Ⓑ Ⓒ Ⓓ	37 Ⓐ Ⓑ Ⓒ Ⓓ
6 Ⓐ Ⓑ Ⓒ Ⓓ	14 Ⓐ Ⓑ Ⓒ Ⓓ	22 Ⓐ Ⓑ Ⓒ Ⓓ	30 Ⓐ Ⓑ Ⓒ Ⓓ	38 Ⓐ Ⓑ Ⓒ Ⓓ
7 Ⓐ Ⓑ Ⓒ Ⓓ	15 Ⓐ Ⓑ Ⓒ Ⓓ	23 Ⓐ Ⓑ Ⓒ Ⓓ	31 Ⓐ Ⓑ Ⓒ Ⓓ	39 Ⓐ Ⓑ Ⓒ Ⓓ
8 Ⓐ Ⓑ Ⓒ Ⓓ	16 Ⓐ Ⓑ Ⓒ Ⓓ	24 Ⓐ Ⓑ Ⓒ Ⓓ	32 Ⓐ Ⓑ Ⓒ Ⓓ	40 Ⓐ Ⓑ Ⓒ Ⓓ

SECTION III

1 Ⓐ Ⓑ Ⓒ Ⓓ	11 Ⓐ Ⓑ Ⓒ Ⓓ	21 Ⓐ Ⓑ Ⓒ Ⓓ	31 Ⓐ Ⓑ Ⓒ Ⓓ	41 Ⓐ Ⓑ Ⓒ Ⓓ	51 Ⓐ Ⓑ Ⓒ Ⓓ
2 Ⓐ Ⓑ Ⓒ Ⓓ	12 Ⓐ Ⓑ Ⓒ Ⓓ	22 Ⓐ Ⓑ Ⓒ Ⓓ	32 Ⓐ Ⓑ Ⓒ Ⓓ	42 Ⓐ Ⓑ Ⓒ Ⓓ	52 Ⓐ Ⓑ Ⓒ Ⓓ
3 Ⓐ Ⓑ Ⓒ Ⓓ	13 Ⓐ Ⓑ Ⓒ Ⓓ	23 Ⓐ Ⓑ Ⓒ Ⓓ	33 Ⓐ Ⓑ Ⓒ Ⓓ	43 Ⓐ Ⓑ Ⓒ Ⓓ	53 Ⓐ Ⓑ Ⓒ Ⓓ
4 Ⓐ Ⓑ Ⓒ Ⓓ	14 Ⓐ Ⓑ Ⓒ Ⓓ	24 Ⓐ Ⓑ Ⓒ Ⓓ	34 Ⓐ Ⓑ Ⓒ Ⓓ	44 Ⓐ Ⓑ Ⓒ Ⓓ	54 Ⓐ Ⓑ Ⓒ Ⓓ
5 Ⓐ Ⓑ Ⓒ Ⓓ	15 Ⓐ Ⓑ Ⓒ Ⓓ	25 Ⓐ Ⓑ Ⓒ Ⓓ	35 Ⓐ Ⓑ Ⓒ Ⓓ	45 Ⓐ Ⓑ Ⓒ Ⓓ	55 Ⓐ Ⓑ Ⓒ Ⓓ
6 Ⓐ Ⓑ Ⓒ Ⓓ	16 Ⓐ Ⓑ Ⓒ Ⓓ	26 Ⓐ Ⓑ Ⓒ Ⓓ	36 Ⓐ Ⓑ Ⓒ Ⓓ	46 Ⓐ Ⓑ Ⓒ Ⓓ	56 Ⓐ Ⓑ Ⓒ Ⓓ
7 Ⓐ Ⓑ Ⓒ Ⓓ	17 Ⓐ Ⓑ Ⓒ Ⓓ	27 Ⓐ Ⓑ Ⓒ Ⓓ	37 Ⓐ Ⓑ Ⓒ Ⓓ	47 Ⓐ Ⓑ Ⓒ Ⓓ	57 Ⓐ Ⓑ Ⓒ Ⓓ
8 Ⓐ Ⓑ Ⓒ Ⓓ	18 Ⓐ Ⓑ Ⓒ Ⓓ	28 Ⓐ Ⓑ Ⓒ Ⓓ	38 Ⓐ Ⓑ Ⓒ Ⓓ	48 Ⓐ Ⓑ Ⓒ Ⓓ	58 Ⓐ Ⓑ Ⓒ Ⓓ
9 Ⓐ Ⓑ Ⓒ Ⓓ	19 Ⓐ Ⓑ Ⓒ Ⓓ	29 Ⓐ Ⓑ Ⓒ Ⓓ	39 Ⓐ Ⓑ Ⓒ Ⓓ	49 Ⓐ Ⓑ Ⓒ Ⓓ	59 Ⓐ Ⓑ Ⓒ Ⓓ
10 Ⓐ Ⓑ Ⓒ Ⓓ	20 Ⓐ Ⓑ Ⓒ Ⓓ	30 Ⓐ Ⓑ Ⓒ Ⓓ	40 Ⓐ Ⓑ Ⓒ Ⓓ	50 Ⓐ Ⓑ Ⓒ Ⓓ	60 Ⓐ Ⓑ Ⓒ Ⓓ

Test 5

I: LISTENING COMPREHENSION

(50 Questions—40 Minutes)

This section of the test requires a demonstration of your ability to understand spoken English. Each of the three parts has special directions. Have a friend read the spoken parts of questions 1 to 50 to you from the script on page 273.

Part A

Directions. In this part of the test, you will hear a brief statement. Each statement will be spoken only once. The statement does not appear in your test booklet. When you have heard a statement, select the answer nearest in meaning to what you have heard. Record your answer on the answer sheet.

Example

You will hear: The Wagners seem to take their large family in stride.

You will read:
  (A) Mr. Wagner comes from a large family.
  (B) Mrs. Wagner comes from a large family.
  (C) Mr. and Mrs. Wagner are the parents of many children.
  (D) The Wagners dislike small families.

The correct answer to the example is (C).

1. (A) The committee made a report before adjourning.
  (B) The next committee meeting has been canceled.
  (C) The committee reported on the adjournment of the meeting.
  (D) The report of the committee was postponed until the next meeting.

2. (A) The family had enough money to buy groceries.
  (B) The family was unable to buy groceries due to the high prices.
  (C) The family was unable to manage their grocery money.
  (D) Sixty dollars was left over after the weekly grocery shopping.

3. (A) Mary exchanged the dress for another one in a different size.
  (B) Mary exchanged the dress because she didn't like it.
  (C) Mary was too late to exchange the dress.
  (D) Mary considered exchanging the dress, but changed her mind.

4. (A) If their wages are not increased, the workers plan to strike.
  (B) The company raised the workers' wages to avoid a strike.
  (C) The company demands that the workers strike.
  (D) The company threatens to pay the workers less.

5. (A) The majority of the students in the class do not speak Spanish.
  (B) Seventy-five percent of the students in the class speak Spanish.

    (C)   About twenty-five percent of the students in the class speak languages other than Spanish.

    (D)   The percentage of students who speak Spanish is less than twenty-five percent.

6. (A) The audience shook the pianist's hand.

    (B)   The audience left before the end of the performance.

    (C)   The audience applauded the pianist's performance.

    (D)   The audience disliked the pianist's performance.

7. (A) Jennifer cannot eat food like pork chops or ham.

    (B)   Jennifer asked me to change my menu to seafood.

    (C)   Seafood is not a good choice to serve on Saturday night.

    (D)   No seafood is available for Saturday night.

8. (A) The man was judged not guilty of killing his wife.

    (B)   The court found a murdered man and his wife.

    (C)   The man was found murdered by his wife.

    (D)   The court decided that the man had killed his wife.

9. (A) It was suggested that the house be painted in warm weather.

    (B)   The contractor said that he would paint the house in spite of the heat.

    (C)   The house should be painted during the winter.

    (D)   The house was too small for the contractor to paint.

10. (A) Mr. Nelson's son doesn't live in a comfortable apartment.

    (B)   Mr. Nelson found his son a comfortable apartment.

    (C)   Mr. Nelson and his son live comfortably.

    (D)   Mr. Nelson's son managed to find a comfortable apartment for his father.

11. (A) We must not write on every line of the paper.

    (B)   The professor will correct our papers in ink.

    (C)   The professor will read our papers, but he will not correct them.

    (D)   We must not write our papers in ink.

12. (A) The job of executive secretary requires more skills than she has.

    (B)   She possesses the firm qualities of an executive secretary.

    (C)   Both she and the executive secretary took a firm position.

    (D)   Firmness is needed to qualify one for position of executive secretary.

13. (A) He thinks that his company manufactures superior products.

    (B)   He convinced his company to put him in charge of production.

    (C)   His company has manufactured inferior products for many years.

    (D)   It took him many years to become a superior in the company.

14. (A) The class started an hour late.

    (B)   The lecturer dismissed the class on time.

    (C)   The lecturer got off the main subject of discussion and did not dismiss the class on time.

    (D)   The class failed to understand what the lecturer was saying.

15. (A) They held the picnic in spite of the rain.

    (B)   They were extremely interested in having the picnic.

    (C)   The picnic was held, but few people showed up.

    (D)   The picnic was put off because of the rain.

16. (A) Bill used to work for a bank, but now he is in the army.
    (B) Bill holds the top position in the bank.
    (C) Bill's boss is first in command at the bank.
    (D) Bill dislikes his work at the bank.

17. (A) An extra person costs four dollars more.
    (B) An extra person costs five dollars more.
    (C) An extra person costs two dollars more.
    (D) An extra person costs nine dollars more.

18. (A) The play began at eight.
    (B) The play began at nine.
    (C) The play began at eight-thirty.
    (D) The play began at seven-thirty.

19. (A) Bob's writing is only average.
    (B) Bob misspells too many words.
    (C) Bob's organization is poor.
    (D) Bob can't stand to write.

20. (A) I refused to lend Mike my car.
    (B) Mike got a speeding ticket while driving my car.
    (C) I knew nothing about Mike's driving record, so I lent him my car.
    (D) Mike drove my car without his driver's license.

Part B

Directions. This section of the Listening Comprehension test consists of fifteen short conversations between two people. When each conversation ends, you will be asked a question by a third voice about what was said. You will hear the question only once and you must choose the answer from the four choices given. When you have chosen what you believe to be the best answer to the question, record your answer on the answer sheet.

Example

You will hear:

(Man) "I've never understood how to use the card catalogue, and I need to get this information today."

(Woman) "Why don't you pick up one of the guidebooks at the front desk? It will help you, I'm sure."

(Third voice): "Where did this conversation most likely occur?"

You will read: (A) At a museum.
(B) In a store.
(C) In a classroom.
(D) In a library.

The correct answer to the example is (D).

21. (A) He thinks that they are of inferior quality.
    (B) He thinks that they are a bargain.
    (C) He thinks that they are overpriced.
    (D) He thinks that they can be purchased at a cheaper price elsewhere.

22. (A) She is full.
    (B) She doesn't want to gain weight.
    (C) She thinks the dessert will be too rich for her.
    (D) She is afraid of spilling the dessert on her clothes.

23. (A) In a museum.
    (B) In a park.
    (C) In a library.
    (D) In an art store.

24. (A) Disconnect his telephone.
    (B) Blow a whistle into the receiver.
    (C) Keep a record of incoming annoyance calls.
    (D) Report his problem to the police.

25. (A) By one o'clock.
    (B) By two o'clock.
    (C) By three o'clock.
    (D) By twelve o'clock.

26. (A) She thinks that the ticket line will be too long.
    (B) She thinks that the speaker won't show up.
    (C) She thinks that no more tickets are available.
    (D) She thinks that the seminar will not be open to the public.

27. (A) A play.
    (B) A movie.
    (C) A lecture.
    (D) A concert.

28. (A) Six weeks.
    (B) Five weeks.
    (C) Four weeks.
    (D) Three weeks.

29. (A) In a hospital.
    (B) In a law office.
    (C) In a plant store.
    (D) In a gift shop.

30. (A) Cooking.
    (B) Eating dinner.
    (C) Writing a check.
    (D) Getting dressed.

31. (A) By plane.
    (B) By bus.
    (C) By car.
    (D) By train.

32. (A) Two.
    (B) Five.
    (C) Seven.
    (D) Nine.

33. (A) Building an office complex.
    (B) Building a clubhouse.
    (C) Building a private residence.
    (D) Building an apartment house.

34. (A) At home.
    (B) In the hospital.
    (C) In the doctor's office.
    (D) At work.

35. (A) He advises that she have them sent C.O.D.
    (B) He tells her to send two dollars in cash now and the rest upon the delivery of the books.
    (C) He advises that she pay for the books with a credit card.
    (D) He advises her to pay for the books by check.

Part C

Directions. In this part of the test, you will be required to listen to several short lectures and conversations. You will hear the lectures and conversations only once. They do not appear in your test booklet. When a question is asked, choose the best answer from the four given. Record your answer on the answer sheet.

36. (A) The State Department.
    (B) The Treasury Department.
    (C) The Department of Commerce.
    (D) The Department of Agriculture.

37. (A) For seven years.
    (B) For seventy years.
    (C) For seventy-seven years.
    (D) For seventeen years.

38. (A) Patent examiners who are trained in technical fields.
    (B) The President of the United States.
    (C) The director of the U.S. Patent Office.
    (D) Government officials from the applicant's home state.

39. (A) One hundred.
    (B) One thousand.
    (C) Six hundred.
    (D) Fifteen hundred.

40. (A) The Department of Commerce.
    (B) The President of the United States.
    (C) The Treasury Department.
    (D) The United States Patent Office.

41. (A) A bird of prey.
    (B) A small kestrel.
    (C) A kind of hawk.
    (D) A type of shotgun.

42. (A) Genghis Khan.
    (B) Europeans.
    (C) Marco Polo.
    (D) Kings.

43. (A) Polo.
    (B) Hunting.
    (C) Preying.
    (D) Hawking.

44. (A) The extinction of the eagle.
    (B) The nobility.
    (C) Modern weaponry.
    (D) The great expense involved.

45. (A) Falcons.
    (B) Insects and mice.
    (C) Exotic birds.
    (D) Deer.

46. (A) Type B hepatitis is more common than Type A.
    (B) Type B hepatitis is always hereditary.
    (C) Type B hepatitis is often found among people who have had blood transfusions.
    (D) Type B hepatitis affects the liver.

47. (A) It can be transmitted from one person to another.
    (B) It occurs more frequently in children.
    (C) It causes fewer deaths than Type A hepatitis.
    (D) It is more common than Type A hepatitis.

48. (A) Through blood transfusions.
    (B) From a new vaccine.
    (C) From chronic carriers.
    (D) From contaminated food and water.

49. (A) A security light goes on automatically and the unit operates on batteries.
    (B) An alarm sounds to notify the homeowner of the power loss.
    (C) The home smoke alarm system fails to operate until power is restored.
    (D) The entire home smoke alarm system must be replaced at once.

50. (A) He can buy one at a large electrical appliance store.
    (B) He can order one from his local fire department.
    (C) He can request one from Underwriters' Laboratories.
    (D) He can purchase one at a hardware store.

II: STRUCTURE AND WRITTEN EXPRESSION

(40 Questions—25 Minutes)

Part A

Directions. In this part of the test each problem consists of an incomplete sentence. Below the sentence are four choices marked (A), (B), (C), and (D). You should find the one choice which best completes the sentence. Mark your choice on your answer sheet.

Example

Because the United States has little tin, _____ produced in the rest of the world.

(A) tin is used
(B) it uses tin
(C) uses of tin
(D) uses tin

The correct answer to the example is (B).

1. Jupiter _____ perhaps the most important planet of the solar system.

   (A) to be
   (B) being
   (C) is
   (D) like

2. The common garden pea, also called the English pea, _____ for its edible seeds.

   (A) to grow
   (B) is grown
   (C) growing
   (D) grown

3. _____, Thomas Edison invented a device to transmit a special signal while he slept.

   (A) He was a night telegraph operator
   (B) That he was a night telegraph operator
   (C) As a night telegraph operator
   (D) Whereas a night telegraph operator

4. Word of the first launching of *Sputnik I* _____ the Observatory Philharmonic on October 4, 1957.

   (A) it reached
   (B) was reached
   (C) has been reaching
   (D) reached

5. Training programs for the United States Peace Corps are conducted in the country or region _____ the volunteer will serve.

   (A) and
   (B) or
   (C) but
   (D) where

6. This vehicle bounces and glides along the ground _____.

   (A) at an average speed of 40 miles per hour
   (B) of 40 miles per hour at an average speed
   (C) at 40 miles per hour of an average speed
   (D) of an average speed at 40 miles per hour

7. _____ famous queens in the history of England: Elizabeth I and Victoria.

   (A) Including two
   (B) There are two
   (C) For two
   (D) Because are two

8. _____, Charles Darwin did much to disprove common theories about biological evolution.

   (A) He was a highly respected naturalist
   (B) Because of he was a highly respected naturalist
   (C) A highly respected naturalist
   (D) A highly respected naturalist he was

9. The African killer bees could not be handled safely, nor _____.

   (A) could their honey be harvested
   (B) their honey could be harvested
   (C) harvested could their honey be
   (D) could not their honey be harvested

10. _____ the first decade of the nineteenth century, the *velocifere,* the forerunner of the modern bicycle, lost favor temporarily.

    (A) While
    (B) It was
    (C) During
    (D) When

11. Playing a major role in the economic life of the United States, _____.

    (A) women currently make up 46 percent of the work force
    (B) the women currently make up 46 percent of the work force
    (C) women currently they make up 46 percent of the work force
    (D) 46 percent percent of the work force is currently made up of women

12. A baby might show fear of an unfamiliar adult, _____ he is likely to smile and reach out to another infant.

    (A) if
    (B) whenever
    (C) so that
    (D) whereas

13. Most psychologists agree that the basic structure of an individual's personality is _____.

    (A) well established extremely by the age of five
    (B) by the age of five it is extremely well established
    (C) extremely well established by the age of five
    (D) by the age of five and extremely well established

14. One of the most beautiful natural wonders in the United States is the Grand Canyon, _____located in northwestern Arizona.

    (A) and
    (B) where
    (C) is
    (D) which is

15. _____ Roman mythology, the god Jupiter was accepted as the most powerful ruler of the heavens.

    (A) Like
    (B) For
    (C) With
    (D) In

Part B

Directions. In each of the following sentences, four words or phrases have been underlined. You should choose the one word or phrase that would not be appropriate in standard written English. Mark your choice on the answer sheet.

Example

The average age <u>at which</u> people <u>begin to need</u> eyeglasses <u>vary</u> <u>considerably</u>.
           A   B   C   D

  (C) is incorrect in standard written English.

16. Dr. Halberstam was <u>the prominent</u> physician <u>who surprised a burglar</u> <u>December last</u> and was shot
                      A   B   C
    twice <u>in the chest</u> with a .32-caliber handgun.
          D

17. No one took cable television <u>seriously</u> fifteen years ago, when it <u>has been</u> no more <u>than a way</u> for
                          A   B   C
    isolated towns to receive <u>television signals.</u>
             D

18. <u>Even though</u> he has already been around <u>the earth</u> once on a bicycle, Lloyd Summer <u>is currently</u>
     A   B   C
    <u>off</u> on a seven-continents marathon.
      D

19. Despite the fact <u>that the South Pole</u> is <u>as snow-covered</u> as the North Pole <u>is</u>, <u>is colder</u> than the
          A   B   C   D
    North Pole.

20. One of the most serious human tragedies in the world <u>continue to unfold</u> <u>in some nations</u>, where
                                                           A   B
famine, conflict, and <u>severe drought</u> <u>have brought</u> millions of people close to starvation.
                     C   D

21. Today, the peanut <u>is cultivated</u> commercially <u>in</u> the southern United States <u>from California to</u>
                    A   B   C
Florida and <u>as far north</u> Washington, D.C.
                 D

22. <u>During the 1940's</u>, as a result of nuclear research, Dr. W. F. Eibby discovered carbon 14, <u>based on</u>
      A   B
radioactive rays <u>present in</u> <u>all plants living</u> and animals.
                      C   D

23. <u>Depriving</u> of the financial means <u>to remain independent</u>, Samuel Johnson was forced to <u>search for</u>
    A   B   C
a job <u>as a scribe</u>.
          D

24. <u>Each year</u>, tourists from <u>all over the world</u> travel to Poland <u>to visit</u> <u>a birthplace of</u> Frederic
    A   B   C   D
Chopin.

25. <u>Despite of</u> his limited <u>educational opportunities</u>, Abraham Lincoln <u>became</u> one of the greatest
      A   B   C
intellectuals <u>the world has ever known</u>.
                       D

26. The <u>most important</u> cause of <u>the War of 1812</u> <u>it was</u> the impressment of American seamen <u>by the</u>
          A   B   C   D
British.

27. <u>In 1955</u>, a huge crowd gathered at the University of Michigan <u>to hear scientists announce</u> that a
   A   B
vaccine against polio <u>had been developed</u> and <u>successful tested</u>.
                            C   D

28. <u>Laying the foundation</u> for world-wide radio, Marconi <u>transmitted</u> long-wave signals without wires
          A   B
in 1895 <u>when only he was</u> <u>twenty-one years old</u>.
               C   D

29. <u>With</u> the possible exception of <u>the termite queen</u>, the cicada <u>is thought to be</u> the <u>longer-living</u>
   A   B   C   D
insect in the world.

30. The second sentence <u>the Declaration of Independence</u> established <u>the foundation</u> for the <u>civil</u>
                          A   B   C
<u>rights</u> now enjoyed by every <u>United States</u> citizen.
                            D

31. Both hard- and soft-shelled clams <u>have</u> a wedge-shaped foot that is <u>too fleshy</u> that they <u>can move</u>
                             A   B   C
<u>easily</u> from <u>one place to another</u> by burrowing in the sand.
                     D

32. Great amounts of energy are required for the massive movements of the air in the atmosphere and
    _____   _____   _____
      A   B   C
    for the exchange of heat and moist between the atmosphere and the earth's land and water
                                  _____
                                            D
    surfaces.

33. Climatic conditions vary widely from place to place and from season to season, but there is a
    _____   _____   _____
       A   B   C
    recognizable order and pattern in this great diversity of various climates.
                                                             _____
                                                                    D

34. A perennial is a plant that grows for more than two consecutive seasons without be replanted.
                            _____ _____   _____   _____
                                A   B   C   D

35. Clouds hold water that evaporates from the land or the sea; later, the water in clouds returned to
                    _____   _____   _____
                            A   B   C
    the land as rain or snow.
            _____
                 D

36. For thousands of years, man has created sweet-smelling substances from wood, herbs, and flowers
                            ___   _____
                             A   B
    and using them for perfume or medicine.
    _____   __
          C   D

37. Cancer researchers have done great progress in the last decade; however, scientists still realize
                     _____   _____   _____
                             A   B   C
    that there are many aspects that need to be studied further.
    ____   _____
     D

38. The cockroach spreads disease and is a serious menace to public health, since it seeks out baker-
                  _____   _____ _____
                         A   B   C
    ies, restaurant kitchens, and it looks for food factories.
                              _____
                                      D

39. The most noticeable feature of tarsiers, small animals which look like monkeys, are their large
    _____   _____   _____
             A   B   C
    eyes that allow them to see well at night.
    ____   _____
     D

40. Although caffeine is a moderately habit-forming drug, coffee is not regarded as harmfully to the
                         _____   _____ _____
                                    A   B   C
    average healthy adult.
            _____
               D

III: READING COMPREHENSION AND VOCABULARY

(60 Questions—45 Minutes)

Part A

Directions. Each problem in this part of the test consists of a sentence in which one word or phrase has been underlined. From the four choices given, you should choose the one word or phrase which could be substituted for the underlined word or phrase without changing the meaning of the sentence. Mark your choice on the answer sheet.

Example

The frown on the man's face showed that he was displeased.

(A) look of fear
(B) look of anger
(C) look of delight
(D) look of surprise

The best answer is (B).

1. Both a person's heredity and his environment help to shape his character.

    (A) relatives
    (B) education
    (C) nationality
    (D) surroundings

2. His natural intelligence and his experience enabled him to cope with the problem.

    (A) grow
    (B) play
    (C) deal
    (D) stay

3. The theory that business could operate totally without the aid of government has proved to be an erroneous belief.

    (A) authentic concept
    (B) argument
    (C) illusion
    (D) asset

4. Many businesses provide a kind of retirement benefit which is paid until the death of the former employee.

    (A) patent
    (B) subsidy
    (C) pension
    (D) bargain

5. The man neglected to file his income tax and therefore had to pay a fine.

    (A) hoped
    (B) failed
    (C) promised
    (D) refused

6. Before beginning classes, each student must fill out many forms.

    (A) complete
    (B) eliminate
    (C) produce
    (D) distribute

7. According to its label, that medicine should take effect in about ten minutes.

    (A) produce results
    (B) dissolve completely
    (C) be administered
    (D) lose its strength

8. She is always diplomatic when she deals with angry students.

    (A) firm
    (B) tactful
    (C) outspoken
    (D) rude

9. The professor dictated the words to her class, who wrote them down in the phonetic alphabet.

    (A) read
    (B) delivered
    (C) handed
    (D) revealed

10. His hobby is collecting stamps from all over the world.

    (A) pastime
    (B) career
    (C) business
    (D) vocation

11. Gradually, the sound of the music and laughter died down.

    (A) became louder
    (B) became softer
    (C) became more irritating
    (D) became more cheerful

12. The climate in the great plains is <u>arid</u>.

    √(A) hot and dry
    (B) hot and wet
    (C) cold and wet
    (D) cold and dry

13. The speaker <u>demonstrated</u> his knowledge of the subject by his excellent lecture.

    (A) corrected
    (B) created
    (C) repeated
    √(D) showed

14. When the bell rang, the chemistry student <u>jerked</u> her hand and spilled the acid.

    √(A) abruptly pulled
    (B) clapped
    (C) gently moved
    (D) rubbed

15. <u>Subsequent</u> events proved the man to be right.

    (A) Few
    (B) Later
    (C) Earlier
    (D) Many

16. He is <u>dubious</u> about the success of the plan.

    (A) confident
    (B) articulate
    (C) indifferent
    (D) doubtful

17. All students should <u>bear in mind</u> that these books must be read by mid-semester.

    (A) remember
    (B) memorize
    (C) decide
    (D) overlook

18. The man listened to reports of the approaching hurricane with mounting <u>anxiety</u>.

    (A) depression
    √(B) uneasiness
    (C) gratification
    (D) absorption

19. The criminal <u>insinuated</u> that he had been roughly treated by the arresting officer.

    (A) suggested indirectly
    (B) denied positively
    (C) argued convincingly
    (D) stated flatly

20. She is a <u>contemporary</u> writer who has received much critical acclaim.

    (A) realistic
    (B) witty
    √(C) modern
    (D) colorful

21. No <u>remnants</u> of the settlement of Roanoke, Virginia, were found by the next group of colonists.

    (A) traces
    (B) survivors
    (C) buildings
    (D) implements

22. The soldier <u>rashly</u> agreed to lead the dangerous expedition.

    (A) resignedly
    (B) heroically
    (C) recklessly
    (D) reluctantly

23. The boy had <u>looked up to</u> his older brother all his life.

    (A) despised
    (B) safeguarded
    (C) admired
    (D) excluded

24. The ambassador <u>verified</u> the report before he called the State Department.

    (A) canceled
    (B) confirmed
    (C) proofread
    (D) initialed

25. The camelia is a tree or shrub with <u>glossy</u> evergreen leaves and waxy, roselike flowers.

   (A) thorny
   (B) sticky
   (C) scaly
   (D) shiny

26. The president appears to have been <u>in earnest</u> when he promised to try to balance the national budget.

   (A) serious
   (B) joking
   (C) lying
   (D) dreaming

27. During the 1930's, a long period of <u>drought</u> turned the Midwestern United States into a dustbowl.

   (A) monsoon winds
   (B) dry weather
   (C) rain and sleet
   (D) flash floods

28. In the 1970's, many governments' efforts to <u>curb</u> inflation were unsuccessful.

   (A) resist
   (B) control
   (C) sustain
   (D) induce

29. After several near disasters, <u>a controversy</u> has raged over the safety of nuclear energy.

   (A) dispute
   (B) seminar
   (C) colloquium
   (D) conversation

30. Smoking is <u>prohibited</u> in many university classrooms in the United States.

   (A) permitted
   (B) taught
   (C) banned
   (D) revoked

Part B

Directions. You will be given a series of different types of reading material (sentences, short paragraphs, advertisements, etc.). Each selection is followed by questions about the meaning of the material. You are to choose the one best answer to each question from the four choices given.

Read the following sample passage.

(1) Marianne Moore was born in St. Louis in 1887 and graduated from Bryn Mawr College in 1909. She taught stenography for a few years and then worked as a librarian in New York. She was a
(5) member of the editorial staff of the famous literary magazine *The Dial* from 1925 to 1929. Although a book of her poems, titled *Observations*, was published in America in 1924, Miss Moore has only recently received the full acclaim
(10) she deserves.

Example I

When did Miss Moore graduate from college?

   (A) 1887
   (B) 1909
   (C) 1925
   (D) 1924

The passage says that Miss Moore graduated from Bryn Mawr in 1909. Therefore, you should choose answer (B).

Example 2

The one profession *not* mentioned as being pursued by Miss Moore is that of

   (A) poet.
   (B) teacher.
   (C) scientist.
   (D) librarian.

The passage mentions that Miss Moore taught stenography, worked as a librarian, and wrote poetry. Therefore, you should choose (C) as the best completion of the sentence.

As soon as you understand the directions, begin work on the problems.

Questions 31–33

(1) W. H. Auden has outlined the English variety of the detective story in "The Guilty Vicarage," and whereas "purgation of guilt" is involved in both the thriller and the detective story, the
(5) methods of purgation and the environments in which they operate make all the difference.

31. W. H. Auden wrote about

   (A) country vicarages.
   (B) the thriller alone.
   (C) detective stories in general.
   (D) English detective stories.

32. "The Guilty Vicarage" states that

   (A) the detective story and the thriller are identical.
   (B) the detective story and the thriller have nothing in common.
   (C) neither the detective story nor the thriller involves "purgation of guilt."
   (D) both the thriller and the detective story involve "purgation of guilt."

33. The word "purgation" (line 3) means most nearly

   (A) freeing from.
   (B) adding to.
   (C) spreading.
   (D) concentrating.

Questions 34–36

(1) The alluvial or floodplain soils of major streams such as the Red, Sabine, Pearl, Atchafalaya, and Mississippi rivers have hardwood vegetation on their better-drained soils and cypress trees in the
(5) swampy areas.

34. According to this passage, the Red, Sabine, Pearl, Atchafalaya, and Mississippi

   (A) are not important streams.
   (B) are important rivers.
   (C) have trees growing in them.
   (D) are surrounded by dry, hot plains.

35. This passage suggests that cypress trees

   (A) do not grow in swamps.
   (B) need well-drained soil to grow.
   (C) are not hardwood trees.
   (D) do not grow near rivers.

36. The alluvial soils of these rivers

   (A) are never flooded.
   (B) have soils that drain and soils that stay swampy.
   (C) are always well-drained.
   (D) have only hardwood vegetation.

Questions 37–41

(1) Just below New Orleans, the parish of St. Bernard spread its fields of cane and corn, its cypress and live oak forests, and its dark swamps under the warm Louisiana sun. Frenchmen had
(5) settled it, and in 1818, only fifteen years after the cession of Louisiana from France to the United States, St. Bernard was proudly and even fiercely French. About twenty miles from the city, in the center of the parish, stood Contreras, the planta-
(10) tion home of the Toutant-Beauregards. Jacques Toutant-Beauregard, the master of Contreras, could trace his French and Welsh lineage back to the thirteenth century. His grandfather, the first of the family to settle in Louisiana, had come out
(15) to the colony in the time of Louis XIV. Jacques numbered among his Louisiana ancestors Cartiers and Ducros, names of distinction in bayou country. His wife was a De Reggio, and had a family tree even more impressive than his. The De
(20) Reggios claimed descent from an Italian noble family, dukes no less, a scion of which migrated to France and founded a French line that eventually ended up in Louisiana.

37. Jacques' wife's ancestry was

   (A) French.
   (B) French and Welsh.
   (C) Italian.
   (D) French and Italian.

38. At the time described in this passage, St. Bernard parish

    (A) was still a part of France.
    (B) was not yet a part of Louisiana.
    (C) had been part of the United States for fifteen years.
    (D) was a part of Louisiana, but not a part of the United States.

39. The first of the Beauregard family to settle in Louisiana was

    (A) Jacques.
    (B) Jacques' grandfather.
    (C) Jacques' father.
    (D) Jacques' great-grandfather.

40. The people of St. Bernard parish were

    (A) ashamed of their French heritage.
    (B) unaware of their French heritage.
    (C) unconcerned with their ancestry.
    (D) proud of their French heritage.

41. Jacques' ancestry was

    (A) less distinguished than his wife's.
    (B) more distinguished than his wife's.
    (C) the most impressive in all of St. Bernard parish.
    (D) as distinguished as his wife's.

Questions 42–46

(1)   There can be little doubt that malaria was prevalent in all American colonies during the seventeenth century. Toward the end of the century and continuing into the eighteenth, a
(5) rising incidence marked parts of Pennsylvania, New Jersey, Maryland, Delaware, and other colonies situated in the coastal plains region, while a corresponding decline characterized New England. The significance of malaria in colonial
(10) history can scarcely be overrated, for it was a major hurdle in the development of the American colonies. To the newly arrived settlers or "fresh Europeans," it frequently proved fatal, and epidemics of pernicious malaria took a heavy toll of
(15) old and new colonists alike. In endemic regions the regular succession of spring and fall outbreaks, with the concomitant sickness and disability, deprived the colonies of much sorely needed labor.

42. Malaria occurred

    (A) only in the spring.
    (B) in almost any season.
    (C) only in the fall.
    (D) in periodic outbreaks.

43. During the late seventeenth and early eighteenth centuries

    (A) the number of malaria cases in Maryland declined.
    (B) the number of malaria cases in New England increased.
    (C) the number of malaria cases in the coastal plains region declined.
    (D) the number of malaria cases in New Jersey increased.

44. The words "endemic regions" (line 15) mean most nearly

    (A) extensive regions.
    (B) regions with poor climate.
    (C) regions where malaria was rare.
    (D) regions where malaria was common.

45. The importance of malaria in colonial history

    (A) is difficult to exaggerate.
    (B) was minimal.
    (C) has never been assessed.
    (D) is difficult to determine.

46. Malaria affected

    (A) only "fresh Europeans."
    (B) only old colonists.
    (C) only newly arrived settlers.
    (D) both old and new colonists.

Questions 47–52 refer to the following recipe.

(1)

PINEAPPLE
UPSIDE DOWN CAKE

¼ cup butter
½ cup brown sugar
(5) 5–7 slices pineapple (No. 2 or 1-lb.-4 oz. can)
Maraschino cherries, optional
1 package white or
yellow cake mix
 for a one-layer
(10) cake (or one-half
 of a regular size package)
Whipped cream

Melt butter, brown sugar, and 2 tablespoons of
pineapple syrup in a saucepan. Remove from heat,
(15) pour into a cake pan, and arrange pineapple and
cherries in mixture.

Prepare batter as directed on cake package. Pour over
mixture in the pan. Bake in a preheated oven of 350
degrees for 40–50 minutes. Let stand 5 minutes. Invert
(20) on serving plate. Allow 2–3 minutes before removing
pan. Serve warm with whipped cream.

47. A regular size package of cake probably
contains

 (A) enough mix for a one-layer cake.
 (B) enough for two two-layer cakes.
 (C) enough for a two-layer cake.
 (D) enough for a one-half layer cake.

48. Directions for preparing the cake batter are

 (A) given in the recipe.
 (B) not given because this recipe is for
  experienced cooks.
 (C) given on the pineapple can.
 (D) given on the cake package.

49. The maraschino cherries

 (A) are essential.
 (B) are used only if the pineapple is
  omitted.
 (C) may be omitted.
 (D) are chopped and added to the batter.

50. A No. 2 can of pineapple probably

 (A) contains about a dozen slices.
 (B) weighs about one pound, four ounces.
 (C) weighs more than one pound, four
  ounces.
 (D) weighs less than one pound, four
  ounces.

51. The phrase "allow 2–3 minutes" means

 (A) loosen 2–3 minutes.
 (B) stir 2–3 minutes.
 (C) shake 2–3 minutes.
 (D) wait 2–3 minutes.

52. The word "invert" (line 18) means

 (A) to remove from the pan.
 (B) to turn upside down.
 (C) to cool.
 (D) to top with whipped cream.

Questions 53–56

(1) Belize City, capital of Belize (once British
Honduras), has always been the country's admin-
istrative, cultural, and geographic center. It is a
unique waterfront community characterized by
(5) large frame houses with rambling, screened verandas. Located on the periphery of the hurricane
zone, and at an average elevation of two feet
above sea level, the city is vulnerable to any tidal
wave. Hence, most buildings are on stilts, and
(10) many others have spartan furnishings at the street
level. The cooling effect of sea breezes in a
community surrounded on three sides by salt
water relieves the otherwise oppressive climate.
Located on the Caribbean coast of Central
(15) America slightly more than eight hundred miles
south of New Orleans and about the same
distance west of Jamaica, Belize City had a
population of nearly six thousand in 1859, ten
thousand in 1900, and thirty thousand in the
(20) 1960's.

53. Jamaica is located

 (A) about eight hundred miles south of
  New Orleans.
 (B) about eight hundred miles east of
  Belize.
 (C) about eight hundred miles west of
  Belize City.
 (D) about eight hundred miles north of
  New Orleans.

54. Because of the danger from tidal waves, the
houses of Belize City

 (A) are on the waterfront.
 (B) have large, screened verandas.

(C)   enjoy cooling sea breezes.
(D)   are built on stilts.

55.   The word "vulnerable" (line 8) means most nearly

(A)   protected against.
(B)   immune to.
(C)   attracted to.
(D)   defenseless against.

56.   According to this passage, Belize City is

(A)   in the center of the hurricane zone.
(B)   well below sea level.
(C)   on the outer edge of the hurricane zone.
(D)   more than two feet above sea level.

Questions 57–60

  Directions. For each of the following questions, choose the answer whose *meaning is closest* to that of the given sentence. Although more than one of the choices may be factually correct, you should choose the one that *most closely restates the original sentence*.

57.   In dense woods where little sunlight penetrates, one is likely to find just about as much moss on the south side as on the north side of a tree trunk.

(A)   When little sunlight comes through the thick forest, the south and the north side of a tree trunk have about the same amount of moss.
(B)   When bright sunlight comes through the dense woods, the moss on the north side of the tree trunk is thicker than that on the south side.
(C)   When not much sunlight penetrates the thick woods, the moss on the south side of the tree trunk is thicker than that on the north side.
(D)   When a great deal of sunlight penetrates the thick forest, very little moss grows on either the south or the north side of the tree trunk.

58.   Lavas from some volcanoes flow for a long distance; others solidify quite quickly, resulting in a mass of jagged blocks.

(A)   All volcanoes produce lavas which sometimes flow for a long distance and sometimes solidify very rapidly.
(B)   Lavas from some volcanoes become solid very rapidly, producing rough blocks, while lavas from other volcanoes flow for long distances.
(C)   Volcanic lavas may flow quickly or slowly, become solid, or stay liquid.
(D)   Some volcanoes produce two types of lavas, quick-flowing lava, and quick solidifying lava.

59.   Viruses are organisms that are much smaller than bacteria and about which very little is known.

(A)   Not much is known about bacteria, but they are much larger organisms than viruses.
(B)   Very little is known about viruses or bacteria except that they are very small organisms.
(C)   Not much is known about viruses, which are much smaller organisms than bacteria.
(D)   Very little is known about bacteria, but viruses are much larger than they are.

60.   Although a mammal, the whale seems fish-like because it lives in water and has a streamlined body.

(A)   The whale seems fish-like because it lives in water and has a streamlined body, so it is a mammal.
(B)   Since the whale lives in water and has a streamlined body, it resembles a fish, but it is a mammal.
(C)   The whale, even though it has a streamlined body and lives in water, is a mammal because it resembles a fish.
(D)   The whale, which lives in water, looks like a fish because of its streamlined body; consequently, it is a mammal.

Test 5—Answer Key

I: LISTENING COMPREHENSION

Part A

1.	A	6.	C	11.	A	16.	C
2.	A	7.	C	12.	A	17.	A
3.	A	8.	A	13.	A	18.	C
4.	A	9.	A	14.	C	19.	B
5.	A	10.	A	15.	D	20.	C

Part B

21.	B	26.	C	31.	B
22.	B	27.	D	32.	C
23.	A	28.	A	33.	C
24.	C	29.	B	34.	B
25.	D	30.	A	35.	D

Part C

36.	C	41.	A	46.	C
37.	D	42.	D	47.	A
38.	A	43.	D	48.	D
39.	B	44.	C	49.	A
40.	B	45.	B	50.	D

II: STRUCTURE AND WRITTEN EXPRESSION

Part A

1.	C	6.	A	11.	A
2.	B	7.	B	12.	D
3.	C	8.	C	13.	C
4.	D	9.	A	14.	D
5.	D	10.	C	15.	D

Part B

16. C	24. D	32. D
17. B	25. A	33. D
18. D	26. C	34. D
19. D	27. D	35. C
20. A	28. C	36. C
21. D	29. D	37. A
22. D	30. A	38. D
23. A	31. B	39. C
		40. C

III: Reading Comprehension and Vocabulary

Part A

1. D	11. B	21. A
2. C	12. A	22. C
3. C	13. D	23. C
4. C	14. A	24. B
5. B	15. B	25. D
6. A	16. D	26. A
7. A	17. A	27. B
8. B	18. B	28. B
9. A	19. A	29. A
10. A	20. C	30. C

Part B

31. D	41. A	51. D
32. D	42. D	52. B
33. A	43. D	53. B
34. B	44. D	54. D
35. C	45. A	55. D
36. B	46. D	56. C
37. D	47. C	57. A
38. C	48. D	58. B
39. B	49. C	59. C
40. D	50. B	60. B

Test 5—Explanatory Answers

II: Structure and Written Expression

1. Jupiter _____ perhaps the most important planet of the solar system.
   (This sentence is made complete by a finite verb.)

   (A) *to be*   *To be* is not a finite verb.
   (B) *being*   *Being* is a present participle rather than a finite verb.
   (C) *is*   CORRECT ANSWER
   (D) *like*   *Like* is a preposition, not a finite verb.

2. The common garden pea, also called the English pea, _____ for its edible seeds.
   (This sentence requires a finite verb.)

   (A) *to grow*   *To grow* is an infinitive, not a finite verb.
   (B) *is grown*   CORRECT ANSWER
   (C) *growing*   *Growing* is not a finite verb, but rather a gerund or a participle.
   (D) *grown*   *Grown* is a past participle, not a finite verb.

3. _____, Thomas Edison invented a device to transmit a special signal while he slept.
   (This sentence uses an introductory phrase to modify the subject, *Thomas Edison*.)

   (A) *He was a night telegraph operator*   This choice is incorrect because it is an independent clause. Two independent clauses may not be joined by a comma in formal written English.
   (B) *That he was a night telegraph operator*   This group of words is a noun clause and must therefore by followed by a finite verb.
   (C) *As a night telegraph operator*   CORRECT ANSWER
   (D) *Whereas a night telegraph operator*   *Whereas* does not make sense in this sentence.

4. Word of the first launching of *Sputnik I* _____ the Observatory Philharmonic on October 4, 1957.
   (This sentence is made complete by the use of a verb in the simple past tense.)

(A)	*it reached*	If *it* occurs before *reached* in the sentence, then an unnecessary subject is present. The answer would be correct if *it* were omitted.
(B)	*was reached*	A passive verb makes no sense in the sentence.
(C)	*has been reaching*	The present perfect continuous tense is grammatically incorrect in this sentence because the exact time of action is known.
(D)	*reached*	**CORRECT ANSWER**

5. Training programs for the United States Peace Corps are conducted in the country or region _____ the volunteer will serve.
   (A subordinating word showing place is needed between the two clauses in this statement.)

(A)	*and*	*And* is used to connect coordinate words, phrases, or clauses. The use of *and* in this choice does not make sense.
(B)	*or*	*Or* is used to connect sentence parts of equal weight. Because *or* indicates choice or alternative, it does not fit well into this particular statement.
(C)	*but*	*But* is used to show an existing contrast between two sentence parts. Since no contrast is apparent in the statement, *but* does not make sense when it is placed between the two clauses.
(D)	*where*	**CORRECT ANSWER**

6. This vehicle bounces and glides along the ground _____.
   (This sentence uses an adverbial phrase containing correct word order.)

(A)	*at an average speed of 40 miles per hour*	**CORRECT ANSWER**
(B)	*of 40 miles per hour at an average speed*	*Of 40 miles per hour* modifies the word *speed* and therefore must be placed after it.
(C)	*at 40 miles per hour of an average speed*	This answer makes no sense because of incorrect word order.
(D)	*of an average speed at 40 miles per hour*	The prepositions *of* and *at* are grammatically incorrect in this answer. See 6(A).

7. _____ famous queens in the history of England: Elizabeth I and Victoria.
   (The expletive *there* followed by a finite verb is used in this sentence.)

(A)	*Including two*	This choice lacks a verb and results in an incomplete sentence.

(B)	*There are two*	CORRECT ANSWER

(C)	*For two*	This choice also has no verb. See 7(A).
(D)	*Because are two*	*Because* is a subordinating conjunction and cannot be used in this answer choice.

8. _____, Charles Darwin did much to disprove common theories about biological evolution.
   (This sentence uses an introductory phrase to rename the subject.)

(A)	*He was a highly respected naturalist*	This choice is incorrect because it is an independent clause.
(B)	*Because of he was a highly respected naturalist*	*Because of* must be followed by a noun phrase rather than by an independent clause.
(C)	*A highly respected naturalist*	CORRECT ANSWER
(D)	*A highly respected naturalist he was*	Because a subject and a finite verb have been placed after the noun phrase, the sentence is grammatically incorrect.

9. The African killer bees could not be handled safely, nor _____.
   (This second independent clause begins with a negative word; therefore, question word order must follow.)

(A)	*could their honey be harvested*	CORRECT ANSWER
(B)	*their honey could be harvested*	This independent clause follows standard statement word order, and therefore cannot be used after the negative word *nor*.
(C)	*harvested could their honey be*	The words in this choice do not follow correct word order.
(D)	*could not their honey be harvested*	*Nor* is a word of negation; therefore, the use of not in this clause is incorrect. Do not use two words of negation in the same clause.

10. _____ the first decade of the nineteenth century, the *velocifere,* the fore-runner of the modern bicycle, lost favor temporarily.
    (This sentence uses a preposition of time, which is followed by a noun phrase.)

(A)	*While*	When *while* occurs in a phrase indicating time, it may not be followed by the word *the.*
(B)	*It was*	*It was* used at the beginning of the sentence makes the introductory phrase a complete sentence. Two complete sentences may not be joined by a comma.
(C)	*During*	CORRECT ANSWER
(D)	*When*	In this choice, a finite verb is needed after the subject *decade* to complete the sentence.

11. Playing a major role in the economic life of the United States, _____.
(The first question you should ask is: Who plays a major role in the economic life of the United States? The answer must be the subject of the independent clause that follows.)

(A) *women currently make up 46 percent of the work force*   CORRECT ANSWER

(B) *the women currently make up 46 percent of the work force*   The definite article *the* preceding *women* is unnecessary. When referring to a group (such as women) in a general sense, do not use *the*.

(C) *women currently they make up 46 percent of the work force*   The word *they* is incorrect in this choice because it repeats the subject of the independent clause, *women*.

(D) *46 percent of the work force is currently made up of women*   *Playing a major role in the economic life of the United States* is an introductory phrase that modifies *women*. Because a modifier should be placed as close as possible to the word it describes, *women*, not *46 percent*, should begin the independent clause.

12. A baby might show fear of an unfamiliar adult, _____ he is likely to smile and reach out to another infant.
(This sentence needs a word to indicate a *contrast* between the two independent clauses.)

(A) *if*   *If* expresses a conditional situation.

(B) *whenever*   *Whenever* indicates a time relationship between two clauses rather than a relationship of contrast.

(C) *so that*   *So that* introduces a dependent clause of purpose or reason.

(D) *whereas*   CORRECT ANSWER

13. Most psychologists agree that the basic structure of an individual's personality is _____.
(This sentence requires an adjective or a noun after the linking verb *is*. Other modifiers must follow correct word order.)

(A) *well established extremely by the age of five*   The word *extremely* is an adverb modifying *well established;* therefore it should be placed before the word it modifies.

(B) *by the age of five it is extremely well established*   The words *it is* should be omitted from the sentence. Only a modifying phrase is needed to complete the meaning.

(C) *extremely well established by the age of five*   CORRECT ANSWER

(D) *by the age of five and extremely well established*   *And* is a connecting word that joins equal parts of a sentence. The parts joined by *and* in this choice are unequal.

14. One of the most beautiful natural wonders in the United States is the Grand Canyon, _____ located in northwestern Arizona.
(In this sentence, a dependent clause is formed by the addition of a subject and a finite verb.)

(A)	*and*	*And* joins equal sentence parts only.
(B)	*where*	The dependent clause requires a subject, which *where* does not supply.
(C)	*is*	*Is* must be preceded by a subject to make the dependent clause complete.
(D)	*which is*	CORRECT ANSWER

15. _____ Roman mythology, the god Jupiter was accepted as the most powerful ruler of the heavens.
(A correct preposition is needed to complete the introductory phrase.)

(A)	*Like*	*Like* means *similar to* and therefore is an unacceptable choice.
(B)	*For*	*For* means *on behalf of* and therefore is an unacceptable choice.
(C)	*With*	*With* is a preposition, but it makes no sense in this sentence.
(D)	*In*	CORRECT ANSWER

16. (C) You should say *last December* since the word *last* modifies the noun *December*.

17. (B) You should use the simple past tense in this sentence since a specific time (fifteen years ago) is mentioned. Change *has been* to *was*.

18. (D) Nouns used as modifiers do not normally appear in the plural form. Change *continents* to *continent*.

19. (D) The subject of the independent clause occurring after the comma is missing. Add *it*, a pronoun referring to *South Pole,* to complete the sentence.

20. (A) The subject of the sentence, *one,* is singular; therefore, a singular verb is required. Change *continue* to *continues*.

21. (D) Because a comparison is being made in this statement, the word *as* should be added after *north* to complete the comparison. Change *as far north* to *as far north as*.

22. (D) The present participle, *living,* should be placed before the word it modifies. Change *all plants living* to *all living plants*.

23. (A) The introductory modifying phrase must contain the past participial form before the preposition *of.* Change *depriving of* to *deprived of*.

24. (D) A person has only one birthplace; therefore, the definite article *the* is required here. Change *a birthplace of* to *the birthplace of*.

25. (A) This phrase does not exist in English. Change *despite of* to *in spite of* or simply *despite*.

26. (C) The finite verb *was* needs only one subject. Omit the word *it*.

27. (D) The past participle *tested,* functioning as a verb in this sentence, must be modified by an adverb, rather than by an adjective. Change *successful* to *successfully*.

28. (C) The adverb *only* is misplaced. *Only* modifies *twenty-one years old* in this statement and therefore the sentence should read ". . . when he was only twenty-one years old."

29. (D) The sentence implies that the cicada lives longer than any other insect except the termite queen. Change the comparative form *longer* to the superlative form *longest*.

30. (A) The word *in* has been omitted and therefore the sentence makes no sense. Place the word *in* after the word *sentence*.

31. (B) An adverbial clause of result is needed to give the sentence meaning. Change *too fleshy* to *so fleshy*.

32. (D) *And* joins two equal sentence parts. *Heat* is a noun. Change *moist*, the adjective form, to *moisture*, the noun form.

33. (D) The word *diversity* implies *variety;* therefore, the word *various* is unnecessary. Omit the word *various* and the sentence maintains its intended meaning.

34. (D) Gerunds commonly follow the prepositions in English. Change *be replanted* to *being replanted*.

35. (C) The simple present tense is needed to express a general fact. Change the past tense verb *returned* to *returns*.

36. (C) This sentence contains incorrect parallel structure. Because *and* is used to connect equal sentence parts, change *using them* to *has used them* or *used them*.

37. (A) The verb *have made* must replace *have done* because, in correct English, the correct expression is "to make progress," not "to do progress."

38. (D) Sentence parts listed in the series must be in parallel form. Omit *it looks for* before *food factories*.

39. (C) *Feature*, the subject of the sentence, is singular. Therefore, change the plural form of the verb *are* to the singular *is*.

40. (C) The adverb *harmfully* is used incorrectly here. Change *harmfully* to the adjective *harmful*, which correctly modifies the noun *coffee*.

III: READING COMPREHENSION AND VOCABULARY

Part A

Following are explanations of questions 1–30. In this section, the correct answers are placed first, so that they can be used to help explain the other choices.

1. (D) CORRECT: *Surroundings* and <u>environment</u> here mean "the total of circumstances surrounding an organism or group of organisms."
   (A) *Relatives* are "those people connected by blood or marriage."

(B)   *Education* means "systematic instruction or training; schooling."

(C)   One's *nationality* refers to one's "membership in a particular nation."

2.   (C) CORRECT: To *deal* with or "handle a problem successfully" is to cope with it."

(A)   To *grow* is "to increase in size or ability."

(B)   To *play* here would mean "to deal or to behave carelessly or indifferently."

(D)   To *stay* with the problem would mean "not to give up; to keep trying."

3.   (C) CORRECT: An *illusion* and an erroneous belief are "false perceptions of reality; delusions."

(A)   An *authentic concept* would be "a true or valid idea," almost the opposite of an erroneous belief.

(B)   An *argument* would be a "debate; dispute."

(D)   An *asset* is a "useful thing or quality." The erroneous belief in the sentence might or might not have been an *asset* to its proponents.

4.   (C) CORRECT: A retirement benefit is called a *pension*.

(A)   A *patent* is "a grant made by a government to an inventor, promising him the sole right to make, use, and sell his invention for a certain period of time."

(B)   A *subsidy* is financial assistance given by one person or government to another.

(D)   A *bargain* here would be "something offered or acquired at a price advantageous to the buyer."

5.   (B) CORRECT: Here *failed* and neglected both suggest that the man has for some reason (forgetfulness or carelessness, perhaps) not paid his tax.

(A)   *Hoped* to file would mean that he "expected or desired" to file.

(C)   *Promised* here would mean that the man had "given his word" that he would pay.

(D)   *Refused* here means a positive rejection of his obligation to pay, something neglect does not suggest.

6.   (A) CORRECT: To *fill out* forms is to *complete* them.

(B)   To *eliminate* the forms would be "to exclude, omit, or leave them out."

(C)   To *produce* here would mean "to make" or "to bring forward; exhibit."

(D)   To *distribute* would mean "to give or hand out; to disperse."

7.   (A) CORRECT: Take effect and *produce results* both mean "to begin to work."

(B)   *Dissolve completely* means "to become a liquid; liquefy."

(C)	*Be administered* means "be given."
(D)	*Lose its strength* means "to become weaker."

8. (B) CORRECT: *Diplomatic* and *tactful* both suggest "smoothness and skill" in dealing with difficult people and situations.

(A) *Firm* in this context would mean "showing determination, strength" and "not yielding under pressure."

(C) *Outspoken* here means "frank, unrestrained in speech."

(D) *Rude* means "discourteous."

9. (A) CORRECT: In this context, *read* can be substituted for dictated.

(B) *Delivered* here would mean "given," not necessarily by "dictating."

(C) *Handed* also means "given" and suggests that a printed list of the words was given to the class.

(D) *Revealed* means "made known," but not necessarily orally.

10. (A) CORRECT: A *pastime* is a hobby, an "enjoyable leisure time activity."

(B) One's *career* is his "profession" and how he succeeds or fails in it.

(C) *Business* here also suggests a full-time, professional activity.

(D) A *vocation* is "one's occupation, business, or profession."

11. (B) CORRECT: *Became softer* here equals died down.

(A) *Became louder* would be the opposite of died down.

(C) *Became more irritating* means became more "annoying" or "disturbing." A sound that grew softer would probably become less, not more, irritating.

(D) *Became more cheerful* means "became happier."

12. (A) CORRECT: Arid means a hot and dry climate.

(B) *Hot and wet* might be "tropical," but not arid.

(C) *Cold and wet* is the exact opposite of arid.

(D) *Cold and dry* does not mean arid.

13. (D) CORRECT: *Showed* means demonstrated here.

(A) *Corrected* means "removed error."

(B) *Created* means "brought into being; originated." Knowledge is not "created."

(C) *Repeated* means "said again."

14. (A) CORRECT: *Abruptly pulled* and jerked both describe a sudden sharp movement.

(B) *Clapped* means "to strike the palms of the hands together."

    (C)   *Gently moved* would describe a slow movement, not the quick movement indicated by "jerk."

    (D)   *Rubbed* here would mean "to move one hand against another with pressure and friction."

15. (B) CORRECT: *Later* and subsequent are synonyms.

    (A)   *Few* means "not many."

    (C)   *Earlier* means almost the opposite of subsequent.

    (D)   *Many* means "a large number."

16. (D) CORRECT: *Doubtful* and dubious both mean "uncertain."

    (A)   *Confident* in this context would mean "certain," the opposite of dubious. Also, "confident" is usually followed by "of."

    (B)   *Articulate* would mean "able to speak clearly and expressively."

    (C)   *Indifferent* suggests that the man doesn't care whether or not the plan is a success. Also, *indifferent* is usually not followed by the preposition "about."

17. (A) CORRECT: To bear in mind is *to remember*, "to be careful not to forget."

    (B)   *Memorize* means "to commit to memory; to learn by heart."

    (C)   *Decide* means "to make up one's mind; to choose."

    (D)   *Overlook* means "to ignore or neglect," almost the opposite of bear in mind.

18. (B) CORRECT: Here, *uneasiness* and anxiety both mean "worry," or "concern."

    (A)   *Depression* would mean "sadness; despondency; dejection."

    (C)   *Gratification* means "satisfaction; pleasure."

    (D)   *Absorption* means "great interest" in this context.

19. (A) CORRECT: Insinuated means "suggested indirectly."

    (B)   *Denied positively* means "stated that something was not true."

    (C)   *Argued convincingly* means "put forward excellent reasons for or against."

    (D)   *Stated flatly* means "said directly."

20. (C) CORRECT: *Modern* and contemporary both suggest the style of the present.

    (A)   *Realistic* in this context would mean "describing things as it is thought they really are."

    (B)   *Witty* would mean "cleverly amusing." Writers of the past or present can be and have been "witty."

    (D)   Here, *colorful* would mean "vivid; full of interest or variety."

21. **(A) CORRECT:** *Traces* and <u>remnants</u> both mean "a surviving vestige, as of a former time or condition."
    (B) *Survivors* is more specific than <u>remnants</u>; it would mean "people remaining at Roanoke."
    (C) *Buildings,* that is, structures such as houses or stores, is too specific here.
    (D) *Implements* would mean "tools" or "utensils" and would also be more specific than <u>remnants</u>.

22. **(C) CORRECT:** <u>Rashly</u> and *recklessly* both mean "headstrong; having no regard for consequences."
    (A) *Resignedly* here would mean "with unresisting acceptance" or "with passive submission."
    (B) *Heroically* would mean "bravely" or "courageously."
    (D) *Reluctantly* means "unwillingly."

23. **(C) CORRECT:** *Admired* and <u>looked up to</u> both mean "had a high opinion of; respected."
    (A) *Despised* means "regarded with contempt," almost the opposite of <u>looked up to</u>.
    (B) *Safeguarded* means "protected."
    (D) *Excluded* here would mean "left out."

24. **(B) CORRECT:** *Confirmed* and <u>verified</u> mean "made certain of the truth of."
    (A) Here *canceled* means "called off."
    (C) *Proofread* here would mean "read over to find the errors."
    (D) *Initialed* would mean "signed by marking with one's own initial or initials."

25. **(D) CORRECT:** *Shiny* and <u>glossy</u> are synonyms meaning "bright and glistening."
    (A) *Thorny* means "having sharp spines."
    (B) *Sticky* means "covered with an adhesive agent; having the property of adhering to a surface."
    (C) *Scaly* means "covered with thin, overlapping parts."

26. **(A) CORRECT:** *Serious* means <u>in earnest</u>.
    (B) *Joking* here would mean "not serious."
    (C) *Lying* would mean "not telling the truth."
    (D) In this context, *dreaming* would suggest that the president was "unrealistic" in his promise.

27. **(B) CORRECT:** In this context, *dry weather* can be substituted for <u>drought</u> without loss of meaning.
    (A) *Monsoon winds* refers to "a wind system that influences large climatic regions and reverses directions seasonally."

(C)	*Rain and sleet* (*sleet* means "frozen rain") would be almost the opposite of <u>drought</u>.
(D)	*Flash floods* would be "sudden violent overflowings of water on land that is normally dry."

28. (B) CORRECT: Here <u>curb</u> means *to control*.

(A)	*Resist* would mean "to work against; fight off; oppose actively."
(C)	*Sustain* would mean "to maintain or prolong."
(D)	*Induce* would mean "to cause."

29. (A) CORRECT: *Dispute* and <u>controversy</u> are synonyms here.

(B)	A *seminar* would be "a meeting for an exchange of ideas; a conference."
(C)	A *colloquium* is "an informal meeting for discussion."
(D)	A *conversation* is "a familiar talk."

30. (C) CORRECT: *Banned* and <u>prohibited</u> both mean "not allowed; forbidden."

(A)	*Permitted* means "allowed," the opposite of <u>prohibited</u>.
(B)	Although the university curriculum in the United States is varied, smoking is not *taught*.
(D)	*Revoked* would mean "canceled or annulled by withdrawing." The law allowing or prohibiting smoking might be "revoked," but smoking cannot be revoked.

Part B

31. This question tests for a main idea in the sentence.

(A)	This is the home of a rural clergyman, usually in the Church of England.
(B)	He has not written about the thriller, but only mentioned it for comparison (lines 3–4).
(C)	See 31(D) below.
(D) CORRECT:	"Variety" in this context means "kind" or "type," so Auden wrote about detective stories of the English type (lines 1–2).

32. This question tests for a main idea of the sentence.

(A)	They have some things in common, but they are not identical (lines 3–6). See 32(D) below.
(B)	See 32(A) above, 32(D) below.
(C)	Both involve purgation of guilt (lines 3–4).
(D) CORRECT:	This is clearly stated in lines 3–4.

33. This question tests for word recognition.

(A) CORRECT: "Purgation of guilt" (line 3) means "a freeing or releasing from guilt."

(B) It means almost the opposite of *adding to*. See 33(A) above.

(C) This would mean involving others in the guilt. See 33(A) above.

(D) This would mean gathering the guilt to one place or person and so intensifying it there. See 33(A) above.

34. This question tests for word recognition.

(A) Line 1 suggests that the Red, Sabine, Pearl, Atchafalaya, and Mississippi rivers are "major streams." In this context, "major streams" means "important rivers."

(B) CORRECT: See 34(A) above.

(C) The trees grow on the alluvial plains, not in the rivers.

(D) *Floodplain* means "an area where a stream periodically overflows its boundaries," and is not a synonym for *plain*.

35. This question tests for the ability to make inferences.

(A) Lines 4–5 specifically say that cypress trees grow "in the swampy areas."

(B) "Swampy areas" are not well-drained. See 35(A) above.

(C) CORRECT: The passage contrasts hardwood trees, which grow in well-drained areas, with cypresses, which grow in swamps. Cypresses must not be hardwoods.

(D) All trees described in this passage grow on the floodplains of rivers.

36. This passage tests for a main idea.

(A) The word "alluvial" means "deposited by flooding."

(B) CORRECT: One of the main ideas of this passage is that floodplains of major rivers have two different types of soils, each producing different types of vegetation.

(C) See 36(A) above.

(D) See 36(B) above.

37. This question tests for attention to detail.

(A) See 37(D) below.

(B) Jacques' ancestry, not his wife's, was *French and Welsh*.

(C) See 37(D) below.

(D) CORRECT: Her family, originally Italian, had lived for generations in France (lines 18–23).

38. This passage tests for word recognition.

(A) *Cession* in the "cession of Louisiana from France to the United States" (lines 5–7) means that the United States had received Louisiana from France. Lines 1–4 make clear that St. Bernard parish is a part of Louisiana.

(B)   See 38(A) above.

(C) CORRECT: See 38(A) above. Lines 5–6 also state that the cession of Louisiana took place fifteen years before 1818, the time described in this passage.

(D)   See 38(A) above.

39. This question tests for attention to detail.

(A)   See 39(B) below.

(B) CORRECT: His grandfather came to Louisiana during the reign of Louis XIV (lines 13–15).

(C)   See 39(B) above.

(D)   See 39(B) above.

40. This question tests for attention to detail.

(A)   See 40(D) below.

(B)   See 40(D) below.

(C)   See 40(D) below.

(D) CORRECT: If, as the author says, they were "proudly and even fiercely French" (lines 7–8), then they were both *aware* of and *concerned* with their heritage, and they were certainly not *ashamed* of it.

41. This question tests for attention to detail.

(A) CORRECT: Her ancestry (her "family tree") was more distinguished ("more impressive") than her husband's (lines 18–19).

(B)   See 41(A) above.

(C)   His wife's was more impressive. See 41(A) above.

(D)   See 41(A) above.

42. This question tests for attention to detail.

(A)   It occurred regularly in both spring and fall (lines 15–17).

(B)   Apparently it occurred normally only in the spring and fall (lines 15–17).

(C)   See 42(A) above.

(D) CORRECT: "Regular succession of . . . outbreaks" (lines 15–17) means "periodic outbreaks."

43. This question tests for attention to detail.

(A)   "A rising incidence" (lines 5–6) in Maryland means that the number of cases *increased*.

(B)   The number of cases in New England *declined* (lines 8–9).

(C)   The cases *increased* in the coastal plains region (lines 5–7).

(D) CORRECT: "A rising incidence" (increase) occurred in New Jersey (lines 5–6).

44. This question tests for word recognition.

   (A)   See 44(D) below.
   (B)   See 44(D) below.
   (C)   See 44(D) below.
   (D) CORRECT: "Endemic" in this context means "consistently present" in a region and identified with the region.

45. This question tests for word recognition.

   (A) CORRECT: "Significance" (line 9) in this context means "importance"; "can scarcely be overrated" (line 10) means that it is almost impossible to exaggerate.
   (B)   The opposite is true. See 45(A) above.
   (C)   The paragraph itself presents an assessment (an estimate or a determination) of its importance.
   (D)   It is *easy* to determine, the author says, that malaria was a major hindrance ("hurdle," line 11) to the development of the colonies.

46. This question tests for attention to detail.

   (A)   It frequently caused the death ("proved fatal") of newly arrived ("fresh") Europeans, but it also "took a heavy toll" among both recently arrived settlers and those who had been in the colonies for years or whose families had lived there for generations. That is, it made very many ill and unable to work (lines 12–15).
   (B)   See 46(A) above.
   (C)   See 46(A) above.
   (D) CORRECT: See 46(A) above.

47. This question tests for the ability to draw inferences.

   (A)   See 47(C) below.
   (B)   See 47(C) below.
   (C) CORRECT: To make a one-layer cake, one should use only "one-half of a regular size package" (lines 10–11). The regular size package, therefore, has enough mix to make a two-layer cake.
   (D)   See 47(C) above.

48. This question tests for attention to detail.

   (A)   See 48(D) below.
   (B)   See 48(D) below.
   (C)   See 48(D) below.
   (D) CORRECT: In line 16, it is clearly stated that one is to prepare the batter "as directed on cake package."

49. This question tests for word recognition.

   (A)   "Optional" (line 6) means that "they are not essential."
   (B)   The recipe requires the pineapple, whether or not one uses the cherries.

(C) CORRECT: They are not necessary (*essential*), but they may be added. See 49(A) above.

(D) No such instructions are given. See 49(A) and 49(C) above.

50. This question tests for the ability to draw inferences.

(A) It probably contains five to seven (line 5).

(B) CORRECT: Since one can use *either* a No. 2 or a one-pound, four-ounce size, they are most likely equivalent.

(C) See 50(B) above.

(D) See 50(B) above.

51. This question tests for word recognition.

(A) In this context, *loosen 2–3 minutes* would mean "to free the cake from the edges of the pan, perhaps by running a knife around the edges."

(B) *Stir 2–3 minutes* would mean "to move a spoon through the cake." Since the cake is already baked, stirring would ruin it.

(C) *Shake 2–3 minutes* would mean "to move the pan from side to side, possibly with the intention of loosening it from the pan."

(D) CORRECT: *Wait 2–3 minutes* has the same sense as "allow 2–3 minutes." Here, the cook is being told to let 2–3 minutes elapse before trying to take the cake from the pan.

52. This question tests for word recognition.

(A) See 52(B) below.

(B) CORRECT: To "invert" means "to turn upside down"; *inverted* means "upside down."

(C) See 52(B) above.

(D) See 52(B) above.

53. This question tests for attention to detail and the ability to draw inferences.

(A) Belize City is located 800 miles south of New Orleans (lines 14–16). See 53(B) below.

(B) CORRECT: If Belize City is about 800 miles west of Jamaica (lines 14–17), then Jamaica is *about 800 miles east of Belize City*.

(C) See 53(B) above.

(D) See 53(B) above.

54. This question tests for attention to detail.

(A) The community is on the waterfront, but not *because* of the danger from tidal waves.

(B) The houses have verandas, but not *because* of the danger from tidal waves.

(C)   The houses are cooled by sea breezes, but not *because* of the danger from tidal waves.

(D) CORRECT: "Vulnerable to" (line 8) means "subject to" or "helpless against." "Hence" (line 9) means, in this context, "therefore." The houses are subject to tidal waves, and therefore they *are built on stilts,* or, *they are built on stilts because* they are subject to tidal waves.

55.   This question tests for word recognition.

(A)   This is opposite the sense of "vulnerable." See 55(D) below.

(B)   See 55(A) above, D below.

(C)   *Attracted to* means "drawn toward." See 55(D) below.

(D) CORRECT: "Vulnerable" means "defenseless against." See 54(D) above.

56.   This question tests for word recognition.

(A)   Lines 6–7 say that Belize City is on the "periphery" of the hurricane zone. Here "periphery" means "edge" or "border," the opposite of *center.*

(B)   Lines 7–8 say that Belize City is located "at an average elevation of two feet above sea level."

(C) CORRECT: See 56(A) above.

(D)   See 56(A) above.

The following questions test for the sense of the sentences.

57.   (A) CORRECT: Both sentences state the effect of meager sunlight on the growth of moss to be the same. "As much" moss on each side means *the same amount* on each side.

(B)   This may be a true statement, but the original sentence does not assert this.

(C)   The amount of moss is *the same* on each side. See 57(A) above.

(D)   The original sentence does not state *how much* moss grows, only that *the same amount* grows on either side. See 57(A) above.

58.   (A)   This sentence states that all volcanoes produce two types of lava, one of which solidifies rapidly and one of which doesn't. See 58(B) below.

(B) CORRECT: Both the original and this sentence state that some volcanoes produce quickly solidifying lava, and that others produce lava that remains fluid longer and flows for long distances.

(C)   This is *part* of what the original sentence asserts, but not all. See 58(B) above.

(D)   See 58(A) and 58(B) above.

59. (A)   Bacteria are larger than viruses, according to the original sentence; but it does not indicate whether much or little is known about bacteria.

(B)   The original states only that very little is known about viruses. See 59(A) above.

(C) CORRECT: See 59(A) and (B) above.

(D)   Both assertions in this sentence are contrary to the original. See 59(A) and 59(B) above.

60. (A)   The original sentence indicates a contrast between being a mammal and seeming fish-like. This sentence indicates a cause-and-effect relation between seeming fish-like and being a mammal.

(B) CORRECT: Both sentences indicate a causal relation between living in water and having a streamlined body and seeming fish-like, and a contrast relation between being a mammal and seeming fish-like.

(C)   This sentence indicates a causal relation between resembling a fish and being a mammal.

(D)   See 60(C) above.

ANSWER SHEET FOR TEST 6

Tear out this answer sheet and use it to record your answers to all the questions in this examination.

SECTION I

1 Ⓐ Ⓑ Ⓒ Ⓓ	11 Ⓐ Ⓑ Ⓒ Ⓓ	21 Ⓐ Ⓑ Ⓒ Ⓓ	31 Ⓐ Ⓑ Ⓒ Ⓓ	41 Ⓐ Ⓑ Ⓒ Ⓓ
2 Ⓐ Ⓑ Ⓒ Ⓓ	12 Ⓐ Ⓑ Ⓒ Ⓓ	22 Ⓐ Ⓑ Ⓒ Ⓓ	32 Ⓐ Ⓑ Ⓒ Ⓓ	42 Ⓐ Ⓑ Ⓒ Ⓓ
3 Ⓐ Ⓑ Ⓒ Ⓓ	13 Ⓐ Ⓑ Ⓒ Ⓓ	23 Ⓐ Ⓑ Ⓒ Ⓓ	33 Ⓐ Ⓑ Ⓒ Ⓓ	43 Ⓐ Ⓑ Ⓒ Ⓓ
4 Ⓐ Ⓑ Ⓒ Ⓓ	14 Ⓐ Ⓑ Ⓒ Ⓓ	24 Ⓐ Ⓑ Ⓒ Ⓓ	34 Ⓐ Ⓑ Ⓒ Ⓓ	44 Ⓐ Ⓑ Ⓒ Ⓓ
5 Ⓐ Ⓑ Ⓒ Ⓓ	15 Ⓐ Ⓑ Ⓒ Ⓓ	25 Ⓐ Ⓑ Ⓒ Ⓓ	35 Ⓐ Ⓑ Ⓒ Ⓓ	45 Ⓐ Ⓑ Ⓒ Ⓓ
6 Ⓐ Ⓑ Ⓒ Ⓓ	16 Ⓐ Ⓑ Ⓒ Ⓓ	26 Ⓐ Ⓑ Ⓒ Ⓓ	36 Ⓐ Ⓑ Ⓒ Ⓓ	46 Ⓐ Ⓑ Ⓒ Ⓓ
7 Ⓐ Ⓑ Ⓒ Ⓓ	17 Ⓐ Ⓑ Ⓒ Ⓓ	27 Ⓐ Ⓑ Ⓒ Ⓓ	37 Ⓐ Ⓑ Ⓒ Ⓓ	47 Ⓐ Ⓑ Ⓒ Ⓓ
8 Ⓐ Ⓑ Ⓒ Ⓓ	18 Ⓐ Ⓑ Ⓒ Ⓓ	28 Ⓐ Ⓑ Ⓒ Ⓓ	38 Ⓐ Ⓑ Ⓒ Ⓓ	48 Ⓐ Ⓑ Ⓒ Ⓓ
9 Ⓐ Ⓑ Ⓒ Ⓓ	19 Ⓐ Ⓑ Ⓒ Ⓓ	29 Ⓐ Ⓑ Ⓒ Ⓓ	39 Ⓐ Ⓑ Ⓒ Ⓓ	49 Ⓐ Ⓑ Ⓒ Ⓓ
10 Ⓐ Ⓑ Ⓒ Ⓓ	20 Ⓐ Ⓑ Ⓒ Ⓓ	30 Ⓐ Ⓑ Ⓒ Ⓓ	40 Ⓐ Ⓑ Ⓒ Ⓓ	50 Ⓐ Ⓑ Ⓒ Ⓓ

SECTION II

1 Ⓐ Ⓑ Ⓒ Ⓓ	9 Ⓐ Ⓑ Ⓒ Ⓓ	17 Ⓐ Ⓑ Ⓒ Ⓓ	25 Ⓐ Ⓑ Ⓒ Ⓓ	33 Ⓐ Ⓑ Ⓒ Ⓓ
2 Ⓐ Ⓑ Ⓒ Ⓓ	10 Ⓐ Ⓑ Ⓒ Ⓓ	18 Ⓐ Ⓑ Ⓒ Ⓓ	26 Ⓐ Ⓑ Ⓒ Ⓓ	34 Ⓐ Ⓑ Ⓒ Ⓓ
3 Ⓐ Ⓑ Ⓒ Ⓓ	11 Ⓐ Ⓑ Ⓒ Ⓓ	19 Ⓐ Ⓑ Ⓒ Ⓓ	27 Ⓐ Ⓑ Ⓒ Ⓓ	35 Ⓐ Ⓑ Ⓒ Ⓓ
4 Ⓐ Ⓑ Ⓒ Ⓓ	12 Ⓐ Ⓑ Ⓒ Ⓓ	20 Ⓐ Ⓑ Ⓒ Ⓓ	28 Ⓐ Ⓑ Ⓒ Ⓓ	36 Ⓐ Ⓑ Ⓒ Ⓓ
5 Ⓐ Ⓑ Ⓒ Ⓓ	13 Ⓐ Ⓑ Ⓒ Ⓓ	21 Ⓐ Ⓑ Ⓒ Ⓓ	29 Ⓐ Ⓑ Ⓒ Ⓓ	37 Ⓐ Ⓑ Ⓒ Ⓓ
6 Ⓐ Ⓑ Ⓒ Ⓓ	14 Ⓐ Ⓑ Ⓒ Ⓓ	22 Ⓐ Ⓑ Ⓒ Ⓓ	30 Ⓐ Ⓑ Ⓒ Ⓓ	38 Ⓐ Ⓑ Ⓒ Ⓓ
7 Ⓐ Ⓑ Ⓒ Ⓓ	15 Ⓐ Ⓑ Ⓒ Ⓓ	23 Ⓐ Ⓑ Ⓒ Ⓓ	31 Ⓐ Ⓑ Ⓒ Ⓓ	39 Ⓐ Ⓑ Ⓒ Ⓓ
8 Ⓐ Ⓑ Ⓒ Ⓓ	16 Ⓐ Ⓑ Ⓒ Ⓓ	24 Ⓐ Ⓑ Ⓒ Ⓓ	32 Ⓐ Ⓑ Ⓒ Ⓓ	40 Ⓐ Ⓑ Ⓒ Ⓓ

SECTION III

1 Ⓐ Ⓑ Ⓒ Ⓓ	11 Ⓐ Ⓑ Ⓒ Ⓓ	21 Ⓐ Ⓑ Ⓒ Ⓓ	31 Ⓐ Ⓑ Ⓒ Ⓓ	41 Ⓐ Ⓑ Ⓒ Ⓓ	51 Ⓐ Ⓑ Ⓒ Ⓓ
2 Ⓐ Ⓑ Ⓒ Ⓓ	12 Ⓐ Ⓑ Ⓒ Ⓓ	22 Ⓐ Ⓑ Ⓒ Ⓓ	32 Ⓐ Ⓑ Ⓒ Ⓓ	42 Ⓐ Ⓑ Ⓒ Ⓓ	52 Ⓐ Ⓑ Ⓒ Ⓓ
3 Ⓐ Ⓑ Ⓒ Ⓓ	13 Ⓐ Ⓑ Ⓒ Ⓓ	23 Ⓐ Ⓑ Ⓒ Ⓓ	33 Ⓐ Ⓑ Ⓒ Ⓓ	43 Ⓐ Ⓑ Ⓒ Ⓓ	53 Ⓐ Ⓑ Ⓒ Ⓓ
4 Ⓐ Ⓑ Ⓒ Ⓓ	14 Ⓐ Ⓑ Ⓒ Ⓓ	24 Ⓐ Ⓑ Ⓒ Ⓓ	34 Ⓐ Ⓑ Ⓒ Ⓓ	44 Ⓐ Ⓑ Ⓒ Ⓓ	54 Ⓐ Ⓑ Ⓒ Ⓓ
5 Ⓐ Ⓑ Ⓒ Ⓓ	15 Ⓐ Ⓑ Ⓒ Ⓓ	25 Ⓐ Ⓑ Ⓒ Ⓓ	35 Ⓐ Ⓑ Ⓒ Ⓓ	45 Ⓐ Ⓑ Ⓒ Ⓓ	55 Ⓐ Ⓑ Ⓒ Ⓓ
6 Ⓐ Ⓑ Ⓒ Ⓓ	16 Ⓐ Ⓑ Ⓒ Ⓓ	26 Ⓐ Ⓑ Ⓒ Ⓓ	36 Ⓐ Ⓑ Ⓒ Ⓓ	46 Ⓐ Ⓑ Ⓒ Ⓓ	56 Ⓐ Ⓑ Ⓒ Ⓓ
7 Ⓐ Ⓑ Ⓒ Ⓓ	17 Ⓐ Ⓑ Ⓒ Ⓓ	27 Ⓐ Ⓑ Ⓒ Ⓓ	37 Ⓐ Ⓑ Ⓒ Ⓓ	47 Ⓐ Ⓑ Ⓒ Ⓓ	57 Ⓐ Ⓑ Ⓒ Ⓓ
8 Ⓐ Ⓑ Ⓒ Ⓓ	18 Ⓐ Ⓑ Ⓒ Ⓓ	28 Ⓐ Ⓑ Ⓒ Ⓓ	38 Ⓐ Ⓑ Ⓒ Ⓓ	48 Ⓐ Ⓑ Ⓒ Ⓓ	58 Ⓐ Ⓑ Ⓒ Ⓓ
9 Ⓐ Ⓑ Ⓒ Ⓓ	19 Ⓐ Ⓑ Ⓒ Ⓓ	29 Ⓐ Ⓑ Ⓒ Ⓓ	39 Ⓐ Ⓑ Ⓒ Ⓓ	49 Ⓐ Ⓑ Ⓒ Ⓓ	59 Ⓐ Ⓑ Ⓒ Ⓓ
10 Ⓐ Ⓑ Ⓒ Ⓓ	20 Ⓐ Ⓑ Ⓒ Ⓓ	30 Ⓐ Ⓑ Ⓒ Ⓓ	40 Ⓐ Ⓑ Ⓒ Ⓓ	50 Ⓐ Ⓑ Ⓒ Ⓓ	60 Ⓐ Ⓑ Ⓒ Ⓓ

Test 6

I: LISTENING COMPREHENSION

(50 Questions—40 Minutes)

This section of the test requires a demonstration of your ability to understand spoken English. Each of the three parts has special directions. Have a friend read the spoken parts of questions 1 to 50 to you from the script on page 281.

Part A

Directions. In this part of the test, you will hear a brief statement. Each statement will be spoken only once. The statement does not appear in the test booklet. When you have heard a statement, select the answer nearest in meaning to what you have heard. Record your answer on the answer sheet.

Example

You will hear: The Wagners seem to take their large family in stride.

You will read:
- (A) Mr. Wagner comes from a large family.
- (B) Mrs. Wagner comes from a large family.
- (C) Mr. and Mrs. Wagner are the parents of many children.
- (D) The Wagners dislike small families.

The correct answer to the example is (C).

1. (A) My car needs some work on it.
   (B) After work every day, I walk five blocks.
   (C) I drive to work in my car every day.
   (D) I have to walk five blocks to get to my car.

2. (A) The children couldn't sleep because of the noise.
   (B) The baby woke up because the children made sounds.
   (C) The baby and the children slept through the noise.
   (D) The noise didn't prevent the baby from sleeping.

3. (A) Eric arrived after the class had begun.
   (B) Eric arrived in class on time.
   (C) Eric is usually late for class.
   (D) Eric arrived in class twenty minutes before it began.

4. (A) I didn't take French last semester.
   (B) Someone offered to teach me French last semester.
   (C) I knew that French was not offered last semester.
   (D) I took French the last semester it was offered.

5. (A) A person is more likely to get a cold in the winter.
   (B) More people have summer colds than winter colds.
   (C) People get colder in the summer than in the winter.
   (D) The winter is much colder than the summer.

6. (A) Tony's boss left the office for two days.
   (B) Tony quit his job after two days.
   (C) Tony took two days off from work.
   (D) Tony's boss agreed to take off for two days.

7. (A) The boss told his secretary to finish the report on time.
   (B) The boss told the secretary not to rush.
   (C) The boss told the secretary to take the report home in order to finish it.
   (D) The boss told the secretary that he would need the report before Thursday.

8. (A) Mr. Riley's customers cannot handle him successfully.
   (B) Mr. Riley finds its difficult to sell to his customers.
   (C) Mr. Riley is a successful salesman of handles to many customers.
   (D) Mr. Riley sometimes has too many customers to take care of.

9. (A) No other student is as smart as Jeanne.
   (B) The class has only three smart students.
   (C) Two students are smarter than Jeanne.
   (D) Jeanne is not as smart as most of the other students.

10. (A) There are few old movies on television.
    (B) Watching old movies on television is enjoyable.
    (C) I dislike watching old movies on television.
    (D) Old televisions and old watches are worth nothing.

11. (A) Mrs. Thompson was a housekeeper.
    (B) Mrs. Thompson made a substantial profit when she sold her house.
    (C) Mrs. Thompson was an architect.
    (D) Mrs. Thompson paid a lot of money to have a servant in her house.

12. (A) The weather report predicted an afternoon rainstorm.
    (B) The weather report predicted rain for the entire day.
    (C) The weather report predicted a cloudy day.
    (D) The weather report predicted a clear afternoon.

13. (A) Most people do not know what the cost of insurance is.
    (B) Insurance rates are decreasing for many people.
    (C) Insurance companies prohibit some people from purchasing insurance.
    (D) One day people may not be able to afford insurance.

14. (A) Times Square is the name of a well-known theater in New York.
    (B) Many famous theaters are located in New York's Times Square.
    (C) New York is in the center of Times Square.
    (D) Many theaters in central New York are open all the time.

15. (A) There is no performance of the ballet on Sunday.
    (B) The ballet is performed six nights a week.
    (C) The ballet is performed twice on Sunday.
    (D) You can see a matinee performance of the ballet any night.

16. (A) He needs more money than he makes.
    (B) He lives on little money.
    (C) He spends more money than he has.
    (D) He wants a raise in salary.

17. (A) The students failed to understand the teacher's instructions.
    (B) The students exchanged seats with the teacher.
    (C) The students followed the teacher's instructions.
    (D) The students sat in the first row, but not in the second.

Test 6 / 205

18. (A) Brett attended only his physics class.
    (B) Brett attended both his biology and physics classes.
    (C) Brett attended only his biology class.
    (D) Brett did not attend any of his classes due to the rain.

19. (A) Martha refuses to lie.
    (B) I lied to Martha.
    (C) Martha does nothing but lie.
    (D) Martha lied to me about something.

20. (A) There were three explosions.
    (B) The first explosion occurred in the cellar.
    (C) Two explosions happened in rapid succession.
    (D) The first explosion was louder than the second.

Part B

Directions. This section of the Listening Comprehension test consists of fifteen short conversations between two people. When each conversation ends, you will be asked a question by a third voice about what was said. You will hear the question only once and you must choose the answer from the four choices given. When you have chosen what you believe to be the best answer to the question, record your answer on the answer sheet.

Example

You will hear:

(Man) "I've never understood how to use the card catalogue, and I need to get this information today."

(Woman) "Why don't you pick up one of the guidebooks at the front desk? It will help you, I'm sure."

(Third voice) "Where did this conversation most likely occur?"

You will read: (A) At a museum.
              (B) In a store.
              (C) In a classroom.
              (D) In a library.

The correct answer to the example is (D).

21. (A) The service is slow.
    (B) There is no salad bar.
    (C) The prices are high.
    (D) The food is poor.

22. (A) A bank deposit.
    (B) An insurance claim.
    (C) A loan.
    (D) An income tax return.

23. (A) The drinks.
    (B) The chicken.
    (C) The ice.
    (D) The transportation.

24. (A) Become a real estate salesperson.
    (B) Get a driver's license.
    (C) Go to a movie.
    (D) Graduate from the university.

25. (A) He suggests that she buy the sweater in another color.
    (B) He suggests that she buy a jacket instead of the sweater.
    (C) He suggests that she buy the sweater at its original price.
    (D) He suggests that she buy the sweater on sale.

26. (A) He ruined the carpet.
    (B) He was not introduced to the governor.
    (B) He broke a punch cup.
    (D) He was not offered any punch.

27. (A) She imagined that she had seen a ghost.
    (B) She hit a bus full of school children.
    (C) She almost collided with a school bus.
    (D) The boulevard was too narrow.

28. (A) In a pet shop.
    (B) In a pediatrician's office.
    (C) In a veterinary clinic.
    (C) In a medical laboratory.

29. (A) In Europe.
    (B) At the university.
    (C) In a photographer's studio.
    (D) In a bank.

30. (A) Go boating.
    (B) Listen to the radio.
    (C) Play tennis.
    (D) Go bicycling.

31. (A) Meat.
    (B) Strawberry pie.
    (C) Potatoes and sour cream.
    (D) Lime sherbet.

32. (A) Hotel manager.
    (B) Steward on a plane.
    (C) Travel agent.
    (D) Librarian.

33. (A) Mend the fence.
    (B) Cut the grass.
    (C) Trim the lawn.
    (D) Clip the hedge.

34. (A) Private rooms.
    (B) Kitchen privileges.
    (C) Noisy students.
    (D) Air-conditioning.

35. (A) It is yellow.
    (B) It is blue and yellow.
    (C) The salesman is asking $150 for it.
    (D) It is damaged.

Part C

Directions. In this part of the test, you will be required to listen to several short lectures and conversations. You will hear the lectures and conversations only once. They do not appear in the test booklet. When a question is asked, choose the best answer from the four given. Record your answer on the answer sheet.

36. (A) Color.
    (B) Cut.
    (C) Carat.
    (D) Clarity.

37. (A) Its defects.
    (B) Its color.
    (C) Its shape.
    (D) Its weight.

38. (A) A clear, bright yellow diamond.
    (B) A slightly gray diamond.
    (C) A white diamond.
    (D) A diamond with a slight yellow cast.

39. (A) Its weight.
    (B) Its shape.
    (C) Its light refraction.
    (D) Its smoothness.

40. (A) Snails.
    (B) Plants.
    (C) Shrimp.
    (D) Dried insects.

41. (A) Dried shrimp.
    (B) Dried insects.
    (C) Commercial goldfish food.
    (D) Snails.

42. (A) They should be fed more than once a day.
    (B) They should be fed fresh food.
    (C) They should be fed at five-minute intervals.
    (D) They should never be fed more than once a day.

43. (A) A U-boat.
    (B) A merchant ship.
    (C) A warship.
    (D) A submarine.

44. (A) In 1917.
     (B) In 1915.
     (C) In 1913.
     (D) In 1918.

45. (A) Britain.
     (B) Ireland.
     (C) Germany.
     (D) The United States.

46. (A) Near Liverpool.
     (B) In a New York port.
     (C) A short distance from the Irish coast.
     (D) In German war territory.

47. (A) Yellowjack.
     (B) Poor appetite.

(C) Exhaustion.
(D) Yellow skin.

48. (A) In Cuba.
     (B) In New Orleans.
     (C) In Africa.
     (D) In Boston.

49. (A) A fever.
     (B) A slave ship.
     (C) A mosquito.
     (D) A virus.

50. (A) In the United States.
     (B) In Africa.
     (C) In Central America.
     (D) In South America.

II: STRUCTURE AND WRITTEN EXPRESSION

(40 Questions—25 Minutes)

Part A

Directions. In this part of the test each problem consists of an incomplete sentence. Below the sentence are four choices, marked (A), (B), (C), and (D). You should find the one choice which best completes the sentence. Mark your choice on the answer sheet.

Example

Because the United States has little tin, _____ produced in the rest of the world.

(A) tin is used
(B) it uses tin
(C) uses of tin
(D) uses tin

The correct answer to the example is (B).

1. An earthquake is a shaking of the ground _____ when masses of rock beneath the surface of the earth change position.

    (A) which occurring
    (B) it occurs

(C) and therefore occurring
(D) that occurs

2. Nervous about flying in planes, _____.

    (A) thirty years ago people knew nothing of space travel
    (B) people knew nothing of space travel thirty years ago
    (C) space travel was unknown by people thirty years ago
    (D) because people knew nothing of space travel thirty years ago

3. _____, authorities allow about one ton to each foot of length.

    (A) To calculate the weight of an average adult whale
    (B) They calculate the weight of an average adult whale
    (C) In the calculation the weight of an average adult whale
    (D) Even though they calculate the weight of an average adult whale

4. Pictures _____ with a telescope are inverted.

   (A) taken
   (B) they took them
   (C) to take
   (D) are taken

5. _____ the exception of institutions controlled by church, municipal, or private corporations, Latin American universities are regulated by federal laws.

   (A) By
   (B) For
   (C) With
   (D) To

6. _____, Harry S. Truman was our nation's thirty-third President.

   (A) He was born and raised in Missouri
   (B) Born and raised in Missouri
   (C) Because he was born and raised in Missouri
   (D) That he was born and raised in Missouri

7. In Austria, where fertile farmland is limited, crops _____.

   (A) are on the sides of mountains often grown
   (B) often are on the sides of mountains grown
   (C) are grown on the sides often of mountains
   (D) are often grown on the sides of mountains

8. _____ pollution control measures are expensive, many industries hesitate to adopt them.

   (A) Although
   (B) However
   (C) Because
   (D) On account of

9. Racial violence erupted throughout the United States _____ Martin Luther King, Jr., was assassinated in April, 1968.

   (A) when
   (B) during
   (C) each time that
   (D) then

10. Francis Ford Coppola, who conceived, co-authored, and _____ *Godfather II*, is one of America's most talented filmmakers.

    (A) director of
    (B) directed
    (C) he directed
    (D) directing

11. _____ is called erosion.

    (A) The wearing away of land
    (B) When land wears away
    (C) Land which wears away
    (D) Wearing away land

12. _____, they continue to overeat and to eat the wrong foods.

    (A) However many overweight people realize that they are threatening their health
    (B) Many overweight people realizing that they are threatening their health
    (C) Because of the fact that many overweight people realize that they are threatening their health
    (D) Even though many overweight people realize that they are threatening their health

13. Firstborn children in a family seem to have a stronger desire to succeed _____.

    (A) than do later-born children
    (B) but later-born children do
    (C) as children born later
    (D) if later-born children do

14. Although the gall bladder is absent from all common members of the deer family, _____.

   (A) but the Asiatic musk deer has this organ
   (B) this organ found in the Asiatic musk deer
   (C) however this organ is found in the Asiatic musk deer
   (D) this organ is found in the Asiatic musk deer

15. _____, we drove the horses into the stable.

   (A) Aware that a tornado was brewing
   (B) Because a tornado brewing
   (C) Although a tornado was brewing
   (D) A tornado was brewing

Part B

Directions. In each of the following sentences, four words or phrases have been underlined. You should choose the one word or phrase that would *not* be appropriate in standard written English. Mark your choice on the answer sheet.

Example

  The average age at which people begin to need eyeglasses vary considerably.
                  A   B   C   D
  (C) is incorrect in standard written English.

16. Scientific prediction of earthquakes remains primitive and haphazard; however, scientists can
                                            A   B
    make general predictions after monitor magnetic changes along principal faults.
                                      C   D

17. People who lose weight with the help of behavioral techniques like weighing themselves regularly
             A   B
    and keeping records of what do they eat seem to need the same techniques to keep the weight off.
                              C   D

18. According to a study of firstborn children, children whose mothers expect them to learn very little as
         A   B
    infants develop more slow than children whose mothers expect them to begin learning immediately.
                      C   D

19. In a report issued by United States Census Bureau, the chemical industry is investing more than
        A   B   C
    any other United States manufacturing industry in fighting pollution.
                                                      D

20. Societies from the primitive to the highly civilized have used food, their most essential resource, in
                                 A   B   C
    social bonding celebrations of all kind and in sacred rituals.
                                  D

21. Throughout the history, the mosquito has been not only a nuisance but a killer, carrying some of
                  A   B   C
    the deadliest diseases known to man.
                            D

22. Recent trends <u>seem to indicate</u> that Americans <u>may come to follow</u> the example of <u>those other</u>
                  A   B   C

    <u>nations</u> where <u>the bicycle it is</u> an important means of transportation.
                         D

23. Exploratory investigations reveal that Alaska is <u>capable to producing</u> 45 to 55 percent of <u>its own</u>
                                         A   B

    <u>requirements</u> of <u>agricultural</u> products, instead of approximately 10 percent, <u>the quantity now</u>
         C

    <u>produced</u>.

24. <u>Between</u> the mountains and the plateau <u>lies</u> the Great Valley, <u>which is rich in</u> fertile crop lands
       A   B

    and <u>apples orchards</u>.
          D

25. The official name of <u>the capital of Mexico</u> is Mexico, D.F., <u>but</u> most people <u>call Mexico City</u> to
                   A   B   C

    distinguish it <u>from</u> the country.
                D

26. <u>Since</u> fireworks <u>are danger</u>, many cities have laws <u>preventing</u> businesses <u>from selling them</u>.
      A   B   C   D

27. The photograph revealed a group of mountain climbers who had <u>strung a</u> <u>twenty-feet</u> rope be-
                                                      A   B

    tween two <u>particularly</u> dangerous peaks.
      C   D

28. <u>During World War II</u>, many Eskimos served <u>in the Army or Navy</u>; <u>another</u> worked on airfields or
           A   B   C

    supplied meat <u>to the armed forces</u>.
               D

29. In spite of all the publicity <u>women pilots</u> had received, <u>no amount</u> of evidence <u>could convince</u> the
                             A   B   C

    War Department <u>allow any of them</u> into the Air Service.
               D

30. <u>There</u> is no doubt that the successful late eighteenth-century improvements in <u>spinning and weav-</u>
      A   B

    ing methods, resulting in increased production of fabrics, <u>have a great effect</u> on the inventors of
                                                          C

    <u>the sewing machine</u>.
          D

31. One of the greatest factors hindering efficient farming and <u>proper agricultural development</u> in
                                                                       A

    these countries since <u>the Second World War</u> <u>have been</u> the lack of information concerning land
                                       B   C

    capability, <u>utilization</u>, and availability.
              D

32. Encephalitis, the only mosquito-borne human disease <u>in this country now active</u>, can kill <u>its</u>
                                                    A   B

    <u>victims</u> <u>or</u> cause them <u>permanent brain damage</u>.
      C   D

33. Over the centuries, women have developed considerate expertise in the techniques of adapting to
    　　A　　　　　　　　　　　　　　　　　　B　　　　　　　　　　　　　　　C
    men, but that ability is not the same as truly understanding male psychology.
    　　　　　　　　　　　　　　　　　　D

34. Often, when a new era began in history, a myth for that era springs up at the same time; the myth
    　　　A　　　　　　　　　　　　　　　　　　　　　　B
    usually contained useful advice for coping with the times ahead.
    　　　　　　C　　　　　　　　　D

35. The aperiodic compass is a magnetic compass which its needle is extremely stable under most
    　　　　　　　　　　　　　　　　　　　　　　　A　　　　　　　B　　　　　C
    flying conditions.
    　　D

36. Every day, at least eight Americans choke to death when food or other objects become lodging in
    　　　　　　　　　　　　　　　　A　　　　　　　　　　　B　　　　　　　C
    their throats.
    　　D

37. The most Americans would benefit by doing more walking; in fact, physicians believe walking to
    　　A　　　　　　　　　B　　　　　　　　　　　　C　　　　　　　　　　　D
    be one of the best forms of exercise.

38. Every city in the United States has traffic problems because the amount of cars on American
    　　　　　　A　　　　　　　　B　　　　　　　　　　　C　　　　　　D
    streets and highways is increasing every year.

39. According to the coroner's report, rock-music idol Elvis Presley died of a heart condition in
    　　　　　　A　　　　　　　　　　　　　　　　　　　　　　B　　　　　　　C
    August 16, 1977, yet medical examiners later found evidence of an unusually high concentration of
    　　　　　　　　　　　　　　　　　D
    dangerous drugs in his body.

40. Thirteen hundred medical professionals, all of which have been trained to treat drug dependency,
    　　　　　　　　　　　　　　　　　A　　　　　　　　　　　B
    attended the annual convention sponsored by the Society to Prevent Drug Abuse.
    　　C　　　　　　　　　　　D

III: READING COMPREHENSION AND VOCABULARY

(60 Questions—45 Minutes)

Part A

Directions. Each problem in this part of the test consists of a sentence in which one word or phrase has been underlined. From the four choices given, you should choose the one word or phrase which could be substituted for the underlined word or phrase without changing the meaning of the sentence. Mark your choice on the answer sheet.

Example

The frown on the man's face showed that he was displeased.

(A) look of fear
(B) look of anger
(C) look of delight
(D) look of surprise

The best answer is (B).

1. When the eye of the hurricane passed over, there was a lull in the storm.

    (A) fresh outburst
    (B) calm interval
    (C) rise in the wind
    (D) freshening

2. The officer compelled the suspect to wait at the scene of the crime.

    (A) allowed
    (B) hired
    (C) beseeched
    (D) forced

3. The young man was so bashful that he did not speak to the pretty girl.

    (A) haughty
    (B) discreet
    (C) shy
    (D) upset

4. He will abide by his promise if he gives it.

    (A) allow for
    (B) renege on
    (C) renew
    (D) stick to

5. The rock was poised on the edge of the cliff.

    (A) balanced
    (B) dangling
    (C) rolling
    (D) perpendicular

6. The Civil Defense evacuated all inhabitants from the area where the storm was predicted to strike.

    (A) aided
    (B) warned
    (C) notified
    (D) removed

7. The student revised his paper carefully, following the professor's suggestions.

    (A) copied
    (B) retyped
    (C) corrected
    (D) outlined

8. We will wind up our business on Friday and take the weekend off.

    (A) discuss
    (B) continue
    (C) conclude
    (D) detail

9. The water trickled over the edge of the basin.

    (A) poured rapidly
    (B) dripped steadily
    (C) rushed
    (D) flooded

10. The judge sentenced the convicted man.

    (A) passed judgment upon
    (B) sympathized with
    (C) gave a pardon to
    (D) gave high praise to

11. The characters in this novel are fictitious.

    (A) symbolic
    (B) believable
    (C) not real people
    (D) identifiable

12. At the battle of Waterloo, Napoleon's forces retreated.

    (A) attacked
    (B) pursued

(C) withdrew
(D) intercepted

13. To everyone but the expert, the painting's defects were <u>invisible</u>.

 (A) unable to be heard
 (B) unable to be seen
 (C) unable to be understood
 (D) unable to be touched

14. The child <u>groped</u> for the light switch.

 (A) reached confidently
 (B) stretched up
 (C) searched blindly
 (D) listened attentively

15. The war ended when the <u>armistice</u> was signed.

 (A) nomination
 (B) charter
 (C) truce
 (D) contract

16. The patient handed the doctor his <u>fee</u>.

 (A) medicine
 (B) money
 (C) bag
 (D) instrument

17. The driver tried to <u>avert</u> the accident by bringing the car to a sudden stop.

 (A) cause
 (B) control
 (C) minimize
 (D) prevent

18. The warmth of the room made the student <u>doze</u>.

 (A) yawn widely
 (B) sweat profusely
 (C) fall asleep
 (D) faint

19. When he heard the news, he was overcome with <u>grief</u>.

 (A) sorrow
 (B) rage
 (C) terror
 (D) emotion

20. At first, the incident seemed to be <u>trivial</u>.

 (A) significant
 (B) momentous
 (C) unimportant
 (D) critical

21. The proposed environmental amendment has not yet been <u>ratified</u> by all fifty states.

 (A) debunked
 (B) approved
 (C) skimmed
 (D) judged

22. Hurricanes often <u>devastate</u> the coffee crop, Haiti's principal export.

 (A) fracture
 (B) scatter
 (C) destroy
 (D) fertilize

23. It is vital to recognize that emotions <u>trigger</u> physiological reactions—and vice versa.

 (A) blunt
 (B) activate
 (C) encounter
 (D) mask

24. The <u>rivalry</u> between the two construction companies was obvious.

 (A) competition
 (B) cooperation
 (C) compromise
 (D) campaign

25. His qualifications for the graduate assistantship are <u>indisputable</u>.

 (A) fraudulent
 (B) invalid

(C) outstanding
(D) unquestionable

26. The <u>collapse</u> of the stock market in 1929 signaled the beginning of the Depression.

(A) rise
(B) failure
(C) rebirth
(D) debt

27. Since federal funds have been <u>reduced</u>, a state program is needed to help landowners improve their forest lands.

(A) cut off
(B) cut back
(C) put off
(D) put back

28. Her style of dress <u>accentuated</u> her extreme slenderness.

(A) betrayed
(B) disfigured
(C) emphasized
(D) revealed

29. The price of gold <u>fluctuates</u> daily.

(A) increases
(B) changes
(C) stabilizes
(D) decreases

30. The Center for Disease Control reported that the epidemic of the viral disease called acute hemorrhagic conjunctivitis shows no signs of <u>abating</u>.

(A) spreading
(B) recurring
(C) worsening
(D) subsiding

Part B

Directions. You will be given a series of different types of reading material (sentences, short paragraphs, advertisements, etc.). Each selection is followed by questions about the

meaning of the material. You are to choose the one best answer to each question from the four choices given.

Read the following sample passage.

(1) Marianne Moore was born in St. Louis in 1887 and graduated from Bryn Mawr College in 1909. She taught stenography for a few years and then worked as a librarian in New York. She was a
(5) member of the editorial staff of the famous literary magazine *The Dial* from 1925 to 1929. Although a book of her poems, titled *Observations*, was published in America in 1924, Miss Moore has only recently received the full acclaim
(10) she deserves.

Example 1

When did Miss Moore graduate from college?

(A) 1887
(B) 1909
(C) 1925
(D) 1924

The passage says that Miss Moore graduated from Bryn Mawr in 1909. Therefore, you should choose answer (B).

Example 2

The one profession *not* mentioned as being pursued by Miss Moore is that of

(A) poet.
(B) teacher.
(C) scientist.
(D) librarian.

The passage mentions that Miss Moore taught stenography, worked as a librarian, and wrote poetry. Therefore, you should choose (C) as the best completion of the sentence.

As soon as you understand the directions, begin work on the problems.

Questions 31–33

The surprisingly abundant life of the Black Sea is confined to the upper layers; the deeper and especially the bottom waters are devoid of oxygen and are often permeated with hydrogen sulfide.

31. The Black Sea waters

    (A) are devoid of life.
    (B) are always permeated with hydrogen sulfide.
    (C) have life only in the upper layers.
    (D) have life only in the lower layers.

32. The sentence suggests that

    (A) observers are surprised at how little life exists in the Black Sea.
    (B) hydrogen sulfide is necessary to life.
    (C) oxygen is necessary to life.
    (D) both oxygen and hydrogen sulfide are necessary to life.

33. The bottom waters of the Black Sea

    (A) have no oxygen.
    (B) have large amounts of oxygen.
    (C) have little oxygen.
    (D) have no hydrogen sulfide.

Questions 34–35

(1) Though reluctant now to accept constitutional changes, the American shows himself ready enough to accept changes in more unyielding realms: the church for example, or class relation-
(5) ships, or higher education.

34. The above sentence implies that Americans

    (A) have always been, and still are, ready to accept constitutional changes.
    (B) have always been slow to accept change of any sort.
    (C) are finally ready to accept constitutional changes.
    (D) are less ready to accept constitutional changes today than they have been in the past.

35. The sentence states that Americans are more willing to change

    (A) the church than higher education.
    (B) class relationships than the Constitution.

    (C) class relationships than the church.
    (D) the Constitution than class relationships.

Questions 36–41 refer to the following weather report.

(1) **Chance of Showers**
     Forecast for Today

The following forecast was issued Saturday night for Baton Rouge and vicinity.
(5) It will be partly cloudy through Monday with a chance of afternoon showers. High Sunday and Monday will be in the mid 80s, with a low Sunday night in the upper 60s. Winds will be southeasterly 10 to 15 miles per hour diminishing at night.
(10) Probability of rain will be 20 percent Sunday.
On the coast, winds will be southeasterly 10 to 15 knots. Seas will run 2–4 feet. Winds and seas will be 3 feet higher near a few thundershowers. High tide at 1 p.m., low tide at 12:24 a.m.
(15) Record high for May 22 was 93 posted in 1956 and record low was 51 recorded in 1954. Normally, temperatures should vary from 86 to 65 degrees.
There will be scattered afternoon thundershowers Tuesday and over the west portion of the state
(20) Thursday. Tuesday through Thursday, lows will be in the mid to upper 70s, with highs in the mid to upper 80s.
High Saturday was 86, with a low of 65.

36. This weather forecast probably appeared in a

    (A) Saturday morning paper.
    (B) Sunday morning paper.
    (C) Sunday evening paper.
    (D) Monday morning paper.

37. This forecast predicts that

    (A) records will be broken.
    (B) there will be no rain in the forecasted period.
    (C) skies will be partially cloudy on Sunday and Monday.
    (D) temperatures will be lower than normal for the time of year.

38. This forecast states that winds

    (A) will be from south to west.
    (B) will decrease their velocity when associated with thundershowers at sea.

(C) will decrease their velocity at night.
(D) will be from a different direction on the coast than in the city.

39. High tides will occur

(A) early in the morning.
(B) late at night.
(C) at 1:00 p.m.
(D) at 12:24 a.m.

40. On the day this forecast was issued, the lowest temperature reached was

(A) 65 degrees.
(B) 51 degrees.
(C) in the upper 60s.
(D) in the mid to upper 70s.

41. If you were planning to play an outdoor game during this period, you should

(A) reschedule the game for better weather.
(B) plan the game for the afternoon.
(C) plan the game for the morning hours.
(D) plan the game for the evening hours.

Questions 42–44

(1)   Output per man-hour has been growing over a long term at an increasing rate. During most of the world's history, productivity grew very slowly indeed, or probably not at all. During the first
(5) half of the nineteenth century, productivity per man-hour in the U.S. may have increased as much as twenty-five percent. In the second half of the century it doubled, and in the first half of the twentieth century it almost trebled. But this
(10) long-run tendency for productivity to rise at an increasing rate is marked by variations in the rate of increase. Thus, during the last hundred years there have been two periods, 1870 or 1880 to about 1910, and 1920 to the present, when growth
(15) in productivity has been rather rapid, and two periods, 1850 to about 1870 or 1880, and 1910 to 1920, when growth has been somewhat slower.

42. The rate of increase for productivity

(A) has been slow, but steady.
(B) has been uniform.
(C) has always been rapid.
(D) has shown frequent variations.

43. In the 1860's, productivity

(A) did not grow at all.
(B) grew particularly rapidly.
(C) grew faster than in 1850 or 1870.
(D) continued to grow, but at a slower rate than the rate after 1880.

44. The first real increase in output per man-hour occurred

(A) from 1800 to 1850.
(B) from 1850 to 1900.
(C) from 1900 to 1950.
(D) after 1950.

Questions 45–49

(1)   The "taint of melancholy" which Edgar Allan Poe throughout his life associated with the more "soulful" aspects of beauty was, of course, one of the familiar moods of romantics everywhere. But
(5) it is somewhat unusual that this particular mood should be so favored by Southern poets. From the defiant anguish reminiscent of Byron to the delicate sadness characteristic of female poets like Mrs. Felicia Hemans, the whole range of melan-
(10) choly feeling could be found in the pages of the *Messenger* during the 1830's. This is not to say that the magazine published only the poems of Southern poetasters who invoked melancholy. The significant point is that the Southern poets
(15) whom the *Messenger* did publish were prone to exploit melancholy. Poems on Poe's favorite subject, the death of a beautiful woman, were numerous enough in the *Messenger* to make us feel some retroactive concern about the durability
(20) of Southern belles.

45. Most poetry published in the South

(A) was cheerful in mood.
(B) was melancholy.

(C) did not reflect one of the familiar moods of the romantics.

(D) was written by Edgar Allan Poe.

46. Poe had a preference for poems that dealt with

(A) the death of a child.
(B) Byronic despair.
(C) Southern belles.
(D) the death of a beautiful woman.

47. The author implies that Southern belles

(A) may often have been delicately sad.
(B) may often have died young.
(C) may have written many poems.
(D) may have lived very melancholy lives.

48. The *Messenger* published

(A) only melancholy poems.
(B) only female poets.
(C) only Southern poets who wrote melancholy poems.
(D) many poems about death.

49. The words *reminiscent of* (line 7) mean most nearly

(A) prominent in.
(B) recalling.
(C) absent in.
(D) favored by.

Questions 50–53

(1) In the early nineteenth century Rousseau's misgivings concerning the progress of civilization were largely forgotten, but his idea of tracing the evolution of human nature from brute-like begin-
(5) nings took hold with a vengeance. Theories of social evolution proliferated like mushrooms. The impetus to their elaboration came less from biology than from a growing awareness of change and improvement in social institutions and a
(10) growing conviction that man's early condition had been a savage one. Taking progress for granted, social scientists endeavored to discover its laws and stages. Auguste Comte, for example, set for "social physics" (or sociology, as he later called

(15) it) the task of discovering "by what necessary chain of successive transformations the human race, starting from a condition barely superior to that of a society of great apes, has been gradually led up to the present stage of European civiliza-
(20) tion." Like Rousseau, Comte regarded man as the only species of animal capable of evolution.

50. The growth of theories of social evolution is compared to the growth of mushrooms because

(A) mushrooms grow in the dark.
(B) mushrooms grow and multiply very rapidly.
(C) mushrooms can be poisonous.
(D) mushrooms are searched for with great care.

51. Sociology was first known as

(A) social science.
(B) Comtism.
(C) social philosophy.
(D) social physics.

52. Rousseau believed

(A) in the inevitability of progress.
(B) that man was the only creature capable of evolution.
(C) that all of nature (animals, plants, and men) was constantly evolving.
(D) that the science of sociology would promote social evolution.

53. Theories of social evolution proliferated because of

(A) advances in biology.
(B) the belief, with Rousseau, that man's condition was showing no real improvement.
(C) respect for Rousseau as a social thinker and philosopher.
(D) the conviction that man's beginnings had been brute-like, but that his condition was showing steady improvement.

Questions 54–56

(1)   William Faulkner of Oxford was not a native of Oxford; nor was he born with the name Faulkner. He was born in New Albany, Mississippi, on September 25, 1897, and the family spelled the
(5) name Falkner. He published his first book when he was twenty-seven. He was awarded the Nobel Prize for Literature when he was fifty-three. He was generally acknowledged as the major American writer of his time when he died on July 6,
(10) 1962. Faulkner or Falkner, he spent almost the whole of his life in the Mississippi town which millions who read his works know not as Oxford but as Jefferson. Even to the people of Oxford, Faulkner was a kind of legend in his own lifetime.
(15) There was, for example, the mystery of who put the "u" in William's last name. For many years the commonly accepted story was that it was a careless printer, in setting type for *The Marble Faun* (1924). Faulkner biographer Carvel Collins
(20) demonstrates that the writer himself added it, and, at least occasionally, as early as 1918.

54.   At the time of his death, Faulkner was

(A)   twenty-seven.
(B)   fifty-three.
(C)   sixty-two.
(D)   sixty-four.

55.   Faulkner lived most of his life in

(A)   Jefferson.
(B)   Oxford.
(C)   New Albany.
(D)   his birthplace.

56.   The "u" in Faulkner's name was added by

(A)   a careless printer.
(B)   Faulkner's biographer Carvel Collins.
(C)   Faulkner himself.
(D)   Faulkner's great-grandfather.

Questions 57–58

Directions. For each of the following questions, choose the answer whose *meaning is closest* to that of the given sentence. Although more than one of the choices may be factually correct, you should choose the one that *most closely restates the original sentence.*

57.   "American uniformity" is an axiom for many Europeans, before and beyond any experience.

(A)   Many Europeans believe in "American uniformity" even before they come to America.
(B)   Many Europeans are more convinced of "American uniformity" after they have been to America.
(C)   Many Europeans believe so strongly in "American uniformity" that no experience can alter their belief.
(D)   The European is clearly correct in his belief in "American uniformity," since that belief is supported by his experience.

58.   Although El Greco's work was popular in Spain, it had little or no effect, strange to say, on the work of other Spanish painters.

(A)   El Greco's work had some effect, although not much, on the painting of other artists.
(B)   It is strange that in spite of its popularity in Spain, El Greco's work did not have much influence on other Spanish painters' work.
(C)   Other Spanish artists did not particularly like El Greco's work, although his work was influential.
(D)   The work of other Spanish painters was strangely influenced by the work of El Greco, a popular painter.

59.   Mars, which lies beyond Earth, is considerably smaller than Venus and is much farther away.

(A)   Mars, which lies beyond Earth, is much farther away and a good bit smaller than Venus.
(B)   Venus, which is a good bit larger than Mars, is much farther away from Earth.

(C) Venus is much farther away from Mars than from Earth, which is considerably smaller.

(D) Lying beyond Earth, Mars is much smaller than Venus, which is much farther away.

60. Greek literature is no exception to the rule that poetry develops before literary prose.

(A) Usually poetry develops before literary prose, except in the case of Greek literature.

(B) In Greece, literary prose developed before poetry.

(C) Greek literature is the exception to the rule that literary prose precedes poetry.

(D) The development of poetry and prose in Greece conforms to the rule that poetry precedes the development of literary prose.

Test 6—Answer Key

I: LISTENING COMPREHENSION

Part A

1.	C	6.	C	11.	A	16.	B
2.	D	7.	B	12.	D	17.	C
3.	A	8.	D	13.	D	18.	A
4.	A	9.	C	14.	B	19.	A
5.	A	10.	C	15.	B	20.	C

Part B

21.	D	26.	C	31.	B
22.	B	27.	C	32.	C
23.	D	28.	C	33.	D
24.	A	29.	B	34.	D
25.	D	30.	A	35.	D

Part C

36.	C	41.	D	46.	C
37.	A	42.	D	47.	A
38.	A	43.	B	48.	B
39.	A	44.	B	49.	C
40.	B	45.	A	50.	B

II: STRUCTURE AND WRITTEN EXPRESSION

Part A

1.	D	6.	B	11.	A
2.	B	7.	D	12.	D
3.	A	8.	C	13.	A
4.	A	9.	A	14.	D
5.	C	10.	B	15.	A

Part B

16.	C	25.	C	34.	B
17.	C	26.	B	35.	A
18.	C	27.	B	36.	C
19.	B	28.	C	37.	A
20.	D	29.	C	38.	C
21.	A	30.	C	39.	C
22.	D	31.	C	40.	A
23.	A	32.	A		
24.	D	33.	B		

III: READING COMPREHENSION AND VOCABULARY

Part A

1.	B	11.	C	21.	B
2.	D	12.	C	22.	C
3.	C	13.	B	23.	B
4.	D	14.	C	24.	A
5.	A	15.	C	25.	D
6.	D	16.	B	26.	B
7.	C	17.	D	27.	B
8.	C	18.	C	28.	C
9.	B	19.	A	29.	B
10.	A	20.	C	30.	D

Part B

31.	C	41.	C	51.	D
32.	C	42.	D	52.	B
33.	A	43.	D	53.	D
34.	D	44.	A	54.	D
35.	B	45.	B	55.	B
36.	B	46.	D	56.	C
37.	C	47.	B	57.	C
38.	C	48.	D	58.	B
39.	C	49.	B	59.	A
40.	A	50.	B	60.	D

TEST 6—Explanatory Answers

II: Structure and Written Expression

1. An earthquake is a shaking of the ground _____ when masses of rock beneath the surface of the earth change position.
   (This sentence is made complete by the addition of an adjective clause after the word *ground*.)

   (A) *which occurring*   A clause contains a finite verb. *Occurring* is not a finite verb.

   (B) *it occurs*   This choice is not an adjective clause. If the word *it* were changed to *which*, the choice would then be correct.

   (C) *and therefore occurring*   *And therefore* would make sense only if followed by a subject and a finite verb.

   (D) *that occurs*   CORRECT ANSWER

2. Nervous about flying in planes, _____.
   (The sentence is completed by the addition of an independent clause beginning with a noun which tells *who* was nervous about flying in planes.)

   (A) *thirty years ago people knew nothing of space travel*   This answer is an independent clause, but the noun *years* does not tell *who* was nervous about flying in planes.

   (B) *people knew nothing of space travel thirty years ago*   CORRECT ANSWER

   (C) *space travel was unknown by people thirty years ago*   This sentence contains a misplaced modifier. See 2(A) above.

   (D) *because people knew nothing of space travel thirty years ago*   The word *because* introduces a dependent clause. An independent clause is needed to complete this sentence.

3. _____, authorities allow about one ton to each foot of length.
   (An introductory phrase or dependent clause is used to modify the subject of the main clause, which is *authorities*.)

   (A) *To calculate the weight of an average adult whale*   CORRECT ANSWER

   (B) *They calculate the weight of an average adult whale*   This group of words, which constitutes an independent clause, will not be correct unless it is followed by a semicolon or a period.

222

| (C) | *In the calculation the weight of an average adult whale* | This group of words lacks a necessary word. Because the calculation relates to the weight of the whale, the word *of* should be placed immediately after the word *calculation*. |
| (D) | *Even though they calculate the weight of an average adult whale* | This choice is grammatically correct; however, *even though* indicates a contrast and therefore does not fit into this particular statement. |

4. Pictures _____ with a telescope are inverted.
(This sentence is made complete by the addition of a modifying word such as a past participle.)

(A)	*taken*	CORRECT ANSWER
(B)	*they took them*	This answer is an independent clause which creates a grammatically incorrect sentence.
(C)	*to take*	The complete infinitive *to take* does not make sense in the sentence.
(D)	*are taken*	The finite verb *are* is not a modifying word. If *are* is omitted, this choice is correct.

5. _____ the exception of institutions controlled by church, municipal, or private corporations, Latin American universities are regulated by federal laws.
(The correct choice of preposition makes this sentence complete.)

(A)	*By*	*By* is an incorrect choice of preposition.
(B)	*For*	According to correct grammatical usage, *for* is an incorrect choice of preposition. *With the exception of* is a phrasal preposition which must be memorized.
(C)	*With*	CORRECT ANSWER
(D)	*To*	*To* is an incorrect choice of preposition.

6. _____, Harry S. Truman was our nation's thirty-third President.
(This sentence is complete as it stands, but an introductory phrase modifying the subject can be added.)

(A)	*He was born and raised in Missouri*	This choice is an independent clause rather than a modifying phrase.
(B)	*Born and raised in Missouri*	CORRECT ANSWER
(C)	*Because he was born and raised in Missouri*	*Because* introduces a dependent clause of reason and therefore makes no sense in this sentence.
(D)	*That he was born and raised in Missouri*	This group of words is a noun clause. A noun clause must be followed immediately by a finite verb.

7. In Austria, where fertile farmland is limited, crops _____.
(A finite verb followed by sentence parts in the correct order is needed to complete this sentence.)

(A)	*are on the sides of mountains often grown*	The order of the words in this choice is grammatically incorrect.
(B)	*often are on the sides of mountains grown*	*Often* is a frequency adverb like *usually, always, seldom, never, sometimes,* etc. Frequency adverbs are placed after the verb *to be.*
(C)	*are grown on the sides often of mountains*	This choice would be correct if the word *often* were placed after the finite verb *are.*
(D)	*are often grown on the sides of mountains*	CORRECT ANSWER

8. _____ pollution control measures are expensive, many industries hesitate to adopt them.
(This sentence is made complete by the addition of a word showing reason.)

(A)	*Although*	This choice is grammatically correct, but *although* indicates contrast rather than reason.
(B)	*However*	*However* must occur *between* two independent clauses. In addition, *however* indicates contrast.
(C)	*Because*	CORRECT ANSWER
(D)	*On account of*	This choice is incorrect because *on account of* must be followed by a noun or noun phrase rather than by a clause.

9. Racial violence erupted throughout the United States _____ Martin Luther King, Jr., was assassinated in April, 1968.
(This sentence requires an adverb of time to connect the two clauses which make up the statement.)

(A)	*when*	CORRECT ANSWER
(B)	*during*	*During* must be followed by a noun phrase rather than by a clause, which contains a subject and a finite verb.
(C)	*each time that*	This time expression may introduce a clause, but since the expression refers to something that happens more than once, it makes no sense in this sentence.
(D)	*then*	*Then* is a transitional connective which relates to time. If *then* is placed between the two clauses as they are written, the logical time sequence of events is reversed. Furthermore, *then* must be preceded by a semicolon or a period to avoid a comma splice error.

10. Francis Ford Coppola, who conceived, co-authored, and _____ *God-father II*, is one of America's most talented filmmakers.
(A finite verb in the past tense to parallel the other two past tense verbs makes this sentence complete.)

(A)	*director of*	This choice would not be parallel because *director of* is not a verb.
(B)	*directed*	CORRECT ANSWER
(C)	*he directed*	A subject is unnecessary before the verb *directed*. If *he* is omitted, this choice is correct.
(D)	*directing*	*Directing* is not a finite verb.

11. _____ is called erosion.
(A subject placed immediately before the finite verb *is* makes this sentence complete.)

(A)	*The wearing away of land*	CORRECT ANSWER
(B)	*When land wears away*	This group of words, a dependent clause, should be followed immediately by an independent clause, which contains a subject and a finite verb.
(C)	*Land which wears away*	This choice would give incorrect information. The land itself is not called erosion, but rather the process of the wearing away of the land.
(D)	*Wearing away land*	See 11(C) above.

12. _____, they continue to overeat and to eat the wrong foods.
(An introductory clause of contrast correctly completes this sentence.)

(A)	*However many overweight people realize that they are threatening their health*	*However* must stand between two independent clauses which are separated by a semicolon or by a period, rather than by a comma.
(B)	*Many overweight people realizing that they are threatening their health*	This choice would be correct if it were followed immediately by a finite verb, rather than by a subject and a finite verb.
(C)	*Because of the fact that many overweight people realize that they are threatening their health*	This answer is grammatically correct, but *because of the fact that* introduces a clause of reason rather than a clause of contrast.
(D)	*Even though many overweight people realize that they are threatening their health*	CORRECT ANSWER

13. Firstborn children in a family seem to have a stronger desire to succeed _____.
(This sentence is completed by the addition of a clause of comparison.)

(A)	*than do later-born children*	CORRECT ANSWER
(B)	*but later-born children do*	*But* shows contrast rather than comparison

(C) *as children born later*   *As* is used only in a simple comparison.

(D) *if later-born children do*   *If* shows condition rather than comparison.

14. Although the gall bladder is absent from all common members of the deer family, _____.
(An independent clause is needed to complete this sentence.)

   (A) *but the Asiatic musk deer has this organ*   The word *but* is unnecessary in this choice.

   (B) *this organ found in the Asiatic musk deer*   This choice is incorrect because it lacks a finite verb.

   (C) *however this organ is found in the Asiatic musk deer*   *However* is an unnecessary word in this choice.

   (D) *this organ is found in the Asiatic musk deer.*   CORRECT ANSWER

15. _____, we drove the horses into the stable.
(An introductory phrase modifying the subject is used to complete the sentence.)

   (A) *Aware that a tornado was brewing*   CORRECT ANSWER

   (B) *Because a tornado brewing*   This choice would be correct if the finite verb *was* were placed before *brewing*.

   (C) *Although a tornado was brewing*   This choice is grammatically correct, but *although* indicates contrast. If *although* were changed to *because,* the choice would be correct.

   (D) *A tornado was brewing*   This choice is an independent clause. The second part of the sentence is also an independent clause, and two independent clauses may not be separated by a comma.

16. (C) Change *monitor* to *monitoring* since the preposition *after* must be followed by a gerund.

17. (C) Omit *do,* since a noun clause used as the object of a preposition is not written in question form.

18. (C) Change *slow* to *slowly.* An adverb is needed to tell how children develop. *Slow* is an adjective.

19. (B) The definite article must be placed before *United States.* The correction would be *the United States.* In English, most countries' names having two words or more are used with the definite article *the.* Single-word names omit the definite article.

20. (D) Since *all* refers to a plural noun, you must use *kinds* rather than *kind.*

21. (A) Since you are speaking of history in general, omit the definite article *the.*

22. (D) The word *it* is unnecessary and therefore should be eliminated.

23. (A) The word *to* is incorrect here. In English, the correct expression is *capable of.*

24. (D) Since *apples* is used as a noun modifier, it should be singular. Change *apples* to *apple*.

25. (C) The pronoun *it* should be placed after the verb *called* because a necessary object has been omitted.

26. (B) An adjective is needed here. Change the noun *danger* to *dangerous*, an adjective.

27. (B) Change *feet* to *foot*. A prenominal modifier must occur in the singular. Note that in the same question *mountain*, used as an adjective before the noun *climbers*, is singular.

28. (C) *Another* refers only to singular nouns. Change *another* to *others*.

29. (C) *Convince* is followed by an object and the complete infinitive. Change *allow* to *to allow*.

30. (C) Since the improvements mentioned in this sentence occurred in the past, the present verb *have* should be changed to the past verb *had*.

31. (C) Because the subject of the sentence is *one*, a singular word, the verb should also be singular. Change *have been* to *has been*.

32. (A) This choice contains an error in word order. *Now active* modifies *disease;* because modifiers should be placed close to the words they describe, change the sentence to read *now active in this country*.

33. (B) The choice of words is incorrect in this answer. Change *considerate* to *considerable*.

34. (B) This statement concerns the past. Change *springs,* a present tense verb, to *sprang,* a past tense verb.

35. (A) A word indicating ownership is needed. Change *which its* to *whose*.

36. (C) A past participle rather than a present participle makes this sentence correct. Change *lodging* to *lodged*.

37. (A) The definite article *the* may not be used before the word *most* when it means *the majority of*. Omit the word *the*.

38. (C) Since *cars* is a countable noun, change *the amount* to *the number*. *The amount* is used only for noncountable nouns.

39. (C) The preposition *in* has been incorrectly used. Change *in* to *on* since both the month and the day have been given.

40. (A) *Professionals* refers to people. Change *all of which* to *all of whom*.

III: READING COMPREHENSION AND VOCABULARY

Part A

Following are explanations of questions 1–30. In this section, the correct answers are placed first, so that they can be used to help explain the other choices.

1. (B) CORRECT: A <u>lull</u> in a storm is a *calm interval* (an *interval* is a "period of time").

(A)	A *fresh outburst* would be a period of renewed activity.
(C)	A *rise in the wind* would mean that the wind increased in speed and force.
(D)	*Freshening* here would also mean "an increase in strength."

2. **(D) CORRECT:** *Forced* and compelled are synonyms.
   (A)   *Allowed* would mean "permitted," but not compelled.
   (B)   *Hired* would mean that the suspect was paid "to wait."
   (C)   *Beseeched* means "begged; implored."

3. **(C) CORRECT:** *Shy* and bashful both mean "to shrink from notice."
   (A)   *Haughty* would mean "proud; arrogant."
   (B)   *Discreet* would mean "prudent; self-restrained."
   (D)   *Upset* would mean "distressed; disturbed."

4. **(D) CORRECT:** To *stick to* a promise is to abide by it or "to keep it."
   (A)   To *allow for* something means "to make a provision for."
   (B)   To *renege on* a promise is "to fail to carry it out," the opposite of abiding by it.
   (C)   To *renew* here would mean "to promise again."

5. **(A) CORRECT:** Poised means *balanced.*
   (B)   *Dangling* would mean "hanging." It would be followed by the preposition "from," not "on."
   (C)   *Rolling* would mean "rocking or swaying from side to side" or "moving forward by repeatedly turning over."
   (D)   *Perpendicular* would mean "vertical; upright."

6. **(D) CORRECT:** In this context, *evacuated* means *removed.*
   (A)   *Aided* means "helped."
   (B)   *Warned* means "cautioned; notified in advance."
   (C)   *Notified* here means "told."

7. **(C) CORRECT:** In this context, *corrected* can be substituted for revised.
   (A)   *Copied* would simply mean "duplicated" with no suggestion of change.
   (B)   *Retyped* would mean "typed for a second time."
   (D)   *Outlined* here would mean "made a preliminary draft or plan."

8. **(C) CORRECT:** Wind up and *conclude* both mean "to finish."
   (A)   *Discuss* means "to talk about."
   (B)   *Continue* means "to keep on; not to stop."
   (D)   Here, *detail* is a verb that means "to tell or spell out item by item."

9. **(B) CORRECT:** *Dripped steadily* has the meaning closest to trickled here.
   (A)   *Poured rapidly* suggests a speed not suggested by trickled.

(C)   *Rushed* also suggests speed.

(D)   In this context, *flooded* would also suggest large amounts of water moving at great speed.

10. (A) CORRECT: *Sentenced* means *passed judgment upon.*

(B)   *Sympathized with* here would mean that the judge "shared or understood" the convicted man's feelings.

(C)   *Gave a pardon to* would mean that the judge "freed the man from punishment."

(D)   *Gave high praise to* would mean that the judge "expressed his admiration" for the man.

11. (C) CORRECT: In novels, *people* who are *not real* may be said to be fictitious.

(A)   *Symbolic* would mean that the characters represented or stood for a particular idea or concept "by reason of association or convention."

(B)   *Believable* would mean that the characters in the novel are "realistically presented."

(D)   *Identifiable* would mean here that the characters in the novel could be "recognized as depictions of real people."

12. (C) CORRECT: *Retreated* and *withdrew* are synonyms here.

(A)   *Attacked* would mean almost the opposite of retreated, "set upon" rather than "withdrew from" the enemy.

(B)   *Pursued* would mean "followed, with the intention of overtaking and capturing."

(D)   *Intercepted* is a transitive verb and therefore must be followed by an object.

13. (B) CORRECT: *Invisible* means *unable to be seen.*

(A)   *Unable to be heard* would be "inaudible."

(C)   *Unable to be understood* would be "incomprehensible."

(D)   *Unable to be touched* would be "intangible."

14. (C) CORRECT: *Groped* means *searched blindly.*

(A)   *Reached confidently* suggests that the child knew exactly where the switch was.

(B)   *Stretched up* suggests that the switch was placed high on the wall.

(D)   *Listened attentively* would make no sense in this context.

15. (C) CORRECT: *Armistice* and *truce* are synonyms.

(A)   A *nomination* is "the act of appointing a person to office."

(B)   A *charter* would be a "written instrument given as evidence of agreement, transfer, or contract; deed."

(D)   A *contract* is an "agreement between two or more parties to do or not to do a certain thing."

16. **(B) CORRECT:** A <u>fee</u> is "*money* paid for professional services."
    (A)   *Medicine* is "a remedy; a substance used in treating a disease."
    (C)   Many doctors do carry a *bag* (a type of briefcase containing their supplies) when visiting patients, but a *bag* is not a <u>fee</u>.
    (D)   An *instrument* would be "an implement" or "a mechanical device."

17. **(D) CORRECT:** *Prevent* and <u>avert</u> are synonyms.
    (A)   *Cause* would mean "to make happen," the opposite of <u>avert</u>.
    (B)   *Control* would mean "to manage or direct."
    (C)   *Minimize* here would mean "to make the accident less serious."

18. **(C) CORRECT:** <u>Doze</u> here means *fall asleep*.
    (A)   *Yawn widely* means "to open the mouth involuntarily to its fullest extent." People yawn when they are sleepy, but yawn does not mean to <u>doze</u>.
    (B)   To "sweat profusely" is "to perspire a great deal." One might sweat in a warm room but to "sweat" does not mean to "doze."
    (D)   To *faint* is "to lose consciousness," but not by the natural process of falling asleep.

19. **(A) CORRECT:** *Sorrow* and "grief" both mean great sadness.
    (B)   *Rage* means "anger," not sorrow.
    (C)   *Terror* means "extreme fear."
    (D)   *Emotion* here would simply mean a strong feeling, not the specific feeling of "grief."

20. **(C) CORRECT:** Trivial means *unimportant* or "insignificant."
    (A)   *Significant* means the opposite of <u>trivial</u>.
    (B)   *Momentous* also means "very important."
    (D)   *Critical* would be "decisive" or "crucial"; hence it would also mean "important."

21. **(B) CORRECT:** In this context, <u>ratified</u> means "approved."
    (A)   *Debunked* would mean "exposed the falseness of."
    (C)   *Skimmed* here would mean "read quickly for the main idea."
    (D)   *Judged* would mean "decided upon" in this context. Of course, the judgment might be to ratify or to reject.

22. **(C) CORRECT:** *Destroy* could be substituted for <u>devastate</u> here. Both mean "to damage beyond repair."
    (A)   To *fracture* is usually used when referring to bones. It means "to break."
    (B)   *Scatter* would mean "to disperse" or "to distribute in all directions."
    (D)   *Fertilize* would mean "to spread or work into the soil some material that would promote growth."

23. **(B) CORRECT:** *Activate* and <u>trigger</u> both mean "to stimulate, initiate, or set off."
    (A) Here, *blunt* would mean "to deaden" or "make less vigorous."
    (C) *Encounter* would mean "to meet."
    (D) *Mask* in this context would mean "to cover up" or "to disguise."

24. **(A) CORRECT:** Here *competition* could be substituted for <u>rivalry</u> without loss of meaning.
    (B) *Cooperation* would mean "willingness to work together."
    (C) *Compromise* would mean "a settlement of differences by each side yielding a little."
    (D) A *campaign* here would be "an operation begun to attain some commercial goal."

25. **(D) CORRECT:** <u>Indisputable</u> and *unquestionable* mean that the matter "cannot be doubted."
    (A) *Fraudulent* means "deceitful."
    (B) *Invalid* means "having no legal force," or "fallacious."
    (C) *Outstanding* in this context would mean "superior."

26. **(B) CORRECT:** Here, *failure* could be substituted for <u>collapse</u>.
    (A) In this context, *rise* would mean "an increase in worth or volume," almost the opposite of <u>collapse</u>.
    (C) A *rebirth* would be a "revival" or "new birth," again, almost the opposite of <u>collapse</u>.
    (D) *Debt* here would mean "money owed."

27. **(B) CORRECT:** *Cut back* in this context means <u>reduced</u>.
    (A) *Cut off* would mean "eliminated completely" here.
    (C) *Put off* would mean "postponed until later."
    (D) *Put back* would mean "replaced."

28. **(C) CORRECT:** <u>Accentuated</u> and *emphasized* both mean "stressed."
    (A) Here, *betrayed* would mean "disclosed something" she wished to conceal.
    (B) *Disfigured* here would mean "made less attractive."
    (D) *Revealed* would mean "made known."

29. **(B) CORRECT:** <u>Fluctuates</u> means *changes*.
    (A) *Increases* would mean that the price of gold "becomes higher."
    (C) *Stabilizes* would mean "becoming resistant to change; maintaining equilibrium."
    (D) *Decreases* would mean that the price of gold "becomes lower."

30. **(D) CORRECT:** Here, both <u>abating</u> and *subsiding* mean "ending."
    (A) *Spreading* would mean "extending over a wider area."
    (B) *Recurring* would mean "happening again."
    (C) *Worsening* would mean "getting more severe."

Part B

31. This question tests for word recognition.

    (A)   The waters contain "abundant life" (line 1). See 31(C)
                   below.
    (B)   Only the "deeper and . . . bottom waters" (lines 2–3)
                   are often (not always) *permeated with hydrogen sulfide.*
    (C) CORRECT: "Confined to" (line 2) in this context means "restricted
                   to" or "only existing in" the upper layers.
    (D)   See 31(C) above.

32. This question tests for the ability to draw inferences.

    (A)   "Surprisingly" (line 1) suggests that life in the Black Sea
                   is *more* abundant than observers might expect.
    (B)   The sentence suggests that hydrogen sulfide may be
                   deadly to life.
    (C) CORRECT: Coming immediately after the assertion in the first main
                   clause that only the upper layers of the Black Sea contain
                   life, the assertion in the second main clause that the
                   bottom waters are devoid of oxygen suggests that the
                   lack of oxygen explains the lack of life.
    (D)   See 32(C) above.

33. This question tests for word recognition.

    (A) CORRECT: "Devoid of" (line 4) in this context means "lacking" or
                   "without" or "empty of." "Waters are devoid of oxy-
                   gen" means "waters lack oxygen."
    (B)   See 33(A) above.
    (C)   See 33(A) above.
    (D)   "Permeated" (line 4) means "saturated," so the bottom
                   waters contain large amounts of hydrogen sulfide.

34. This question tests for the ability to draw inferences.

    (A)   See 34(D) below.
    (B)   They are willing to accept many kinds of changes (lines
                   2–5).
    (C)   They are less ready now than before to accept constitu-
                   tional changes. See 34(D) below.
    (D) CORRECT: "*Though reluctant now* to accept constitutional changes"
                   implies that Americans were more willing to accept such
                   changes in the past than they are now.

35. This question tests for a main idea of the sentence.

    (A)   See 35(B) below.
    (B) CORRECT: The sense of the sentence is that Americans are more
                   willing to accept changes in class relations, or in the
                   church, or in higher education than in the Constitution.
    (C)   See 35(B) above.
    (D)   See 35(B) above.

36. This question tests for attention to detail and for the ability to draw inferences.

(A) See 36(B) below.
(B) CORRECT: The forecast was issued Saturday night, too late for the Saturday morning paper (line 3). The high temperature Sunday "*will be* in the mid 80s" (lines 6–7). The future tense here would have been inappropriate in either the Sunday evening or Monday morning papers.
(C) See 36(B) above.
(D) See 36(B) above.

37. This question tests for attention to detail.

(A) The report neither states nor implies that *records will be broken*. It predicts normal weather for the time of year (lines 16–17, 23).
(B) There is some chance of rain on Sunday, Monday, Tuesday, and Thursday (lines 5–6, 10, 18–20).
(C) CORRECT: The report, issued Saturday night, predicts "partly cloudy" skies "through Monday" (line 5), which means Sunday and Monday.
(D) See 37(A) above.

38. This question tests for attention to detail.

(A) Winds will be "southeasterly" both inland and on the coast (lines 8–9, 11–12), that is, they will blow from the southeast—and therefore *to* the northwest.
(B) Under these conditions, winds will "increase" their velocity (lines 12–13).
(C) CORRECT: "Diminishing at night" (lines 8–9) means "*decreasing* at night."
(D) See 38(A) above.

39. This question tests for attention to detail.

(A) See 39(C) below.
(B) See 39(C) below.
(C) CORRECT: This is clearly stated in lines 13–14.
(D) This is the time of "low" tide (line 14).

40. This question tests for attention to detail.

(A) CORRECT: The forecast was issued Saturday night (line 3), and the lowest temperature Saturday was 65 (line 23).
(B) This is the lowest recorded temperature (recorded in 1954) for the date of May 22 (lines 15–16).
(C) This is the range predicted for the low temperature on Sunday night (lines 7–8).
(D) This is the range predicted for the low temperatures on Tuesday through Thursday (lines 20–21).

41. This question tests for the ability to draw inferences.

    (A)   Temperatures will be moderate during this period, and there will only be occasional rain ("showers") and probably not everywhere—the showers will be "scattered" (line 18).

    (B)   Afternoon rain is predicted for most of the days covered by this forecast (lines 5–6, 18–19).

    (C) CORRECT: Temperatures are likely to be cooler during the mornings, and rain is not predicted for any morning during this period.

    (D)   See 41(B) above.

42. This question tests for the main idea of the paragraph.

    (A)   Through most of history, there was probably no increase in productivity per man-hour (lines 2–4). Since the early nineteenth century, the rate has increased greatly (lines 4–7).

    (B)   See 42(A) above, 42(D) below.

    (C)   See 42(A) above, 42(D) below.

    (D) CORRECT: In the second half of the paragraph (lines 9–17), the author describes the variations in the rate of increase.

43. This question tests for attention to detail.

    (A)   Productivity grew, but at a slower rate than in earlier and later periods (lines 15–17).

    (B)   See 43(A) above, 43(D) below.

    (C)   The paragraph does not contain sufficiently specific information to make these comparisons.

    (D) CORRECT: The rate of increase in productivity continued to grow in the 1860's, but at a slower rate than occurred during the period of growth following 1880. See lines 12–17.

44. This question tests for attention to detail.

    (A) CORRECT: During the first half of the nineteenth century (1800–1850), U.S. productivity per man-hour increased by as much as twenty-five percent (lines 4–7). This is the first increase noted in the paragraph.

    (B)   See 44(A) above.

    (C)   See 44(A) above.

    (D)   There were several significant increases in output per man-hour before 1950. See 44(A) above.

45. This question tests for the main idea of the paragraph.

    (A)   The author suggests that most of the poetry was not cheerful but melancholy.

    (B) CORRECT: This fact is stated or implied in every sentence of the paragraph.

    (C)   The poetry did reflect one of the romantics' familiar moods—melancholy (lines 1–6).

    (D)   This *might* be true—it probably is not—but the paragraph contains no information on this point.

46. This question tests for attention to detail.

    (A)   See 46(D) below.
    (B)   See 46(D) below.
    (C)   See 46(D) below.
    (D) CORRECT: The author states that this was Poe's *favorite* subject for poems (lines 16–17).

47. This question tests for word recognition and for the ability to draw inferences.

    (A)   See 47(B) below.
    (B) CORRECT: "Durability" (line 19) in this context means "ability to endure or to survive." The *Messenger* published so many poems by Southern writers on the subject of the death of a beautiful woman, the author states, that we must wonder whether this unhappy event was a frequent occurrence in the South. We feel concern that "Southern belles" (line 20)—young, attractive, unmarried Southern women—were rarely strong enough to live past their youth.
    (C)   See 47(B) above. The author makes no mention of how many of the poems he discusses were written by Southern women.
    (D)   This is a possible implication of the author's comments, but not the most immediate or obvious one. See 47(B) above.

48. This question tests for attention to detail.

    (A)   Lines 11–13 suggest that the *Messenger* published poems invoking moods other than melancholy.
    (B)   The author does not mention the gender of the poets he discusses, and that they were exclusively female is highly unlikely.
    (C)   See 48(A) above.
    (D) CORRECT: The assertion is clearly presented in lines 14–20.

49. This question tests for word recognition.

    (A)   *Reminiscent* in this context implies that "defiant anguish" is a prominent quality of Byron's work, but the word does not mean "prominent in." See 49(B) below.
    (B) CORRECT: "Defiant anguish" (line 7) in these poems reminds one of—or "recalls"—Byron because this attitude is present in much of his work.
    (C)   See 49(A) and 49(B) above. This is contrary to the sense of the word.
    (D)   See 49(A) and 49(B) above.

50. This question tests for the ability to perceive analogies.

    (A)   This is true, but not the characteristic of mushrooms referred to here. The author is not suggesting that the theories grew in the dark.

(B) CORRECT: "Proliferated" means in this context that the number of such theories increased greatly, as mushrooms increase their numbers quickly.

(C)   See 50(A) and 50(B) above.

(D)   See 50(A) and 50(B) above.

51. This question tests for attention to detail.

(A)   See 51(D) below.

(B)   This term might be used to refer specifically to Comte's theories. See 51(D) below.

(C)   See 51(D) below.

(D) CORRECT: If Comte "later" (line 14) called *social physics* sociology, then "social physics" is an earlier name for "sociology."

52. This question tests for attention to detail.

(A)   He may have believed this, but it is not so stated in the paragraph. That he had "misgivings"(line 2) concerning progress suggests either that he was unsure as to whether it would continue, or that he believed "progress" to bring not only gain but also loss, not only advance, but also regression, and so to be not entirely "progress."

(B) CORRECT: Both Rousseau and Comte believed this (lines 20–21).

(C)   Inconsistent with the correct answer. See 52(B) above.

(D)   The paragraph makes no mention of this point.

53. This question tests for attention to detail.

(A)   The author says that this was *not* the main cause of their proliferation (lines 5–8).

(B)   This idea of Rousseau's had been largely forgotten during the time that these theories proliferated.

(C)   The author does not state this to be the cause of the proliferation.

(D) CORRECT: The author states that these two ideas gave the impetus (the *starting force*) for this proliferation (lines 6–11).

54. This question tests for attention to detail.

(A)   See 54(D) below.

(B)   See 54(D) below.

(C)   See 54(D) below.

(D) CORRECT: Faulkner was born on September 25, 1897, and died on July 6, 1962—that is, about a month and a half before he would have celebrated his sixty-fifth birthday.

55. This question tests for attention to detail.

(A)   This is the name he gave a town that often appears in his writings, and that is a fictional portrayal of Oxford (lines 12–13).

(B) CORRECT: This is stated in lines 10–13.

(C)   This is the town in which he was born (line 3).

(D)   See 55(C) and 55(B) above.

56.   This question tests for attention to detail.

    (A)   This was a commonly accepted but "untrue" story (lines 15–21).

    (B)   Collins showed that Faulkner himself added it (lines 19–21).

    (C) CORRECT: This is stated in lines 20–21.

    (D)   *Faulkner's great-grandfather* is not mentioned in the paragraph.

The following questions test for the sense of the sentences.

57.   (A)   The original makes this assertion, *and more.*

    (B)   This is possibly true, but the statement does not compare Europeans' convictions before and after they have visited America.

    (C) CORRECT: The original statement says that many Europeans hold this conviction so strongly before they visit America, or have any contradictory experience, that no experience can change their belief.

    (D)   This is inconsistent with the original. See 57(C) above.

58.   (A)   The original refers only to Spanish painters, on which El Greco's work had *little or no effect.*

    (B) CORRECT: El Greco's work was popular in Spain, but did not affect in any noticeable way other Spanish painters. His lack of influence on these artists is not what one would expect and is difficult to explain.

    (C)   The original does not say how the artists regarded his work. See 58(B) above.

    (D)   This is contrary, in its main assertion, to the original.

59.   (A) CORRECT: Mars is farther from Earth than Venus, and is smaller than Venus.

    (B)   Mars is farther away.

    (C)   The original does not compare the distance from Venus to Mars and from Venus to Earth, as this sentence does.

    (D)   See 59(B) above.

60.   (A)   Greek literature is *no exception* to the rule; that is, it conforms to the rule.

    (B)   This statement is contrary to the original. See 59(C) below.

    (C)   The rule is that poetry precedes prose. Greek literature conforms to this rule.

    (D) CORRECT: See 59(C) above.

PART III
APPENDIX

Test 1

LISTENING COMPREHENSION SCRIPT

These are the same 50 questions included in Test 1 on pages 21 to 25. The answers for this test are on page 36. Have a friend read you the material in parentheses once only. Be sure to observe the time limit for this test.

Part A

Directions. In this part of the test, you will hear a brief statement. Each statement will be spoken only once. The statement does not appear in your test booklet. When you have heard a statement, select the answer nearest in meaning to what you have heard. Record your answer on the answer sheet.

1. (Mrs. Jones is out of coffee.)

   (A) Mrs. Jones went out to buy coffee.
   (B) Mrs. Jones doesn't have any coffee.
   (C) Mrs. Jones has a great deal of coffee.
   (D) Mrs. Jones has a little coffee.

2. (The question is too important to forget.)

   (A) We must ask the question.
   (B) We must remember the question.
   (C) The question is not important.
   (D) We must try to forget the question.

3. (The woman wanted to keep her accident quiet.)

   (A) The woman wanted to hide her accident.
   (B) The woman wanted to explain her accident to her friends.
   (C) The woman wanted to report her accident.
   (D) The woman wanted to talk about her accident quietly.

4. (I'm going to do away with these clothes.)

   (A) I'm going to wear these clothes.
   (B) I'm going to keep these clothes.
   (C) I'm going to wash these clothes.
   (D) I'm going to discard these clothes.

5. (Bill has no business going to New York next December.)

   (A) Bill went to New York in December.
   (B) Bill runs a business in New York.
   (C) Bill will open a business in New York in December.
   (D) Bill shouldn't go to New York.

6. (The teacher called off the test completely.)

   (A) The teacher gave the test.
   (B) The teacher postponed the test.
   (C) The teacher canceled the test.
   (D) The teacher gave the test orally.

7. (When I told Mark the news, he blew up.)

   (A) Mark became curious.
   (B) Mark became worried.
   (C) Mark became angry.
   (D) Mark became nervous.

8. (The sole survivor of the plane crash was Mary Peters.)

   (A) All of the passengers on the train were killed.
   (B) Mary Peters was the only passenger killed.

(C)   None of the train's passengers were killed.

(D)   Mary Peters was the only passenger not killed in the plane crash.

9.   (The company turned down Bill's offer.)

(A)   The company offered Bill a job.
(B)   The company rejected Bill's offer.
(C)   The company accepted Bill's offer.
(D)   The company discussed Bill's offer.

10.   (Mr. Black makes a living repairing sinks.)

(A)   Mr. Black is a mechanic.
(B)   Mr. Black is a plumber.
(C)   Mr. Black is an electrician.
(D)   Mr. Black is a builder.

11.   (Mary's suggestion to the teacher was out of the question.)

(A)   Mary asked the teacher a question.
(B)   Mary's idea was reasonable.
(C)   Mary's question was off the subject.
(D)   Mary's idea was impossible.

12.   (One way to avoid being robbed is not to advertise your money in a public place like a bank or a store.)

(A)   After you get your money at the bank, go to the store.
(B)   Banks and stores are often robbed.
(C)   Keep your money hidden in public places.
(D)   Keep your money in a bank, not in a store.

13.   (William read ten short stories and a couple of novels during his freshman English course.)

(A)   William must do a lot of reading during his next English course.
(B)   William read some short stories but no novels.
(C)   English is a refreshing course for William to take.
(D)   William read more short stories than novels.

14.   (If your plane leaves at eight, you must arrive thirty minutes ahead of time to check in at the ticket counter.)

(A)   You should buy your ticket at eight.
(B)   The plane departs at eight.
(C)   The plane is arriving at seven-thirty.
(D)   You should go to the ticket counter as soon as the plane leaves.

15.   (In order to cash a check at many banks, one must show a valid driver's license with his photograph on it.)

(A)   Many banks offer photographs to drivers.
(B)   Almost all banks photograph their customers.
(C)   Many banks require customer identification.
(D)   Banks must have a valid license in order to cash checks.

16.   (On their trip to New York, John and Bill took turns driving.)

(A)   The boys took a wrong turn during the trip.
(B)   Bill did most of the driving during the trip.
(C)   John drove Bill to New York.
(D)   The boys divided the driving time.

17.   (The test was difficult to say the least.)

(A)   The test was not the least bit difficult.
(B)   The test was the least difficult of all.
(C)   The test was very difficult.
(D)   The test was as difficult as previous ones.

18.   (The truck is practically as cheap as the van.)

(A)   The van and the truck are the same price.
(B)   The van is more expensive than the truck.
(C)   The truck is as practical as the van.
(D)   The truck is a little more expensive than the van.

19. (Our children are hard on furniture.)

   (A) Our children hardly use the furniture.
   (B) Our children dislike the furniture.
   (C) Our children treat the furniture roughly.
   (D) Our children want us to replace the furniture.

20. (Bill outdoes his brother John in math.)

   (A) Bill surpasses John in math.
   (B) John surpasses Bill in math.
   (C) Bill always does John's math for him.
   (D) John and Bill make the same grades in math.

Part B

   Directions. This section of the Listening Comprehension test consists of fifteen short conversations between two people. When each conversation ends, you will be asked a question by a third voice about what was said. You will hear the question only once and you must choose the answer from the four choices given. When you have chosen what you believe to be the best answer to the question, record your answer on the answer sheet.

21.   (Man)   "I'm sorry, Madam. The train is somewhat behind schedule. Take a seat, and I'll notify you as soon as we know something definite."

   (Woman)   "Thank you. I'll just sit here and read a magazine in the meantime."

   (Third voice)   "What can you conclude about the train from the conversation?"

   (A) The train is crowded.
   (B) The train is late.
   (C) The train is empty.
   (D) The train is on time.

22.   (Man)   "Everyone hide in the next room and when John comes in, jump out."

   (Woman)   "Perhaps we should turn on a few lights so he won't be too suspicious."

   (Third voice)   "What are the people in the conversation most likely planning?"

   (A) A surprise party.
   (B) A picnic.
   (C) A meeting.
   (D) An appointment.

23.   (Man)   "I was terribly embarrassed when some members of the audience got up and left in the middle of the performance."

   (Woman)   "Well, some people just can't seem to appreciate live drama."

   (Third voice)   "What did the people in the conversation attend?"

   (A) A movie.
   (B) A lecture.
   (C) A play.
   (D) A speech.

24.   (Woman)   "My name is Helen Ware. W-A-R-E. Can I get a class card for biology today?"

   (Man)   "Oh, no. Registration for students whose last names begin with "W" doesn't start until tomorrow."

   (Third voice)   "What has happened to the woman?"

   (A) She misplaced her class card for biology.
   (B) She arrived for registration too early.
   (C) She missed registration.
   (D) The man cannot spell her name.

25.   (Man)   "That was such an interesting movie! I hope you enjoyed it as much as I did."

   (Woman)   "I must admit that I dozed off after the first thirty minutes."

(Third voice) "How did the woman in the conversation feel about the movie?"

(A) She found it interesting.
(B) She found it boring.
(C) She found it informative.
(D) She found it enjoyable.

26. (Woman) "During the last thunderstorm, I noticed several leaks in my living room ceiling."

(Man) "Maybe you have some broken shingles. I have the number of a good roofing company."

(Third voice) "What can we conclude from this conversation?"

(A) The woman is afraid of thunderstorms.
(B) The man works for a roofing company.
(C) The roof of the woman's house needs repairing.
(D) The man's roof is leaking.

27. (Man) "I'm in charge of buying the fruit for the children at our church. I'm so happy to find that apples and plums are in season. Give me two dozen of each."

(Woman) "I hope that they're as good as they look."

(Third voice) "How many apples did the man buy?"

(A) 12.
(B) 48.
(C) 36.
(D) 24.

28. (Man) "This is Mr. Jones. My heater is not getting any power and the temperature is going to get down below freezing. Could you come over and fix it?"

(Woman) "This is our busiest time of the year, but I'll speak to one of our men about getting over there sometime today."

(Third voice) "Who has Mr. Jones called to come over?"

(A) A plumber.
(B) An electrician.
(C) A salesman.
(D) A telephone repairman.

29. (Man) "The guests are leaving for New York today on the ten o'clock flight. We need someone to get them to the airport on time."

(Woman) "Ordinarily, I'd be happy to, but my car is in the garage."

(Third voice) "How are the guests going to New York?"

(A) By bus.
(B) By plane.
(C) By car.
(D) By train.

30. (Man) "I want to see about getting a private room as soon as possible. Also, please put a 'No Visitors' sign on my door when you leave."

(Woman) "I'll take care of both things, but first I have to give you an examination so that I can fill out your chart."

(Third voice) "Where is the man in the dialogue?"

(A) In a hotel.
(B) At home.
(C) In a hospital.
(D) In a dentist's office.

31. (Man) "Did you see that fabulous documentary on U.S. hospitals on Channel 4 last night?"

(Woman) "No, I decided to watch the movie on Channel 8 instead. Afterwards, I fell asleep."

(Third voice) "Why did the woman miss the documentary?"

(A) She was at the movies.
(B) She was in bed.
(C) She was in the hospital.
(D) She was watching another channel.

32. (Man) "Have you decided where you are going to live when you get married?"

(Woman) "I would like to live in the city near my work, but my fiancé wants a house in the suburbs to save on expenses."

(Third voice) "Why does the woman want to live in the city?"

(A) Life is less expensive in the city.
(B) Jobs are easier to find in the city.
(C) Her job is in the city.
(D) Living in the suburbs is expensive.

33. (Man) "Would you like to go to the beach this afternoon? Bill and Mary are coming, too."

(Woman) "I'm sorry, but I was just going out shopping. I need to get the blouse that goes with my pants suit. They had to order it, and it just arrived yesterday."

(Third voice) "What is the woman going to buy downtown?"

(A) A newspaper.
(B) A suit.
(C) A coat.
(D) A blouse.

34. (Man) "How did you like the performance?"

(Woman) "Generally speaking, it was very good. The part of the maid was played beautifully, but I thought the man who played the salesman was too dramatic to be realistic."

(Third voice) "How does the woman feel about the salesman in the play?"

(A) The woman thinks the salesman was realistic.
(B) The woman thinks the salesman exaggerated his part.
(C) The woman thinks the salesman was not dramatic enough.
(D) The woman thinks the salesman played his part well.

35. (Man) "I saw your ad in the morning paper concerning some cameras you have on sale. Could I see the X-20 model, please?"

(Woman) "Of course. It's an excellent buy. The price includes the tripod."

(Man) "The lens seems to be excellent and the tripod is not bad. However, the price on this model seems a little steep. Does it include the flash attachment?"

(Third voice) "What does the man dislike about the camera?"

(A) The model.
(B) The lens.
(C) The price.
(D) The flash attachment.

Part C

Directions. In this part of the test, you will be required to listen to several short lectures and conversations. You will hear the lectures and conversations only once. They do not appear in your test booklet. When a question is asked, choose the best answer from the four given. Record your answer on the answer sheet.

Questions 36–38 are based on the following lecture.

Born Cassius Clay in Louisville, Kentucky, in 1942, Muhammad Ali retired from boxing in 1980. As an amateur, he won 100 out of 108 fights. Later, as a professional boxer, Ali was trained by Angelo Dundee, who pushed him on to face champion boxer Sonny Liston in 1964; in this exciting match, Liston was unable to continue the fight after the sixth round.

After winning the championship fight against Liston, Ali announced that he had joined the Black Muslim religion. At the time, the Vietnam War was in progress. When Ali claimed to be a conscientious objector to the war, based on religious grounds, he was denied exemption from military service. Refusing to be inducted into the U.S. Army, he was stripped of his right to box and was given a five-year prison sentence, a conviction that was reversed three years later. Once again able to enter the ring, Muhammad Ali became the first man to win the world's heavyweight boxing title three times.

36. (According to the lecture, what was the result of Ali's 1964 fight against Sonny Liston?)

(A) Liston was claimed winner by decision after only two rounds.
(B) Ali knocked Liston out in the seventh round.
(C) Liston was unable to answer the bell in the ninth round.
(D) Ali was proclaimed champion after six rounds.

37. (What happened to Ali when he refused to enter the United States Army during the Vietnam War?)

(A) He spent five years in prison.
(B) He was accepted into the Black Muslim religious group.
(C) He was denied his boxing rights.
(D) He was immediately exempted from military service.

38. (When did Ali announce that he had become a Black Muslim?)

(A) He announced that he had become a Black Muslim after defeating Liston in a championship fight.
(B) He announced that he had become a Black Muslim while he was still an amateur boxer.
(C) He announced that he had become a Black Muslim after the Vietnam War.
(D) He announced that he had become a Black Muslim when he retired from boxing in 1980.

Questions 39–40 are based on the following lecture.

People usually regard the presence of even a single volcano in their particular geographical region as a cause of great concern. But the inhabitants of the island of Lanzarote live in the shadows of over two hundred volcanoes, most of which now lie sleeping. Lanzarote, one of the Canary Islands belonging to Spain, is located about eighty miles off the western coast of Morocco.

The inhabitants of Lanzarote are known for their courage and adaptability. Their island is an arid, treeless land. But its agricultural output is impressive. Because there is very little rain, farmers use volcanic cinder to capture and retain wetness in the earth. They even dare to plant crops in the desert sand that is a condition of their daily existence. An unusual land, Lanzarote proves man's ability to overcome the obstacles in his natural environment.

Further, Lanzarote provides a unique landscape, which, oddly enough, might be compared to that of the moon. In the past, producers of science-fiction movies have used this interesting island for location shooting for their movies.

39. (According to the speaker, what is the present condition of the volcanoes on Lanzarote?)

(A) The majority of the volcanoes are inactive.
(B) Most of the volcanoes present a threat to the inhabitants of the island.

(C) A great many of the volcanoes are still exploding.
(D) The presence of the volcanoes is making agriculture difficult, if not impossible, on the island.

40. (Which of the following statements contradicts the information given in the lecture?)

(A) Lanzarote's inhabitants are a brave and flexible people.
(B) Lanzarote is a dry land without trees.
(C) Lanzarote's landscape closely parallels that of the moon.
(D) Lanzarote is located off the southern coast of Africa.

Questions 41–45 are based on the following lecture.

One of the most feared occurrences in nature is the tornado. The area most frequently the target of this violent windstorm is the Great Plains, the region extending from the Rockies to the Mississippi, and from Canada down through Texas. When warm, moist air meets with cooler, drier air at low levels, a tornado often occurs. Prior to the formation of the familiar funnel-shaped cloud, the sky is very clear. Then, a black line suddenly appears. As this black area moves in, the fast wind becomes hot and moist and a deep stillness encircles the landscape. Because the air pressure drops steadily during a tornado, breathing becomes difficult. Insects fall to the ground, unable to balance themselves in flight. Suddenly, a black funnel resembling a giant whip dips down out of the sky, destroying what it touches, and then retreats. Although a tornado usually destroys property rather than lives, an average of 120 people die yearly as a result of these violent storms. It is obvious why the tornado is feared throughout the Great Plains.

41. (What is the appearance of the sky just prior to the formation of a tornado?)

(A) The air has a yellowish tinge.
(B) The sky is very dark.
(C) The sky is cloudless.
(D) A red line stretches across the horizon.

42. (What effect does a tornado have on insects?)

(A) They fly above the darkened clouds to safety.
(B) They are unable to navigate.
(C) Their rate of breathing is increased.
(D) They die instantly due to low atmospheric pressure.

43. (On the average, how many people are killed by tornadoes annually?)

(A) 83.
(B) 120.
(C) 300.
(D) 250.

44. (What atmospheric conditions bring about the formation of a tornado?)

(A) Warm, damp air encounters cooler, arid air.
(B) Extremely hot, dry air meets with warm, dry air.
(C) Damp air connects with extremely wet air.
(D) Cold, damp air encounters hot, dry air.

45. (Why does breathing become more difficult for humans just before a tornado strikes?)

(A) They are knocked to the ground.
(B) The wind becomes fast, hot, and humid.
(C) Air pressure gets progressively lower.
(D) The black area moves closer.

Questions 46–50 are based on the following conversation.

Woman: "Good afternoon. Melrose Apartments. May I help you?"

Man: "Yes, I'm interested in renting a one-bedroom apartment. Do you have any available?"

Woman: "No, I'm sorry. None are available at this time, but I expect a vacancy in about three weeks. Could I interest you in a two-bedroom?"

Man: "Well, I'm a student and I have to cut corners. How much more would a two-bedroom apartment cost me?"

Woman: "The one-bedroom rents for $250 a month and the two-bedroom is only $35 more."

Man: "Is the two-bedroom a great deal larger than the one-bedroom?"

Woman: "Yes, it is. Also, I might tell you that the one-bedroom doesn't have a dishwasher. All of our two-bedroom apartments do."

Man: "What about signing a lease?"

Woman: "We do require a six-month lease on all our apartments, and there is a deposit of $100 in case any damage is done to the apartment."

Man: "Is there a pool?"

Woman: "No, I'm sorry, there isn't. We do have a recreation area and a sauna. Also, there are tennis courts adjacent to our building."

Man: "When could I see an apartment?"

Woman: "How about later this afternoon? Let's see. I have an appointment at three-thirty and another one at four. How about five o'clock this afternoon?"

Man: "That would be fine. I'll pick my wife up from work, and we'll come right over."

Woman: "I'll be looking forward to seeing you then."

Man: "Thank you. Good-bye."

Woman: "Good-bye."

46. (What is one thing the apartment building which the woman describes does not have?)

(A) Tennis courts.
(B) A recreation area.
(C) A sauna.
(D) A swimming pool.

47. (If the student decides to rent an apartment from the woman, what will his deposit be?)

(A) One hundred dollars.
(B) Thirty-five dollars.
(C) Fifty dollars.
(D) Two hundred fifty dollars.

48. (Why is a deposit required at Melrose Apartments?)

(A) To secure a two-bedroom apartment.
(B) To renew a six-month lease.
(C) To pay for a dishwasher.
(D) To cover property damage.

49. (How long will the student have to wait for a one-bedroom apartment?)

(A) For a week.
(B) For two weeks.
(C) For three weeks.
(D) For a month.

50. (When will the student go to see the apartment?)

(A) At three-thirty.
(B) At one-thirty.
(C) At four o'clock.
(D) At five o'clock.

Test 2

LISTENING COMPREHENSION SCRIPT

These are the same 50 questions included in Test 2 on pages 57 to 61. The answers for this test are on page 73. Have a friend read you the material in parentheses once only. Be sure to observe the time limit for this test.

Part A

Directions. In this part of the test, you will hear a brief statement. Each statement will be spoken only once. The statement does not appear in your test booklet. When you have heard a statement, select the answer nearest in meaning to what you have heard. Record your answer on the answer sheet.

1. (My rent is due on the first of the month, but I rarely pay my other bills until the fifteenth.)

   (A) I pay my rent before the middle of each month.
   (B) I do not pay my rent until after the fifteenth of the month.
   (C) I have fifteen bills a month, including my rent.
   (D) I rarely pay my rent when it is due.

2. (The green checked bedspread is prettier, but the solid blue one is cheaper.)

   (A) Both bedspreads cost the same amount.
   (B) The green bedspread is the same size as the blue one.
   (C) The blue bedspread isn't as pretty as the other one.
   (D) One of the bedspreads has blue checks.

3. (Mary told me that she would graduate in June if she could get the chemistry course she needs out of the way.)

   (A) Mary will graduate in June, and then she's going away.
   (B) Mary intends to do graduate work in chemistry after June.
   (C) Mary won't graduate in June because of chemistry.
   (D) Mary must take another chemistry course before she can graduate in June.

4. (To operate the machine properly, you must keep the top closed while the machine is spinning.)

   (A) The machine does not spin if you close the top.
   (B) The top of the machine spins during operation.
   (C) Do not open the machine when it is spinning.
   (D) The operation of the machine requires you to spin.

5. (It's a shame John eats sweets whenever he gets the chance.)

   (A) John likes to take chances.
   (B) John dislikes eating sweets.
   (C) John never turns down sweets when they are offered to him.
   (D) John will not take a chance on eating sweets.

6. (We would have had a better time at the party if we had known some of the other guests.)

  (A) We knew almost every person at the party.
  (B) We knew none of the people at the party.
  (C) We guess we had a better time at the party than the other people.
  (D) We had a good time with the guests at the party.

7. (Tigers eat human beings only on rare occasions when food is scarce.)

  (A) Tigers occasionally consume human beings when they are hungry.
  (B) People rarely scare tigers.
  (C) Tigers are scarce today, just like food.
  (D) Food is available for human beings but not for tigers.

8. (I'm only an acquaintance of Bill Jones, but he seems a likeable fellow.)

  (A) I like Bill Jones, but he doesn't like me.
  (B) Bill Jones and I don't know each other very well.
  (C) Most fellows are acquainted with Bill Jones.
  (D) Bill Jones is a well-known, likeable fellow.

9. (The shoe shop is on the east side of the shopping center, close to the cafeteria.)

  (A) The shoe shop is not located in the shopping center.
  (B) The cafeteria is on the east side of the shopping center.
  (C) The shoe shop closes at the same time as the cafeteria.
  (D) The shoe shop near the cafeteria is closed.

10. (Peter wishes to be an architect like his father.)

  (A) Peter wants his father to be an architect.

  (B) Peter and his father wish to become architects.
  (C) Peter would like to be an architect.
  (D) Peter wants the architect to like his father.

11. (After Mary was almost asleep, she realized that she had forgotten to set the alarm.)

  (A) Mary got into bed without setting the alarm.
  (B) Mary was alarmed when she couldn't get to sleep.
  (C) Mary's sleep was interrupted by the alarm.
  (D) Mary almost slept through the alarm.

12. (If Carolyn doesn't improve in math this semester, she'll have to find a tutor.)

  (A) Carolyn is a better math student than her tutor.
  (B) Tutors cannot be found this semester.
  (C) Carolyn needs to do better in math.
  (D) Carolyn has improved in math this semester.

13. (What he did came as no surprise to me.)

  (A) He was surprised when I came.
  (B) I was not surprised by his actions.
  (C) He told me that he was not surprised.
  (D) His behavior surprised me.

14. (Twice as many men as women are insurance agents.)

  (A) More men than women have insurance.
  (B) Male insurance agents outnumber female agents.
  (C) Women are twice as likely as men to have insurance.
  (D) Insurance is twice as difficult to sell to women as to men.

15. (When Mr. Moore returned to his office after lunch, his secretary had a message for him from his lawyer.)

  (A) Mr. Moore's secretary delivered the lawyer's message.

(B) Mr. Moore and his lawyer had lunch together in the office.
(C) Mr. Moore advised his secretary to deliver lunch to his lawyer.
(D) The lawyer asked the secretary to have lunch with him.

16. (The plane was supposed to land at 6:00, but the flight was thirty minutes ahead of schedule.)

(A) The plane landed at 5:30.
(B) The plane was on time.
(C) The landing was delayed for half an hour.
(D) The plane didn't land until 6:30.

17. (Frank doesn't care if Harriet leaves or stays.)

(A) Frank wants Harriet to stay.
(B) Harriet will stay, but Frank wants her to leave.
(C) Harriet wants to leave unless Frank stays.
(D) Whatever Harriet does is all right with Frank.

18. (I remembered his face when I ran into him, but his name escaped me.)

(A) When I saw him, he tried to escape.
(B) His face seemed unfamiliar to me when I saw him.
(C) When I saw him, I couldn't recall his name.
(D) As soon as I saw him, I remembered his name.

19. (I understand that Susan has broken her engagement to Walter, but she doesn't seem at all upset about it.)

(A) Walter is sorry about his engagement to Susan.
(B) Susan has decided not to marry Walter.
(C) Susan is upset that Walter broke their engagement.
(D) Susan and Walter regret their marriage.

20. (Mr. Conner always wore old clothes although he had a sizable bank account.)

(A) Mr. Conner wore old clothes to the bank.
(B) Mr. Conner's bank was old and large.
(C) Mr. Conner wore old clothes in a large size.
(D) Mr. Conner did not spend money on clothes.

Part B

Directions. This section of the Listening Comprehension test consists of fifteen short conversations between two people. When each conversation ends, you will be asked a question by a third voice about what was said. You will hear the question only once and you must choose the answer from the four choices given. When you have chosen what you believe to be the best answer to the question, record your answer on your answer sheet.

21. (Man) "What did you think of the final exam?"
(Woman) "I was expecting it to be easy, but at the end of the first hour, I was still on the first page. I barely had time to get to the last question."
(Third voice) "What can we conclude from the above conversation?"

(A) The test consisted of one page.
(B) The exam was difficult for the woman.
(C) The woman found the exam easy.
(D) The woman completed the exam in one hour.

22. (Woman) "Your room is a mess! Your clothes are all over the floor and your bed is unmade. And when was the last time you picked up your toys?"
(Man) "You ought to try to be neater. Clean it up now, and when you're finished, we'll all go on a picnic."

(Third voice) "Who might these two speakers be?"

(A) Parents.
(B) A teacher and a student.
(C) Two friends.
(D) A parent and a child.

23. (Woman) "Can you accompany me on the piano while I sing?"
    (Man) "I don't play very well, but I'll give it a try."
    (Third voice) "What does the woman want the man to do?"

(A) Play the piano.
(B) Learn to sing.
(C) Keep her company.
(D) Teach her to sing.

24. (Man) "The telephone company says that they can send a man between one and three tomorrow afternoon. But someone has to be at home to let him in."
    (Woman) "Well, I guess I'll have to take off from work at noon. We can't go any longer without a telephone."
    (Third voice) "What does the woman need to do tomorrow?"

(A) Leave work early.
(B) Call the telephone company at noon.
(C) Go to work during the afternoon.
(D) Go to the telephone company between one and three.

25. (Man) "Can you bill me later?"
    (Woman) "I'm sorry, I can't. You're a new patient, so the fee for the first examination is due now. You can pay by cash, credit card, or check."
    (Third voice) "Where did this conversation most likely take place?"

(A) On a college campus.
(B) In a bank.
(C) In a doctor's clinic.
(D) In a hardware store.

26. (Woman) "I don't understand how you got a ticket. I always thought you were a careful driver."
    (Man) "I usually am, but I thought I could get through the intersection before the light turned."
    (Third voice) "Why did the man get a ticket?"

(A) He was speeding.
(B) He ran a red light.
(C) He went through a stop sign.
(D) He turned a corner too fast.

27. (Woman) "I can't decide whether to buy a new car or try to find a second-hand one."
    (Man) "If you buy a new one, you'll probably save money in the long run."
    (Third voice) "What does the man suggest to the woman?"

(A) To save her money for a long time.
(B) To buy a new car.
(C) To purchase a used car.
(D) To get a second car.

28. (Woman) "There isn't enough punch to go around."
    (Man) "I know you told me to get more, but there were only two gallons left on the shelf."
    (Third voice) "What is the woman complaining about?"

(A) Her guests don't like punch.
(B) The man left two gallons of punch on the shelf.
(C) She has too many gallons of punch.
(D) She will run out of punch.

29. (Woman) "This is the third time you've been late this week, Robert. You'll have to do better than that, or I might find it necessary to let you go."

(Man) "It won't happen again, I assure you."
(Third voice) "Who spoke to Robert?"

(A) His advisor.
(B) His teacher.
(C) His partner.
(D) His boss.

30. (Woman) "It's a miracle that Frank came out of the accident alive."
(Man) "That's true. His car is a total loss, you know."
(Third voice) "What do we learn from the above conversation?"

(A) Frank's car was accidentally lost.
(B) Frank was killed in a car accident.
(C) Frank fell out of a car.
(D) Frank survived a car accident.

31. (Man) "My blue jeans are so old I hate to wear them anymore."
(Woman) "If you get some blue dye, they should come out like new."
(Third voice) "What's probably wrong with the blue jeans?"

(A) They are faded.
(B) They are dirty.
(C) They are dyed.
(D) They are blue.

32. (Woman) "Have Todd and Lisa Taylor started a family yet? They've been married for two years now."
(Man) "Todd indicated to me that they'd postpone having children until he gets his law degree."
(Third voice) "How do the Taylors feel about children?"

(A) They have two children already.
(B) Mrs. Taylor wishes to have children, but her husband doesn't.

(C) They will start a family as soon as they get married.
(D) They don't want children for the time being.

33. (Woman) "There was a new quiz show on television last night, but we were just sitting down to dinner when it came on."
(Man) "I watched it and it was great! The first four contestants won only small prizes, but the fifth left with a new luxury car."
(Third voice) "What happened last night?"

(A) Four contestants failed to win prizes.
(B) The man ate during the show.
(C) The woman missed the show.
(D) Five contestants won cars.

34. (Woman) "Does Tom like his new high-rise apartment near the lakes?"
(Man) "He says the view of the mountains from the tenth floor is terrific, but that he's so afraid of a fire breaking out he wants to change to another floor."
(Third voice) "What will Tom probably do?"

(A) Change apartments.
(B) Look for a less expensive place to live.
(C) Move to the mountains.
(D) Find an older apartment away from the lakes.

35. (Man) "I have a terrible chest cold, and I can't stop coughing. What do you take for a cold, Phyllis?"
(Woman) "Well, over-the-counter medicines never help me, and the doctor refuses to prescribe antibiotics, so I usually rely on old home remedies like honey and whiskey."

(Third voice)   "What does Phyllis suggest for a cold?"

(A)   Cough medicine.
(B)   Honey and whiskey.
(C)   Antibiotics.
(D)   Over-the-counter remedies.

Part C

Directions.   In this part of the test, you will be required to listen to several short lectures and conversations. You will hear the lectures and conversations only once. They do not appear in your test booklet. When a question is asked, choose the best answer from the four given. Record your answer on the answer sheet.

Questions 36–39 are based on the following lecture.

The state of Kansas is called the "Bread Basket of America" because it ranks first in wheat growing and flour milling. In addition, there are hundreds of cattle ranches in western Kansas, some of which cover 50,000 acres. The state is larger than most states, but rather sparsely populated.

In pioneer days, many settlers passed through Kansas seeking rich land and gold farther west. Looking upon Kansas as a "useless waste of land," they refused to settle there. However, when Kansas joined the Union in 1861 as a free state opposed to slave labor, the population began to increase. Finally, the railroads helped to attract settlers by selling them inexpensive land.

36.   (What did the early pioneers think about Kansas?)

(A)   They thought there was gold in western Kansas.
(B)   They found slave labor too expensive.
(C)   They considered the land unproductive.
(D)   They liked the rich soil.

37.   (How did the railroads attract settlers?)

(A)   By giving away gold.
(B)   By offering cheap land.

(C)   By constructing flour mills.
(D)   By opposing slave labor.

38.   (Which of the following descriptions fits Kansas best?)

(A)   The population is small, but the state is large.
(B)   It is a large state with a large population.
(C)   The state is small and it has few people.
(D)   Its sparse population inhabits 50,000 acres.

39.   (What is the chief occupation of most Kansans?)

(A)   Farming.
(B)   Running railroads.
(C)   Weaving baskets.
(D)   Mining.

Questions 40–42 are based on the following lecture.

One of the main complaints of city residents, surprisingly, is the number of stray dogs and cats roaming the streets. It has been estimated by Friends of Animals, Inc., a nationwide volunteer agency, that over 30 million dogs and cats are wandering through the streets and alleyways of the nation's cities. Each year, approximately a fifth of these animals are destroyed.

A survey of 41 cities by Friends of Animals reports that as much as 15 million dollars is spent annually to capture and kill strays. One city alone, Chicago, spends $1 million a year to control its animal population.

New York, on the other hand, which spends large amounts of money on other programs, does not appropriate tax money to animal control. The American Society for the Prevention of Cruelty to Animals, a non-governmental agency, deals with the problem in New York.

40.   (What is the source of most of the statistics presented in this talk?)

(A)   A survey done by Friends of Animals, Inc.

(B)   A report prepared by the city of Chicago.

(C)   A survey sponsored by the federal government.

(D)   A study done by the city of New York.

41.   (What is Friends of Animals, Inc.?)

(A)   A tax-funded organization.
(B)   A society that roams the streets.
(C)   A control center for destroying strays.
(D)   An agency interested in animals.

42.   (Which of the following does not take an official interest in animal control?)

(A)   Chicago.
(B)   New York City.
(C)   Friends of Animals, Inc.
(D)   The American Society for the Prevention of Cruelty to Animals.

Questions 43–46 relate to the following lecture.

Five bodies of water make up the chain of lakes called the Great Lakes. Each of these five lakes is among the fifteen largest lakes in the world. The largest of these lakes is Lake Superior, followed by Huron, Michigan, Erie, and Ontario.

Lake Michigan is located entirely within the United States, but the other four lakes form a part of the boundary running between the United States and Canada. These freshwater lakes form a waterway more than 1,000 miles long, which is as busy as, if not busier than, any other waterway in the world. Canals have been dug to make the lakes a better waterway. These canals permit large, ocean-going vessels loaded with grain, iron ore, and coal to reach the lakes.

43.   (Which statement is true of the Great Lakes?)

(A)   All of the lakes are located within the United States.
(B)   The lakes have salty water.
(C)   Many ships sail the lakes.
(D)   Lake Superior is the fifteenth largest lake in the world.

44.   (Which of the following is *not* a name of one of the Great Lakes?)

(A)   Erie.
(B)   Michigan.
(C)   Huron.
(D)   Canada.

45.   (The canals were dug for what purpose?)

(A)   To improve the lakes as a waterway.
(B)   To form a boundary between the United States and Canada.
(C)   To make all of the lakes among the fifteen largest lakes in the world.
(D)   To keep fresh water in the lakes running.

46.   (Which of the five Great Lakes is the largest?)

(A)   Huron.
(B)   Ontario.
(C)   Superior.
(D)   Erie.

Questions 47–50 relate to the following conversation.

A: Professor Jones, may I see you a moment?

B: Of course, Gus. Come in and have a seat. I have about a half hour before my faculty meeting. Let me move this chair closer to my desk.

A: Thanks. I've come to talk to you about my grade on my last economics project. I want to know why I was given an "F."

B: Well, Gus, your approach was so similar to that of another student in the class that I seriously doubted that you'd done the calculations yourself.

A: I did work closely with my roommate Steve, but let me explain why. A week before the project was due, I was too sick to do my research. Steve agreed to help me with the project the night before it was due. We stayed up all night in order to finish it on time. The calculations were really my own.

B: Well, you'd been given a month to work on the project. Wouldn't it have been better to get a head start rather than to wait until the last minute? Each student was supposed to prepare this project individually. I'm afraid that my decision remains the same. However, next week we will be studying the government's role in running the economy. If you're willing to make an oral presentation about the subject, I'll give you extra credit.

A: Thank you, Professor Jones. I'll have my oral report ready for class on Friday.

47. (Where does this conversation most likely occur?)

    (A) In the library on campus.
    (B) In a classroom.
    (C) In the professor's office.
    (D) In the corridor between classes.

48. (How long had the student been given to complete the project?)

    (A) Eight weeks.
    (B) Six weeks.

(C) Four weeks.
(D) Two weeks.

49. (Why has the professor given the student a failing grade on his project?)

    (A) The professor believes that the student's work was not completely his own.
    (B) The professor believes that the student's work is inferior to that of the other students in the class.
    (C) The professor believes that the student's project is incomplete.
    (D) The professor believes that the student should discuss his project at the faculty meeting.

50. (What must the student do to receive credit?)

    (A) Write a report.
    (B) Revise his project.
    (C) Give a talk to the class.
    (D) Take an examination.

Test 3

LISTENING COMPREHENSION SCRIPT

These are the same 50 questions included in Test 3 on pages 93 to 97. The answers to this test are on page 109. Have a friend read you the material in parentheses once only. Be sure to observe the time limit for this test.

Part A

Directions. In this part of the test, you will hear a brief statement. Each statement will be spoken only once. The statement does not appear in your test booklet. When you have heard a statement, select the answer nearest in meaning to what you have heard. Record your answer on the answer sheet.

1. (You can't pick up your film today because it's not developed yet, and since we're closed tomorrow, the earliest you can get it is Friday.)

    (A) You can pick up your film in two days.
    (B) You can get your film tomorrow.
    (C) Your film is ready now.
    (D) You can pick up your film either today or tomorrow.

2. (The tank is almost empty, but I think there's a gas station about twenty miles up the road.)

    (A) We need to get some gas soon.
    (B) We have about twenty gallons of gas left.
    (C) We have traveleJd about twenty miles so far.
    (D) There are about twenty gas stations on this road.

3. (If you aren't able to pay cash for the television set, you can make arrangements with the credit manager for twelve payments.)

    (A) You can buy the television set on credit.
    (B) You can arrange to use the television set for twelve months.
    (C) You must pay cash for the television set.
    (D) You can return the television set to the credit manager after twelve months.

4. (I don't intend to stop by the post office, but I will go to the grocery store and to the cleaners after I see the doctor.)

    (A) The woman will go to the doctor's office first.
    (B) The woman will go to the post office first.
    (C) The woman will go to the grocery store first.
    (D) The woman will go to the cleaners first.

5. (I had to stand in line for two hours to get a first-row seat for the performance.)

    (A) The performance lasts two hours.
    (B) The man got a seat in the second row.
    (C) The man got a seat in the front row.
    (D) The man failed to get a ticket to the performance.

6. (Jack can't go to the movies with you because he needs to brush up on his notes.)

    (A) Jack must memorize his notes.
    (B) Jack must review his notes.
    (C) Jack must type his notes.
    (D) Jack must summarize his notes.

7. (With thirty seconds to go in the football game, the Harvard halfback scored a touchdown to beat Yale.)

    (A) Yale won the game.
    (B) The score of the game was 30–30.
    (C) A player from Yale scored the winning touchdown.
    (D) Harvard won the game.

8. (An assembled lawn mower costs $125, but it's only $100 if you put it together yourself.)

    (A) The total price of the lawn mower is $225.
    (B) There is no charge to assemble the lawn mower.
    (C) A lawn mower comes assembled for $100.
    (D) The price is cheaper if you assemble the lawn mower yourself.

9. (Dave had to take a cut in pay to keep from losing his job.)

    (A) Dave lost his job.
    (B) Dave had an accident on the job.
    (C) Dave's salary was lowered.
    (D) Dave was given a salary increase.

10. (Bill was on the verge of speeding when he saw the patrolman.)

    (A) Bill was given a speeding ticket by the patrolman.
    (B) Bill was speeding when he saw the patrolman.
    (C) Bill was about to speed when he saw the patrolman.
    (D) Bill told the patrolman that he (Bill) had not been speeding.

11. (Instead of waiting until tomorrow or Wednesday, Bob wants to get right to work.)

    (A) Bob wants to begin work immediately.
    (B) Bob wants to begin working tomorrow.
    (C) Bob wants to forget about the work.
    (D) Bob wants to begin working on Wednesday.

12. (I took more time on the last question than I did on the first four.)

    (A) I answered only the first question.
    (B) The last question was the most difficult for me.
    (C) I failed to get to the last question.
    (D) I found the final question easier than the other questions.

13. (We're closed on Sundays, but we stay open from 8 until 6 on weekdays and from 8 until 12 on Saturdays.)

    (A) On Tuesdays, the store closes at 8.
    (B) On Tuesdays, the store closes at 6.
    (C) On Tuesdays, the store closes at 4.
    (D) On Tuesdays, the store closes at 12.

14. (The student kept on talking even though the teacher had asked him to stop.)

    (A) The student continued talking.
    (B) The student asked for permission to talk.
    (C) The student stopped talking.
    (D) The student prevented the teacher from talking.

15. (Because she wanted to take a walk, Mrs. Jones asked Linda to keep an eye on the baby.)

    (A) Mrs. Jones asked Linda to bathe the baby.
    (B) Mrs. Jones asked Linda to walk the baby.
    (C) Mrs. Jones asked Linda to feed the baby.
    (D) Mrs. Jones asked Linda to take care of the baby.

16. (Before finding out that a neighbor had broken his window, the father scolded his child for having done it.)

    (A) The father broke the window.
    (B) The father mistakenly accused his child of breaking the window.
    (C) The child was responsible for breaking the window.
    (D) The father never learned who had broken the window.

17. (The hostess made every effort to see that her guests got the food and drinks they wanted.)

    (A) The hostess was reluctant to offer her guests food and drinks.
    (B) The hostess tried hard to please her guests.
    (C) The guests refused the food and drinks prepared by the hostess.
    (D) Neither the guests nor the hostess had food or drinks.

18. (John attended kindergarten and grade school in New York City and high school in Washington, but he received his higher education in Chicago.)

    (A) John attended college in New York City.
    (B) John attended college in Chicago.
    (C) John received a poor education in school.
    (D) John studied education in college.

19. (It's hard to believe that Bill is a sophomore at Memphis State University.)

    (A) Bill is studying more this year.
    (B) Bill is in his second year of college.
    (C) Bill made a statement about the university.
    (D) Bill is in his fourth year of college.

20. (Mark hasn't touched a book since the semester began.)

    (A) Mark hasn't gone to the library.
    (B) Mark hasn't begun the semester.
    (C) Mark hasn't studied at all this semester.
    (D) Mark hasn't bought any books.

Part B

Directions. This section of the Listening Comprehension test consists of fifteen short conversations between two people. When each conversation ends, you will be asked a question by a third voice about what was said. You will hear the question only once and you must choose the answer from the four choices given. When you have chosen what you believe to be the best answer to the question, record your answer on your answer sheet.

21. (Woman) "Here's this week's schedule. On Monday, there's the board meeting. Your speech at the Lion's Club is on Tuesday. Then, on Wednesday, you're supposed to see the dentist."

    (Man) "I'm glad I don't have to travel to the business conference until next week."

    (Third voice) "What will the man do on Tuesday?"

    (A) He must see the dentist.
    (B) He must give a speech.
    (C) He has a meeting to attend.
    (D) He must travel to a business conference.

22. (Man) "They may be proud of their new facility, but frankly I'm disappointed. The nurses are friendly, but everything seems to be running behind schedule."

    (Woman) "Not to mention the fact that it's noisy because no one observes visiting hours."

    (Third voice) "What are the people in the dialogue discussing?"

    (A) A new restaurant.
    (B) A new hotel.
    (C) A new hospital.
    (D) A new airport.

23.   (Man)   "I'm tired of Bill's remarks. I don't know why he wants to look at everything in such a negative way."

    (Woman)   "Why don't you do what I do, John, and take his comments with a grain of salt?"

    (Third voice)   "According to the woman, what should John do about Bill?"

(A) John should not talk to Bill anymore.
(B) John should tell Bill not to think negatively.
(C) John should take Bill's remarks seriously.
(D) John should pay little attention to what Bill says.

24.   (Man)   "Your new dresses are beautiful. Where did you find them?"

    (Woman)   "Well, I bought three of them while I was on vacation in Chicago, but I made the other one myself."

    (Third voice)   "What can we conclude from the above conversation?"

(A) The woman buys all her clothes in Chicago.
(B) The woman purchased no dresses in Chicago.
(C) The woman can sew.
(D) The woman bought one dress in Chicago.

25.   (Man)   "I'm disgusted with the way the subway is running. I've been waiting for an hour."

    (Woman)   "Well, so have I, but we should be boarding soon."

    (Third voice)   "What is the man unhappy about?"

(A) He arrived at the subway station late.
(B) The subway is not on time.
(C) The subway left an hour ago.
(D) The woman kept him from boarding the subway.

26.   (Man)   "It's been raining since Monday, but clear weather is forecast for tomorrow."

    (Woman)   "I'm glad to hear that because I always play golf on Thursdays and I like to have good weather."

    (Third voice)   "What will the weather probably be like on Thursday?"

(A) It will probably rain.
(B) It will probably be foggy.
(C) It will probably not rain.
(D) It will probably be cold.

27.   (Man)   "Mrs. Johnson, you must take two pills every four hours without fail. And don't forget to finish the bottle."

    (Woman)   "Don't worry, Doctor. I want to get well as quickly as I can."

    (Third voice)   "What will the woman probably do?"

(A) Take four pills.
(B) Hesitate to take any pills.
(C) Take the doctor's advice.
(D) Take eight pills.

28.   (Woman)   "London is a gorgeous city. From here you can see the palace guards."

    (Man)   "Wait until we get to Paris and Madrid. And don't forget about Rome!"

    (Third voice)   "Where did this conversation take place?"

(A) In Rome.
(B) In Paris.
(C) In London.
(D) In Madrid.

29.   (Man)   "I'm going to visit my brother in Seattle. I told him to meet me at the airport at five. I can almost see the city from here."

(Woman) "Seattle is a nice place. I think you'll enjoy your visit there."

(Third voice) "How are the people in the dialogue traveling?"

(A) By plane.
(B) By car.
(C) By bus.
(D) By train.

30. (Man) "Look at those colorful birds over there. I think you can teach them to talk."

(Woman) "Yes, but look at the price tag on them. Frankly, I'd rather have a hamster for two-fifty."

(Third voice) "Where did this conversation take place?"

(A) In a park.
(B) In a museum.
(C) In a zoo.
(D) In a pet store.

31. (Woman) "Could you tell me how to get to the bus station from here?"

(Man) "Go straight until you come to the stoplight. Turn to the left and go about three miles. When you get to the Argo Grocery Store, turn right. You can't miss it."

(Third voice) "What is the woman trying to do?"

(A) Get directions to the bus station.
(B) Get to the grocery store.
(C) Give the man directions to the bus station.
(D) Find out where the stoplight is.

32. (Man) "My family and I will be leaving on January 5. Is there anything we need to do to the apartment before we leave?"

(Woman) "If you want your fifty-dollar deposit back, you'll have to clean the stove and the refrigerator. Also, we ask that you vacuum carefully before leaving."

(Third voice) "What does the woman in the dialogue do for a living?"

(A) She's a maid.
(B) She sells stoves and refrigerators.
(C) She's an apartment manager.
(D) She's a real estate agent.

33. (Man) "The transmission in your car must be replaced. A transmission job is about four hundred dollars, but since the car is still under warranty, you'll have to pay only a small service charge."

(Woman) "That's good news. How long do you think it'll take?"

(Third voice) "How much will it cost the woman to get her car fixed?"

(A) Four hundred dollars.
(B) A little less than four hundred dollars.
(C) No money at all.
(D) A great deal less than four hundred dollars.

34. (Man) "How do Jane and Bill like their new home?"

(Woman) "It's really comfortable, but they're tired of having to hear the jets go over their house at all hours."

(Third voice) "What is located close to Jane and Bill's new home?"

(A) A bus station.
(B) An airport.
(C) A super highway.
(D) A train station.

35.   (Man)   "I was sorry to hear about Bill's being fired. I know he was sick a lot and that he usually got to work late."

        (Woman)   "Oh, it wasn't that. Bill made a big error in last month's accounting. Even though it wasn't really his fault, his boss was very angry.

        (Third voice) "Why did Bill lose his job?"

    (A) He got angry with his boss.
    (B) He always got to work late.
    (C) He was frequently sick and absent from work.
    (D) He prepared a financial report incorrectly.

Part C

Directions. In this part of the test, you will be required to listen to several short lectures and conversations. You will hear the lectures and conversations only once. They do not appear in your test booklet. When a question is asked, choose the best answer from the four given. Record your answer on the answer sheet.

Questions 36–38 are based on the following lecture.

Before Helen Keller was two years old, she lost her sight and her hearing. She lived in a world of confusion until the arrival of Anne Mansfield Sullivan, the woman who was to change Helen's life. On March 3, 1887, Miss Sullivan arrived at the Keller home. It was three months before Helen's seventh birthday. Miss Sullivan worked closely with her new student. At times, the teacher became frustrated. Eventually, Miss Sullivan's efforts were rewarded. The deaf and blind Helen Keller learned to communicate verbally.

36. (How old was Helen when Miss Sullivan arrived?)

    (A) Six years old.
    (B) Two years old.
    (C) Three months old.
    (D) Seven years old.

37. (What does the lecturer mean when she says that Miss Sullivan's efforts were rewarded?)

    (A) Helen's hearing was restored.
    (B) Helen learned to speak.
    (C) Helen's sight was restored.
    (D) Helen was able to teach other blind children.

38. (When did Miss Sullivan arrive at the Keller home?)

    (A) In 1887.
    (B) In 1830.
    (C) In 1867.
    (D) In 1840.

Questions 39–41 are based on the following conversation.

(Man)   "May I help you?"

(Woman)   "Yes, my nephew is graduating from college next week and I'd like to get him a nice gift."

(Man)   "What price gift are you interested in? We'll need to know that before we begin looking."

(Woman)   "Well, I usually spend about twenty dollars for a gift. Do you have anything nice for that price?"

(Man)   "How about a pen and pencil? We could engrave his initials on them."

(Woman)   "No, my brother gave him that for his birthday last year."

(Man)   "Well, then, would he enjoy a chess set?"

(Woman)   "No, he doesn't go in much for chess, but he is quite athletic."

(Man)   "Then you could get him a handball set."

(Woman)   "That's a good idea. I'll take it."

39. (Who is the woman buying the gift for?)

    (A) Her son.
    (B) Her brother.
    (C) Her father.
    (D) Her nephew.

40. (How much does the woman want to spend on the gift?)

    (A) Fifty dollars.
    (B) Ten dollars.
    (C) Thirty dollars.
    (D) Twenty dollars.

41. (What is the first gift the clerk suggests to the woman?)

    (A) A chess set.
    (B) A pen and pencil set.
    (C) A book on athletics.
    (D) A handball set.

Questions 42–45 are related to the following lecture.

The rattlesnake, often considered the deadliest of all North American snakes, has often been the subject of research and discussion among naturalists. This snake earns its name from the presence of rings of tough skin on its tail that remain when sloughing, or the dropping off of skin, occurs. Whenever a rattlesnake is agitated, it begins to move its tail, a motion that causes the rings of hardened skin to make a rattling noise.

Most naturalists believe that this noise is an involuntary reaction that results from the nervousness of the reptile; they do not think that the rattlesnake is attempting to convey a warning to its possible victim. Studies have revealed that the rattlesnake is the only venomous snake that gives a signal before striking, and, in fact, this reptile is the only species that has rattles. However, both the bull snake and the fox snake also vibrate their tails rapidly whenever they become nervous. Whether or not the rattlesnake should be called "the gentleman among snakes" because of the noise it makes before striking is an interesting question.

42. (Which of the following statements about the rattlesnake is untrue?)

    (A) The rattlesnake is a dangerous snake.
    (B) The rattlesnake's rattles are rings of hardened skin.
    (C) The rattlesnake is the only species of snake that has rattles.
    (D) The rattlesnake is one of many poisonous snakes that give warning before they strike.

43. (What eventually happens to the skin of the rattlesnake?)

    (A) The snake sheds its skin.
    (B) The skin becomes transparent.
    (C) The skin hardens and releases a poisonous liquid.
    (D) The snake forms an additional protective skin over the original.

44. (How do naturalists regard the rattle of the rattlesnake?)

    (A) They believe that the snake is able to control the rattle.
    (B) They believe that the snake is unaware of its rattle.
    (C) They believe that the rattle is a nervous action.
    (D) They believe that the rattle is a deliberate warning.

45. (What other species of snake moves its tail rapidly when it becomes agitated?)

    (A) The water snake.
    (B) The bull snake.
    (C) The cobra.
    (D) The cat snake.

Questions 46–50 are based on the following lecture.

Although twins have always been a source of curiosity, they are not so uncommon statistically, since they occur once in every 86 births.

About one-third of all twins are identical, or single-egg, twins. Identical twins have the same genes and, hence, the same sex, hair, eyes, blood type, and bone and tooth structure. Some identical twins are mirror images of each other. For example, one may be left-handed, the other right-handed. As young children, some identical twins may develop their own private language. Identical twins have an especially keen intuition, and they often seem to think and dress alike even when away from each other. In fact, even when they are separated at birth and raised apart, identical twins develop startling similarities. They may pursue the same careers, have the same interests, or die within days of each other.

In contrast to identical twins, fraternal twins

inherit a separate assortment of genes and are not necessarily of the same sex. In some families there is a hereditary tendency to produce fraternal twins, but identical twins occur at random in the population.

46. (About what proportion of twins are identical?)

(A) One-half.
(B) One-fourth.
(C) One-third.
(D) Two-thirds.

47. (Which of the following statements is true of fraternal twins?)

(A) They always have the same blood type.
(B) They occur at random in the population.
(C) They can be of different sexes.
(D) They have the same genes.

48. (What is another term for identical twins?)

(A) Single-egg twins.
(B) Mirror twins.
(C) Fraternal twins.
(D) Separate-egg twins.

49. (When they are young, what do some identical twins develop?)

(A) A secret language.
(B) The same genes.
(C) The same careers.
(D) A different bone structure.

50. (What does the talk seem to concentrate on?)

(A) How twins are born.
(B) Fraternal twins and their parents.
(C) Characteristics of identical twins.
(D) The marriages of twins.

Test 4

LISTENING COMPREHENSION SCRIPT

These are the same 50 questions included in Test 4 on pages 129 to 133. The answers to this test are on page 145. Have a friend read you the material in parentheses once only. Be sure to observe the time limit for this test.

Part A

Directions. In this part of the test, you will hear a brief statement. Each statement will be spoken only once. The statement does not appear in your test booklet. When you have heard a statement, select the answer nearest in meaning to what you have heard. Record your answer on the answer sheet.

1. (Once John realized that he had made a mistake, he went back and corrected it.)

   (A) John forgot that he needed to correct a mistake.
   (B) John corrected the mistake which he had made.
   (C) Going back was the mistake John made.
   (D) John corrected one mistake but neglected the others.

2. (Unlike her husband, Alice believes that it is useless to subscribe to more than one news magazine.)

   (A) Alice subscribes to more news magazines than her husband.
   (B) Alice told her husband that he should like news magazines.
   (C) Alice's husband considers it worthwhile to subscribe to several news magazines.
   (D) Neither Alice nor her husband reads news magazines.

3. (The medicine made him drowsy, so he wasn't able to drive while taking it.)

   (A) He was too sleepy to take the medicine.
   (B) He took the medicine while he was driving.
   (C) He couldn't drive while he took the medicine.
   (D) He felt drowsy, so he didn't have to take the medicine.

4. (The flight attendant took control of the plane after the pilot had had a heart attack.)

   (A) The flight attendant piloted the plane.
   (B) The airplane went out of control.
   (C) The pilot assisted the flight attendant.
   (D) The flight attendant suffered a heart attack.

5. (He makes a better husband than father.)

   (A) Fathers are usually good husbands.
   (B) He is more successful as a husband than as a father.
   (C) His father is better than her husband.
   (D) He tries to be a good husband and father.

6. (After several months, the problem continues to be discussed.)

   (A) The problem was solved after several months' discussion.
   (B) The discussion of the problem ceased several months ago.

265

(C) Several new problems have arisen and must be discussed.
(D) The discussion of the problem is not over yet.

7. (I'd like to know more about the religions of the world.)

(A) I like all world religions.
(B) I'm a very religious person.
(C) World religions do not concern me.
(D) I'm interested in learning more about world religions.

8. (Richard shouldn't have forgotten that yesterday was his wife's birthday.)

(A) Richard's wife forgot her own birthday.
(B) Richard had a birthday which his wife forgot.
(C) Yesterday, Richard remembered when his wife's birthday was.
(D) Richard failed to remember the date of his wife's birthday.

9. (Mr. Grant told his family that he was opposed to purchasing an additional television set.)

(A) Mr. Grant is against buying another television set.
(B) The family is sorry that Mr. Grant bought a television set.
(C) The family enjoys watching television more than Mr. Grant does.
(D) Mr. Grant advised his family to find a television set.

10. (I was born in Canada, but my parents brought me to the United States shortly afterwards.)

(A) I used to live in the United States.
(B) I came to the United States when I was a small child.
(C) My family lived in the United States for a short time.
(D) I lived in Canada much longer than in the United States.

11. (The secret to success is hard work.)

(A) Working hard ensures success.
(B) One must work hard to keep secrets.
(C) One cannot succeed if he has secrets.
(D) If you keep your work secret, you will succeed.

12. (After two appointments with the eye doctor and a new pair of glasses, Carol's sight still hasn't improved.)

(A) The doctor gave Carol two pairs of glasses.
(B) Carol's vision is no better now than it was before she went to the doctor.
(C) Carol has visited two eye doctors.
(D) Carol's eyesight improved when she went to the doctor.

13. (There is no difference between the twin girls except their height.)

(A) The twins are exactly the same.
(B) Both twins are overweight.
(C) One twin is taller than the other.
(D) The twins have different opinions concerning weight.

14. (The man had his dirty car washed at last.)

(A) The car got dirty last week.
(B) The man's dirty car did not last.
(C) The man got dirty when he washed his car.
(D) Someone finally washed the man's car.

15. (Catching fish is lots of fun, but I can do without cleaning them.)

(A) I'd rather catch fish than clean them.
(B) I don't know how to clean the fish I catch.
(C) I enjoy cleaning fish.
(D) It's no fun to catch fish.

16. (The lecture to be held in the auditorium is open to the public and free of charge.)

    (A) The auditorium will not be open for the lecture.
    (B) The public auditorium charged a fee for the lecture.
    (C) The lecture is an open discussion of public matters.
    (D) Admittance to the lecture is free.

17. (Mr. Butler usually goes to work by subway, but this morning he took the bus.)

    (A) Mr. Butler rarely takes the subway to work.
    (B) Mr. Butler usually goes to work by bus.
    (C) Mr. Butler missed the bus this morning, so he took the subway.
    (D) Mr. Butler almost always takes the subway to work.

18. (The whole neighborhood likes Mrs. Capps in spite of her odd habits.)

    (A) Mrs. Capps lives in a strange neighborhood.
    (B) Everyone in the neighborhood wears caps.
    (C) Mrs. Capps is a popular person in the neighborhood.
    (D) The neighbors act oddly toward Mrs. Capps.

19. (The weather has been generally cold all week, but a slight increase in temperature is expected tomorrow.)

    (A) The temperature will probably rise.
    (B) The temperature will probably remain cold.
    (C) The temperature will probably fall.
    (D) The temperature will probably stay warm.

20. (The more money Don makes, the more his wife spends.)

    (A) Don spends more money than his wife.
    (B) Don's wife keeps spending more money.
    (C) Don and his wife both make money.
    (D) Don spends the money his wife makes.

Part B

Directions. This section of the Listening Comprehension test consists of fifteen short conversations between two people. When each conversation ends, you will be asked a question by a third voice about what was said. You will hear the question only once and you must choose the answer from the four choices given. When you have chosen what you believe to be the best answer to the question, record your answer on the answer sheet.

21. (Woman) "Paul is so busy lately, I never have a chance to talk to him anymore. How's he doing?"
    (Man) "He had a collection of verse published last year, and now he's trying to get a novel about the automobile industry accepted."
    (Third voice) "What does Paul do?"

    (A) He publishes books.
    (B) He is an author.
    (C) He collects automobiles.
    (D) He works in industry.

22. (Woman) "How's your new job with the book company?"
    (Man) "It seemed promising at first, but I guess I'm no salesman. And to add fuel to the fire, the boss and I have our differences."
    (Third voice) "What do we know about the man's job?"

    (A) He has a promising career.
    (B) He can't sell books.
    (C) He and his boss get along well.
    (D) He prefers to be a fireman.

23.   (Man)   "Here's your report, Susan."

          (Woman)   "I'm really shocked. I never thought I'd receive a 'C.' "

          (Man)   "If you'd turned in the report a week ago as scheduled, you would have received a grade higher."

          (Third voice)   "What grade would Susan have received if she had submitted her report on time?"

(A) She would've received an A.
(B) She would've received a C.
(C) She would've received a D.
(D) She would've received a B.

24.   (Woman)   "Hi, Bill. Have you been playing much golf lately?"

          (Man)   "Hello, Joan. I play as often as I can get out of the house. And by the way, I have a new set of clubs. They seem to have helped my game, though they're much heavier than my old set."

          (Third voice)   "What does Bill tell Joan?"

(A) He prefers his old set of clubs.
(B) He has little chance to play golf.
(C) He's playing better golf recently.
(D) He's too old to play much golf.

25.   (Man)   "How's your French class coming?"

          (Woman)   "Slowly, I'm afraid. I spend hours going over the lessons in the text, but I don't seem to be able to carry on a decent conversation in French."

          (Man)   "You should take some private lessons from the new Belgian student. You'd surely make progress then."

          (Third voice)   "What advice does the man give the woman?"

(A) He suggests that she visit Belgium.
(B) He suggests that she spend more time studying her textbook.
(C) He suggests that she spend more time in the language laboratory.
(D) He suggests that she get a tutor.

26.   (Man)   "Your yard is always so beautiful, Cathy. You must have a gardener."

          (Woman)   "Oh, no. It would cost at least $50 a month to hire someone to do the work, so I do most of it myself. The flowers I enjoy taking care of, but I have to force myself to do the weeding and cut the grass."

          (Third voice)   "What does Cathy like to do?"

(A) Mow the lawn.
(B) Weed the flowers.
(C) Pay $50 a month for a gardener.
(D) Work in the flowerbeds.

27.   (Man)   "Did you find what you wanted? You've been gone all afternoon."

          (Woman)   "I looked all over town, but couldn't find any bookcases on sale. They're so expensive. I guess I'll wait a while longer."

          (Third voice)   "What is obvious from the conversation?"

(A) The man and woman shopped all over town.
(B) The woman went to many different stores.
(C) The woman bought some bookcases on sale.
(D) The man sold the woman some expensive bookcases.

28.   (Woman)   "These hogs look fine! Are you raising them for the market?"

          (Man)   "Not this year. With the cost of feed and the low

profit, it doesn't seem worthwhile. I'll just slaughter them for my own consumption."

(Third voice) "Where did this conversation probably occur?"

(A) On a farm.
(B) In a slaughterhouse.
(C) In a market.
(D) In a feed store.

29. (Woman) "Professor Horton, have you heard the morning news report? Lindsay resigned his post as defense secretary."

(Man) "I didn't turn on the radio this morning, but I did see the headlines. If you remember, he threatened to leave office at the last cabinet meeting."

(Third voice) "How did the professor learn that the defense secretary had resigned?"

(A) He read the newspaper.
(B) One of his students told him.
(C) He listened to a radio report.
(D) He attended a cabinet meeting.

30. (Man) "Is your baby on solid food yet? Ours isn't."

(Woman) "Oh, yes. He's had rice cereal and mashed banana so far, and I'm going to try him on vegetables next week."

(Third voice) "What does the woman's baby eat now?"

(A) Vegetables.
(B) Cereal and vegetables.
(C) Cereal and banana.
(D) Rice and mashed fruit.

31. (Woman) "Does everything look right to you? I want it to be perfect."

(Man) "I think you've made a mistake. Don't the napkins

go on the left and the silverware on the right?"

(Third voice) "What are the two people discussing?"

(A) Setting the table.
(B) Polishing silver.
(C) Sewing napkins.
(D) Stocking a pantry.

32. (Woman) "I see that Vincent is smiling again."

(Man) "Yes. He decided to speak to his boss's mother about his problem at work rather than to go directly to his boss."

(Woman) "That was certainly an unusual way of handling the situation, but it did bring good results."

(Third voice) "How did Vincent solve his problem?"

(A) He went directly to the boss with his problem.
(B) He decided to keep the problem to himself.
(C) He let his mother speak to the boss about the problem.
(D) He told his boss's mother about the problem.

33. (Woman) "Are you going to the post office for stamps or to pick up a package?"

(Man) "Neither. I left a letter for the postman to take yesterday, but he left it clipped to the mailbox. And this check has got to be in the mail today. I'd better hurry."

(Third voice) "Why is the man going to the post office?"

(A) To mail a letter.
(B) To buy stamps.
(C) To get a package.
(D) To deliver a check to the postman.

34. (Woman) "I don't think that Anita will ever sign another contract."
     (Man) "Why do you say that?"
     (Woman) "She broke the one that she had with her health club and lost her hundred-dollar deposit."
     (Third voice) "According to the conversation, what happened to Anita?"

(A) She lost a hundred dollars on the way to the health club.
(B) She received a refund of one hundred dollars from the health club.
(C) She refused to sign a contract with the health club.
(D) She failed to keep her contract with the health club.

35. (Man) "Will you be teaching this summer?"
     (Woman) "No. I'm going to take the summer off. I plan to go to Paris to work on a novel."
     (Man) "Then I'll look forward to seeing you in the fall."
     (Third voice) "What does the woman intend to do during the summer?"

(A) She plans to teach.
(B) She plans to write a book.
(C) She plans to do a great deal of reading.
(D) She plans to stay at home and rest.

Part C

Directions. In this part of the test, you will be required to listen to several short lectures and conversations. You will hear the lectures and conversations only once. They do not appear in your test booklet. When a question is asked, choose the best answer from the four given. Record your answer on the answer sheet.

Questions 36–39 relate to the following talk.

Birds of paradise have brighter colors than any other birds in the world. With their gay colors, it would be difficult to guess that they are cousins of the common crow. However, only the male birds of paradise have bright-colored feathers; the feathers of the female are very dull. The more than 30 different kinds of birds of paradise inhabit mostly the hot, rainy forests of New Guinea, although a few species are found in Australia.

As long ago as 500 years, the skins of these birds were used in trading in the East Indies. Before their skins were used, their feet were always cut off, leading to the misconception that the birds never had feet. There was a popular story told that these beautiful creatures were not able to stop flying until they died. The scientist Linnaeus even gave them a name which means "without feet."

36. (What kind of feathers does the female bird of paradise have?)

(A) Gaily colored.
(B) Very plain.
(C) Like the common crow's.
(D) Symmetrically shaped.

37. (What was a common misconception about the birds?)

(A) They had no scientific name.
(B) Their skins were used in trading.
(C) They were related to the crow.
(D) They kept flying until they died.

38. (Where are most birds of paradise found?)

(A) New Guinea.
(B) Australia.
(C) The East Indies.
(D) Linnaeus.

39. (What does the scientific name of the birds of paradise mean?)

(A) Bright colors.
(B) Flying creatures.
(C) Without feet.
(D) Dancing skins.

Questions 40–43 are based on the following lecture.

According to a recent poll, a large majority of Americans are in favor of retaining the present 55-mile-an-hour speed limit. This speed limit was imposed in 1973 when fuel shortages became crucial. Seventy-five percent of the persons surveyed think that the law is a good one. They point to the decrease in the highway death rate or to the saving of fuel as reasons for their opinion. Easterners and older people, rather than young adults, are more likely to argue for retention of the law.

Likewise, only 23 percent of the people surveyed favor a higher speed limit for trucks. The trucking industry contends that truck engines work more efficiently at higher speeds and that trucks traveling at higher speeds reach markets more quickly, thereby saving consumers money. Some of the persons polled argue that trucks on certain highways are already involved in a disproportionate number of fatal highway acidents.

40. (What was the principal reason for the original imposition of the 55-mile-per-hour speed limit?)

    (A) A majority of Americans voted for it.
    (B) Large trucks were causing many accidents.
    (C) There was a sudden increase in highway deaths.
    (D) A fuel shortage was developing.

41. (Which of the following are less likely to favor retaining the 55-mile-per-hour speed limit?)

    (A) Easterners.
    (B) Westerners.
    (C) Older persons.
    (D) Automobile industry workers.

42. (How many of the people surveyed believe that the law is a good one?)

    (A) 75 percent.
    (B) 23 percent.
    (C) 55 percent.
    (D) 66 percent.

43. (Why do truckers want a higher speed limit for trucks?)

    (A) Trucks do not use crucial fuel.
    (B) Few trucks are involved in accidents.
    (C) Most trucks do not transport consumer goods.
    (D) Trucks run better at higher speeds.

Questions 44–47 are based on the following talk.

Laird Gogins is a fifty-seven-year-old inventor who has developed a device to harness the power of the wind. He claims that his invention could eventually provide all the electrical power needed by the United States. A network of his wind machines across country could transfer electricity produced in a windy spot to a place where the air is still. Just one of Gogins' wind machines will produce eighty megawatts of electricity, which is ten times the power produced by all the windmills in the United States today. In addition, the wind machine is cheaper to build than a windmill. Gogins says that if just one percent of the available wind power in the United States were captured, it could provide one hundred percent of the electrical power now consumed. However, the inventor admits that the wind will probably never become the country's sole power source.

44. (What is Laird Gogins' profession as stated in the talk?)

    (A) He's a scientist.
    (B) He's an electrical engineer.
    (C) He's an inventor.
    (D) He's a chemist.

45. (What does Gogins' device harness in nature?)

    (A) Still air.
    (B) Electricity.
    (C) The power of the wind.
    (D) Solar energy.

46. (Which of the following sentences concerning Gogins' machine is *not* true?)

    (A) It is cheaper to construct than a windmill.

(B) It will produce eighty megawatts of electricity.
(C) It could produce much more power than the windmill.
(D) It is currently providing all of the electrical power needed by the United States.

47. (What does Gogins admit about his invention?)

(A) He believes that the windmill is more practical than his machine.
(B) He believes that a network of his machines would be incapable of transferring electricity from one place to another.
(C) He believes that his machine will probably never be the only device used to produce power in the United States.
(D) He believes that his machine will never be popular outside the United States.

Questions 48–50 relate to the following conversation.

(Man)   "Hello. Are you the person who has a house for sale?"

(Woman)   "Yes, I am."

(Man)   "Well, the ad says that it has four bedrooms and three baths, just what I need for my family of six. May I ask how much you want for it?"

(Woman)   "I prefer not to quote a price over the phone, but let's say it's in the neighborhood of $150,000. I would also require a down payment of $40,000. Why don't you come by and take a look?"

(Man)   "Well, I'm not sure I can afford such a large down payment, but I guess it wouldn't hurt to see the house. If you can tell me how to get to Churchill Avenue from South Florida Street, my wife and I'll be over."

48. (How large is the prospective buyer's family?)

(A) It consists of a couple and four children.
(B) It includes a man and his wife.
(C) It has four members.
(D) It has three members.

49. (How did the man learn about the house?)

(A) He read about it in the newspaper.
(B) He saw it on South Florida Street.
(C) His wife told him about it.
(D) He saw it while riding down Churchill Avenue.

50. (What is the man most worried about?)

(A) The size of the house.
(B) The location of the house.
(C) The appearance of the house.
(D) The down payment on the house.

Test 5

LISTENING COMPREHENSION SCRIPT

These are the same 50 questions included in Test 5 on pages 165 to 169. The answers for this test are on page 181. Have a friend read you the material in parentheses once only. Be sure to observe the time limit for this test.

Part A

Directions. In this part of the test, you will hear a brief statement. Each statement will be spoken only once. The statement does not appear in your test booklet. When you have heard a statement, select the answer nearest in meaning to what you have heard. Record your answer on the answer sheet.

1. (Having submitted its report, the committee adjourned until the next meeting.)

   (A) The committee made a report before adjourning.
   (B) The next committee meeting has been canceled.
   (C) The committee reported on the adjournment of the meeting.
   (D) The report of the committee was postponed until the next meeting.

2. (Although groceries were high, the family managed to get by on sixty dollars a week.)

   (A) The family had enough money to buy groceries.
   (B) The family was unable to buy groceries due to the high prices.
   (C) The family was unable to manage their grocery money.
   (D) Sixty dollars was left over after the weekly grocery shopping.

3. (Mary thought that the dress would fit, but she had to exchange it later.)

   (A) Mary exchanged the dress for another one in a different size.
   (B) Mary exchanged the dress because she didn't like it.
   (C) Mary was too late to exchange the dress.
   (D) Mary considered exchanging the dress, but changed her mind.

4. (The workers are threatening to go on strike unless the company raises the hourly wage.)

   (A) If their wages are not increased, the workers plan to strike.
   (B) The company raised the workers' wages to avoid a strike.
   (C) The company demands that the workers strike.
   (D) The company threatens to pay the workers less.

5. (Slightly more than 25 percent of the students in the class come from Spanish-speaking countries.)

   (A) The majority of the students in the class do not speak Spanish.
   (B) Seventy-five percent of the students in the class speak Spanish.
   (C) About twenty-five percent of the students in the class speak languages other than Spanish.
   (D) The percentage of students who speak Spanish is less than twenty-five percent.

6. (When the pianist had finished, the audience stood up and gave him a hand.)

    (A) The audience shook the pianist's hand.
    (B) The audience left before the end of the performance.
    (C) The audience applauded the pianist's performance.
    (D) The audience disliked the pianist's performance.

7. (Jennifer is allergic to seafood, so I'll have to change my menu for Saturday night.)

    (A) Jennifer cannot eat food like pork chops or ham.
    (B) Jennifer asked me to change my menu to seafood.
    (C) Seafood is not a good choice to serve on Saturday night.
    (D) No seafood is available for Saturday night.

8. (The court found the man innocent of murdering his wife.)

    (A) The man was judged not guilty of killing his wife.
    (B) The court found a murdered man and his wife.
    (C) The man was found murdered by his wife.
    (D) The court decided that the man had killed his wife.

9. (The contractor advised the couple not to paint their house until the weather warmed up a little.)

    (A) It was suggested that the house be painted in warm weather.
    (B) The contractor said that he would paint the house in spite of the heat.
    (C) The house should be painted during the winter.
    (D) The house was too small for the contractor to paint.

10. (It's too bad Mr. Nelson's son couldn't have found a more comfortable apartment to live in.)

    (A) Mr. Nelson's son doesn't live in a comfortable apartment.
    (B) Mr. Nelson found his son a comfortable apartment.
    (C) Mr. Nelson and his son live comfortably.
    (D) Mr. Nelson's son managed to find a comfortable apartment for his father.

11. (The professor suggests that we write in ink on alternate lines so that he can make corrections in pencil.)

    (A) We must not write on every line of the paper.
    (B) The professor will correct our papers in ink.
    (C) The professor will read our papers, but he will not correct them.
    (D) We must not write our papers in ink.

12. (She is unqualified to fill the position as executive secretary of the firm.)

    (A) The job of executive secretary requires more skills than she has.
    (B) She possesses the firm qualities of an executive secretary.
    (C) Both she and the executive secretary took a firm position.
    (D) Firmness is needed to qualify one for position of executive secretary.

13. (Having worked for the same company for many years, he is convinced of the superiority of its products.)

    (A) He thinks that his company manufactures superior products.
    (B) He convinced his company to put him in charge of production.
    (C) His company has manufactured inferior products for many years.
    (D) It took him many years to become a superior in the company.

14. (Because the lecturer failed to come to the point quickly, the class was dismissed an hour late.)

   (A) The class started an hour late.
   (B) The lecturer dismissed the class on time.
   (C) The lecturer got off the main subject of the discussion and did not dismiss the class on time.
   (D) The class failed to understand what the lecturer was saying.

15. (Although there was a lack of interest to begin with, the main reason that they postponed the picnic was the rain.)

   (A) They held the picnic in spite of the rain.
   (B) They were extremely interested in having the picnic.
   (C) The picnic was held, but few people showed up.
   (D) The picnic was put off because of the rain.

16. (At the bank, Bill is second in command.)

   (A) Bill used to work for a bank, but now he is in the army.
   (B) Bill holds the top position in the bank.
   (C) Bill's boss is first in command at the bank.
   (D) Bill dislikes his work at the bank.

17. (The price of the room for two is twenty-five dollars, but with one extra person, it'll be twenty-nine dollars.)

   (A) An extra person costs four dollars more.
   (B) An extra person costs five dollars more.
   (C) An extra person costs two dollars more.
   (D) An extra person costs nine dollars more.

18. (The play should have begun at eight, but the curtain didn't rise until half past eight.)

   (A) The play began at eight.
   (B) The play began at nine.
   (C) The play began at eight-thirty.
   (D) The play began at seven-thirty.

19. (I find your grammar and organization above average, Bob, but your spelling could stand some improvement.)

   (A) Bob's writing is only average.
   (B) Bob misspells too many words.
   (C) Bob's organization is poor.
   (D) Bob can't stand to write.

20. (I would never have lent Mike my car if I had known that he had a past record of driving violations.)

   (A) I refused to lend Mike my car.
   (B) Mike got a speeding ticket while driving my car.
   (C) I knew nothing about Mike's driving record, so I lent him my car.
   (D) Mike drove my car without his driver's license.

Part B

   Directions. This section of the Listening Comprehension test consists of fifteen short conversations between two people. When each conversation ends, you will be asked a question by a third voice about what was said. You will hear the question only once and you must choose the answer from the four choices given. When you have chosen what you believe to be the best answer to the question, record your answer on the answer sheet.

21. (Man) "Look at the low prices on these turntables. Don't you think that they're a fantastic buy?"

   (Woman) "Yes, but quality is more important than price. Let's look elsewhere before making a decision."

   (Third voice) "How does the man feel about the turntables?"

   (A) He thinks that they are of inferior quality.
   (B) He thinks that they are a bargain.

(C) He thinks that they are overpriced.
(D) He thinks that they can be purchased at a cheaper price elsewhere.

22. (Man) "I think I'll order the chocolate mousse. I know it's rich, but I didn't eat lunch earlier today."

(Woman) "No dessert for me. I can hardly get into my clothes as it is."

(Third voice) "Why won't the woman order dessert?"

(A) She is full.
(B) She doesn't want to gain weight.
(C) She thinks the dessert will be too rich for her.
(D) She is afraid of spilling the dessert on her clothes.

23. (Man) "Isn't that a replica of one of Columbus' ships?"

(Woman) "Yes, I believe so. And over there you can see some very valuable paintings, but those areas are roped off to the public. We can't even take photographs!"

(Third voice) "Where did this conversation probably occur?"

(A) In a museum.
(B) In a park.
(C) In a library.
(D) In an art store.

24. (Man) "I've been having annoyance calls for two weeks. When I answer the phone, the other party hangs up without saying anything. I've tried everything including blowing a whistle into the receiver."

(Woman) "Beginning today, we want you to keep a record of the time each call occurs. From this chart, we can get information to help us trace the

calls. If necessary, the telephone company can contact the police."

(Third voice) "What does the woman suggest that the man do?"

(A) Disconnect his telephone.
(B) Blow a whistle into the receiver.
(C) Keep a record of incoming annoyance calls.
(D) Report his problem to the police.

25. (Man) "Have you finished your term paper? I handed mine in last Friday."

(Woman) "I finished typing mine at three o'clock this morning. I have to submit it by noon today."

(Third voice) "When must the girl turn in her term paper?"

(A) By one o'clock.
(B) By two o'clock.
(C) By three o'clock.
(D) By twelve o'clock.

26. (Man) "Saturday's speaker is supposed to be wonderful. Are you going to attend the seminar that day?"

(Woman) "Yes, but I haven't gotten my ticket yet. Since the lecture is open to the public, I imagine that the tickets may already be sold out."

(Third voice) "Why is the woman afraid that she won't be able to attend the seminar?"

(A) She thinks that the ticket line will be too long.
(B) She thinks that the speaker won't show up.
(C) She thinks that no more tickets are available.
(D) She thinks the seminar will not be open to the public.

27.
(Man) "I'd like to buy a ten-dollar ticket to Friday's concert."

(Woman) "Your ticket will be for the orchestra section. The tickets in the lower balcony are five dollars while the upper balcony seats are two-fifty."

(Third voice) "What event is the man going to?"

(A) A play.
(B) A movie.
(C) A lecture.
(D) A concert.

28.
(Man) "You've passed the written test. Stand over here about three feet from the camera and we'll take your picture. We're going to issue you a temporary license. You'll receive your permanent license in about six weeks."

(Woman) "Thank you. Here's the five-dollar fee."

(Third voice) "How long will it take the woman's permanent license to arrive?"

(A) Six weeks.
(B) Five weeks.
(C) Four weeks.
(D) Three weeks.

29.
(Man) "My sister is in the hospital and I'd like to send her a plant she can use later in the law office where she's employed."

(Woman) "How about a nice cactus? They always make lovely gifts."

(Third voice) "Where does the man's sister work?"

(A) In a hospital.
(B) In a law office.
(C) In a plant store.
(D) In a gift shop.

30.
(Man) "I haven't read the newspaper yet. When you're finished, may I see it?"

(Woman) "I'll give it to you right now. I have to check on dinner anyway."

(Third voice) "What is the woman doing besides reading the newspaper?"

(A) Cooking.
(B) Eating dinner.
(C) Writing a check.
(D) Getting dressed.

31.
(Woman) "You're going to Chicago tomorrow, aren't you?"

(Man) "Yes. I thought I'd fly, but then I decided that taking a bus would be cheaper than driving or flying."

(Third voice) "How will the man get to Chicago?"

(A) By plane.
(B) By bus.
(C) By car.
(D) By train.

32.
(Woman) "Every time I see you, Bob, you are wearing a different tie."

(Man) "That's because I have one for every day of the week."

(Third voice) "How many ties does the man have?"

(A) Two.
(B) Five.
(C) Seven.
(D) Nine.

33.
(Woman) "I can't wait to move into our new house! When do you think that the painters will be finished, Mr. Lee?"

(Man) "I expect them to stop work tomorrow. Then we will have to call in the electrician and the plumber. Tell your movers to be ready by the fifteenth, and

I'll make sure that every-thing, including your kitchen, is just the way you want it."

(Third voice) "What are the two people in the dialogue discussing?"

(A) Building an office complex.
(B) Building a clubhouse.
(C) Building a private residence.
(D) Building an apartment house.

34. (Woman) "When do you think that I can go home, Dr. Smith?"
(Man) "Well, you came in on Monday and today is Friday. I'd say that you could probably leave tomorrow, but I don't want you to go back to work for several weeks."
(Third voice) "Where is the woman in the conversation?"

(A) At home.
(B) In the hospital.
(C) In the doctor's office.
(D) At work.

35. (Woman) "I've just decided to order some books from this catalogue. I wonder how I should pay for them."
(Man) "It says here that C.O.D.'s are not accepted. However, you can save two dollars by paying in cash or by check instead of using a credit card. If I were you, I'd send them a check."
(Third voice) "How does the man suggest that the woman pay for the books?"

(A) He advises that she have them sent C.O.D.
(B) He tells her to send two dollars in cash now and the rest upon the delivery of the books.
(C) He advises that she pay for the books with a credit card.
(D) He advises her to pay for the books by check.

Part C

Directions. In this part of the test, you will be required to listen to several short lectures and conversations. You will hear the lectures and conversations only once. They do not appear in your test booklet. When a question is asked, choose the best answer from the four given. Record your answer on the answer sheet.

Questions 36–40 are related to the following lecture.

A patent is a government grant of certain exclusive rights to an inventor who chooses to make his invention public. A patent in the United States is granted for seventeen years. During this time, other people are prevented from making, using, or selling the invention without the permission of the inventor. When this period ends, anyone can use the invention.

The United States Patent Office, an agency of the Department of Commerce in Washington, is responsible for administering the patent laws. The Commissioner of Patents is appointed by the President of the United States. More than one thousand patent examiners, all of whom are people with technical training, work in the Patent Office. These examiners study applications to determine whether the applicant has followed the established rules and patent laws.

36. (What United States agency controls the Patent Office?)

(A) The State Department.
(B) The Treasury Department.
(C) The Department of Commerce.
(D) The Department of Agriculture.

37. (For how long is a patent in the United States granted?)

(A) For seven years.
(B) For seventy years.
(C) For seventy-seven years.
(D) For seventeen years.

38. (Who is responsible for making certain that an applicant for a patent has followed the proper patent regulations?)

    (A) Patent examiners who are trained in technical fields.
    (B) The President of the United States.
    (C) The director of the U.S. Patent Office.
    (D) Government officials from the applicant's home state.

39. (Approximately how many patent examiners are employed in the U.S. Patent Office?)

    (A) One hundred.
    (B) One thousand.
    (C) Six hundred.
    (D) Fifteen hundred.

40. (Who appoints the Commissioner of Patents?)

    (A) The Department of Commerce.
    (B) The President of the United States.
    (C) The Treasury Department.
    (D) The United States Patent Office.

Questions 41–45 are based on the following lecture.

Falconry is the art of training birds of prey, such as falcons, other hawks, and occasionally eagles, to hunt game. This sport, often called hawking, is an ancient pastime. In fact, Marco Polo observed the followers of the Mongol Genghis Khan training and flying large numbers of birds of prey.

The kinds of birds employed in falconry range from the small kestrel, whose normal prey is insects and mice, to the magnificent Golden Eagle, a bird of great courage and strength, which may attack deer or wolves.

During the Middle Ages, training swift birds for hunting was a favorite sport of European aristocracy. However, only kings were allowed to fly the noble eagle.

The invention of the shotgun changed the pattern of hunting, and falconry began to decline. Nevertheless, the sport still enjoys some popularity among a few people, who go to great expense to use their falcons to hunt rare and exotic prey.

41. (What is the Golden Eagle?)

    (A) A bird of prey.
    (B) A small kestrel.
    (B) A kind of hawk.
    (D) A type of shotgun.

42. (Who flew the noble eagle during the Middle Ages?)

    (A) Genghis Khan.
    (B) Europeans.
    (C) Marco Polo.
    (D) Kings.

43. (What is another name for falconry?)

    (A) Polo.
    ((B) Hunting.
    (C) Preying.
    (D) Hawking.

44. (What caused the sport of falconry to decline?)

    (A) The extinction of the eagle.
    (B) The nobility.
    (C) Modern weaponry.
    (D) The great expense involved.

45. (What is the usual prey of the small kestrel?)

    (A) Falcons.
    (B) Insects and mice.
    (C) Exotic birds.
    (D) Deer.

Questions 46–48 are based on the following talk.

Hepatitis is a liver disease that is sometimes fatal. There are two types of hepatitis: Type A, usually contracted from contaminated food and water, and Type B, formerly called "serum hepatitis," because it is often found among people who have undergone blood transfusions.

It is Type B that causes the most deaths, and it is for this type that a new vaccine should be available soon. This vaccine is considered important in controlling hepatitis because up to ten percent of those patients infected with Type B become chronic carriers and can transmit the disease to others.

Type A causes many more cases of hepatitis than Type B, particularly in children. The prospects of a vaccine for Type A are promising, especially since scientists recently succeeded in reproducing large quantities of the Type A virus in the laboratory.

46. (Why was Type B hepatitis formerly called "serum hepatitis"?)

   (A) Type B hepatitis is more common than Type A.
   (B) Type B hepatitis is always hereditary.
   (C) Type B hepatitis is often found among people who have had blood transfusions.
   (D) Type B hepatitis affects the liver.

47. (Which of the following statements is true of Type B hepatitis?)

   (A) It can be transmitted from one person to another.
   (B) It occurs more frequently in children.
   (C) It causes fewer deaths than Type A hepatitis.
   (D) It is more common than Type A hepatitis.

48. (How does one get Type A hepatitis?)

   (A) Through blood transfusions.
   (B) From a new vaccine.
   (C) From chronic carriers.
   (D) From contaminated food and water.

Questions 49–50 are based on the following talk.

With the ever-increasing threat of home fires, Americans are choosing smoke alarm systems that can be easily installed as warning devices in residences. One such alarm is battery-operated, so it continues to function when power fails. The security light on the unit goes on automatically when a power failure occurs. This unit can be unplugged and used as a rechargeable flashlight and as a night light. Smoke alarm systems of this kind are listed by Underwriters' Laboratories and can be bought at hardware stores.

49. (What happens to the smoke alarm system when a power failure occurs?)

   (A) A security light goes on automatically and the unit operates on batteries.
   (B) An alarm sounds to notify the homeowner of the power loss.
   (C) The home smoke alarm system fails to operate until power is restored.
   (D) The entire smoke alarm system must be replaced at once.

50. (According to the lecture, how can a homeowner obtain a smoke alarm system for his residence?)

   (A) He can buy one at a large electrical applicance store.
   (B) He can order one from his local fire department.
   (C) He can request one from Underwriters' Laboratories.
   (D) He can purchase one at a hardware store.

Test 6

LISTENING COMPREHENSION SCRIPT

These are the same questions included in Test 6 on pages 203 to 207. The answers for this test are on page 220. Have a friend read you the material in parentheses once only. Be sure to observe the time limit for this test.

Part A

Directions. In this part of the test, you will hear a brief statement. Each statement will be spoken only once. The statement does not appear in your test booklet. When you have heard a statement, select the answer nearest in meaning to what you have heard. Record your answer on the answer sheet.

1. (If I didn't have a car, I'd have to walk five blocks to work every day.)

   (A) My car needs some work on it.
   (B) After work every day, I walk five blocks.
   (C) I drive to work in my car every day.
   (D) I have to walk five blocks to get to my car.

2. (The baby slept soundly even with the noise the children made.)

   (A) The children couldn't sleep because of the noise.
   (B) The baby woke up because the children made sounds.
   (C) The baby and the children slept through the noise.
   (D) The noise didn't prevent the baby from sleeping.

3. (Eric is usually on time for his ten o'clock class, but today he arrived twenty minutes late.)

   (A) Eric arrived after the class had begun.
   (B) Eric arrived in class on time.
   (C) Eric is usually late for class.
   (D) Eric arrived in class twenty minutes before it began.

4. (I might've taken French last semester if I'd known it was offered.)

   (A) I didn't take French last semester.
   (B) Someone offered to teach me French last semester.
   (C) I knew that French was not offered last semester.
   (D) I took French the last semester it was offered.

5. (Most people get fewer colds in the summer than in the winter.)

   (A) A person is more likely to get a cold in the winter.
   (B) More people have summer colds than winter colds.
   (C) People get colder in the summer than in the winter.
   (D) The winter is much colder than the summer.

6. (Tony's boss gave him permission to take two days off.)

   (A) Tony's boss left the office for two days.
   (B) Tony quit his job after two days.
   (C) Tony took two days off from work.
   (D) Tony's boss agreed to take off for two days.

7. (When the secretary said that the report would be ready by Thursday, the boss told her to take her time.)

   (A) The boss told his secretary to finish the report on time.
   (B) The boss told the secretary not to rush.
   (C) The boss told the secretary to take the report home in order to finish it.
   (D) The boss told the secretary that he would need the report before Thursday.

8. (A very successful salesman, Mr. Riley often has more customers than he can handle.)

   (A) Mr. Riley's customers cannot handle him successfully.
   (B) Mr. Riley finds it difficult to sell to his customers.
   (C) Mr. Riley is a successful salesman of handles to many customers.
   (D) Mr. Riley sometimes has too many customers to take care of.

9. (In the class of twenty, Jeanne is the third best student.)

   (A) No other student is as smart as Jeanne.
   (B) The class has only three smart students.
   (C) Two students are smarter than Jeanne.
   (D) Jeanne is not as smart as most of the other students.

10. (I'd rather do nothing than watch old movies on television.)

   (A) There are few old movies on television.
   (B) Watching old movies on television is enjoyable.
   (C) I dislike watching old movies on television.
   (D) Old televisions and old watches are worth nothing.

11. (Mrs. Thompson attended to the domestic details of the house, for which she received a substantial salary.)

   (A) Mrs. Thompson was a housekeeper.
   (B) Mrs. Thompson made a substantial profit when she sold her house.
   (C) Mrs. Thompson was an architect.
   (D) Mrs. Thompson paid a lot of money to have a servant in her house.

12. (Despite the weather report that the skies would clear at midmorning, the rain continued throughout the day and into the night.)

   (A) The weather report predicted an afternoon rainstorm.
   (B) The weather report predicted rain for the entire day.
   (C) The weather report predicted a cloudy day.
   (D) The weather report predicted a clear afternoon.

13. (Insurance rates are rising so fast that the cost may soon be prohibitive.)

   (A) Most people do not know what the cost of insurance is.
   (B) Insurance rates are decreasing for many people.
   (C) Insurance companies prohibit some people from purchasing insurance.
   (D) One day people may not be able to afford insurance.

14. (Times Square is the center of many well-known theaters in New York.)

   (A) Times Square is the name of a well-known theater in New York.
   (B) Many famous theaters are located in New York's Times Square.
   (C) New York is in the center of Times Square.
   (D) Many theaters in central New York are open all the time.

15. (You may see the ballet any night but Sunday, when there is a matinee performance.)

    (A) There is no performance of the ballet on Sunday.
    (B) The ballet is performed six nights a week.
    (C) The ballet is performed twice on Sunday.
    (D) You can see a matinee performance of the ballet any night.

16. (His wages are small, and so are his needs.)

    (A) He needs more money than he makes.
    (B) He lives on little money.
    (C) He spends more money than he has.
    (D) He wants a raise in salary.

17. (The students heeded the instructions of the teacher and took their places in the first two rows.)

    (A) The students failed to understand the teacher's instructions.
    (B) The students exchanged seats with the teacher.
    (C) The students followed the teacher's instructions.
    (D) The students sat in the first row, but not in the second.

18. (Brett sat through his physics class in his rain-soaked clothes, but decided to go home rather than to attend biology class.)

    (A) Brett attended only his physics class.
    (B) Brett attended both his biology and physics classes.
    (C) Brett attended only his biology class.
    (D) Brett did not attend any of his classes due to the rain.

19. (Martha said she would do anything for me but lie.)

    (A) Martha refuses to lie.
    (B) I lied to Martha.
    (C) Martha does nothing but lie.
    (D) Martha lied to me about something.

20. (Another explosion occurred seconds after the first.)

    (A) There were three explosions.
    (B) The first explosion occurred in the cellar.
    (C) Two explosions happened in rapid succession.
    (D) The first explosion was louder than the second.

Part B

Directions. This section of the Listening Comprehension test consists of fifteen short conversations between two people. When each conversation ends, you will be asked a question by a third voice about what was said. You will hear the question only once and you must choose the answer from the four choices given. When you have chosen what you believe to be the best answer to the question, record your answer on the answer sheet.

21. (Man) "Where shall we have lunch? All I want is a salad. Isn't there a new cafeteria in the mall?"

    (Woman) "I've been there a few times. It's quick, and the price is right, but the food isn't anything to speak of."

    (Third voice) "What is the woman's opinion of the cafeteria?"

    (A) The service is slow.
    (B) There is no salad bar.
    (C) The prices are high.
    (D) The food is poor.

22. (Woman) "Have you received the check from the company to cover the damage to your car?"

    (Man) "No, not yet, but I expect to within the next few days."

    (Third voice) "What is the most likely subject of this conversation?"

(A) A bank deposit.
(B) An insurance claim.
(C) A loan.
(D) An income tax return.

23. (Woman) "I want to do my part for the picnic on Thursday. What should I bring?"

    (Man) "Well, let's see. Art is bringing the drinks, Buddy is getting the ice, and Paul is going to pick up the chicken. You could take care of seeing that the buses stop for all of the students."

    (Third voice) "What does the man want the woman to be in charge of?"

(A) The drinks.
(B) The chicken.
(C) The ice.
(D) The transportation.

24. (Woman) "You certainly must've been busy lately. It's been a month since you called."

    (Man) "I haven't had a spare minute. I've been studying for my realtor's exam every night and holding down a job with the university besides. But we'll take in a movie just as soon as I pass the test and get my license."

    (Third voice) "What does the man want to do first?"

(A) Become a real estate salesperson.
(B) Get a driver's license.
(C) Go to a movie.
(D) Graduate from the university.

25. (Woman) "I'm crazy about the blue cashmere sweater in the window. Could I see it, please?"

    (Man) "We're about to mark down all of our winter mer-chandise, including our jackets, suits, and cash-mere sweaters in several colors. Why don't you wait until Friday?"

    (Third voice) "What does the man sug-gest that the woman do?"

(A) He suggests that she buy the sweater in another color.
(B) He suggests that she buy a jacket instead of the sweater.
(C) He suggests that she buy the sweater at its original price.
(D) He suggests that she buy the sweater on sale.

26. (Woman) "Did you have a good time at the reception? I wish I had had a chance to meet the governor."

    (Man) "An embarrassing thing happened. I was helping myself to some punch when the cup slipped out of my hand. The carpet can be cleaned, thank goodness, but the cup is in a hundred pieces."

    (Third voice) "What happened to the man at the party?"

(A) He ruined the carpet.
(B) He was not introduced to the gover-nor.
(C) He broke a punch cup.
(D) He was not offered any punch.

27. (Man) "Mary, you're trembling. And you're as pale as a ghost. What happened?"

    (Woman) "I nearly had a terrible accident. I was driving down Glenmore Boulevard in the right-hand lane when a school bus pulled over in front of me. I had to run off the road to keep from get-ting hit."

    (Third voice) "What is the woman upset about?"

(A) She imagined that she had seen a ghost.
(B) She hit a bus full of school children.
(C) She almost collided with a school bus.
(D) The boulevard was too narrow.

28. (Woman) "I'm here to pick up Taffy. Is she all right?"

(Man) "I think she ought to stay here for at least another twenty-four hours. She still has an infection in her hind leg that should be watched carefully. Why don't you telephone tomorrow morning?"

(Third voice) "Where does this conversation most likely take place?"

(A) In a pet shop.
(B) In a pediatrician's office.
(C) In a veterinary clinic.
(D) In a medical laboratory.

29. (Woman) "If I leave for Europe in two months, as I've been planning, I'd better get my passport picture taken soon. Is there a photographer nearby?"

(Man) "There's one just off campus, but he's expensive. I think there's a cheaper one near the downtown bank, but I could be mistaken. Why don't you check around?"

(Third voice) "Where does this conversation probably take place?"

(A) In Europe.
(B) At the university.
(C) In a photographer's studio.
(D) In a bank.

30. (Woman) "There was a storm warning on the radio this morning. Did you happen to be listening?"

(Man) "No, but what a shame. I guess we'll have to change our sailing plans. Would

you rather play tennis or go bicycle riding?"

(Third voice) "What had the couple planned to do before the storm warning was issued?"

(A) Go boating.
(B) Listen to the radio.
(C) Play tennis.
(D) Go bicycling.

31. (Woman) "I can't decide what to serve for dessert tonight. We're having roast beef, baked potatoes with sour cream, and a Caesar salad. Any suggestions?"

(Man) "Well, I really like your strawberry pie, but strawberries are out of season now. Why not serve something simple like lime sherbet?"

(Third voice) "What probably will not be served tonight?"

(A) Meat.
(B) Strawberry pie.
(C) Potatoes and sour cream.
(D) Lime sherbet.

32. (Woman) "I need to purchase two tickets to Nassau for the last week in April. Also, try to see if you can book a room for me at the Royal Princess and arrange transfers from the airport."

(Man) "We do have some fantastic island packages for the spring. Do you prefer single or double accommodations?"

(Third voice) "What is most probably the man's profession?"

(A) Hotel manager.
(B) Steward on a plane.
(C) Travel agent.
(D) Librarian.

33. (Woman) "I see that you have the lawnmower out. Are you going to cut grass in this heat?"

(Man) "Well, it has to be done, but I need to trim the box hedge next to the fence before I mow the lawn."

(Third voice) "What will the man do first?"

(A) Mend the fence.
(B) Cut the grass.
(C) Trim the lawn.
(D) Clip the hedge.

34. (Man) "How can you stand living in the dormitory? All that noise would drive me crazy. And the heat this time of year!"

(Woman) "Oh, it's not so bad. I do have a room by myself and access to a small kitchen down the corridor."

(Third voice) "What does the dormitory *not* have?"

(A) Private rooms.
(B) Kitchen privileges.
(C) Noisy students.
(D) Air-conditioning.

35. (Woman) "Now this chair I like. It would go perfectly with my blue carpet and new blue and yellow draperies. But I don't see a price tag."

(Man) "Well, there's a small hole on the back side of the cushion. See? It regularly sells for $150, but we will gladly make an adjustment if you want it."

(Third voice) "What do we know about the chair?"

(A) It is yellow.
(B) It is blue and yellow.
(C) The salesman is asking $150 for it.
(D) It is damaged.

Part C

Directions. In this part of the test, you will be required to listen to several short lectures and conversations. You will hear the lectures and conversations only once. They do not appear in your test booklet. When a question is asked, choose the best answer from the four given. Record your answer on the answer sheet.

Questions 36–39 are based on the following lecture.

The value of a diamond is estimated according to four qualities—carat, clarity, color, and cut. However, only carat, a unit of weight, is an objective measure, since a diamond's weight in carats can be determined by an electronic scale. The remaining characteristics have a partly subjective basis.

Clarity refers to the external cracks or to the internal flaws left in the diamond when it is formed under intense heat and pressure.

The third quality is color, and, in general, the less the color, the better the diamond. A tinge of gray or yellow can lower a diamond's value. On the other hand, a clear, bright yellow diamond, called a "fancy yellow," commands a higher price than the top-quality white diamonds.

Finally, the cut of a diamond is judged by the shape of the stone, its light refraction, and how well it is polished.

36. (What quality of a diamond can be determined objectively?)

(A) Color.
(B) Cut.
(C) Carat.
(D) Clarity.

37. (What does the clarity of a diamond involve?)

(A) Its defects.
(B) Its color.
(C) Its shape.
(D) Its weight.

38. (Which diamond is the most valuable?)

    (A) A clear, bright yellow diamond.
    (B) A slightly gray diamond.
    (C) A white diamond.
    (D) A diamond with a slight yellow cast.

39. (Which of the following does not refer to the cut of a diamond?)

    (A) Its weight.
    (B) Its shape.
    (C) Its light refraction.
    (D) Its smoothness.

Questions 40–42 relate to the following talk.

  Because goldfish can be kept easily in small ponds and aquariums, they make good pets, but like any other pets, they must have proper care and the right kind of place to live.

  A two-inch fish requires a minimum of two gallons of water containing sufficient oxygen to support life. Some oxygen will make its way into the water of an aquarium from the air that touches the surface; plants in an aquarium also help to furnish oxygen. Snails help to keep an aquarium clean. Thus, with plenty of plants and snails, the water in an aquarium does not have to be changed frequently.

  It is important that goldfish not be overfed. They can be fed such things as dried insects and shrimp in addition to commercially prepared goldfish food, but they should never be fed more than once a day. Even then, they should not be given more food than can be consumed in about five minutes.

40. (Which of the following helps supply goldfish with oxygen?)

    (A) Snails.
    (B) Plants.
    (C) Shrimp.
    (D) Dried insects.

41. (All but which of the following are commonly used as goldfish food?)

    (A) Dried shrimp.
    (B) Dried insects.

(C) Commercial goldfish food.
(D) Snails.

42. (What is important to remember when feeding goldfish?)

    (A) They should be fed more than once a day.
    (B) They should be fed fresh food.
    (C) They should be fed at five-minute intervals.
    (D) They should never be fed more than once a day.

Questions 43–46 are based on the following lecture.

  On May 7, 1915, the British liner *Lusitania* was sunk without warning by a German submarine. The sinking of the *Lusitania* contributed to the entry of the United States into World War I two years later.

  At the time of the unprovoked attack, the 32,000-ton ship was sailing on her regular run from New York to Liverpool in spite of the war. She had a full load of passengers and a cargo that included munitions. The ship was unarmed. Her speed was 18 knots, a speed much greater than that of contemporary submarines. Therefore, it was only with much luck that the German U-boat was able to get into torpedo range and fire at the *Lusitania*.

  When she was only a few miles off the coast of Ireland, the *Lusitania* sank. Of the almost 2,000 passengers, more than 1,000 persons drowned, among them 128 American citizens.

43. (What kind of ship was the *Lusitania*?)

    (A) A U-boat.
    (B) A merchant ship.
    (C) A warship.
    (D) A submarine.

44. (When did the *Lusitania* sink?)

    (A) In 1917.
    (B) In 1915.
    (C) In 1913.
    (D) In 1918.

45. (Which country did the *Lusitania* belong to?)

   (A) Britain.
   (B) Ireland.
   (C) Germany.
   (D) The United States.

46. (Where was the *Lusitania* located when she sank?)

   (A) Near Liverpool.
   (B) In a New York port.
   (C) A short distance from the Irish coast.
   (D) In German war territory.

Questions 47–50 are based on the following lecture.

Yellow fever, a severe disease transmitted by mosquitoes, is characterized by general aches, high fever, hemorrhage, vomiting, fatigue, loss of appetite, and yellowness of the skin. It was first observed in Boston in 1658, and the final outbreak in the United States occurred in New Orleans in 1905.

It was believed at first that yellow fever, or yellowjack, as it is sometimes called, came from Central or South America, but scientific investigations now indicate a West African origin. The current theory is that the *Aedes aegypti,* infected with the yellow fever virus, came to the New World aboard slave ships. The female *Aegypti* bit humans on the ships, and the infectious cycle was underway.

Until 1881, many causes of yellow fever were suspected, such as filth in the streets or even noxious gases. But then a Cuban, Dr. Carlos Finlay, proposed the theory of propagation of the disease by means of the mosquito.

47. (Which of the following is *not* a symptom of yellow fever?)

   (A) Yellowjack.
   (B) Poor appetite.
   (C) Exhaustion.
   (D) Yellow skin.

48. (According to the lecture, where was the last yellow fever epidemic in America?)

   (A) In Cuba.
   (B) In New Orleans.
   (C) In Africa.
   (D) In Boston.

49. (What is the *Aedes aegypti*?)

   (A) A fever.
   (B) A slave ship.
   (C) A mosquito.
   (D) A virus.

50. (Where did yellow fever probably originate?)

   (A) In the United States.
   (B) In Africa.
   (C) In Central America.
   (D) In South America.

Glossary of Correct Usage

The following glossary contains words or phrases which may cause you special difficulty.

1. **accept, except.** *Accept* is a verb; *except* is a preposition.

   WRONG: They excepted my invitation to dinner.
   RIGHT: They *accepted* my invitation to dinner.

   WRONG: Everyone attended the meeting accept the secretary.
   RIGHT: Everyone attended the meeting *except* the secretary.

2. **advice, advise.** *Advice* is a noun; *advise* is a verb.

   WRONG: His advise was very useful.
   RIGHT: His *advice* was very useful.

   WRONG: I was adviced to purchase an economical car.
   RIGHT: I was *advised* to purchase an economical car.

3. **affect, effect.** *Affect* is a verb; it means "to influence." *Effect* may be a verb or a noun. The verb *effect* means "to cause to happen." The noun *effect* means "the result."

   WRONG: Pollution effects everyone.
   RIGHT: Pollution *affects* everyone.

   WRONG: Your tears do not effect me.
   RIGHT: Your tears do not *affect* me.

   WRONG: What is the affect of that drug?
   RIGHT: What is the *effect* of that drug?

4. **almost, most.** *Most* is an adjective; *almost* is an adverb.

   WRONG: Most everyone has a desire to succeed.
   RIGHT: *Almost* everyone has a desire to succeed.

   WRONG: The student was most finished when the bell rang.
   RIGHT: The student was *almost* finished when the bell rang.

   WRONG: The children ate most all of the pie.
   RIGHT: The children ate *almost* all of the pie.
   or
   The children ate *most* of the pie.

5. **already, all ready.** *Already* means "before the time specified." *All ready* means "completely prepared."

   WRONG: The movie had all ready begun by the time we arrived.
   RIGHT: The movie had *already* begun by the time we arrived.

   WRONG: Are you already to go?
   RIGHT: Are you *all ready* to go?

6. **altogether, all together.** *Altogether* means "thoroughly." *All together* means "in a group."

   WRONG: All together confused, he asked me to explain the word again.
   RIGHT: *Altogether* confused, he asked me to explain the word again.

   WRONG: The passengers stood altogether in the station.
   RIGHT: The passengers stood *all together* in the station.

7. **amount, number.** Use *amount* to refer to things which cannot be counted. *Number* refers to the countable.

   WRONG: He checked out a large amount of books from the library.

289

RIGHT: He checked out a large *number* of books from the library.

WRONG: I was amazed by the amount of people present.

RIGHT: I was amazed by the *number* of people present.

WRONG: Elephants can consume a large number of food.

RIGHT: Elephants can consume a large *amount* of food.

8. **anywheres, somewheres, everywheres.** Omit the *s*.

WRONG: We can talk anywheres.
RIGHT: We can talk *anywhere*.

WRONG: I lost my umbrella somewheres in the store.

RIGHT: I lost my umbrella *somewhere* in the store.

9. **about, around.** *Around* refers to place. *About* means "approximately."

WRONG: The mail arrived around ten o'clock.
RIGHT: The mail arrived *about* ten o'clock.

WRONG: He is around six feet tall.
RIGHT: He is *about* six feet tall.

10. **because, because of.** *Because* is a subordinating conjunction; it is followed by a clause. *Because of* is a preposition; it is followed by a noun or a noun phrase.

WRONG: The game was canceled because of it was raining.
RIGHT: The game was canceled *because of* the rain.

WRONG: We could not see because the poor lighting.
RIGHT: We could not see *because* the lighting was poor.

WRONG: He can move the furniture easily because of he is strong.
RIGHT: He can move the furniture easily *because of* his strength.

11. **beside, besides.** *Beside* means "next to." *Besides* means "in addition to."

WRONG: Beside Tommy, Helen and I attended the concert.
RIGHT: *Besides* Tommy, Helen and I attended the concert.

WRONG: He was sitting besides the pretty girl.
RIGHT: He was sitting *beside* the pretty girl.

WRONG: We visited California beside Oregon.
RIGHT: We visited California *besides* Oregon.

or

We visited California. *Besides,* we visited Oregon.

12. **between, among.** *Between* is used with two persons or things. *Among* is used with three or more persons or things.

WRONG: The law was debated between the senators, the representatives, and the judges.
RIGHT: The law was debated *among* the senators, the representatives, and the judges.

WRONG: There is a dispute between the local union members.
RIGHT: There is a dispute *among* the local union members.

WRONG: You must choose among the two plans.
RIGHT: You must choose *between* the two plans.

13. **but, hardly, scarcely.** These words are negative. Do not use them with another negative word.

WRONG: I couldn't hardly see him in the dark.
RIGHT: I *could hardly* see him in the dark.

WRONG: She didn't earn but thirty dollars last week.
RIGHT: She *earned but* thirty dollars last week.

WRONG: He doesn't spend scarcely any money on clothes.

RIGHT: He *spends scarcely* any money on clothes.

14. **different from** (not **different than**).

WRONG: The result was much different than what I expected.

RIGHT: The result was much *different from* what I expected.

15. **do, make.** These words have different meanings.

WRONG: They did a peaceful agreement.
RIGHT: They *made* a peaceful agreement.

WRONG: I never do fun of other people.
RIGHT: I never *make* fun of other people.

WRONG: It's time to do the sandwiches.
RIGHT: It's time *to make* the sandwiches.

WRONG: Rarely does he do a mistake.
RIGHT: Rarely does he *make* a mistake.

WRONG: I'll do the arrangements for the party.
RIGHT: I'll *make* the arrangements for the party.

WRONG: Will you make me a small favor?
RIGHT: Will you *do* me a small favor?

WRONG: Before she left the house, she did her bed.
RIGHT: Before she left the house, she *made* her bed.

WRONG: The president did an interesting speech, didn't he?
RIGHT: The president *made* an interesting speech, didn't he?

WRONG: My father refuses to make business with dishonest people.
RIGHT: My father refuses to *do* business with dishonest people.

WRONG: The teacher did the examination difficult.

RIGHT: The teacher *made* the examination difficult.

16. **equally as** + adjective is not correct. Use either *equally* + adjective or *as* + adjective + *as*.

WRONG: The second lesson was equally as difficult as the third.
RIGHT: The second and the third lessons were *equally difficult*.
    or
    The second lesson was *as difficult as* the third.

WRONG: Jim and his brother-in-law are equally as tall.
RIGHT: Jim and his brother-in-law are *equally tall*.
    or
    Jim is *as tall as* his brother-in-law.

17. **expect, suppose, think.** *Suppose* and *think* are not followed by infinitives. *Expect* is not followed by a noun clause.

WRONG: He thinks to graduate in May.
RIGHT: He *expects* to graduate in May.
    or
    He *thinks* (or *supposes*) that he will graduate in May.

WRONG: I suppose to see you tomorrow.
RIGHT: I *expect* to see you tomorrow.
    or
    I *suppose* (or *think*) that I will see you tomorrow.

WRONG: I expect that he is busy now.
RIGHT: I *think* (or *suppose*) that he is busy now.

18. **farther, further.** *Farther* refers to distance; *further* is used to express additional time, degree, or quantity.

WRONG: Chicago is further north than Fort Worth.
RIGHT: Chicago is *farther* north than Fort Worth.

WRONG: I can give you farther information about this later.

RIGHT: I can give you *further* information about this later.

WRONG: How much further did he run than she did?

RIGHT: How much *farther* did he run than she did?

19. **few, a few.** *Few* has a negative implication; it means *not many. A few* has an affirmative meaning; it means *some.*

WRONG: He was so tired that he stopped playing for few minutes.

RIGHT: He was so tired that he stopped playing for *a few* minutes.

WRONG: There were a few chairs left, so I had to stand up.

RIGHT: There were *few* chairs left, so I had to stand up.

WRONG: The meeting was canceled because a few members attended.

RIGHT: The meeting was canceled because *few* members attended.

WRONG: Most people in Mexico speak Spanish, but few speak English.

RIGHT: Most people in Mexico speak Spanish, but *a few* speak English.

20. **fewer, less.** *Fewer* refers to the countable. *Less* refers to value, degree, or amount.

WRONG: The class consists of less than fifteen students.

RIGHT: The class consists of *fewer* than fifteen students.

WRONG: He spends fewer time on his studies than on his golf game.

RIGHT: He spends *less* time on his studies than on his golf game.

WRONG: It is true that less girls than boys become engineers.

RIGHT: It is true that *fewer* girls than boys become engineers.

21. **had better, would rather** are followed by the short infinitive.

WRONG: You had better to pay attention to the details.

RIGHT: You *had better pay* attention to the details.

WRONG: I had better not to play tennis this afternoon.

RIGHT: I *had better not play* tennis this afternoon.

WRONG: Which movie would you rather to see?

RIGHT: Which movie *would you rather see?*

WRONG: She says that she would rather not to have dessert.

RIGHT: She says that she *would rather not have* dessert.

22. **hanged, hung.** *Hanged* refers to executions.

WRONG: The British hung Nathan Hale as a spy.

RIGHT: The British *hanged* Nathan Hale as a spy.

WRONG: He hanged his suit in the closet.

RIGHT: He *hung* his suit in the closet.

WRONG: My mother hanged her children's pictures on the wall.

RIGHT: My mother *hung* her children's pictures on the wall.

23. **in, into.** *In* indicates "location within." *Into* indicates "motion or direction."

WRONG: She stepped carefully in the car.

RIGHT: She stepped carefully *into* the car.

WRONG: He jumped off his bicycle and ran in the library.

RIGHT: He jumped off his bicycle and ran *into* the library.

24. **in regards to** is not correct. Say *in regard to, as regards,* or *regarding.*

WRONG: I am writing in regards to your letter of May 10.

RIGHT: I am writing *in regard to* (or *as regards, regarding*) your letter of May 10.

25. **in spite of, despite** are prepositions. They cannot be followed by a clause.

WRONG: I was able to concentrate despite the room was noisy.
RIGHT: I was able to concentrate *despite* the noisy room.

WRONG: In spite of it was cold, he didn't wear a coat.
RIGHT: *In spite of* the cold, he didn't wear a coat.

26. **its, it's.** *Its* is a possessive pronoun. *It's* is a contraction of *it is.*

WRONG: Its essential that we leave on time.
RIGHT: *It's* essential that we leave on time.

WRONG: The human body and it's organs are interesting to study.
RIGHT: The human body and *its* organs are interesting to study.

WRONG: The dog wagged it's tail when it saw the food.
RIGHT: The dog wagged *its* tail when it saw the food.

27. **kind, sort,** and **type** are singular words. They must be modified by singular adjectives. The plural forms are *kinds, sorts,* and *types.*

WRONG: You should avoid making these kind of mistakes.
RIGHT: You should avoid making *these kinds* of mistakes.
or
You should avoid making *this kind* of mistake.

WRONG: Those kind of insects are harmful to man.
RIGHT: *Those kinds* of insects are harmful to man.
or
That kind of insect is harmful to man.

28. **kind of a, sort of a, type of a.** Omit *a.*

WRONG: What kind of a telephone did the company install?
RIGHT: What *kind of* telephone did the company install?

WRONG: The vicuna is a shy type of an animal.
RIGHT: The vicuna is a shy *type of* animal.

29. **later, latter.** *Later* is the comparative of *late.* *Latter* refers to the last named of two things or people.

WRONG: Jefferson and Lincoln are two famous presidents. The later was assassinated while in office.
RIGHT: Jefferson and Lincoln are two famous presidents. *The latter* was assassinated while in office.

30. **lay, lie.** The verb *lay* has an object; the verb *lie* does not have an object. The principal parts of the verb *lay* are: *lay* (present), *laid* (past), *laid* (past participle), and *laying* (present participle). The principal parts of the verb *lie* are; *lie* (present), *lay* (past), *lain* (past participle), and *lying* (present participle).

WRONG: I always lay down after I eat dinner.
RIGHT: I always *lie* down after I eat dinner. (present tense)

WRONG: He laid down because he had a headache.
RIGHT: He *lay* down because he had a headache. (past tense)

WRONG: The books are laying on the table.
RIGHT: The books are *lying* on the table. (present participle)

WRONG: The teacher lay her books on the table when she entered the room.
RIGHT: The teacher *laid* her books on the table when she entered the room. (past tense)

WRONG: The boys have laid under the trees for hours.
RIGHT: The boys have *lain* under the trees for hours. (present participle)

31. **lend, loan.** *Lend* is a verb; *loan* is a noun.

WRONG: Would you mind loaning me your pencil?
RIGHT: Would you mind *lending* me your pencil?

WRONG: I needed money, so John loaned me some.
RIGHT: I needed money, so John *lent* me some.

32. **little, a little.** *Little* means "not much." *A little* means "some."

WRONG: He has had difficulty in finding a job because he has a little education.
RIGHT: He has had difficulty in finding a job because he has *little* education.

WRONG: This machine is easy to operate; you need a little skill.
RIGHT: This machine is easy to operate; you need *little* skill.

WRONG: Learning to ski is difficult; little effort is required.
RIGHT: Learning to ski is difficult; *a little effort* is required.

WRONG: Please give me little more time to finish writing.
RIGHT: Please give me *a little* more time to finish writing.

33. **like, as, as if.** *Like* is a preposition; *as, as if* (or *as though*) are conjunctions. *As* is also a preposition when it means "in the capacity of."

WRONG: She doesn't study like she should.
RIGHT: She doesn't study *as* she should.

WRONG: You ought to write as me.
RIGHT: You ought to write *like* me.

WRONG: Like the coach said, the team performed well.
RIGHT: *As* the coach said, the team performed well.

WRONG: She acts like she doesn't understand.
RIGHT: She acts *as if* (or *as though*) she doesn't understand.

WRONG: Like a full-time student, you must register for at least four courses a semester.
RIGHT: *As* a full-time student, you must register for at least four courses a semester.

34. **lose, loose.** *Lose* is a verb; the past tense of *lose* is *lost*. *Loose* is an adjective which means "not tight."

WRONG: She will loose weight if she goes on a diet.
RIGHT: She will *lose* weight if she goes on a diet.

WRONG: One of the knobs on the drawer is lose.
RIGHT: One of the knobs on the drawer is *loose*. (meaning "not tight")
or
One of the knobs on the drawer is *lost*. (meaning "missing")

35. **maybe, may be.** *Maybe* means "perhaps." *May be* is a verb.

WRONG: May be the sun will come out tomorrow.
RIGHT: *Maybe* the sun will come out tomorrow.

WRONG: The secretary maybe out to lunch.
RIGHT: The secretary *may be* out to lunch.

36. **myself, himself, herself, yourself, ourselves, themselves,** and **yourselves** are reflexive pronouns. They are used when the subject of the verb also receives the action of the verb or when emphasis is needed.

WRONG: Only Bill and myself witnessed the accident.

RIGHT: Only Bill and *I* witnessed the accident.

WRONG: The tires of the car are bad, but itself is in good condition.

RIGHT: The tires of the car are bad, but *the car itself* is in good condition.

WRONG: They did the work by theirselves.

RIGHT: They did the work by *themselves*.

WRONG: The little boy was extremely intelligent; he taught him to read.

RIGHT: The little boy was extremely intelligent; he taught *himself* to read.

37. **passed, past.** *Passed* is the past tense of the verb *pass*. *Past* is either an adjective or a noun.

WRONG: When I asked, she past me the sugar.

RIGHT: When I asked, she *passed* me the sugar.

WRONG: I past his house on the way to the post office.

RIGHT: I *passed* his house on the way to the post office.

WRONG: In passed times, salt was often used as money.

RIGHT: In *past* times, salt was often used as money.

WRONG: One can learn from passed experiences.

RIGHT: One can learn from *past* experiences.
or
One can learn from experiences in his *past*.

38. **percentage, percent.** Use *percent* after a number.

WRONG: A large percent of his salary is spent on food.

RIGHT: A large *percentage* of his salary is spent on food.

WRONG: Almost fifty percentage of our energy resources come from abroad.

RIGHT: Almost fifty *percent* of our energy resources come from abroad.

39. **prefer** and **superior** are not followed by the preposition *than*.

WRONG: Many students prefer history than mathematics.

RIGHT: Many students prefer history *to* mathematics.
or
Many students prefer history *rather than* mathematics.

WRONG: I believe that a microwave oven is superior than a conventional oven.

RIGHT: I believe that a microwave oven is superior *to* a conventional oven.

40. **principal, principle.** *Principal* is a noun or an adjective meaning "chief official or main." *Principle* is a noun meaning "fundamental truth."

WRONG: In his research he followed basic scientific principals.

RIGHT: In his research he followed basic scientific *principles*.

WRONG: The principle side effect of decongestants is drowsiness.

RIGHT: The *principal* side effect of decongestants is drowsiness.

WRONG: The chairman pointed out his principle objections.

RIGHT: The chairman pointed out his *principal* objections.

41. **quiet, quite.** *Quiet* means "silent." *Quite* means "completely."

WRONG: We must be quite inside the library.

RIGHT: We must be *quiet* inside the library.

WRONG: Your answer was quiet wrong.
RIGHT: Your answer was *quite* wrong.

42.   **raise, rise.** The verb *rise* does not have an object. The verb *raise* has an object. The principal parts of the verb *rise* are: *rise* (present), *rose* (past), *risen* (past participle), and *rising* (present participle). The principal parts of the verb *raise* are: *raise* (present), *raised* (past), *raised* (past participle), and *raising* (present participle).

WRONG: He rose his hand before asking a question.
RIGHT: He *raised* his hand before asking a question. (past tense)

WRONG: Having finished lunch, he raised from the table.
RIGHT: Having finished lunch, he *rose* from the table. (past tense)

WRONG: The sun is raising high in the sky.
RIGHT: The sun is *rising* high in the sky. (present participle)

WRONG: Some questions were risen about taxes.
RIGHT: Some questions were *raised* about taxes. (past participle)

WRONG: My grandfather raises early every morning.
RIGHT: My grandfather *rises* early every morning. (present tense)

WRONG: Private income has raised steadily for the past decade.
RIGHT: Private income has *risen* steadily for the past decade. (past participle)

43.   **reason . . . because** is not correct. Say *reason . . . that.*

WRONG: The reason he makes poor grades is because he never studies.
RIGHT: The reason he makes poor grades is *that* he never studies.

WRONG: My reason for using a typewriter is because my handwriting is poor.

RIGHT: My reason for using a typewriter is *that* my handwriting is poor.

44.   **seldom ever, seldom or ever** are incorrect. Use *seldom if ever* or *hardly ever.*

WRONG: Tigers seldom ever eat human beings.
RIGHT: Tigers *seldom if ever* (or *hardly ever*) eat human beings.

45.   **some, somewhat.** *Some* is an adjective; *somewhat* is an adverb.

WRONG: Students find that mathematical concept some difficult.
RIGHT: Students find that mathematical concept *somewhat* difficult.

WRONG: His shirt looks some dirty.
RIGHT: His shirt looks *somewhat* dirty.

46.   **sit, set.** *Sit* does not take an object; *set* takes an object. The principal parts of the verb *sit* are: *sit* (present), *sat* (past), *sat* (past participle), and *sitting* (present participle). The principal parts of the verb *set* are: *set* (present), *set* (past), *set* (past participle), and *setting* (present participle).

WRONG: The old man is setting on the porch.
RIGHT: The old man is *sitting* on the porch. (present participle)

WRONG: The woman sat the groceries on the table.
RIGHT: The woman *set* the groceries on the table. (past tense)

WRONG: Exhausted, the hiker set down to rest.
RIGHT: Exhausted, the hiker *sat* down to rest. (past tense)

WRONG: Please set here if you're tired.
RIGHT: Please *sit* here if you're tired. (present tense)

47.   **so that** refers to "purpose." Do not omit "that."

WRONG: He came here so he could study English.

RIGHT: He came here *so that* he could study English.

WRONG: The spider spins a web so it can catch insects.

RIGHT: The spider spins a web *so that* it can catch insects.

48.   **such, so.** Avoid using these words instead of the word "very."

WRONG: Taxes are so high today.
RIGHT: Taxes are *very* high today.
or
Taxes are *so* high today *that* some people try to cheat on their tax returns.

WRONG: Professor Davis is such a good lecturer.

RIGHT: Professor Davis is a *very* good lecturer.
or
Professor Davis is *such* a good lecturer *that* students enjoy being in his class.

49.   **sure** and **try** are not followed by *and.*

WRONG: You should try and write legibly.
RIGHT: You should *try to* write legibly.

WRONG: I am going to try and get some sleep tonight.
RIGHT: I am going to *try to* get some sleep tonight.

WRONG: Be sure and bring a pencil to class tomorrow.
RIGHT: Be sure *to bring* a pencil to class tomorrow.

50.   **that.** Do not omit *that* in noun clauses. Be especially careful when there is more than one noun clause.

WRONG: My objection to smoking is it is dangerous to health.
RIGHT: My objection to smoking is *that* it is dangerous to health.

WRONG: Everyone knows Greenland is an island and it is located to the north.

RIGHT: Everyone knows *that* Greenland is an island and *that* it is located to the north.

51.   **their, there, they're.**

WRONG: I am interested in they're habits.
RIGHT: I am interested in *their* habits.

WRONG: Their coming later this afternoon.
RIGHT: *They're* coming later this afternoon.

WRONG: They're coming surprised us.
RIGHT: *Their* coming surprised us.

WRONG: They're several ways to use the word correctly.
RIGHT: *There* are several ways to use the word correctly.

52.   **too, enough.** *Too* means "to an excessive degree." *Enough* means "adequate or sufficient for the purpose desired."

WRONG: Your brother is too old to know better.
RIGHT: Your brother is old *enough* to know better.

WRONG: The window was dirty enough to see through.
RIGHT: The window was *too* dirty to see through.

WRONG: I am too sick to miss class.
RIGHT: I am sick *enough* to miss class.

WRONG: John is too clever to solve the problem.
RIGHT: John is clever *enough* to solve the problem.

53.   **used to, supposed to.** Do not omit the *d.*

WRONG: I use to enjoy gardening.
RIGHT: I *used to* enjoy gardening.

WRONG: My uncle has trouble breathing; he isn't suppose to smoke.
RIGHT: My uncle has trouble breathing; he isn't *supposed to* smoke.

54. **very.** Do not use this word instead of the word *too*.

WRONG: This book is very old to use anymore.

RIGHT: This book is *too* old to use anymore.

WRONG: The weather is very cold to go swimming.

RIGHT: The weather is *too* cold to go swimming.

WRONG: The actor is very nervous to go on stage.

RIGHT: The actor is *too* nervous to go on stage.

55. **wait on** means "to serve." Do not confuse with *wait for*.

WRONG: My friend was late; I had to wait on him for half an hour.

RIGHT: My friend was late; I had to *wait for* him for half an hour.

WRONG: Good clerks are happy to wait for their customers.

RIGHT: Good clerks are happy to *wait on* their customers.

56. **want** is not followed by a noun clause. It is often followed by an infinitive.

WRONG: She wants that she can pass the test.

RIGHT: She *wants to pass* the test.

WRONG: My father wants that I do well in school.

RIGHT: My father *wants me to do* well in school.

57. **where** refers to place. Avoid using *where* as a synonym for *that*.

WRONG: I read in the newspaper where crime is on the increase.

RIGHT: I read in the newspaper *that* crime is on the increase.

WRONG: Have you noticed where people are smoking less than they used to?

RIGHT: Have you noticed *that* people are smoking less than they used to?

58. **which** is a relative pronoun that refers to things and never to people.

WRONG: The person with which I had the argument was the chairman.

RIGHT: The person with *whom* I had the argument was the chairman.

WRONG: The scientist which invented the electric light was Thomas Edison.

RIGHT: The scientist *who* invented the electric light was Thomas Edison.

WRONG: I was annoyed by the salesman which came to my door.

RIGHT: I was annoyed by the salesman *who* came to my door.

59. **while** usually refers to time. Avoid using *while* to show contrast.

WRONG: While my family is not rich, we have many advantages.

RIGHT: *Although* my family is not rich, we have many advantages.

WRONG: While I was not busy, I couldn't help him.

RIGHT: *Although* I was not busy, I couldn't help him.

WRONG: While teaching seems like a good profession, I would prefer to be a lawyer.

RIGHT: *Although* teaching seems like a good profession, I would prefer to be a lawyer.

60. **who, whom.** *Who* is a subject pronoun. *Whom* is an object pronoun.

WRONG: Who did you speak to about your problem?

RIGHT: *Whom* did you speak to about your problem? (*Whom* is the object of the preposition *to*.)

WRONG: Whom did you say ruled the country at that time?

RIGHT: *Who* did you say ruled the country at that time? (*Who* is the subject of the verb *ruled*.)

WRONG: John Kennedy was a man who many people admired.

RIGHT: John Kennedy was a man *whom* many people admired. (*Whom* is the object of the verb *admired*.)

61. **who's, whose.** *Who's* means *who is*. *Whose* is possessive.

WRONG: The counselor was the person who's advice I took.

RIGHT: The counselor was the person *whose* advice I took.

WRONG: Do you remember whose in charge of preparing the menu?

RIGHT: Do you remember *who's* in charge of preparing the menu?

62. **would.** Although this word is the past tense form of *will*, it is often used to show action occurring in the present time. It is also used frequently in noun clauses when the principal verb is in the past tense.

WRONG: Will you like a cup of coffee now?

RIGHT: *Would* you like a cup of coffee now?

WRONG: I have never met your parents, but I will like to know them.

RIGHT: I have never met your parents, but I *would* like to know them.

WRONG: My boss told me that he will increase my salary next year.

RIGHT: My boss told me that he *would* increase my salary next year.

WRONG: We heard on the radio that it will rain tomorrow.

RIGHT: We heard on the radio that it *would* rain tomorrow.

Review of Basic Grammatical Structures

LIST OF STRUCTURES

Review of Basic Grammatical Structures

ADJECTIVES AND ADVERBS

Adjectives modify nouns and pronouns. Adverbs modify verbs, adjectives, and other adverbs. Study the following list of trouble spots related to the use of adjectives and adverbs:

(1) Linking verbs are followed by adjectives, not adverbs. Here is a list of common linking verbs:

be	remain
become	feel
appear	smell
look	sound
seem	taste

Note that some of the verbs listed as linking verbs may sometimes function as verbs of action:

Adjectives	Adverbs
I feel *tired*.	I felt my way *slowly* in the darkness.
He looked *angry*.	He looked about the room *angrily*.
The pie tastes *delicious*.	She tasted the pie *cautiously*.

(2) Verbs are modified by adverbs, not by adjectives:

Mr. Jackson is a *good* teacher.	Mr. Jackson teaches *well*.
Her brother is a *bad* driver.	He drives *badly*.
There has been a *considerable* change in the weather.	The weather has changed *considerably*.
My sister is a *superb* dancer.	My sister dances *superbly*.
The teacher gave a *quick* explanation of the problem.	The teacher explained the problem *quickly*.
This is a *slow* exercise.	This exercise must be done *slowly*.

WRONG: The girl looks *intelligently*.
RIGHT: The girl looks *intelligent*.

WRONG: That perfume smells *sweetly*, doesn't it?
RIGHT: That perfume smells *sweet*, doesn't it?

WRONG: The physician appeared *nervously* when he talked to the patient.
RIGHT: The physician appeared *nervous* when he talked to the patient.

WRONG: This bed seems very *comfortably*.
RIGHT: This bed seems very *comfortable*.

301

WRONG:	I felt *badly* about forgetting the appointment.
RIGHT:	I felt *bad* about forgetting the appointment.

WRONG:	We all agreed that the new film was *real* good.
RIGHT:	We all agreed that the new film was *really* good.

WRONG:	The students found the physics examination *extreme* difficult.
RIGHT:	The students found the physics examination *extremely* difficult.

WRONG:	If you speak *firm,* he will listen to you.
RIGHT:	If you speak *firmly,* he will listen to you.

WRONG:	He made *considerable* more progress than I.
RIGHT:	He made *considerably* more progress than I.

WRONG:	The professor presented an *obvious* important point in class.
RIGHT:	The professor presented an *obviously* important point in class.

WRONG:	He said that the medicine tasted *terribly.*
RIGHT:	He said that the medicine tasted *terrible.*

WRONG:	It rained *steady* all day yesterday.
RIGHT:	It rained *steadily* all day yesterday.

WRONG:	The dog remained *faithfully* to its master until the end.
RIGHT:	The dog remained *faithful* to its master until the end.

WRONG:	He can do the job *easier* than you can.
RIGHT:	He can do the job *more easily* than you can.

WRONG:	The problem seemed *exceeding* complex to me.
RIGHT:	The problem seemed *exceedingly* complex to me.

(3) Negative adverbs, such as *hardly, seldom, rarely,* and *never,* should not be used with other negatives.

WRONG:	He *hasn't never* seen a copy of our latest book.
RIGHT:	He *has never* seen a copy of our latest book.

or

He *hasn't ever* seen a copy of our latest book.

WRONG:	He rarely eats at that restaurant, *doesn't* he?
RIGHT:	He rarely eats at that restaurant, *does* he?

WRONG:	I *can't* scarcely believe it's true.
RIGHT:	I *can* scarcely believe it's true.

WRONG:	I *hadn't* hardly gotten out the door when the phone rang again.
RIGHT:	I *had* hardly gotten out the door when the phone rang again.

(4) When *these* and *those* are used as demonstrative adjectives, they must be followed by a *plural* noun.

WRONG:	*These combination* of chemicals can be dangerous.
RIGHT:	*These combinations* of chemicals can be dangerous.

WRONG:	Those *kind* of jackets are very popular.
RIGHT:	Those *kinds* of jackets are very popular.

or

That *kind* of jacket is very popular.

(5) Some adjectives and adverbs have the same form, such as *fast, hard, right, straight,* and *late.*

WRONG: Several people arrived too *lately* to be admitted to the performance.
RIGHT: Several people arrived too *late* to be admitted to the performance.

WRONG: The horse ran *fastly* enough to win the race.
RIGHT: The horse ran *fast* enough to win the race.

WRONG: The architect worked *hardly* to finish his drawings by the next day.
RIGHT: The architect worked *hard* to finish his drawings by the next day.

ADVERBIAL CLAUSES

Below is a list of six of the most important kinds of adverbial clauses. Be especially careful with the verbs in adverbial clauses of time.

(1) Reason or Purpose
The soccer game was called off *because the weather was bad.*
Since most students go out on Saturday nights, the dormitories are usually quiet then.
I carried some extra money with me *so that I wouldn't be short of cash.*

(2) Result
I found the house dark, *so I turned on a few lights.*
The coffee was so black *that the guests had trouble drinking it.*
It was such an informative lecture *that many of the students wanted to tape it.*

(3) Time
When I visited Nashville, I toured the famous Parthenon.
I will wait at home *until Mike calls.* (not *until Mike will call.*)
(Express future action by using *only the simple present tense* of the verb after words such as *when, before, after, as soon as, whenever, until.*)
When I visit Nashville, I will tour the famous Parthenon.
Before I lock the doors, I will make certain that all of the lights have been turned off.
He talked about his travels to Europe *whenever he visited his relatives in New York.*

(4) Place
Wherever he walked, people stared at him in amazement.
Please leave the key *where it belongs.*

(5) Opposition (Contrast)
Although he had studied diligently for several months, he was unable to pass the examination.
He dressed poorly and drove an old car *despite the fact that he had recently inherited three million dollars.*

(6) Comparison

The food is better in the cafeteria today *than it was yesterday*.

I don't swim as well *as she does*.

WRONG: Unless Terry *will pass* his chemistry course, he won't graduate this semester.

RIGHT: Unless Terry *passes* his chemistry course, he won't graduate this semester.

WRONG: *Although* it was raining, Anita refused to take her swimming lesson.
RIGHT: *Because* it was raining, Anita refused to take her swimming lesson.

WRONG: Vincent will wait on the corner until the bus *will come*.
RIGHT: Vincent will wait on the corner until the bus *comes*.

WRONG: We will continue the game after the rain *will stop*.
RIGHT: We will continue the game after the rain *stops*.

WRONG: He carefully taped the chemistry lecture so that he *can listen* to it again.

RIGHT: He carefully taped the chemistry lecture so that he *could listen* to it again.

WRONG: As soon as he *will get* his check, he can buy the books he needs.
RIGHT: As soon as he *gets* his check, he can buy the books he needs.

WRONG: Police officers stop citizens when they *will drive* too fast.
RIGHT: Police officers stop citizens when they *drive* too fast.

WRONG: Before you go to bed, *you will turn off* the lights.
RIGHT: Before you go to bed, *turn off* the lights.

WRONG: If anyone *will have* a question, I'll be happy to answer it.
RIGHT: If anyone *has* a question, I'll be happy to answer it.

AGREEMENT OF PRONOUN AND ANTECEDENT

The antecedent of a pronoun (the noun to which the pronoun refers) determines the person, number, and gender of the pronoun. Study the rules given in the section on *Agreement of Subject and Verb*. These rules are also important for pronoun-antecedent agreement. In short, the pronoun must be singular if its antecedent is singular; the pronoun must be plural if its antecedent is plural.

WRONG: Neither of the two women wants *their* office renovated.
RIGHT: Neither of the two women wants *her* office renovated.

WRONG: I always give each of my students the attention *they* need.
RIGHT: I always give each of my students the attention *he* needs.

WRONG: He is one of those speakers who make *his* ideas perfectly clear.
RIGHT: He is one of those speakers who make *their* ideas perfectly clear.

WRONG: No one would wish to lose all of *their* money in the stock market.
RIGHT: No one would wish to lose all of *his* money in the stock market.

WRONG: Neither the members of the committee nor the chairman submitted *their* reports on time.

RIGHT: Neither the members of the committee nor the chairman submitted *his* reports on time.

WRONG: My insurance company has recently increased *their* premiums on liability policies.

RIGHT: My insurance company has recently increased *its* premiums on liability policies.

WRONG: One can find a great deal of information on world religions if *they* go to the library.

RIGHT: One can find a great deal of information on world religions if *he* goes to the library.

WRONG: A parent should never allow *themselves* to neglect *their* children.
RIGHT: A parent should never allow *himself* to neglect *his* children.

WRONG: The state of Texas has changed *their* laws on adoption.
RIGHT: The state of Texas has changed *its* laws on adoption.

WRONG: If anyone has a question, I'll see *them* after class.
RIGHT: If anyone has a question, I'll see *him* after class.

WRONG: Which student forgot to sign *their* name in the proper place?
RIGHT: Which student forgot to sign *his* name in the proper place?

WRONG: In inflationary times a person ought to spend *their* money wisely.
RIGHT: In inflationary times a person ought to spend *his* money wisely.

WRONG: A baby tiger lives with its mother for two years, but at the age of seven months *they* can kill for *themselves*.

RIGHT: A baby tiger lives with its mother for two years, but at the age of seven months *it* can kill for *itself*.

WRONG: Neither the man nor the woman carried *their* luggage with *them*.
RIGHT: Neither the man nor the woman carried *her* luggage with *her*.

WRONG: A lawyer must deal honestly with *their* clients if *they* wish to maintain a good reputation.

RIGHT: A lawyer must deal honestly with *his* clients if *he* wishes to maintain a good reputation.

WRONG: Many people enjoy reading about the Netherlands and *their* people.
RIGHT: Many people enjoy reading about the Netherlands and *its* people.

WRONG: Any senior can rent *their* cap and gown for graduation from the bookstore.

RIGHT: Any senior can rent *his* cap and gown for graduation from the bookstore.

CASE OF PRONOUNS

Be especially careful to distinguish between the subjective case (*I, you, he, she, it, we, they, who*) and the objective case (*me, you, him, her, it, us, them, whom.*) Study the following rules:

(1) The subjective case of the pronoun must be used if the pronoun is the subject of a verb, an appositive of a subject or a predicate nominative, or a predicate nominative.

(2) The objective case of the pronoun must be used if the pronoun is a direct or indirect object, the object of a preposition, or an appositive of a direct object, indirect object, or object of a preposition.

WRONG: John and *me* took the last two seats.
RIGHT: John and *I* took the last two seats.

WRONG: Janet is much more charming than *him*.
RIGHT: Janet is much more charming than *he*.

WRONG: We, you and *me*, are responsible for sending out the newsletter.
RIGHT: We, you and *I*, are responsible for sending out the newsletter.

WRONG: *Whom* do you believe is to blame?
RIGHT: *Who* do you believe is to blame?

WRONG: You may invite *whoever* you choose.
RIGHT: You may invite *whomever* you choose.

WRONG: It was *them* who participated in the strike.
RIGHT: It was *they* who participated in the strike.

WRONG: I gave the keys to them—Susan and *she*.
RIGHT: I gave the keys to them—Susan and *her*.

WRONG: Let's you and *I* decide who caused the accident.
RIGHT: Let's you and *me* decide who caused the accident.

WRONG: People like him and *she* should be punished.
RIGHT: People like him and *her* should be punished.

WRONG: Everyone but Don and *he* accepted the player's excuse for being late.
RIGHT: Everyone but Don and *him* accepted the player's excuse for being late.

WRONG: Between you and *I*, the new proposal seems to be poorly written.
RIGHT: Between you and *me*, the new proposal seems to be poorly written.

WRONG: Carole, unlike *they*, understood the mathematical equation.
RIGHT: Carole, unlike *them*, understood the mathematical equation.

WRONG: The chairman refused to acknowledge either John or *I*.
RIGHT: The chairman refused to acknowledge either John or *me*.

WRONG: Be sure to speak to my husband or *I* about your suggestion.
RIGHT: Be sure to speak to my husband or *me* about your suggestion.

WRONG: Please remind *whomever* comes in first to open the windows.
RIGHT: Please remind *whoever* comes in first to open the windows.

WRONG: *Us* teachers are accustomed to spending hours preparing classes.
RIGHT: *We* teachers are accustomed to spending hours preparing classes.

COMMA SPLICES AND RUN-TOGETHER SENTENCES

Comma splices and run-together sentences are considered to be very serious errors. Following are some examples:

(1) Marla rode the horse for several hours then she walked him around the ring. (run-together sentence)

(2) The test was difficult, he couldn't pass it. (comma splice)

(3) They had a flat tire on the way to the airport they arrived on time. (run-together sentence)

(4) He had checked the yard for footprints, he entered the den to question the family members. (comma splice)

There are four basic methods that can be used to correct comma splices (two independent clauses connected by a comma) and run-together sentences (two independent clauses without any connection). Study the four methods listed below:

(1) Separate the two independent clauses with a period.

Example: Marla rode the horse for several hours. Then she walked him around the ring.

(2) Connect the two independent clauses by a semicolon if they are closely related. Or use a transitional connective (*however, thus, therefore,* etc.) to show the relationship between the two clauses.

Example: The test was difficult; as a result, he couldn't pass it.

(3) Place a coordinating conjunction (*and, but, for, or, nor, yet,* or *so*) after the comma.

Example: They had a flat tire on the way to the airport, but they arrived on time.

(4) Make one of the clauses into a dependent clause. Use a subordinating conjunction, such as *when, although, because, since, if, after,* etc. or a relative pronoun to introduce the dependent clause.

Example: After he had checked the yard for footprints, he entered the den to question the family members.

WRONG: The children were tired their mother put them to bed.
RIGHT: The children were tired, so their mother put them to bed.
                                         or
          Since the children were tired, their mother put them to bed.

WRONG: The spider is an insect, it spins a web.
RIGHT: The spider is an insect which spins a web.

WRONG:	Greenland is a large island few people live there.
RIGHT:	Greenland is a large island, but few people live there.

or

Although Greenland is a large island, few people live there.

or

Greenland is a large island; however, few people live there.

WRONG:	The Vikings ate fish they drank ale.
RIGHT:	The Vikings ate fish; they drank ale.

or

The Vikings ate fish and drank ale.

WRONG:	George Washington Carver was a slave, he became a famous man.
RIGHT:	George Washington Carver was a slave who became a famous man.

WRONG:	Vesuvius is a famous volcano, it is located near Naples, Italy.
RIGHT:	Vesuvius is a famous volcano which is located near Naples, Italy.

WRONG:	Many snakes are poisonous people avoid them.
RIGHT:	Many snakes are poisonous; thus, people avoid them.

or

People avoid snakes because many of them are poisonous.

WRONG:	John Kennedy is a well-known person he established the Peace Corps.
RIGHT:	John Kennedy, who established the Peace Corps, is a well-known person.

or

John Kennedy is a well-known person who established the Peace Corps.

WRONG:	That boy speaks German fluently he knows English too.
RIGHT:	That boy speaks German fluently; moreover, he knows English.

or

That boy speaks German fluently, and he knows English too.

or

That boy not only speaks German fluently but also knows English.

COMPARISON

Most adjectives and adverbs are compared by adding *-er* or *-est,* or by using *more* or *most* in front of the adjective or adverb. Most short modifiers are compared by adding *-er* or *-est* to the positive form. In general, *more* and *most* are used before "long" adjectives and adverbs (adjectives and adverbs of more than two syllables).

List 1.   Some adjectives and adverbs that are compared regularly

POSITIVE	COMPARATIVE	SUPERLATIVE
lazy	lazier	the laziest
tall	taller	the tallest
cheap	cheaper	the cheapest

expensive	more expensive	the most expensive
intelligent	more intelligent	the most intelligent
quickly	more quickly	the most quickly
easily	more easily	the most easily
useful	more useful	the most useful
common	more common	the most common

List 2. Some adjectives and adverbs that are compared irregularly

POSITIVE	COMPARATIVE	SUPERLATIVE
bad, badly	worse	the worst
far	{ farther	the farthest (distance)
	{ further	the furtherest
good, well	better	the best
little	less	the least
many, much	more	the most

WRONG: This shirt is *more cheaper* than that one.
RIGHT: This shirt is *cheaper* than that one.

WRONG: The Thai student speaks English as *fluent* as the Frenchman.
RIGHT: The Thai student speaks English as *fluently* as the Frenchman.

WRONG: My information is *better that* theirs.
RIGHT: My information is *better than* theirs.

WRONG: She looks a great deal *taller as* he.
RIGHT: She looks a great deal *taller than* he.

WRONG: I ran much *further* than the other contestants.
RIGHT: I ran much *farther* than the other contestants.

WRONG: I hope that you drive *more carefuler* than he does.
RIGHT: I hope that you drive *more carefully* than he does.

WRONG: Was my composition *the most longest* that you read?
RIGHT: Was my composition *the longest* that you read?

WRONG: Tokyo is *larger city* than New York.
RIGHT: Tokyo is *a larger city* than New York.

WRONG: He made *few mistakes* as I.
RIGHT: He made *as few mistakes* as I.

WRONG: Your pronunciation is *the worse* that I have ever heard.
RIGHT: Your pronunciation is *the worst* that I have ever heard.

WRONG: He usually does as *less* work as he can.
RIGHT: He usually does as *little* work as he can.

Additional notes on comparison:

(1)   Use the comparative degree when only two people or things are compared.

(2)   Use *any other* rather than *any* when comparing people or things of the same type or class.

(3)   Be sure to make your comparisons logical.

WRONG:	He is the *most successful* of the two businessmen.
RIGHT:	He is the *more successful* of the two businessmen.

WRONG:	Of the twins, Susan was the *most talkative*.
RIGHT:	Of the twins, Susan was the *more talkative*.

WRONG:	I looked at the two games and then chose the *easiest* one.
RIGHT:	I looked at the two games and then chose the *easier* one.

WRONG:	Soccer is more popular than *any* sport on our campus.
RIGHT:	Soccer is more popular than *any other* sport on our campus.

WRONG:	Calculus 102 is harder than *any* course in the mathematics department.
RIGHT:	Calculus 102 is harder than *any other* course in the mathematics department.

WRONG:	Are Kennedy's children more famous than *Nixon?*
RIGHT:	Are Kennedy's children more famous than *Nixon's?*

WRONG:	Her skin is as soft as *a baby*.
RIGHT:	Her skin is as soft as *a baby's*.

WRONG:	I like animals more than *most adults*.
RIGHT:	I like animals more than *most adults do*.

or

I like animals more than *I do most adults*.

CONDITIONAL SENTENCES

There are three basic types of conditional sentences:

(1) *You will (might) get sick if you eat too much*. This sentence means that something will occur if a certain condition is fulfilled. (future-probable)

(2) *You would (could, might) get sick if you ate too much*. This sentence means that something is unlikely to occur. (present-unreal)

(3) *You would have (could have, might have) gotten sick if you had eaten too much*. This sentence means that something did not occur because a certain condition was not fulfilled. (past-unreal)

Remember the following important points in writing conditional sentences:

(1) Do not use *will*, *would*, or *would have* in the *if* clause.

(2) Use the subjunctive form *were* instead of *was* in the *if* clause.

(3) *Unless* means "if not."

WRONG: If you study hard, you *pass* the next test. •
RIGHT: If you study hard, you *will* pass the next test.

WRONG: You might have enjoyed yourself if you *would have gone* with us.
RIGHT: You might have enjoyed yourself if you *had gone* with us.

WRONG: If I *lived* during the seventeenth century, I could have known Sir Isaac Newton.
RIGHT: If I *had lived* during the seventeenth century, I could have known Sir Isaac Newton.

WRONG: The woman could explain these sentences if she *was* a teacher.
RIGHT: The woman could explain these sentences if she *were* a teacher.

WRONG: If my friends *would have* a car, they would certainly pick me up.
RIGHT: If my friends *had* a car, they would certainly pick me up.

WRONG: He *could* use the machine unless it is broken.
RIGHT: He *can* use the machine unless it is broken.

WRONG: If you *will need* help, I'll be happy to help you.
RIGHT: If you *need* help, I'll be happy to help you.

WRONG: He *didn't understand* you unless you had spoken slowly.
RIGHT: He *wouldn't have understood* you unless you had spoken slowly.

WRONG: If you *would have called*, I would have gone out with you.
RIGHT: If you *had called*, I would have gone out with you.

WRONG: Plants *don't* grow if the sun didn't shine.
RIGHT: Plants *wouldn't grow* if the sun didn't shine.

WRONG: The dog will bite you if you *will enter* the gate.
RIGHT: The dog will bite you if you enter the gate.

WRONG: If dinner *was* ready, I'd eat now.
RIGHT: If dinner *were* ready, I'd eat now.

WRONG: I wouldn't have paid the money unless I *would have owed* it.
RIGHT: I wouldn't have paid the money unless I *had owed* it.

WRONG: He *doesn't change* his mind unless he were wrong.
RIGHT: He *wouldn't change* his mind unless he were wrong.

Additional notes on conditional sentences:

(1) When the agreement of another person is needed or requested, *will* is used after *if*.

Example: If you will be quiet, I'll try to explain. (If you agree to be quiet, I'll try to explain).
Example: I can help you if you will wait a minute. (I can help you if you agree to wait a minute).
Example: If you will play the piano, I'll sing. (If you agree to play the piano, I'll sing).

(2) In addition to *if,* some other conjunctions are often used in conditional sentences.

Example: He acts *as if* he were rich. (But he really isn't rich.)

Example: *As long as* it doesn't rain, we'll have the picnic. (*As long as* means "if.")

Example: He will pay the rent *provided that* he gets his check. (*Provided that* means "if.")

Example: *Supposing that* you were a lawyer, would you give me some legal advice? (*Supposing that* means "if.")

Example: She looks *as though* she is ill. (She might be ill.)

Example: *In the event that* it had rained, the game would have been postponed. (*In the event that* means "if.")

Example: *If only* I had known you were coming, I would have prepared lunch. (The word *only* is used for emphasis.)

(3) In past-unreal conditional sentences, or in present-unreal conditional sentences which contain the verb *were,* the conjunction *if* is sometimes omitted.

Example: *Had she had* time, she probably would have finished the letter. (*Had she had time* means "if she had had time.")

Example: *Had you failed* the exam, you might not have passed the course. (*Had you failed* means "if you had failed.")

Example: *Were he* a counselor, he could give me some good advice. (*Were he a counselor* means "if he were a counselor.")

Example: *Were the speech* intelligible, I might understand it. (*Were the speech intelligible* means "if the speech were intelligible.")

DANGLING MODIFIERS

Modifiers should be placed as close as possible to the words they modify. When related parts of a sentence are needlessly separated, a dangling modifier may occur. Correct dangling modifiers by making the dangling part of the sentence modify the subject of the main clause.

WRONG: *On arriving at the picnic,* the moon was high in the sky.
RIGHT: On arriving at the picnic, the group (the campers, we, etc.) found the moon high in the sky.

WRONG: *When in grammar school,* his teachers taught him to read.
RIGHT: When in grammar school, he was taught to read (by his teachers.)

WRONG: *Discovered many years ago,* we find uranium a useful metal.
RIGHT: Discovered many years ago, uranium is a useful metal.

WRONG: *To dance well,* practice is needed.
RIGHT: To dance well, one needs practice.

WRONG: *Watching the slides carefully,* many familiar scenes appeared.
RIGHT: Watching the slides carefully, we (the girls, they, etc.) saw many familiar scenes.

WRONG: *Hurrying to class,* an accident happened in my car.
RIGHT: Hurrying to class, I had an accident in my car.

WRONG: *Having traveled at a high speed,* a ticket was issued to the motorist.
RIGHT: Having traveled at a high speed, the motorist was issued a ticket.

WRONG: *After considering the plan for several days,* it was adopted.
RIGHT: After considering the plan for several days, we (the committee, the representatives, etc.) adopted it.

WRONG: *With a great deal of effort,* his courses were passed.
RIGHT: With a great deal of effort, he passed his courses.

WRONG: *When sick,* see a doctor at once.
RIGHT: When sick, you should see a doctor at once.

WRONG: *While cooking dinner,* her finger was burned badly.
RIGHT: While cooking dinner, she burned her finger badly.

WRONG: *If not eaten,* you should throw away the dessert.
RIGHT: If not eaten, the dessert should be thrown away.

WRONG: *By looking in the telephone book,* his number can be found.
RIGHT: By looking in the telephone book, you (she, I, etc.) can find his number.

WRONG: *Shopping in the department store,* a pretty blouse came to my attention.
RIGHT: Shopping in the department store, I noticed a pretty blouse.

GERUNDS AND INFINITIVES

List 1. Some common verbs followed by a gerund.

admit	mind (negatives and questions)
allow	miss
appreciate	practice
can't help	put off (= postpone)
can't stand	remember (= recall)
consider	resent
delay	risk
deny	stop (= cease)
dislike	
enjoy	
finish	

WRONG: I will never consider *to leave* this job.
RIGHT: I will never consider *leaving* this job.

WRONG: Many people avoid *to wear* safety belts when they drive.
RIGHT: Many people avoid *wearing* safety belts when they drive.

WRONG: A busy person can't stand *to wait* in line.
RIGHT: A busy person can't stand *waiting* in line.

WRONG: Do you enjoy *to be* in the United States?
RIGHT: Do you enjoy *being* in the United States?

WRONG: Students must practice *to use* different words.
RIGHT: Students must practice *using* different words.

WRONG: John finished *to iron* his shirt a few minutes ago.
RIGHT: John finished *ironing* his shirt a few minutes ago.

WRONG: Would you please stop *to talk* so loudly?
RIGHT: Would you please stop *talking* so loudly?

List 2.   Some common verbs followed by an infinitive.

agree	need
attempt	offer
decide	plan
demand	prepare
expect	pretend
happen	promise
hesitate	refuse
hope	remember (= not to forget)
intend	seem
learn	want
manage	wish
mean	

WRONG: Do you hope *getting* your degree by next year?
RIGHT: Do you hope *to get* your degree by next year?

WRONG: I hesitate *saying* what I mean.
RIGHT: I hesitate *to say* what I mean.

WRONG: Birds have to learn *using* their wings.
RIGHT: Birds have to learn *to use* their wings.

WRONG: Men of peace have attempted *putting* an end to war.
RIGHT: Men of peace have attempted *to put* an end to war.

WRONG: Can that student demand *seeing* his grades?
RIGHT: Can that student demand *to see* his grades?

WRONG: He surely expects *paying* all of his bills.
RIGHT: He surely expects *to pay* all of his bills.

WRONG: My father is planning *changing* jobs shortly.
RIGHT: My father is planning *to change* jobs shortly.

WRONG: Did the cook remember *adding* salt?
RIGHT: Did the cook remember *to add* salt?

List 3.   Some common verbs followed by either a gerund or an infinitive with no change in meaning.

begin	love
continue	prefer
hate	start
like	

WRONG: Almost everyone loves *have* free time.
RIGHT: Almost everyone loves *having* free time.

or

                Almost everyone loves *to have* free time.

WRONG: The homesick child started *think* about his family.
RIGHT: The homesick child started *thinking* about his family.

or

                The homesick child started *to think* about his family.

WRONG: It should begin *rain* before midnight.
RIGHT: It should begin *raining* before midnight.

or

                It should begin *to rain* before midnight.

List 4.   Some common verb/preposition combinations followed by a gerund.

approve of	look forward to
argue about	insist on
complain about	keep on
concentrate on	object to
depend on	plan on
decide on	rely on
feel like	succeed in
forget about	think about
give up	worry about

WRONG: Don't worry about *make* a mistake.
RIGHT: Don't worry about *making* a mistake.

WRONG: Did Paul object to *pick* you up?
RIGHT: Did Paul object to *picking* you up?

WRONG: We're looking forward to *visit* our friends.
RIGHT: We're looking forward to *visiting* our friends.

WRONG: I haven't succeeded in *find* a job yet.
RIGHT: I haven't succeeded in *finding* a job yet.

WRONG: The Browns are planning on *to buy* more furniture.
RIGHT: The Browns are planning on *buying* more furniture.

WRONG: Most teachers insist on *to correct* their students' mistakes.
RIGHT: Most teachers insist on *correcting* their students' mistakes.

WRONG: He rarely complains about *to have* to get up early.
RIGHT: He rarely complains about *having* to get up early.

WRONG: You must concentrate on *to do* your best.
RIGHT: You must concentrate on *doing* your best.

List 5.   Some common adjectives followed by an infinitive.

afraid	lucky
ashamed	pleased
considerate	prepared
disappointed	proud
eager	qualified

foolish	ready
fortunate	sorry
happy	surprised

WRONG: I'm afraid *drive* alone at night.
RIGHT: I'm afraid *to drive* alone at night.

WRONG: The actress seems eager *going* on stage.
RIGHT: The actress seems eager *to go* on stage.

WRONG: Citizens ought to feel lucky *be* able to vote.
RIGHT: Citizens ought to feel lucky *to be* able to vote.

WRONG: Were you disappointed not *win* the race?
RIGHT: Were you disappointed not *to win* the race?

WRONG: The parents are proud *having* a healthy child.
RIGHT: The parents are proud *to have* a healthy child.

WRONG: He was not at all surprised *hearing* the news.
RIGHT: He was not at all surprised *to hear* the news.

WRONG: I'm looking for someone qualified *type* a thesis.
RIGHT: I'm looking for someone qualified *to type* a thesis.

List 6.   Some common adjective/preposition combinations followed by a gerund.

accustomed to	interested in
afraid of	opposed to
ashamed of	proud of
bored with	responsible for
capable of	sorry about
disappointed in (with)	successful in
essential to	surprised at
excited about	tired from (= physically tired)
famous for	tired of (= mentally tired)
fond of	used to
hopeful of	worried about
intent on	

WRONG: Police soon get accustomed to *arrest* criminals.
RIGHT: Police soon get accustomed to *arresting* criminals.

WRONG: Are you capable of *complete* the work within an hour?
RIGHT: Are you capable of *completing* the work within an hour?

WRONG: Eli Whitney is famous for *invent* the cotton gin.
RIGHT: Eli Whitney is famous for *inventing* the cotton gin.

WRONG: The driver was intent on *to pass* the other car.
RIGHT: The driver was intent on *passing* the other car.

WRONG: The treasurer is responsible for *to keep* the books.
RIGHT: The treasurer is responsible for *keeping* the books.

WRONG: Ornothologists are interested in *to learn* about birds.
RIGHT: Ornothologists are interested in *learning* about birds.

WRONG: Jonas Salk was successful in *find* a vaccine against polio.
RIGHT: Jonas Salk was successful in *finding* a vaccine against polio.

WRONG: No one is opposed to *reduce* taxes.
RIGHT: No one is opposed to *reducing* taxes.

List 7.   Some common verbs followed by the short infinitive (the infinitive without *to*).

            let   make   have

WRONG: Would you let me *to use* your pencil?
RIGHT: Would you let me *use* your pencil?

WRONG: The company made the customer *to pay* his bill.
RIGHT: The company made the customer *pay* his bill.

WRONG: I had an electrician *to repair* the wiring.
RIGHT: I had an electrician *repair* the wiring.

List 8.   Some common verbs followed by a present participle or by a short infinitive. (Although the present participle is an "-ing" form, it is not a true gerund. Therefore, it cannot have a possessive form before it.)

WRONG: I heard *John's knocking* at the door.
RIGHT: I heard *John knocking* at the door.
                            or
               I heard *John knock* at the door.

WRONG: Have you ever seen *a tiger's attacking* a human being?
RIGHT: Have you ever seen *a tiger attacking* a human being?
                            or
               Have you ever seen *a tiger attack* a human being?

WRONG: Did you notice *the car's moving?*
RIGHT: Did you notice *the car moving?*
                          or
               Did you notice *the car move?*

WRONG: Parents enjoy watching *their children's playing.*
RIGHT: Parents enjoy watching *their children playing*.
                          or
               Parents enjoy watching *their children play.*

Additional notes on gerunds and infinitives:

(1)   The gerund is a noun. Therefore, it is logical to put a possessive form before it.

WRONG: Why do you dislike *me* cooking?
RIGHT: Why do you dislike *my* cooking?

WRONG: I can't remember *the teacher* announcing a test.
RIGHT: I can't remember *the teacher's* announcing a test.

WRONG: Will you forgive *us* leaving early?
RIGHT: Will you forgive *our* leaving early?

WRONG: *Paul* winning the race surprised everyone.
RIGHT: *Paul's* winning the race surprised everyone.

WRONG: The movie is not worth *you* paying four dollars to see.
RIGHT: The movie is not worth *your* paying four dollars to see.

WRONG: I won't insist on *him* wearing formal clothes.
RIGHT: I won't insist on *his* wearing formal clothes.

WRONG: The doctor has recommended *my father* having an operation.
RIGHT: The doctor has recommended *my father's* having an operation.

WRONG: Every *citizen* casting a vote is important.
RIGHT: Every *citizen's* casting a vote is important.

Wrong: The boss excused *his secretary* failing to come to work.
RIGHT: The boss excused *his secretary's* failing to come to work.

(2)   With the verb *need*, the gerund or the passive infinitive is often used.

WRONG: His hair needs *cut*.
RIGHT: His hair needs *cutting*.
                         or
His hair needs *to be cut*.

WRONG: Does the bed need *to make*?
RIGHT: Does the bed need *making*?
                         or
Does the bed need *to be made*?

WRONG: My pencil needed *to sharpen*.
RIGHT: My pencil needed *sharpening*.
                         or
My pencil needed *to be sharpened*.

IRREGULAR VERBS

Remember that the past participle is the form of the verb used with *have*, *has*, or *had* to form the past perfect or the present perfect tense.

PRESENT	PAST	PAST PARTICIPLE
become	became	become
begin	began	begun
blow	blew	blown
break	broke	broken
choose	chose	chosen
come	came	come
do	did	done
drink	drank	drunk
drive	drove	driven
eat	ate	eaten
fall	fell	fallen
fly	flew	flown
forget	forgot	forgot(ten)
go	went	gone
give	gave	given

know	knew	known
ring	rang	rung
run	ran	run
see	saw	seen
sing	sang	sung
sink	sank	sunk
speak	spoke	spoken
steal	stole	stolen
swim	swam	swum
take	took	taken
tear	tore	torn
throw	threw	thrown
wear	wore	worn
write	wrote	written

WRONG: He shouldn't have been *chose* as secretary.
RIGHT: He shouldn't have been *chosen* as secretary.

WRONG: He *swum* across the river without any difficulty.
RIGHT: He *swam* across the river without any difficulty.

WRONG: The girl's arm was *broke* in the car accident.
RIGHT: The girl's arm was *broken* in the car accident.

WRONG: After he had *ate* dinner, he rested on the sofa.
RIGHT: After he had *eaten* dinner, he rested on the sofa.

WRONG: I have *saw* that movie several times.
RIGHT: I have *seen* that movie several times.

WRONG: He had knocked at the door and *rang* the doorbell for ten minutes before someone answered.
RIGHT: He had knocked at the door and *rung* the doorbell for ten minutes before someone answered.

WRONG: Have you ever *took* pictures with this kind of camera?
RIGHT: Have you ever *taken* pictures with this kind of camera?

WRONG: Having *ran* out of gas, we stopped to fill up the car.
RIGHT: Having *run* out of gas, we stopped to fill up the car.

WRONG: The speaker has just *began* his talk.
RIGHT: The speaker has just *begun* his talk.

WRONG: Many people died when the boat *sunk*.
RIGHT: Many people died when the boat *sank*.

WRONG: He's already prepared and *drank* a cup of tea.
RIGHT: He's already prepared and *drunk* a cup of tea.

WRONG: Have you ever *wrote* a letter in green ink?
RIGHT: Have you ever *written* a letter in green ink?

WRONG: Had I *drove* eighty miles an hour, I would have been arrested.
RIGHT: Had I *driven* eighty miles an hour, I would have been arrested.

WRONG: I believe that someone has *took* my books.
RIGHT: I believe that someone has *taken* my books.

WRONG: He has made and *broke* promises to his friends all of his life.
RIGHT: He has made and *broken* promises to his friends all of his life.

WRONG: Her husband hasn't *gave* her a birthday present yet.
RIGHT: Her husband hasn't *given* her a birthday present yet.

WRONG: He *come* in at midnight last night.
RIGHT: He *came* in at midnight last night.

WRONG: Having *spoke* to the audience for an hour, the speaker left the auditorium.
RIGHT: Having *spoken* to the audience for an hour, the speaker left the auditorium.

MISPLACED CLAUSES, WORDS, AND PHRASES

Be sure to place modifying elements in the sentence correctly so that the meaning is perfectly clear.

WRONG: It *only* took two days to get there by train.
RIGHT: It took *only* two days to get there by train.

WRONG: He was hoping to *by the end of the year* find a job.
RIGHT: He was hoping to find a job *by the end of the year*.

WRONG: I *nearly* saw 100 bears at the zoo.
RIGHT: I saw *nearly* 100 bears at the zoo.

WRONG: To *logically* think in English is my goal.
RIGHT: To think *logically* in English is my goal.

WRONG: The tiger escaped from the cage *which came from Africa*.
RIGHT: The tiger *which came from Africa* escaped from the cage.

WRONG: We *almost* have written twenty compositions this semester.
RIGHT: We have written *almost* twenty compositions this semester.

WRONG: The woman went to the dentist *with a toothache*.
RIGHT: The woman *with a toothache* went to the dentist.

WRONG: He was asked *to later sharpen* his pencil.
RIGHT: He was asked *to sharpen* his pencil *later*.

WRONG: I intend to after class *go shopping*.
RIGHT: I intend to *go shopping* after class.

WRONG: The school children learned *in 1492* that Columbus had discovered America.
RIGHT: The school children learned that Columbus had discovered America *in 1492*.

WRONG: The carpenter makes furniture for people *of any size*.
RIGHT: The carpenter makes furniture *of any size* for people.

WRONG: *Hiding in the bushes,* the policeman found the robber.
RIGHT: The policeman found the robber *hiding in the bushes.*

WRONG: The vicuna has beautiful, silky hair *which lives high in the mountains of Peru.*
RIGHT: The vicuna, *which lives high in the mountains of Peru,* has beautiful, silky hair.

WRONG: The mansion was constructed by a new company *which the governor lives in.*
RIGHT: The mansion *which the governor lives in* was constructed by a new company.

WRONG: *Jumping from branch to branch,* I was fascinated by a squirrel.
RIGHT: I was fascinated by a squirrel *jumping from branch to branch.*

OMISSIONS

Do not omit words that are a necessary part of the sentence. Study the following points carefully:

(1) Be certain to include the correct article if one is needed.

WRONG: On the way to *office,* Richard stopped to buy a morning paper.
RIGHT: On the way to *the office,* Richard stopped to buy a morning paper.

WRONG: Lying on the beach were a towel, a red ball, and *broken* tennis racket.
RIGHT: Lying on the beach were a towel, a red ball, and *a broken* tennis racket.

WRONG: It was so pleasant *day* that we sat on the patio for hours.
RIGHT: It was so pleasant *a day* that we sat on the patio for hours.

(2) Do not omit necessary prepositions.

WRONG: He is both interested in and *dedicated* cancer research.
RIGHT: He is both interested in and *dedicated to* cancer research.

WRONG: The person I *spoke* was a native of Raceland, Louisiana.
RIGHT: The person I *spoke to* was a native of Raceland, Louisiana.

WRONG: The thing that I was most *surprised* was his attitude.
RIGHT: The thing that I was most *surprised at* was his attitude.

(3) Do not omit important verb parts.

WRONG: The glasses were washed and the *silver polished.*
RIGHT: The glasses were washed and the *silver was polished.*

WRONG: I wanted her to help me, but she must not have *wanted.*
RIGHT: I wanted her to help me, but she must not have *wanted to.*

WRONG: Laziness in people always *has* and always will be one of my pet peeves.

RIGHT: Laziness in people always *has been* and always will be one of my pet peeves.

(4) Do not omit *that* from a dependent clause if there is a possibility that the reader will misunderstand the sentence.

WRONG: We saw Alex, if not warned, would drive off the highway and onto the shoulder.

RIGHT: We saw *that* Alex, if not warned, would drive off the highway and onto the shoulder.

WRONG: It is believed, especially in the capital, the government is gaining strength.

RIGHT: It is believed, especially in the capital, *that* the government is gaining strength.

(5) Do not omit necessary words in comparisons.

WRONG: The traffic in New Orleans is heavier than Baton Rouge.

RIGHT: The traffic in New Orleans is heavier than *that of* Baton Rouge.

or

The traffic in New Orleans is heavier than *in* Baton Rouge.

WRONG: Earl is as tall, if not taller than, Wade.

RIGHT: Earl is as tall *as,* if not taller than, Wade.

WRONG: Owning a house is more expensive today.

RIGHT: Owning a house is more expensive today *than it was in the past.*

WRONG: Teaching young children is not so different from teenagers.

RIGHT: Teaching young children is not so different from *teaching teenagers.*

PARALLEL STRUCTURE

By parallelism, we mean equal or similar grammatical structure. You should connect a noun with a noun, an infinitive with an infinitive, an active verb with an active verb, a preposition with a preposition, a clause with a clause, and an adjective with an adjective.

WRONG: The day is dark, with cloudy skies and has a high humidity.

RIGHT: The day is *dark, cloudy, and humid.*

WRONG: As a teenager, she had babysat, working in a restaurant, and typing for her mother.

RIGHT: As a teenager, she had *babysat, worked in a restaurant, and typed for her mother.*

WRONG: The statesman died loved by his friends, feared by his enemies, and everyone respected him.

RIGHT: The statesman died *loved by his friends, feared by his enemies, and respected by everyone.*

WRONG: I am studying the sources of educational theory and how educational theory has evolved.

RIGHT: I am studying *the sources and the evolution of educational theory.*

WRONG: I read Hegel for the profound ideas in his philosophy but not his style of writing.

RIGHT: I read Hegel *for the profound ideas in his philosophy but not for his style of writing.*

WRONG: In his hands he was holding a book and interesting magazine.

RIGHT: In his hands he was holding *a book and an interesting magazine.*

WRONG: He was not only sympathetic but also knew when to be considerate.

RIGHT: He was *not only sympathetic but also considerate.*

WRONG: Not only did he enjoy the movie but also the play.

RIGHT: He enjoyed *not only the movie but also the play.*

WRONG: He was successful both as a church architect and writing poetry.

RIGHT: He was successful both as *a church architect and a poet.*

WRONG: Playing tennis is more strenuous than to ride a bicycle.

RIGHT: *Playing tennis* is more strenuous than *riding a bicycle.*

WRONG: I was concerned about the price of the car and if it was comfortable.

RIGHT: I was concerned about *the price and the comfort of the car.*

WRONG: Their homeland was cold and with many mountains.

RIGHT: Their homeland was *cold and mountainous.*

WRONG: Neither does he speak Spanish nor Helen.

RIGHT: *Neither he nor Helen* speaks Spanish.

WRONG: She wanted the roof repaired and to paint the fence.

RIGHT: She wanted *the roof repaired and the fence painted.*

WRONG: John decided to go to the university rather than a job.

RIGHT: John decided *to go to the university rather than to get a job.*

WRONG: John Higgenbotham is a man of many ideas and who knows how to express them.

RIGHT: John Higgenbotham is a man *who has many ideas and who knows how to express them.*

WRONG: He is a poor teacher but who treats his students fairly.

RIGHT: *He is a poor teacher, but he treats* his students fairly.

WRONG: For my birthday he gave me a watch and which I really like.

RIGHT: For my birthday he gave me *a watch which I really like.*

WRONG: The vicuna is a timid animal and which lives in Peru.

RIGHT: The vicuna is *a timid animal which lives in Peru.*

or

The vicuna is *an animal which is timid and which lives in Peru.*

WRONG: I learned that he was young, but he was, nevertheless, ambitious.

RIGHT: I learned *that he was young, but that he was, nevertheless, ambitious.*

PAST PERFECT TENSE

The past perfect tense describes an action which occurred before some particular past moment which is in mind.

WRONG: They said that they *didn't meet* him before.
RIGHT: They said that they *hadn't met* him before.

WRONG: We heard that the president *gave* a speech on television.
RIGHT: We heard that the president *had given* a speech on television.

WRONG: I was surprised to learn that she *was* injured in an accident.
RIGHT: I was surprised to learn that she *had been* injured in an accident.

WRONG: The librarian wanted to know where I *lost* the book.
RIGHT: The librarian wanted to know where I *had lost* the book.

WRONG: We found out that our friend *went* to California.
RIGHT: We found out that our friend *had gone* to California.

WRONG: The robber wouldn't say where he *spent* all the money.
RIGHT: The robber wouldn't say where he *had spent* all the money.

WRONG: When I saw him later, he *gained* over fifty pounds.
RIGHT: When I saw him later, he *had gained* over fifty pounds.

WRONG: Mr. Smith *just left* when his wife called.
RIGHT: Mr. Smith *had just left* when his wife called.

WRONG: She was hurt to learn that her boyfriend *forgot* her birthday.
RIGHT: She was hurt to learn that her boyfriend *had forgotten* her birthday.

WRONG: He asked me what countries I *visited*.
RIGHT: He asked me what countries I *had visited*.

WRONG: I discovered that someone *drank* all the milk.
RIGHT: I discovered that someone *had drunk* all the milk.

WRONG: I saw that my wallet *was stolen* when I opened my purse.
RIGHT: I saw that my wallet *had been* stolen when I opened my purse.

WRONG: The clerk assured me that she *told* the manager about my complaint.
RIGHT: The clerk assured me that she *had told* the manager about my complaint.

WRONG: It *already began* to rain when we started for the beach.
RIGHT: It *had already begun* to rain when we started for the beach.

WRONG: The little girl asked what *happened* to her dog.
RIGHT: The little girl asked what *had happened* to her dog.

WRONG: The senator declared that he *voted* for the new amendment.
RIGHT: The senator declared that he *had voted* for the new amendment.

PERFECT INFINITIVES AND PERFECT PARTICIPLES

are used only when they show action which happened prior to the action of the main verb.

PRESENT INFINITIVE	PERFECT INFINITIVE	PRESENT PARTICIPLE	PERFECT PARTICIPLE
to be	to have been	being	having been
to do	to have done	doing	having done
to go	to have gone	going	having gone
to see	to have seen	seeing	having seen
to write	to have written	writing	having written

WRONG: I seem *to leave* my key in the car last night.
RIGHT: I seem *to have left* my key in the car last night.

WRONG: He would like *to live* during the eighteenth century.
RIGHT: He would like *to have lived* during the eighteenth century.

WRONG: *Eating* lunch, he took a nap.
RIGHT: *Having eaten* lunch, he took a nap.

WRONG: She is happy *to meet* John when he was here.
RIGHT: She is happy *to have met* John when he was here.
or
She was happy *to meet* John when he was here.

WRONG: *Driving* for ten hours, we stopped to rest.
RIGHT: *Having driven* for ten hours, we stopped to rest.

WRONG: I would have been afraid *to have touched* the lion at the zoo yesterday.
RIGHT: I would have been afraid *to touch* the lion at the zoo yesterday.

WRONG: My mother would have liked *to have been* in Florida last week.
RIGHT: My mother would have liked *to be* in Florida last week.
or
My mother would like *to have been* in Florida last week.

PRESENT PERFECT TENSE

The present perfect tense is probably used more frequently than any other tense in English. This tense belongs to present time and must never be used if a definite past time is stated or suggested.

WRONG: I *have bought* a new hat last weekend.
RIGHT: I *bought* a new hat last weekend.

WRONG: We *don't have* a meeting since last month.
RIGHT: We *haven't had* a meeting since last month.

WRONG: Where *is he* all day?
RIGHT: Where *has he been* all day?

WRONG: They *are waiting* in the hall for half an hour.
RIGHT: They *have been waiting* in the hall for half an hour.

WRONG: The architect *has finished* his plans a week ago.
RIGHT: The architect *finished* his plans a week ago.

WRONG: *Have you written* your composition last night?
RIGHT: *Did you write* your composition last night?

WRONG: I *don't see* John since last Monday.
RIGHT: I *haven't seen* John since last Monday.

WRONG: He's looking for a wife, but he *doesn't find* one yet.
RIGHT: He's looking for a wife, but he *hasn't found* one yet.

WRONG: The foreign student *doesn't meet* many Americans so far.
RIGHT: The foreign student *hasn't met* many Americans so far.

WRONG: I *am already speaking* to her about that matter.
RIGHT: I *have already spoken* to her about that matter.

WRONG: What *are you doing* since yesterday?
RIGHT: What *have you been doing* since yesterday?

WRONG: They *don't see* a movie in a year.
RIGHT: They *haven't seen* a movie in a year.

WRONG: He *likes* me ever since we met.
RIGHT: He *has liked* me ever since we met.

WRONG: My wife *has died* over six months ago.
RIGHT: My wife *died* over six months ago.

WRONG: The girl *is practicing* the piano since early this morning.
RIGHT: The girl *has been practicing* the piano since early this morning.

WRONG: I still *don't learn* to speak English very well.
RIGHT: I still *haven't learned* to speak English very well.

WRONG: Shakespeare *has written* many dramas.
RIGHT: Shakespeare *wrote* many dramas.

REFERENCE OF PRONOUNS

Every pronoun must refer to a definite noun (its antecedent), or the meaning of the sentence may be unclear. Study the following points:

(1) Do not use two nouns as possible antecedents.

(2) Do not use *which, this,* or *that* to refer to an entire idea.

(3) Do not use the personal pronouns *you, they, them,* or *it* unless they refer to a particular noun.

WRONG: Sally told Linda that *she* was overweight.
RIGHT: Sally told Linda, "*You* are overweight."
or

Sally told Linda, "*I* am overweight."

WRONG: Mr. Daniel always challenges everything I say, *which* unnerves me.
RIGHT: Mr. Daniel always challenges everything I say, *a habit which* unnerves me.

WRONG: Oswald assassinated President John Kennedy. *This* shocked the world.
RIGHT: Oswald assassinated President John Kennedy. *This crime* shocked the world.

WRONG: Mr. Young said that he would sell his farm at a very cheap price. *It* surprised all of the members of the Farm Bureau.
RIGHT: Mr. Young said that he would sell his farm at a very cheap price. *This statement* surprised all of the members of the Farm Bureau.

WRONG: In college *you* have to study more than you do in high school.
RIGHT: In college *one* has to study more than he does in high school.

WRONG: He is bad at tennis because he can't hit *them* across the net.
RIGHT: He is bad at tennis because he can't hit *the balls* across the net.

WRONG: When John was painting the garage, some of *it* spilled on his pants.
RIGHT: When John was painting the garage, some of *the paint* spilled on his pants.

WRONG: In Chicago *they* have snow during the winter.
RIGHT: In Chicago *the people* have snow during the winter.

WRONG: In the newspaper *it* said that a new tax law had been passed.
RIGHT: The newspaper reported that a new tax law had been passed.

NOTE: *It* is used correctly in the following sentences:
   (1) *It is clear* that the students understood the lesson.
   (2) *It was suggested* that he keep his old textbooks.
   (3) *It is fifty miles* to the next town.
   (4) *It was foggy* almost all morning.
   (5) *It was the clerk* who made the mistake.
   (6) I think that *it is time* for us to begin.

RESTRICTIVE (IDENTIFYING) AND NON-RESTRICTIVE (NON-IDENTIFYING) ADJECTIVE CLAUSES

Study the following sentences with restrictive adjective clauses:

(1) A student *who studies hard* usually learns quickly.
             that studies hard

(2) I want a car *which is economical* to drive.
             that is economical

(3) Thomas Edison was the scientist *who invented the electric light.*
                       that invented the electric light.

(4)   I have already finished the lesson *which the teacher assigned.*
that the teacher assigned.

(5)   The man *whom you recommended* did an excellent job.
that you recommended

Study the following sentences with non-restrictive adjective clauses:

(1)   John Morgan, *who studies hard,* usually learns quickly.

(2)   I want a Toyota, *which is economical to drive.*

(3)   Thomas Edison, *who invented the electric light,* was a scientist.

(4)   I have already finished Lesson Two, *which the teacher assigned.*

(5)   San Peters, *whom you recommended,* did an excellent job.

Remember the following important points about restrictive and non-restrictive adjective clauses:

(1)   Restrictive adjective clauses *identify* the noun which they modify.

(2)   Non-restrictive adjective clauses *describe,* but do not identify, the noun which they modify.

(3)   The relative pronoun *that* cannot be used in non-restrictive adjective clauses.

(4)   Commas are used to set off non-restrictive adjective clauses.

WRONG: Iowa, *that* lies in the north-central section of the United States, is between the Mississippi and Missouri rivers.
RIGHT: Iowa, *which* lies in the north-central section of the United States, is between the Mississippi and Missouri rivers.

WRONG: The chief city of Hungary is Budapest, to *that* great damage was done during World War II.
RIGHT: The chief city of Hungary is Budapest, to *which* great damage was done during World War II.

WRONG: The Iowa country was first visited in 1673 by Joliet and Marquette, *that* were French explorers.
RIGHT: The Iowa country was first visited in 1673 by Joliet and Marquette, *who* were French explorers.

WRONG: Some important discoveries about gravitation were made by Sir Issac Newton, *that* was a seventeenth-century scientist.
RIGHT: Some important discoveries about gravitation were made by Sir Issac Newton, *who* was a seventeenth-century scientist.

WRONG: The impala, *that* is one of the fastest and most graceful of antelopes, is found wild only in Africa.
RIGHT: The impala, *which* is one of the fastest and most graceful of antelopes, is found wild only in Africa.

WRONG: Most of the world's supply of dates comes from Iraq, *that* is rapidly becoming an important modern country.

RIGHT: Most of the world's supply of dates comes from Iraq, *which* is rapidly becoming an important modern country.

WRONG: Kentucky was the home of Abraham Lincoln, *that* was president during the Civil War.

RIGHT: Kentucky was the home of Abraham Lincoln, *who* was president during the Civil War.

SHIFT IN TENSE

In narrative writing, you should keep the tense of verbs consistent. If you begin with one tense, you should not change to another tense without a good reason.

WRONG: After the bell rings, it *was* time to close the door.
RIGHT: After the bell rings, it *is* time to close the door.

WRONG: Everyone in class knew that the examination *is* going to include six chapters.
RIGHT: Everyone in class knew that the examination *was* going to include six chapters.

WRONG: When I spoke to him, he *is* just getting ready to leave.
RIGHT: When I spoke to him, he *was* just getting ready to leave.

WRONG: As soon as I finish biology, I *take* chemistry.
RIGHT: As soon as I finish biology, I *will take* chemistry.

WRONG: She once heard a record of his, but she never *sees* him in person.
RIGHT: She once heard a record of his, but she *has never seen* him in person.

WRONG: As the ship sank, he jumped overboard and *tries* to keep himself afloat.
RIGHT: As the ship sank, he jumped overboard and *tried* to keep himself afloat.

WRONG: He had a serious operation while he *is* in the hospital.
RIGHT: He had a serious operation while he *was* in the hospital.

WRONG: I will answer the phone if it *rang*.
RIGHT: I will answer the phone if it *rings*.

WRONG: Like almost all teachers, she was well prepared and never *comes* to class late.
RIGHT: Like almost all teachers, she was well prepared and never *came* to class late.

WRONG: When we reached the station, it *is* well after midnight.
RIGHT: When we reached the station, it *was* well after midnight.

WRONG: When you got home, *do* you notice what time it was?
RIGHT: When you got home, *did* you notice what time it was?

WRONG: That essay is very timely even though it *is* written two hundred years ago.
RIGHT: That essay is very timely even though it *was* written two hundred years ago.

WRONG: If you had told her that she was wrong, she *would be* angry.
RIGHT: If you had told her that she was wrong, she *would have been* angry.

WRONG: When Napoleon *loses* the Battle of Waterloo, he was exiled to the island of St. Helena.
RIGHT: When Napoleon *lost* the Battle of Waterloo, he was exiled to the island of St. Helena.

SIMPLE PRESENT AND PRESENT CONTINUOUS TENSES

The simple present tense, which occurs in spoken English far less frequently than the present continuous tense, describes action which is permanent or habitual. The present continuous tense, or real present, describes action which is occurring *now* (at the moment of speaking).

WRONG: I see that you *wear* your new coat today.
RIGHT: I see that you *are wearing* your new coat today.

WRONG: The sun *is giving* us light.
RIGHT: The sun *gives* us light.

WRONG: He *sleeps* because he worked very hard this morning.
RIGHT: He *is sleeping* because he worked very hard this morning.

WRONG: When I go to work, I generally *am meeting* many school children.
RIGHT: When I go to work, I generally *meet* many school children.

WRONG: I *listen,* but I cannot hear a sound.
RIGHT: I *am listening,* but I cannot hear a sound.

WRONG: He needs to wear warm clothes today because it *freezes.*
RIGHT: He needs to wear warm clothes today because it *is freezing.*

WRONG: How often *are you studying* in the library?
RIGHT: How often *do you study* in the library?

WRONG: That man who *talks* to the policeman just got a ticket.
RIGHT: That man who *is talking* to the policeman just got a ticket.

WRONG: Policemen *are issuing* tickets to speeders.
RIGHT: Policemen *issue* tickets to speeders.

WRONG: Look! That woman *runs* to catch the bus.
RIGHT: Look! That woman *is running* to catch the bus.

WRONG: They *are sitting* in class everyday for several hours.
RIGHT: They *sit* in class everyday for several hours.

WRONG: When the student wants to ask a question, he *is raising* his hand.
RIGHT: When the student wants to ask a question, he *raises* his hand.

WRONG: Why *do you wash* your car this morning?
RIGHT: Why *are you washing* your car this morning?

WRONG: Bad students usually *are not working* hard.
RIGHT: Bad students usually *do not work* hard.

WRONG: I almost always think in English, but today I *think* in my native language.
RIGHT: I almost always think in English, but today I *am thinking* in my native language.

SUBJECT-VERB AGREEMENT

A verb must agree in number with its subject. Keep the following rules in mind when making certain that subjects and verbs agree:

(1)   A prepositional phrase that comes between a subject and a verb does not affect the verb form.

(2)   Some indefinite pronouns are always singular and therefore require singular verbs. The ones that are most likely to be used incorrectly with a plural verb include *one, each, everyone, either,* and *neither.*

(3)   Two or more subjects joined by "and" usually require a plural verb.

(4)   When the conjunctions "or" and "nor" and the pairs of conjunctions "either . . . or," "neither . . . nor," and "not only . . . but also" are used to join subjects, the verb agrees in number with the part of the subject nearest the verb.

(5)   When normal word order (subject-verb) is inverted (verb-subject) either by simply placing the subject after the verb or by beginning the sentence with "there," the verb agrees in number with the true subject following the verb. Remember, however, that a verb does not agree with its complement or object.

(6)   Collective nouns (army, audience, committee, etc.) usually take singular verbs, but require a plural verb when the collective noun refers to the *members of the group* and not to the group *as a unit.*

(7)   Expressions referring to quantity or extent (miles, liters, pounds, etc.) take singular verbs when the amount is considered as a unit and plural verbs when the amount is considered as a number of individual units.

(8)   "Number" may be singular or plural. *The* number refers to the total sum and takes a singular verb; *a* number refers to the individual units and takes a plural verb.

(9)   Words ending in "-ics" (mathematics, acoustics, athletics, etc.) take a singular verb when they refer to a science, art, or body of knowledge; they take a plural verb when they refer to physical activities or qualities.

(10) The verb in clauses that begin "one of _____ (who, which, or that)" is plural.

Examples:

WRONG: The man, as well as his wife and children, *were* injured in the accident.
RIGHT: The man, as well as his wife and children, *was* injured in the accident.

WRONG: One of the students in the class *are* absent today.
RIGHT: One of the students in the class *is* absent today.

WRONG: A crate of apples and oranges *have* been delivered to our doorstep.
RIGHT: A crate of apples and oranges *has* been delivered to our doorstep.

WRONG: His grasp of many areas of radio and television technology *make* it easy for him to find a job.
RIGHT: His grasp of many areas of radio and television technology *makes* it easy for him to find a job.

WRONG: Each man and each woman *have* to consider how to react to such an emergency.
RIGHT: Each man and each woman *has* to consider how to react to such an emergency.

WRONG: Every one of the employees *are* angry about the new contract.
RIGHT: Every one of the employees *is* angry about the new contract.

WRONG: The man and his assistant *is* pleased with the new office.
RIGHT: The man and his assistant *are* pleased with the new office.

WRONG: My friend and teacher *are* my mother.
RIGHT: My friend and teacher *is* my mother.

WRONG: Either the students or the teacher *have* made a mistake.
RIGHT: Either the students or the teacher *has* made a mistake.

WRONG: The parent or the children *inherits* the estate.
RIGHT: The parent or the children *inherit* the estate.

WRONG: Buried under the floorboards *are* the murdered man.
RIGHT: Buried under the floorboards *is* the murdered man.

WRONG: There *is* at least fifteen angry demonstrators outside.
RIGHT: There *are* at least fifteen angry demonstrators outside.

WRONG: The best time to take a nap *are* the two hours after lunch.
RIGHT: The best time to take a nap *is* the two hours after lunch.

WRONG: The jury *agree* on the verdict.
RIGHT: The jury *agrees* on the verdict.

WRONG: The jury *disagrees* on the verdict.
RIGHT: The jury *disagree* on the verdict.

WRONG: Ten miles *are* not far to go for a delicious meal.
RIGHT: Ten miles *is* not far to go for a delicious meal.

WRONG: Thirty dollars *are* too much to pay for that purse.
RIGHT: Thirty dollars *is* too much to pay for that purse.

WRONG: A number of students *fails* every test.
RIGHT: A number of students *fail* every test.

WRONG: The number of students who pass *are* increasing.
RIGHT: The number of students who pass *is* increasing.

WRONG: Economics, my major, *are* difficult.
RIGHT: Economics, my major, *is* difficult.

WRONG: The acoustics of the building *is* good.
RIGHT: The acoustics of the building *are* good.

WRONG: One of the men who *is* being considered for the job is from this university.
RIGHT: One of the men who *are* being considered for the job is from this university.

UNINFLECTED VERBS

The uninflected form of the verb (the simple infinitive) in a dependent noun clause is used after some particular verbs or expressions. Study the list of verbs and expressions below which are often followed by a noun clause with an uninflected verb:

ask	require
advise	request
command	suggest
insist	urge
order	essential that
prefer	important that
propose	necessary that
recommend	urgent that

WRONG: The director advises that we *are* on time for the next meeting.
RIGHT: The director advises that we *be* on time for the next meeting.

WRONG: The counselor has insisted that Tommy *takes* time to relax.
RIGHT: The counselor has insisted that Tommy *take* time to relax.

WRONG: Did the general urge that his troops *fought?*
RIGHT: Did the general urge that his troops *fight?*

WRONG: My father suggested that I *didn't buy* a used car.
RIGHT: My father suggested that I *not buy* a used car.

WRONG: It is essential that each camper *brings* his own equipment.
RIGHT: It is essential that each camper *bring* his own equipment.

WRONG: Is it important that she *finishes* the typing today?
RIGHT: Is it important that she *finish* the typing today?

WRONG: Was it recommended that the young woman *didn't drive* after dark?
RIGHT: Was it recommended that the young woman *not drive* after dark?

WRONG: It seemed urgent that the meeting *began* immediately.
RIGHT: It seemed urgent that the meeting *begin* immediately.

WRONG: Your request that the test *is delayed* has been denied.
RIGHT: Your request that the test *be delayed* has been denied.

WISH CLAUSES

Notice the meaning of the following sentences with the verb *wish:*

(1) I wish that he *were* here today.
     (But he isn't here today.)

(2) The boys wish that they *had won* the game.
     (But they didn't win the game.)

(3) She wishes that he *could understand* Japanese.
     (But she can't understand Japanese.)

(4) Farmers wish it *would rain* soon.
     (Farmers want it to rain soon.)

(5) I wish you *would eat* your food.
     (But you won't eat your food. You refuse to eat your food.)

Remember the following important points in writing sentences with the verb *wish:*

(1) In a *wish* clause, the verb is never in the present tense. Therefore, you can never use *will* or *can* in the *wish* clause.

(2) The word *that* is often omitted in the *wish* clause.

(3) Instead of *was*, use *were* in the *wish* clause.

(4) Do not use *would have* in the *wish* clause. Use *had.*

WRONG: I wish you *would have called* me yesterday.
RIGHT: I wish you *had called* me yesterday.

WRONG: The student wishes that he *took* English in high school.
RIGHT: The student wishes that he *had taken* English in high school.

WRONG: I wish it *rains* more in this area during the spring.
RIGHT: I wish it *rained* more in this area during the spring.

WRONG: Don't you wish you *can dance* better?
RIGHT: Don't you wish you *could dance* better?

WRONG: I wish I *knew* you ten years ago.
RIGHT: I wish I *had known* you ten years ago.

WRONG: The secretary wishes that she *has* time to type the letter now.
RIGHT: The secretary wishes that she *had* time to type the letter now.

WRONG: I wish you *won't interrupt* me while I'm talking.
RIGHT: I wish you *wouldn't interrupt* me while I'm talking.

WRONG: She wishes that she *was* a good actress.
RIGHT: She wishes that she *were* a good actress.

WORDINESS

Avoid wordiness by choosing economical constructions to express ideas clearly and concisely and by eliminating all unnecessary words.

WORDY: There are several causes of malnutrition, one of which is vitamin deficiency.
CONCISE: Vitamin deficiency is one cause of malnutrition.

WORDY: I think that *Being There* is Peter Sellers' best movie, superior to all others.
CONCISE: I think that *Being There* is Peter Sellers' best movie.

WORDY: Regarding the subject of laws governing motorists, many people feel that the speed limit should be increased to sixty-five miles per hour.
CONCISE: Many people feel that the speed limit should be increased to sixty-five miles per hour.

WORDY: The novel was neither interesting nor was it well written.
CONCISE: The novel was neither interesting nor well written.

WORDY: The famous singing group, "The Rolling Stones," is known internationally throughout the world.
CONCISE: "The Rolling Stones" is an internationally known singing group.

WORDY: The reason why he left New York two days early was that he had to attend a conference in Miami.
CONCISE: He left New York two days early to attend a conference in Miami.

WORDY: There are various and sundry reasons why one should avoid discussing religion.
CONCISE: There are various reasons why one should avoid discussing religion.

WORDY: The bridge stretched across the vast swampland, and the bridge was twenty-five miles long.
CONCISE: The twenty-five-mile-long bridge stretched across the vast swampland.

WORDY: It was clearly evident that the grass had been cut.
CONCISE: It was evident (or *it was clear*) that the grass had been cut.

WORDY: She is a tennis player who plays tennis regularly.
CONCISE: She plays tennis regularly.

WORDY: I picked up the heavy tools with my two hands.
CONCISE: I picked up the heavy tools with my hands.

WORDY: Sir Thomas More was a writer who wrote *Utopia*.
CONCISE: Sir Thomas More wrote *Utopia*.

WORDY: There is a society called the Audubon Society, which was named in honor of John Audubon, the great artist.
CONCISE: The Audubon Society was named in honor of John Audubon, the great artist.

WORD ORDER

The order of most adverbs in English is very flexible, and their position is often changed. Notice the following general rules:

(1) The normal position for most adverbs is at the end of the sentence. An adverb of manner will come first, followed by an adverb of place, and finally, an adverb of time.

(2) The verb and object are never separated by an adverb.

(3) The adverb of time often comes at the beginning of a sentence.

(4) With verbs of movement, the place adverb follows the verb.

WRONG: He spoke at the meeting *knowledgeably* this morning.
RIGHT: He spoke *knowledgeably* at the meeting this morning.

WRONG: The family came *in 1975* to the United States by boat.
RIGHT: The family came to the United States by boat *in 1975*.

WRONG: I read *quickly* the letter from my parents.
RIGHT: I read the letter from my parents *quickly*.

WRONG: The student spent in the library *six hours* yesterday.
RIGHT: The student spent *six hours* in the library yesterday.

WRONG: Do you want to go *tonight* to the movies?
RIGHT: Do you want to go to the movies *tonight*?

WRONG: The Arab speaks *very well* English.
RIGHT: The Arab speaks English *very well*.

WRONG: She does *completely* her assignments every night.
RIGHT: She does her assignments *completely* every night.

WRONG: My husband prefers to eat *at home* his lunch at noon.
RIGHT: My husband prefers to eat his lunch *at home* at noon.

Additional notes on word order:

(1) In noun clauses introduced by a question word, use statement word order.

Example: I'm not sure *what he bought* at the store.

(2) Place the frequency adverb in front of the principal verb of the sentence except for the verb "be."

Example: The chairman *is always* on time.
Example: The children *never quarrel* with each other.
Example: We *have often visited* them.

(3) When a sentence begins with a negative or near-negative word or phrase, use question word order.

Example: Never *do the children quarrel* with each other.
Example: Only at the zoo *can you see* monkeys.

WRONG: I *forget sometimes* my phone number.
RIGHT: I *sometimes forget* my phone number.

WRONG: We *just have finished* eating.
RIGHT: We *have just finished* eating.

WRONG: The highways *usually are crowded* on the weekend.
RIGHT: The highways *are usually crowded* on the weekend.

WRONG: Rarely *I have been* to court.
RIGHT: Rarely *have I been* to court.

WRONG: Almost *never he irons* his own clothes.
RIGHT: Almost *never does he iron* his own clothes.

WRONG: Hardly ever *they attend* church.
RIGHT: Hardly ever *do they attend* church.

WRONG: Not only *he broke* two glasses, but also he left the table dirty.
RIGHT: Not only *did he break* two glasses, but also he left the table dirty.

WRONG: Nowhere in this city *you will find* high fashion.
RIGHT: Nowhere in this city *will you find* high fashion.

WRONG: Do you know why *is he* so angry?
RIGHT: Do you know why *he is* so angry?

WRONG: It is unclear how *did he escape.*
RIGHT: It is unclear how *he escaped.*

WRONG: He doesn't know when *will he be* here again.
RIGHT: He doesn't know when *he will be* here again.

WRONG: Please show me how *does this machine work.*
RIGHT: Please show me how *this machine works.*

WRONG: I'm never quite sure whom *can I trust.*
RIGHT: I'm never quite sure whom *I can trust.*

WRONG: I need to know what time *is it.*
RIGHT: I need to know what time *it is.*

WRONG: Can you tell me where *is his house?*
RIGHT: Can you tell me where *his house is?*

WRONG: I wonder why *did he tell* a lie.
RIGHT: I wonder why *he told* a lie.

Vocabulary Building

In order to understand what you are reading, you must know the meanings of the words that are used. Very often you can guess at the meaning from the rest of the sentence, but that method is not completely reliable. The sentence itself is important for determining which of the word's several meanings is intended, but you usually have to have some idea of the word itself.

How can you build a larger vocabulary? You could sit down with a long list of words and try to memorize it, or perhaps go through the dictionary page by page. This procedure, however, is very time consuming and very boring. Memorizing words is probably the least successful way of building a vocabulary.

Words are best remembered when they are understood and used, when they are part of your own experience. Here are some ways in which you can build your vocabulary.

Learn a little etymology. Approximately 70 percent of all English words consist of roots and prefixes derived from Latin and Greek. "Prefixes" are letter combinations which appear at the beginning of a word. "Suffixes" are letter combi-nations which occur at the end of a word. "Roots" carry the basic meaning of a word and are combined with each other and with prefixes and suffixes to create other words with related meanings. If you learn prefixes, suffixes, and roots you will have a clue to the meanings of thousands of words. For example, the Latin root *voc* (meaning "to call") appears in the words advocate, voca-tion, irrevocable, vociferous, etc. The root *port* (meaning "to carry") is found in the words report, export, support, porter, etc. Learn to look for the roots of words, and for familiar parts of words you meet. For your convenience, here is a list of the most common prefixes, suffixes, and roots. With prefixes and suffixes, which you study first, there are examples of word formation, with meanings, and additional examples. If you find any unfamil-iar words among the sample, consult your diction-ary to look up their meanings.

The list of roots is accompanied by words in which the letter combinations appear. Here again, use the dictionary to look up any words which are not clear in your mind.

Etymology—A Key to Word Recognition.

PREFIX	MEANING	EXAMPLE	PREFIX	MEANING	EXAMPLE
ab,a	away from	absent, amoral	mal	bad	malcontent
ad, ac, ag, at	to	advent, accrue, aggressive, attract	mis	wrong	misnomer
an	without	anarchy	non	not	nonentity
ante	before	antedate	ob	against	obstacle
anti	against	antipathy	per	through	permeate
bene	well	beneficent	peri	around	periscope
bi	two	bicameral	poly	many	polytheism
circum	around	circumspect	post	after	postmortem
com, con, col	together	commit, confound, collate	pre	before	premonition
contra	against	contraband	pro	forward	propose
de	from, down	descend	re	again	review
dis, di	apart	distract, divert	se	apart	seduce
ex, e	out	exit, emit	semi	half	semicircle
extra	beyond	extracurricular	sub	under	subvert
in, im, il, ir, un	not	inept, impossible, illicit, irregular, unknown	super	above	superimpose
			sui	self	suicide
inter	between	interpose	trans	across	transpose
intra, intro, in	within	intramural, introspective	vice	instead of	vice-president

SUFFIX	MEANING	EXAMPLE	SUFFIX	MEANING	EXAMPLE
able, ible	capable of being	capable, reversible	ence	relating to	confidence
			er	one who	adviser
age	state of	storage	ic	pertaining to	democratic
ance	relating to	reliance	ious	full of	rebellious
ary	relating to	dictionary	ize	to make like	harmonize
ate	act	confiscate	ment	result	filament
ation	action	radiation	ty	condition	sanity

Latin and Greek Roots.

STEM	MEANING	EXAMPLE	STEM	MEANING	EXAMPLE
ag, ac	do	agenda, action	arch	chief, rule	archbishop
agr	farm	agriculture	astron	star	astronomy
aqua	water	aqueous	auto	self	automatic
cad, cas	fall	cadence, casual	biblio	book	bibliophile
cant	sing	chant	bio	life	biology
cap, cep	take	captive, accept	chrome	color	chromosome
capit	head	capital	chron	time	chronology
cede	go	precede	cosmo	world	cosmic
celer	speed	celerity	crat	rule	autocrat
cide, cis	kill, cut	suicide, incision	dent, dont	tooth	dental, indent
clud, clus	close	include, inclusion	eu	well, happy	eugenics
cur, curs	run	incur, incursion	gamos	marriage	monogamous
dict	say	diction	ge	earth	geology
duct	lead	induce	gen	origin, people	progenitor
fact, fect	make	factory, perfect	graph	write	graphic
fer, lat	carry	refer, dilate	gyn	women	gynecologist
fring, fract	break	infringe, fracture	homo	same	homogeneous
frater	brother	fraternal	hydr	water	dehydrate
fund, fus	pour	refund, confuse	logy	study of	psychology
greg	group	gregarious	meter	measure	thermometer
gress, grad	move forward	progress, degrade	micro	small	microscope
homo	man	homicide	mono	one	monotony
ject	throw	reject	onomy	science	astronomy
jud	right	judicial	onym	name	synonym
junct	join	conjunction	pathos	feeling	pathology
lect, leg	read, choose	collect, legend	philo	love	philosophy
loq, loc	speak	loquacious, interlocutory	phobia	fear	hydrophobia
manu	hand	manuscript	phone	sound	telephone
mand	order	remand	pseudo	false	pseudonym
mar	sea	maritime	psych	mind	psychic
mater	mother	maternal	scope	see	telescope
med	middle	intermediary	soph	wisdom	sophomore
min	lessen	diminution	tele	far off	telepathic
mis, mit	send	remit, dismiss	theo	god	theology
mort	death	mortician	thermo	heat	thermostat
mote, mov	move	remote, remove	sec	cut	dissect
naut	sailor	astronaut	sed	remain	sedentary
nom	name	nomenclature	sequ	follow	sequential
pater	father	paternity	spect	look	inspect
ped, pod	foot	pedal, podiatrist	spir	breathe	conspire
pend	hang	depend	stat	stand	status

STEM	MEANING	EXAMPLE
plic	fold	implicate
port	carry	portable
pos, pon	put	depose, component
reg, rect	rule	regicide, direct
rupt	break	eruption
scrib, scrip	write	inscribe, conscription
anthrop	man	anthropology

STEM	MEANING	EXAMPLE
tact, tang	touch	tactile, tangible
ten	hold	retentive
term	end	terminal
vent	come	prevent
vict	conquer	evict
vid, vis	see	video, revise
voc	call	convocation
volv	roll	devolve

Read—everything, anything. try to find at least one new word every day.

Use the dictionary—frequently and extensively. Look up the meaning of a word you do not know, and try to identify its root. If you do not have a good dictionary, you should buy one. Any one of the following is highly recommended:

> *Standard College Dictionary* (Funk and Wagnalls)
> *Webster's New Collegiate Dictionary* (Merriam-Webster)
> *American College Dictionary* (Random House)
> *The New Method English Dictionary* (Longmans)

The New Method English Dictionary is written especially for persons whose native language is not English. It explains new words and idioms by using a carefully controlled vocabulary of words which you already know.

Listen to persons who speak English well. Do not be afraid to ask them the meaning of a word they use that is unfamiliar to you. They will be glad to help.

Make a personal word list of your new words. Make it on index cards so that you can play a "flash card" game with yourself.

Use the new words you learn each day. When you talk or write, try to use as many new words as you can. A word used is a word remembered.

To do well in any Reading Comprehension test you must develop your reading skill by systematic practice. The gains you make will become apparent not only in a higher score on the TOEFL, but also in your reading for study.

Here are five steps to use when working out any comprehension question. If you apply them calmly, you should arrive at the right answer most of the time.

1. Survey selection—Read the entire selection quickly to get the general sense and main idea.
2. Survey the questions—but not the choice of answers.
3. Reread selectively—Reread the selection, concentrating on the parts which seem to be related to the questions.
4. Concentrate on each question—Now look at the first question with its four possible answers and cross out any answer which is obviously ridiculous, irrelevant, or impossible. You should be left with two or three answers that seem possible.
5. Go back to the selection—Reread only the part of the selection that applies to the question, and base your choice on information actually given and not on your personal opinion or prejudice. Some questions require your making a judgment which must also be based on the information as given.

Some seemingly acceptable choices are so qualified as to be incorrect. For example, the following sentence may appear in the reading selection: "When you get caught in the rain, you may catch cold." One possible answer may be: "When you get caught in the rain, you *always* catch cold." The assertion in the reading selection is not that one who gets caught in the rain *always* catches cold, but only that he *may* do so.

You can apply the above steps, with slight modifications, whenever you read. If you keep these steps in mind and practice them consistently when reading newspaper articles, magazines, and books, you will follow them automatically on a test. Your scores on tests, and your grades in your university classes, will show marked improvement.

Recommended Review Texts for Structure and Written Expression

If you feel that you need to review important points related to Structure and Written Expression, use the list below as a guideline.

TOEFL Grammar Workbook
Phyllis Lim and Mary Kurtin. Laurie Wellman, Consulting Editor.
ARCO Publishing, Inc.
215 Park Avenue South
New York, New York 10003

Mastering American English
Grant Taylor, Consulting Editor
McGraw-Hill, Inc.
1221 Avenue of the Americas
New York, New York 10020

Let's Write English
By George Wishon and Julia Burks
American Book Company
450 W. 33rd Street
New York, New York 10001

English Sentence Structure
By Robert Krohn and the Staff of the English Language Institute
The University of Michigan Press
Ann Arbor, Michigan 48106

Mastering American English
By Rebecca Hayden, Dorothy Pilgrim, and Aurora Haggard
Prentice-Hall, Inc.
Englewood Cliffs, New Jersey 07632

A Workbook for Writers
Form D
By Harry J. Sachs, Harry M. Brown, and P. Joseph Canavan
D. Van Nostrand Company
450 W. 33rd Street
New York, New York 10001

The Most Common Mistakes in English Usage
By Thomas Elliott Berry
McGraw-Hill, Inc.
1221 Avenue of the Americas
New York, New York 10020

Harbrace College Workbook
Form 9 A
By Sheila Y. Graham
Harcourt Brace Jovanovich, Inc.
757 Third Avenue
New York, New York 10017

The Writer's Handbook
By Allan B. Lefcowitz
Prentice-Hall, Inc.
Englewood Cliffs, New Jersey 07632

TOEFL
TEST OF ENGLISH AS A FOREIGN LANGUAGE

This 90-minute Cassette Tape will improve your performance on the Listening Comprehension section of the TOEFL

TOEFL

TEST OF ENGLISH AS A FOREIGN LANGUAGE

SIDE 1

Test 1
Test 2
Parts A & B

LISTENING COMPREHENSION SECTION
ARCO PUBLISHING, INC. All rights reserved.

$7.95

Using Arco's TOEFL Listening Comprehension Cassette Tape allows you to take the first three practice tests in our TOEFL preparation book under the same conditions as you will take the actual TOEFL.

Although you can have a friend read the test questions to you from the Listening Comprehension Scripts included in this book, the whole purpose of this section of the TOEFL is to measure your comprehension of idiomatic English as it is spoken in North America. There is really no substitute for the sound of a native English speaker's voice, which is exactly what you will hear when you take your test.

For the best possible preparation for the TOEFL Listening Comprehension section, use Arco's TOEFL Cassette. To order, mail in the form below with your check or money order.